KNOWLEDGE MANAGEMENT AND ORGANIZATIONAL LEARNING

A Reader

Edited by

**Laurence Prusak and
Eric Matson**

OXFORD
UNIVERSITY PRESS

OXFORD
UNIVERSITY PRESS

Great Clarendon Street, Oxford OX2 6DP
Oxford University Press is a department of the University of Oxford.
It furthers the University's objective of excellence in research, scholarship,
and education by publishing worldwide in
Oxford New York
Auckland Cape Town Dar es Salaam Hong Kong Karachi
Kuala Lumpur Madrid Melbourne Mexico City Nairobi
New Delhi Shanghai Taipei Toronto
With offices in
Argentina Austria Brazil Chile Czech Republic France Greece
Guatemala Hungary Italy Japan South Korea Poland Portugal
Singapore Switzerland Thailand Turkey Ukraine Vietnam

ISBN 978-0-19-929180-9

Printed in the United Kingdom by
Lightning Source UK Ltd., Milton Keynes

Acknowledgements

Robert Grant, 'Knowledge Management and the Knowledge-Based Economy'. Reprinted with permission from *General Management Review*, vol. 3, January–March 2002. Every effort has been made to contact the holders of copyright of this piece. Any omissions will be rectified in future printings if notice is given to the publisher.

Michael H. Zack, 'Developing a Knowledge Strategy'. Reprinted with permission from the *California Management Review*, 1999. © University of California, 1999.

Atul Gawande, 'The Learning Curve'. Reprinted from *The New Yorker*, 2002, with kind permission of the author.

Gerardo Patriotta, 'Knowledge-In-The-Making: The "Construction" of Fiat's Melfi Factory'. From *Organizational Knowledge in the Making*, Oxford University Press, 2003. Reprinted with permission. © Gerardo Patriotta, 2003.

Dorothy Leonard and Walter Swap, 'Generating Creative Options'. Reprinted with permission from *When Sparks Fly*, Harvard Business Press, 1999.

Salvatore Parise and Laurence Prusak, 'Partnerships for Knowledge Creation'. Paper given at the World Bank Conference on Evaluation and Development, reprinted by permission of the World Bank.

Arnold Kransdorff and Russell Williams, 'Swing Doors and Musical Chairs'. Reprinted from *Business Horizons*, May–June 1999, © 1999, with permission from Elsevier.

Linda Argote, 'Organizational Memory'. Reprinted with permission from *Organizational Learning: Creating, Retaining, and Transferring Knowledge*, Kluwer Academic Publishers, 1999.

John Seely Brown and Paul Duguid, 'Balancing Act: How to Capture Knowledge Without Killing It'. Reprinted with permission from the *Harvard Business Review*, 2000. © 2000 by the President and Fellows of Harvard College.

Kenneth T. Derr, 'Managing Knowledge the Chevron Way'. Speech made to the World Summit on Knowledge Management, 1999. Reprinted with permission of the Chevron Corporation.

Acknowledgements

Gabriel Szulanski and Sidney Winter, 'Getting it Right the Second Time'. Reprinted with permission from the *Harvard Business Review*, 2002. © 2002 Harvard Business School Publishing Corporation.

Lowell L. Bryan, 'Making a Market in Knowledge'. This article was originally published in *The McKinsey Quarterly*, 2004, and can be found on the publication's web site: www.mckinseyquarterly.com © 2004 McKinsey & Company. All rights reserved. Reprinted with permission.

Eric Matson and Laurence Prusak, 'The Performance Variability Dilemma'. Reprinted with permission from the *MIT Sloan Management Review*, 2003. © Massachusetts Institute of Technology, 2003.

Anil K. Gupta and Vijay Govindarajan, 'Knowledge Management's Social Dimension: Lessons from Nucor Steel'. Reprinted with permission from the *MIT Sloan Management Review*, 2000. © Sloan Management Review Association, Alfred P. Sloan School of Management, 2000.

W. Chan Kim and Renée Mauborgne, 'Fair Process: Managing in the Knowledge Economy'. Reprinted with permission from the *Harvard Business Review*, 1997. © 2003 Harvard Business School Publishing Corporation.

Etienne C. Wenger and William M. Snyder, 'Communities of Practice: The Organizational Frontier'. Reprinted with permission from the *Harvard Business Review*, 1999. © 1999 by the President and Fellows of Harvard College.

Rob Cross, Andrew Parker, Laurence Prusak, and Stephen P. Borgatti, 'Knowing What we Know: Supporting Knowledge Creation and Sharing in Social Networks'. Reprinted from *Organizational Dynamics*, vol. 30, pp. 100–20. © 2001, with permission from Elsevier.

Peter F. Drucker, 'Knowledge-Worker Productivity: The Biggest Challenge'. Reprinted with permission from the *California Management Review*, 1999. © University of California, 1999.

Thomas H. Davenport and John Glaser, 'Just-in-Time Delivery Comes to Knowledge Management'. Reprinted with permission from the *Harvard Business Review*, 2002. © 2002 Harvard Business School Publishing Corporation.

Leigh Weiss and Laurence Prusak, 'Seeing Knowledge Plain: How to Make Knowledge Visible'. From *New Frontiers of Knowledge Management*, edited by Kevin C. Desouza (Palgrave, 2005), reproduced with permission of Palgrave Macmillan.

Michael Idinopulos and Lee Kempler, 'Do you Know who your Experts are?' This article was originally published in *The McKinsey Quarterly*, 2003, and can be found on the publication's web site: www.mckinseyquarterly.com © 2003 McKinsey & Company. All rights reserved. Reprinted with permission.

Jeffrey H. Dyer and Nile W. Hatch, 'Using Supplier Networks to Learn Faster'. Reprinted with permission from the *MIT Sloan Management Review*, 2004. © Massachusetts Institute of Technology, 2004.

Contents

Contents

List of Contributors

Linda Argote, Tepper School of Business, Carnegie Mellon University

Stephen P. Borgatti, Organization Studies Department, Boston College

John Seely Brown, Independent consultant and author

Lowell L. Bryan, McKinsey & Company

Rob Cross, McIntire School of Commerce, University of Virginia

Thomas Davenport, Babson College

Kenneth T. Derr, Citigroup Inc.

Peter F. Drucker, Claremont Graduate University in Claremont, California

Paul Duguid, School of Information Management and Systems (SIMS), University of California, Berkeley

Jeffrey H. Dyer, Marriott School of Management, Brigham Young University

Atul Gawande, Harvard School of Public Health and Brigham and Women's Hospital

John Glaser, Partners Healthcare System

Vijay Govindarajan, Tuck School of Business at Dartmouth

Robert Grant, McDonough School of Business, Georgetown University

Anil K. Gupta, Robert H. Smith School of Business, University of Maryland

Nile W. Hatch, College of Business, University of Illinois

Michael Idinopulos, McKinsey & Company

Lee Kempler, McKinsey & Company

W. Chan Kim, INSEAD

Arnold Kransdorff, Pencorp Group

Dorothy Leonard, Harvard Business School

Eric Matson, McKinsey & Company

Renée Mauborgne, INSEAD

Salvatore Parise, Babson College

Andrew Parker, Stanford University

Laurence Prusak, Babson College

Gerardo Patriotta, Nottingham University Business School

William M. Snyder, Social Capital Group

Walter Swap, Department of Psychology, Tufts University

Gabriel Szulanski, INSEAD

Leigh Weiss, McKinsey & Company

Etienne C. Wenger, Independent consultant and author

Russell Williams, University of Aberdeen Business School

Sidney Winter, Wharton School, University of Pennsylvania

Michael H. Zack, Northeastern University College of Business Administration

Introduction and Overview

Eric Matson and Laurence Prusak

The claim that we live and work in a 'knowledge economy' or 'knowledge society' has been made so frequently in recent years that it almost seems a cliché. Repetition has not made it less true, however, or guaranteed that the implications of those phrases are fully understood.

Not so many years ago, we talked more about the 'post-industrial' or 'information' society, but over the past decade knowledge and learning (or variations on those terms) have emerged as the hallmarks of the twenty-first century society and economy as the keys to economic success and perhaps social health, and as a focus of thinking about organizational effectiveness and innovation. For the sake of clarity, we will call our subject the knowledge and learning movement. It incorporates knowledge management, the learning organization, organizational social capital, and other, related approaches.

Academics and practitioners have been talking increasingly about and experimenting with knowledge and learning for at least the past two decades. Of course, diverse thinkers have been pondering knowledge and learning for centuries. In the eighteenth century, Adàm Smith's emphasis on the division of labor as a way for workers to gain expertise by repeating the same well-defined task was indeed a knowledge theory. His ideas were also applied to government and policy—to the business of nations. More than 2,000 years earlier, Aristotle defined different types of knowledge and discussed how they are acquired in arguments still very much worth reading.

So the subject is far from new, but it has unquestionably moved more into the management spotlight in recent years. An overwhelming majority of large organizations now engage in a wide range of knowledge and learning activities and nearly all have programs and personnel explicitly dedicated to these tasks. It is always risky to try to explain why some topics emerge in management discourse (as well as why they disappear). The effort is further complicated in this case by the impact of the vendors and consultants who promote—and often distort—knowledge and learning ideas in pursuit of their own self-interested goals. But understanding why these ideas rose to prominence beginning in the early 1990s can contribute to understanding the ideas themselves, so the effort is worth making.

One reason is clearly the realization within the developed Western economies and Japan that they were producing and profiting from more and more services and making fewer and fewer tangible goods. Capital market analysts, popular journalists, sociologists, and business school professors began to claim in their writings (and government statistics proved) that a substantial economic shift was occurring. The world's appetite for material goods had not lessened, of course, but their manufacture was increasingly moving to nations that had formerly been considered less-developed. These countries, including Ireland, Malaysia, India, Mexico, and of course China, developed the capacity and capability to carry out complex manufacturing at substantially lower cost than the former 'industrialized' nations. They had embarked on a knowledge revolution that has still not been completely documented, though it has changed the world and has powerfully influenced thinking about an emerging knowledge society.

A gradual but continuing change in how organizations understand what differentiates them from current and potential competitors has also driven interest in knowledge and learning. The industrial economics model of strategy and organizations was firmly entrenched by 1980 (it continues to hold on in many organizations), when academics began to discuss alternate strategic models of success based more on a firm's competences and capabilities—organizational capacities that depend on knowledge—than on its material and financial resources. This new perspective was inspired by Edith Penrose's book, *The Theory of the Growth of the Firm* and then by Nelson and Winter's *A Theory of Economic Evolution*. As these ideas began to seep into more popular management journals, business leaders slowly began to realize that their most valuable resources and potential competitive advantage resided in the brains of their employees, not necessarily their factories and stocks of raw materials.

A third force, though somewhat removed from practice, was the literature of 'learning by doing,' launched by Kenneth Arrow in his classic article, 'Learning by Doing,' and furthered by Robert Solow, another Nobel-prize winning economist. This influential work still reverberates in human resource and strategy discussions and has important truths to tell us about how expertise develops in practice. Other learning theories, sociology, and social psychology have also contributed to the knowledge and learning movement in a variety of more diffuse ways.

Fourth, the fact that so many organizations are globally dispersed and depend on virtual teams for critical work necessarily requires executives to devote organizational attention to how people can better understand one another, share ideas, and make decisions in a cyber-environment—essential knowledge and learning movement questions.

Finally (though this list is by no means exhaustive), there has been a proliferation of tools to manage knowledge and learning. Knowledge-related technology, though undoubtedly important for global organizations and a global economy, has been a source of dispute and disappointment as vendors and consultants have pushed technology-driven 'solutions' on often willing executives who find it easier to think of knowledge and learning as basically technological issues, or issues that lend themselves to technological fixes. A strong consensus exists among researchers and practitioners, however, that technology contributes most effectively to knowledge and learning activities when it supports and is subordinated to more managerial efforts including strategy, incentives, organizational designs, and other actions that focus on people and processes. Practice has shown that technology-led efforts are less often successful than more balanced approaches, and theory has shown why this is so.

Unlike some of the other subjects in this series, knowledge and learning have seen an ongoing fruitful interchange between the academic and practitioner adherents, often through the intermediation of consultants. Early knowledge and learning initiatives at the World Bank, British Petroleum, and Xerox, for example, formed the basis of articles and books which then influenced the next stage of practice. Not surprisingly, many knowledge and learning practitioners have a taste for theory and follow the more accessible academic literature.

The Readings

After years of discussion and experiment, practitioners and theorists have come to a consensus on defining the key knowledge and learning activities that organizations need to engage in or enhance. These activities occur in the key areas of knowledge development, knowledge retention, knowledge transfer, and the fostering of a knowledge-friendly culture characterized by norms of trust and cooperation. (These are the terms most common in practice, but we could as accurately talk about knowledge creation, knowledge embedding, and knowledge distribution.)

The goal of this volume is to bring together the latest examples of these activities and their impact. The articles are contemporary, predominantly from the last five years, and filled with case studies. Our intention is to provide both students and practitioners with practical examples to guide their thinking.

The volume begins with a section emphasizing the importance of knowledge and learning in today's economy. The next three sections dive into greater detail on the methods required for effective development, retention, and transfer of knowledge, drawing on examples from industries as diverse as petroleum, pharmaceuticals, and pizza making. In the subsequent section, we pay particular attention to the social dimensions of knowledge sharing, describing the importance of such elements as networks and trust. Finally, we discuss potential future directions for knowledge and learning, ranging from just-in-time delivery to visualization.

The Strategic Importance of Knowledge and Learning

Knowledge has always been an important driver of competitive advantage, but changes in the economy have made it increasingly so. As it becomes harder to obtain privileged access to land, labor, and capital, a firm's proprietary knowledge remains difficult for other firms to replicate. Grant, in his article 'Knowledge Management and the Knowledge-based Economy' (2002), argues that the bursting of the 'New Economy' bubble did not lessen this fact. He describes the fundamental drivers of change in the digital economy and the resulting importance of recognizing the firm's key knowledge and converting it into goods and services.

In order for knowledge to provide competitive advantage, it must be explicitly integrated into a firm's strategy. Zack, in 'Developing a Knowledge Strategy' (1999), describes a framework for linking knowledge management to a firm's strategic needs. Zack believes that every strategic position requires a specific set of intellectual resources and capabilities. Updating the traditional SWOT framework, he suggests that a firm must map its existing knowledge against external opportunities and threats in order to identify strategic knowledge gaps and guide its knowledge management efforts.

Knowledge Development and Individual Learning

Knowledge development lies at the heart of organizational innovation and growth, essential goals for many organizations. Knowledge work in this area often consists of team and network design or incentives for creation. One of the primary vehicles for creating knowledge within organizations is learning from individual experience, leading to the importance of 'embodying' knowledge in people—focusing on traditional human capital practices that use education, training, work experience, and mentoring to help individuals learn and absorb useful knowledge in a measurable or observable way. Of course, building experience requires deliberate practice, taking risks, and making mistakes along the way. Gawande's 'The Learning Curve' (2002) describes in painful detail the process by which surgeons learn from experience, using the insertion of a central line into the vena cava as an example.

Patriotta's chapter on 'Knowledge-in-the-Making' (2003) provides a unique lens into how such learning occurs in the workplace. The author describes the construction of Fiat's car manufacturing plant in Melfi, which was built with unusually active involvement from its workforce. The example shows how the workers learned about their role through formal training, learned about the different activities and equipment by helping to build the site, and about the work methods by disassembling and reassembling key products.

Individual experience is not the only vehicle for developing knowledge, however. Leonard and Swap's chapter on 'Generating Creative Options' (1999) shows how knowledge development can be as much a group process as an individual one—if the right conditions are met. After discussing the barriers to group creativity, such as an overly directive leadership style or insularity, the authors describe how to encourage knowledge creations through a set of practical ground rules and techniques.

In addition to developing knowledge in-house, firms can acquire knowledge from strategic alliances—such exchanges frequently include technological know-how or customer knowledge as well as more general employee expertise. Parise and Prusak, in 'Partnerships for Knowledge Creation' (2001), describe why it is difficult and how organizations can successfully acquire knowledge from alliances through actions designed to foster trust, build transparency, and communicate learning objectives.

Knowledge Retention and Organizational Learning

As we discussed earlier, individual experience is a foundation of learning—but in order to be effective, this learning must be generalized and retained by the broader organization. When turnover rates are high, this experience base is continually disappearing, making it critical to document knowledge from individual heads. Kransdorff and Williams' 'Swing Doors and Musical Chairs' (1999) describes the new flexible labor market and the resulting need to retain employee knowledge through oral debriefings, using examples from Glaxo Wellcome, Kraft, Ford, and BP. Although such debriefings often focus on employee departures or transitions, a subset called 'after action reviews' or 'learning histories' is used at more regular intervals to ensure key lessons are not forgotten over time.

Organizational learning can be captured in other ways as well. Knowledge retention often occurs through 'embedding' or building knowledge into an organizational process or routine so that it can be available for use in a transparent and effective way—so that, in fact, properly carrying out the process or routine means getting the benefit of the organizational knowledge embedded in a technical or human system. Argote's chapter on 'Organizational Memory' (1999) uses examples from pizza stores and manufacturing plants to show how 'retention bins' like technology or routines can contribute to productivity gains.

This spectrum of ways to learn raises a critical dilemma. As employees learn from experience, it is tempting for the organization to document the lessons in explicit routines or processes that must be followed by all. But there will always be improvisations required by changing conditions and driven by tacit knowledge exchange—the key is to make room for social mechanisms to create and vet those changes. Brown and Duguid, in 'Balancing Act: How to Capture Knowledge without Killing It' (2000), discuss the difference between process and practice using Xerox 'tech reps' as an example, exchanging war stories about tricky problems with copiers and improvising solutions together.

Knowledge Transfer and Dissemination

Knowledge transfer is the strategic goal of many knowledge and learning initiatives. It involves taking a successful knowledge-based practice or essential knowledge that exists in one part of the organization and reproducing it in another part where it can be put to use. (Sometimes knowledge is transferred from outside the firm, but usually less successfully than when the sources and recipients are internal.) Kenneth Derr, in his speech on 'Managing Knowledge the Chevron Way' (1999), describes a range of methods that firm uses including full-time 'process masters', part-time 'natural teams', in-house conferences, and a best-practices newsletter. He provides examples of the financial benefits of sharing best practices such as reducing Chevron's energy costs by $200 million per year.

Several constraints make this transfer process more difficult than practitioners and theorists initially expect. These include the barriers of low trust and limited understanding between the parties of the hoped-for knowledge exchange and the difficulty of capturing valuable knowledge in documents and databases. Because technology does little to remove these barriers, many organizations that have taken a technology-heavy approach to knowledge transfer have often been disappointed with the results. Szulanski and Winter, in 'Getting It Right the Second Time' (2002), show the problems that occur during the transfer of practices across different units, using examples from Bank One, Rank Xerox, and Intel to show the benefit of copying practices as closely as possible.

Many transfer problems can be solved by using a market perspective to encourage both supply and demand of knowledge. Lowell Bryan, in 'Making a Market in Knowledge' (2004), describes the characteristics of effective firm-wide knowledge markets, such as valuable knowledge objects, an effective 'pricing' or reward system, an efficient exchange mechanism, market-clearing facilitators, and a set of standards to encourage confidence in the system.

Ironically, there is risk that a firm will be too successful at replicating its successes and thus decrease the experimentation that will allow new learning to emerge. Some authors have argued that replication and innovation must be housed in separate parts of the organization in order to thrive, but Matson and Prusak, in 'The Performance Variability Dilemma' (2003), argue for an integrated approach to replication and innovation using examples from Shell, World Bank, and Clarica Life Insurance.

Social Perspectives

Developing a knowledge-friendly culture is in many ways the holy grail of knowledge and learning activities. Much recent social science literature has identified trust as a key component of a healthy knowledge culture. Economists, political scientists, and sociologists agree that it is difficult to engage employees in any but the most rudimentary knowledge and learning activities if they do not trust each other or trust the leadership of their organization.

It is difficult to generalize about actions that promote a knowledge-friendly culture, since they are contingent on an organization's existing culture, history, industry, and competitive environment. In general, though, actions that promote social norms of sharing, responsiveness, and generalized reciprocity include rewarding and demonstrating trustworthy and collaborative behaviors, telling stories of successful knowledge sharing, encouraging the formation of informal communities, and providing adequate time and space and appropriate technology for people to locate and communicate with each other. Gupta and Govindarajan, in 'Knowledge Management's Social Dimension: Lessons from Nucor Steel' (2000), provide examples of that firm's 'social ecology', such as high-powered incentives based on production output as well as the performance of peers, a high degree of accountability, and periodic visits to other mills. However, even high-powered incentives will be useless if employees feel their ideas are being misused or not taken seriously. Kim and Mauborgne, in 'Fair Process: Managing in the Knowledge Economy' (1997), describe three key aspects to building trust with employees: engaging them by asking for their ideas on key decisions, explaining why a decision was made, and then clarifying expectations based on the decision.

Another important social element to knowledge sharing is the role of groups—both small communities and broader networks. The movement initially focused on individuals and their knowledge actions, but some disappointing results along with careful observations led practitioners to recognize the profoundly social nature of knowledge, learning, and knowledge-based work. This insight created a new focus on the group as the unit of analysis for the knowledge movement. The change influenced and was in turn influenced by a growing body of writing on knowledge communities, practices (in the sense of professional groups), and networks, which has proved extremely fruitful. Social network analysis, a tool imported from sociology that charts informal connections among people, has helped organizations understand the networks and communities in which organizational knowledge moves and grows.

Wenger and Snyder, in their article on 'Communities of Practice: The Organizational Frontier' (2000), define a community of practice, explain its value in organizational learning, and suggest how they can be nurtured with support and infrastructure. A complementary way in which to develop knowledge is through broader networks—employees frequently ask a range of co-workers for help, especially in solving problems and creating new knowledge. Cross, Parker, Prusak, and Borgatti, in 'Knowing What We Know: Supporting Knowledge Creation and Sharing in Social Networks' (2002), describe the characteristics of relationships that facilitate knowledge flow, such as knowledge about what another person knows, the ability to access them, and the willingness of that person to engage in problem solving.

Future Directions

Although the examples earlier demonstrate a great deal of progress, our ability to use knowledge and learning to improve the productivity of knowledge workers is almost non-existent compared to the progress that has been made with manual workers over the last century. As Peter Drucker explains in 'Knowledge Worker Productivity: The Biggest Challenge' (1999), knowledge worker productivity is critical to improvement, but not currently well understood. He suggests the key questions we should be asking, such as how to define the task and how to measure output of knowledge workers.

One key challenge will be getting the knowledge to the right person at the right time. Davenport and Glaser, in 'Just-in-time Delivery Comes to Knowledge Management' (2002), describe a system at Partners Healthcare that provides physicians with just-in-time advice while they order prescriptions and lab tests, reducing search time and error rates.

Another key challenge will be communicating knowledge in the most useful format. Most organizational knowledge is displayed in the form of drab-looking lists that convey only a portion of the needed context and meaning. Knowledge searches can be vastly improved by making knowledge more visible: Weiss and Prusak in 'Seeing Knowledge Plain' (2004) describe examples such as Sony's map of its music catalog and Motorola's timeline of its product histories.

When knowledge remains tacit, the key challenge is for the organization to know who has it. Most 'yellow pages' systems—whether in print or online—do not do this effectively, rapidly becoming outdated and useless. Idinopulos and Kempler in 'Do You Know Who Your Experts Are?' (2003) describe a new way to identify experts within organizations by leveraging existing data sets such as accounting, recruiting, and professional development files.

Another challenge is to know how and when to open the boundaries of an organization to share learning with customers and suppliers. In 'Using Supplier Networks to Learn Faster' (2004), Dyer and Hatch describe how Toyota has established networks of suppliers to enable knowledge sharing, resulting in dramatic improvements in worker output and product quality.

Recently, observers and practitioners have also come to see space as a critical variable in knowledge and learning activities. In addition to considering the design of the physical spaces where people work, researchers have begun to explore the characteristics of social space, cognitive space, cyberspace, and that elusive Japanese concept, 'baa,' a space—part mental, part physical, and perhaps part spiritual—where shared meaning and context are built. Several large organizations are investing significant efforts and resources in designing and building office spaces according to developing knowledge principles. Novartis, who is building what is in effect a knowledge campus or small city in Basel, Switzerland, is one striking example. Although we did not include an article on this topic, we suspect it will be an important topic in future writings.

Additional Readings

Due to space constraints, we were unable to include dozens of articles that provide valuable perspectives on knowledge and learning; here are just a few.

We did not touch at all on measuring intangible assets, a topic that gets comprehensive treatment in John Hand and Baruch Lev's reader on *Intangible Assets: Values, Measures, and Risks* (Oxford University Press 2003).

To supplement Grant's piece on the drivers and implications of the knowledge economy, we would recommend David Teece on 'Capturing Value from Knowledge: The New Economy, Markets for Know-How, and Intangible Assets' (California Management Review 1998). Another fascinating piece on the upsides and downsides of the knowledge economy is Peter Drucker's 'The Next Society' (*The Economist* 2001).

An interesting description of the shared context in which knowledge is created can be found in Nonaka, Toyama, and Nagata's 'A Firm as a Knowledge-creating Entity: A New Perspective on the Theory of the Firm' (Industrial and Corporate Change 2000). This article also describes the knowledge-creating modes of socialization, externalization, combination, and internalization first introduced by Nonaka and Takeuchi in 1995.

For more on individual learning, see Chris Argyris on the need for successful people to accept failure in 'Teaching Smart People How to Learn' (Harvard Business Review 1991). A broader perspective on organizational learning can be found in Peter Senge's 'The Leader's New Work: Building Learning Organizations,' (Sloan Management Review 1990) or Steven Prokesch's 'Unleashing the Power of Learning: An Interview with BP's John Browne' (Harvard Business Review 1997).

Finally, for more on social perspectives, a great example of a working community of practice can be found in W. E. Fulmer's 'The World Bank and Knowledge Management: The Case of the Urban Services Thematic Group' (Harvard Business School Publishing 2001).

Concluding Thoughts

After re-reading the chosen articles and many other worthy candidates whom we considered, we are left with several observations that we feel are worth sharing, though they may seem self-evident to some.

- Knowledge and learning have become an integral part of the dynamic conversation focused on organizational strategy, management, behavior, and human resources. This ongoing discourse between academics, practitioners, and consultants is where new ideas are developed, tested, and embedded. Knowledge and learning, however labeled, are now a part of this dialog.
- Within the past few decades, the subject has entered the discipline of economics, where it filters down (or across) to business schools. It has always been a part of sociology, psychology, philosophy, and anthropology—other disciplines that have some influence on management thinking.

- People in organizations are experimenting with a variety of ways to make knowledge and learning more efficient, effective, or innovative. The latest surveys show that these efforts are globally widespread among large organizations and that the 'practice' of knowledge and learning is fairly established, though often under varying functions and names.
- There is a general acceptance among theorists and practitioners regarding what the processes focused on knowledge and learning look like. We have tried to mirror these in our chapter divisions as development and individual learning, retention and organizational learning, and transfer and dissemination.
- There is also a growing acceptance as to what the most useful unit of analysis is when doing knowledge and learning projects. The group, as opposed to individuals or the entire organization, would appear to be the consensus choice among both practitioners and theorists. Not surprisingly, this group is described by several different labels (such as community, practice, or network), but it is clearly a distinct entity that connotes commonality of understanding, connections, sharing, identity, and emotions.

Over time, the symbiotic relationship between theory and practice has generated a growing body of insights into the essentials of organizational knowledge and learning, though, needless to say, there will be additions, revisions, and dissensions as long as the movement continues. Given the macro-economic forces that continue to put a premium on knowledge, it is likely to continue for a long time—probably throughout our lifetimes—though the labels and rhetorics used to describe it may change.

I. THE STRATEGIC IMPORTANCE OF KNOWLEDGE AND LEARNING

Knowledge Management and the Knowledge-Based Economy

Robert Grant

Summary

With the bursting of the dotcom bubble and the onset of recession in much of the industrialised world, optimism over the 'New Economy' has evaporated and doubts have grown over the potential for knowledge management to unlock new sources of productivity. In this chapter, I point to the need to identify the fundamental drivers of technological change in the digital economy and explore their impact on industry structure and competition. While the implications for profitability are largely unfavourable, this reinforces the quest for competitive advantage for companies. Here knowledge management can play a key role—especially if it focuses upon the fundamental questions of 'What are the key knowledge processes through which the firm creates value?' and 'What are the characteristics of the knowledge used?'

The economic events of 18 months up to the end of October 2001 have been salutary for the proponents of the 'New Economy'. The upward trend of US productivity and the profitability has come to a dramatic halt and the once-booming technology-media-telecommunications sector is in the doldrums, and the bursting of the Internet bubble has resulted in the ruin of many once promising e-commerce start-ups. The final act of the 'Cinderella economy' has been revealed: Cinderella is chased away by the angry bears. What are the implications of these developments for recent ideas of 'the new knowledge economy' and for the role of knowledge management within it? My intention in this paper is to reassess, in the light of recent events, first the nature of the contemporary economy and second the contribution of knowledge management as a tool of current management practice.

....

Whatever Happened to the New Economy?

The period of intense economic and technological change beginning in the latter part of the 1990s has been described as the 'third industrial revolution'—following the first industrial revolution that began in Britain at the end of the 18th century and was associated with the mechanization of production, and the second industrial revolution that began in the US at the end of the 19th century and was associated with the rise of the modern corporation and the introduction of the telephone, automobile, and electrical power. As with prior industrial revolutions, the period 1995–2000 was one of prosperity and opportunity, especially for companies in North America and western Europe. These opportunities have been closely associated with knowledge—information technologies in particular. Although the micro-electronics revolution dates back to the invention of the integrated circuit and the rise of the personal computer industry, it was not until the 1990s when the full impact of the digital revolution has been felt by the world of business—not least because of the revolutionary impact of the Internet. New opportunities for trade, investment, and entrepreneurship have also sprung from rapid globalization: worldwide privatisation and deregulation, increased freedom of trade following the creation of the World Trade Organization, and the formation of regional free-trade areas (NAFTA, Mercosur, and the enlarged European Union).

The telecommunications sector reflects the combined impact of these forces more clearly than almost any other industry. Beginning with the breakup of AT&T, privatization of British Telecom, and advent of wireless telephony at the beginning of the 1990s, the industry has been propelled into a hyper competitive ferment. Globalization, digitalization and fiber optics, the development of the Internet and Internet protocols, privatization and deregulation, and the convergence of telecommunication with entertainment and information technology have created a state of permanent revolution. Giants, such as AT&T have been slain; upstarts such as Vodaphone, DoCoMo, and Worldcom have emerged as leading players. In the current turmoil with telecom service companies and telecom hardware companies crippled by debt, massive overcapacity in existing technologies, and uncertainty over emerging third-generation technologies, there is little consensus as to what the industry will look like in five years time.

From Exuberance to Depression

During the late 1990s, the term 'New Economy' was used to refer to this emerging industrial revolution. In its narrower sense, New Economy is associated with the industries most heavily impacted by digital technologies and knowledge-based production—primarily the TMT sector (technology, media, and telecommunication)—as opposed to the 'Old Economy' of mature, established industries. In its wider sense, the New Economy referred to the new economic conditions that resulted from the diffusion of new technologies and new business models and the transition to a knowledge-based economy. The resulting surge in labour productivity—especially in the US—permitted an unprecedented combination of growth and price stability.

The events of 2001 show that the promise of the New Economy was greatly overhyped. Surging productivity appeared to be primarily a US phenomenon with little follow-on in Europe and even less in Asia. As for a new era of profitable growth, virtually all the evidence pointed towards the New Economy generating profitless growth. Most of the TMT sector was associated with intense price competition resulting from low-entry barriers, lack of product differentiation, and extreme scale economies. The telecommunications sector is a classic case of phenomenal growth and rapid erosion of margins. By February 2001, long-distance prices in the US had fallen to two cents a minute, from 15 cents a minute four years earlier.

During 2001, few of the world's leading telecom companies were expected to earn positive economic profits. Meanwhile, in e-commerce, the demise of Web-Van, eToys, Pets.com, and a host of other prominent Internet start-ups raised doubts about the viability of even the most securely established e-commerce businesses. The impact of the New Economy on profitability in the Old Economy also seemed to be mainly negative. The Internet provides a new avenue for communication and distribution that facilitated new entry into existing markets, lowered consumers' costs of search and switching, and increased the transparency of prices. Hence, for all the growth opportunities that the New Economy made possible, it appeared that the major impact of the new economic conditions of the new millennium was a tougher economic environment for most companies in terms of greater competition, greater uncertainty, and lower profitability.

What do these development imply about the nature of today's economic environment?

....

The Nature of the Knowledge Economy

The key characteristics of the New Economy—innovation, rapid productivity growth, new business opportunities—are closely associated with the increasing role of knowledge in production. However, this prominence of knowledge as the critical factor of production is hardly a new phenomenon. Every significant increase in productivity since the transition from a hunter-gather to agrarian economy some five thousand years ago has been the result of new knowledge. Are mature industries such as automobiles, paper, agriculture, and winemaking less knowledge intensive than the new industries of computer software, telecommunications, and e-commerce? Similarly, are today's 'knowledge workers'—computer programers, management consultants, and web designers—any more knowledge dependent than the knowledge workers of previous eras—Titian, Stradevalio, Benjamin Franklin, and James Watt?

Stanford economist, Paul Romer (1986, 1994, 1998), identifies the increased accumulation of knowledge over time and downplays the idea that the knowledge-based economy is a new phenomenon. He points to the transition from a mechanised economy to a software-based economy as a feature of the 20th century as a whole. Among the different types of software, the most important in terms of contributing to productivity growth have been 'recipes' for producing goods and services. These include Henry Ford's mass manufacturing system, McDonald's system for producing fast food in thousands of locations throughout the world, and Wal-Mart's system of retailing. A key feature of software—whether it is a movie, a book, a computer program, or a business system—is that its initial cost of creation is very high, but subsequent copies cost much less. Increasing returns in the modern economy are also a consequence of the fact that new knowledge complements older knowledge and every investment in knowledge makes us better at discovering new knowledge.

So what is different about the past decade? The key feature of the recent 'information revolution' is the diffusion of digital technologies. These technologies reinforce the scale economies associated with the software economy. Digital software products such as Microsoft Windows XP, Pixar's Toy Story, or the Vienna Philharmonic's 14-CD recording of Wagner's Ring Cycle are very expensive to create, but they can be replicated at negligible cost (see Shapiro and Varian 1998).

The potential for the mass low-cost replication of digital products on a global scale offers enormous productivity gains, but the ability for companies to appropriate these gains may be limited by the intensity of competition. If the fixed costs of developing the product can only be amortised over a huge sales-base, firms will compete vigorously for a market share. The intensity of competition between

Netscape and Microsoft in the market for Internet browsers resulted in the price falling to zero—the companies gave the product away.

The effect of extreme scale economies in driving competition in the digital economy has been exacerbated by the influences of network externalities and competition for standards. Networks of consumers and producers are a common feature of many information-based markets giving rise to network externalities—where the value of a product to a user depends on the number of other users of that product. These network effects provide further incentives for market dominance. Network effects encourage convergence around a single technical standard, reinforcing the tendency to a single firm or coalition of firms to establish dominant market leadership. Competition for standards—such as exists in digital music formats, wireless telephony, operating systems for handheld computers, and digital image storage—encourages strategies that rapidly build market presence through liberal licensing to multiple users. The result is that all competitors dissipate the potential gains from ultimate market leadership (see Shapiro and Varian 1999; Kelley 1998).

At the same time, accelerating rates of technological change implying rapidly declining unit costs and shortening product life cycles. Nowhere is this more evident than in semiconductors where Moore's law predicts a doubling of the density of transistors on a integrated circuit every two years. As the cost of developing new technology-based products increases, the time window for exploiting them becomes shorter. This greatly increases the level of business risk. Although market leaders, such as Intel in microprocessors and Cisco in Internet hardware can use their stronger cash flows to pressure less well-resourced rivals by continually driving the pace of technological change and new product introduction, even the market leaders are not insulated from these risks. Despite its market dominance, Sony looks unlikely to recoup the multi-billion dollar development and launch costs of its Playstation2.1. The lesson to draw from the economic circumstances of the past 18 months is not that the knowledge-based, New Economy was a myth, but that the process of economic change requires careful, penetrating analysis. The propensity for business managers, investment analysts, and economists to abandon their analytic tools in favour of a fairy-tale romance with the wonders of the Cinderella economy and dotcom start-ups seems remarkable in the aftermath of the Internet bust. The danger is that we lurching from irrational exuberance to irrational pessimism and fail to recognize the economic and strategic implications of current and impending technologic changes. Continued innovation in digital technologies will inevitably drive productivity increase—even if these gains are offset by global recession. However, the most interesting issues concern impact of these technologies on industry structure, the basis of competitive advantage, and the dynamics of competition. The combination of extreme scale economies, network externalities, and fast-paced innovation creates 'winner-take-all' markets where each competitor is willing to incur substantial losses to gain the change to emerge as the industry winner. The browser wars between Netscape and Microsoft, the on-line auction battle in Europe between eBay and QXL, and the competition between Palm, Symbian, and Microsoft in operating systems for handheld digital devices are examples of such extreme competition. These same forces of extreme scale economies and network externalities also create strong pressures for globalization. If new technology-based products cost billions of dollars to develop, it is imperative that they are rolled out globally. Similarly, there are strong pressures on individual countries to adopt global standards, or run the risk of isolation from the onward march of technology.

Reassessing the Contribution of Knowledge Management

Enthusiasm for the 'new knowledge economy' has been paralleled by a surge of interest in knowledge management. Among practicing managers, awareness of the need to manage companies' knowledge assets more effectively has been triggered by recognition of the woeful inefficiency with which knowledge assets are deployed. Initial interest focused on the use of information technology, especially intranets, groupware, and databases, for storing, analysing, and disseminating information. Subsequent developments in knowledge management have been concerned less with data and more with the transfer of best practices, the pursuit of organizational learning, the fostering of creativity, and the management of intellectual property. The broadening scope of knowledge management is indicated by the number of large corporations that have created positions of Chief Knowledge Officer. Meanwhile, within business schools, interest in the role of knowledge in economic organization has developed from several streams of literature that has culminated in the knowledge-based view of the firm—an emerging concept of the firm as a set of knowledge assets where the primary purpose of the firm is to add value through creating and deploy these knowledge assets.

Amidst the shattered dreams of the New Economy, there is a risk that knowledge management may be dismissed as mere fad. Certainly, some of the manifestations of knowledge management are suspect. Saatchi & Saatchi's director of knowledge management was reported to be 'absorbing everything under the sun', including the implications of breakthrough products such as Japanese panty hose 'embedded with millions of microcapsules of vitamin C and seaweed extract that burst when worn to provide extra nourishment for the limbs' (*Wall Street Journal* 1997). Lucy Kellaway of the *Financial Times* notes that beyond the simple truth that 'companies that are good at sharing information have an advantages [sic] over companies that are not. ... The subject [of knowledge management] has attracted more needless obfuscation and woolly thinking by academics and consultants than any other' (Kellaway 1999).

Undoubtedly, knowledge management, along with virtually every other management trend of the past two decades (including total quality management and business process reengineering), as attracted its fair share of naifs and charlatans. At its core, however, knowledge management and the knowledge-based view of the firm represent important extensions of our theoretical and practical tools of management. As a resource, knowledge is acknowledged to be the overwhelming important productive resource—indeed the value of people and machines is primarily because of the knowledge they embody. In terms of strategy, knowledge is a particularly interesting strategic property that make it critically important to establishing and sustaining competitive advantage. The tools of knowledge management can offer us insight into the architecture of organizational capability and uncover fundamental issues as to how capability can be created, developed, maintained, and replicated. The key is to avoid over-hyped notions of 'revolutionary management practices for a knowledge-based revolutionary era' (as one knowledge management consultant pontificated) and to focus upon fundamentals. At its core, knowledge management is about recognizing the characteristics of the knowledge that the firm owns, recognizing the processes through which knowledge is converted into goods and services, and adapting management practices (including organizational structures) to these factors.

Types of Knowledge

The single most useful contribution of knowledge management is the recognition that different types of knowledge have very different characteristics. The distinction between knowing how and knowing about corresponds to the tacit/explicit distinction. While know-how is primarily tacit in nature, knowing about is primarily explicit—it comprises facts, theories, and sets of instructions. The different characteristics of tacit and explicit knowledge with regard to transferability have far-reaching implications for management. While explicit knowledge is transferable across individuals, space, and time (low-cost replicability), tacit knowledge cannot be easily articulated or codified and its transfer between people is slow, costly, and uncertain. As a result, explicit knowledge is seldom a foundation of sustainable competitive advantage: unless protected by intellectual property rights (patents, copyrights, and trade secrets), or secrecy, it leaks to competitors. The challenge of tacit knowledge is the reverse—the problem is not the ease of knowledge transfer to competitors, but the difficulty of knowledge transfer, even within the firm itself. If Ms Jenkins is an outstandingly successful salesperson, how can the company transfer her selling skills to the rest of its sales force?

The tacit/explicit distinction also has important implications for the distribution of decision-making authority within the company. If the knowledge relevant to decisions is explicit, then it can be easily transferred and assembled in one place, hence permitting centralized decision-making (treasury activities within companies are typically centralized). If knowledge is primarily tacit, then it cannot be transferred and decision-making needs to be located among the people where the knowledge lies. If the each salesperson's knowledge of how to make sales is based on their intuition and their understanding of their customers' idiosyncrasies, such knowledge cannot be easily transferred to their sales managers. It follows that decisions about their working hours and selling strategies should be made by them, not by the sales manager.

The distinction is also relevant to the ways in which organizational managers work together. If tacit knowledge cannot be easily communicated, how can different specialists combine their different knowledge bases? For processes that cannot be readily routinized, organizational arrangements that permit flexible, close-knit patterns of working are likely to be conducive to effective knowledge integration. As we shall explore further in the next section, team-based structures appear to be effective for the processes of knowledge development and integration. In new product development from automobiles (Fujimoto and Clark 1991) to computer software (Cusumano 1997) such team-based structures predominate. Unstructured, flexible patterns of knowledge exchange may parallel the formal structure: communities of practice have been identified as effective informal structures through which workers with common interests in developing and sharing knowledge interact (Brown and Duguid 1991; Wenger and Snyder 2000).

Types of Knowledge Process

The second major component of knowledge management is the recognition of the processes through which knowledge is developed and applied. Two categories of knowledge processes can be identified: those that are concerned with increasing the stock of knowledge available to the organization, and those, concerned with the application of the organization's knowledge. J. C. Spender (1992) refers to the former as knowledge generation and the latter as knowledge application.

James March's (1991) distinction between exploration and exploitation recognizes a similar dichotomy. Within these two broad areas we can identify a number of different knowledge processes each of which has been associated with particular techniques and approaches to knowledge management.

The best-developed and most widely applied techniques of knowledge management have focused upon some of the most basic aspects of knowledge application and exploitation. For example:

- In the area of knowledge identification, companies are increasingly assembling and systematizing information on their knowledge assets. These include assessments and reviews of patent portfolios and providing personnel data that allow each employee to identify the skills and experience of other employees in the organization. A key aspect of such knowledge identification is the recognition of knowledge that is being created in the organization so that it can subsequently be stored for future use. Such knowledge identification is especially important in project-based organizations to ensure that knowledge that is developed in one project is not lost to the organization. Systematic post-project reviews are a central theme in the US Army's 'lessons learned' procedure.

  At the Army's National Training Center, the results of practice maneuvers and simulated battles are quickly identified then distilled into tactical guidelines and recommended procedures by the Center for Army Lessons Learned. A similar systematized learning process is applied to identifying knowledge generated from actual operations. During the military intervention in Bosnia in 1995, the results of every operation were forwarded to the Center for Lessons Learned to be collected and codified, and lessons learned were distributed to active units every 72 hours (*Wall Street Journal* 1997). By the late 1990s, virtually every major management consulting firm had introduced a system whereby the learnings of each consulting project had to be identified, written-up, and submitted into a common database.

- Knowledge measurement involves the difficult task of applying metrics to the organization's stock of knowledge and its utilization. The pioneer of measurement has been Skandia, the Swedish insurance company, with its system of intellectual capital accounting (Edvinsson and Malone 1997; Marchand and Roos 1996). Dow Chemical's system of intellectual capital management also relies on quantitative tools to link its intellectual property portfolio to the shareholder value using a balanced scorecard approach.

- For knowledge to be efficiently utilized within the organization, then knowledge storage and organization is critical. The key contribution of information technology to knowledge management has been in creating databases for storing information, for organizing information, and for accessing and communicating information, accessing and facilitating the transfer of and access to knowledge. The backbone of the Booz-Allen & Hamilton's 'Knowledge-On-Line' system (Harvard Business School 1997a), Accenture's (formerly Anderson Consulting) 'Knowledge Xchange', AMS's 'Knowledge Express' (Harvard Business School 1997b) is an IT system typically using groupware (such as Lotus Notes) and a company intranet to allow employees to input, and access information. Knowledge sharing and replication involves the transfer of knowledge from one part of the organization (or from one person) to be replicated in another part (of by another individual). A central function of IT-based knowledge management systems is to achieve precisely that. However, tacit knowledge is not amenable to codification within an IT system. The traditional answer to the problem of replicating tacit knowledge embodied within individuals is to use apprenticeships and other forms of on-the-job training. Recently, organizations have discovered the important role played by informal networks in transferring experiential knowledge. These initially self-organizing communities-of-practice are increasingly being deliberately established and managed as a means of facilitating knowledge sharing and group learning (Wenger and Snyder 1999). Replicating capabilities pose an even greater challenge. Gabriel Szulanski (1996) shows that transferring best practices within companies is not simply about creating appropriate incentives; it is the complexity of the knowledge involved that constitutes the most significant barrier.

• Knowledge integration represents one of the greatest challenges to any company. Ultimately, producing a good or service requires bringing together the knowledge of many people, establishing organizational processes, which allow this to be achieved efficiently, is a daunting task. The task of knowledge integration is central to many organizational processes. For example, a strategic planning system may be seen as a vehicle for integrating the different knowledge bases of managers at different levels of the organization and from different functions in order to create the best strategy for the company; similarly with new product development. The key is to integrate the knowledge of many technical experts and across a range of functions. Our developing understanding of these processes points to the key role of project teams in achieving effective knowledge integration (Imai et al. 1985; Fujimoto and Clark 1991).

In the area of knowledge generation, it is possible to distinguish between the internal creation of knowledge (knowledge creation) and the search to identify and absorb existing knowledge from outside the organization (knowledge acquisition). The mechanisms through which knowledge is acquired from outside the organization are typically well known: hiring skilled employees, acquiring companies or their knowledge resources, benchmarking companies that are recognized as 'best-in-class' for certain practices, and learning through alliances and joint ventures. Creativity remains a key challenge for most companies. While most studies of creativity emphasize the role of the individual and the types of environment conducive to individual creativity, Dorothy Leonard has explored the role of groups and group processes in stimulating innovation (Leonard 1995; Leonard and Rayport 1997; Leonard and Sensiper 1998).

Knowledge Conversion

In practice, knowledge generation and application are not distinct. For example, the application of existing knowledge creates opportunities for learning which increase the stock of knowledge. Nonaka's theory of knowledge creation identifies the processes of knowledge conversion—between tacit and explicit, and between individual and organizational knowledge—as central to the organization's building of their knowledge base (Nonaka and Takeuchi 1995). Nonaka's specifies four types of knowledge conversion. Of these, knowledge conversion between tacit and explicit dimensions is particularly interesting. Nonaka notes how intuition and know-how can be communicated among the members of cross-functional product development teams by means of analogy and metaphor. For example, a member of Canon's mini-copier development team used a beer can to explain his concept of a drum cylinder. More widespread knowledge diffusion and replication is possible through converting tacit into explicit knowledge through systematization. Fundamental to the success of many multinational corporations is the huge amounts of value created from systematizing tacit knowledge and then replicating it globally. Consider the following examples:

- Henry Ford's Model T was initially produced on a small scale by skilled metal workers one car at a time. Ford's assembly line mass production technology systematized that tacit knowledge, built it into machines and a business process, and replicated it in Ford plants throughout the world. With the knowledge built into the system, the workers no longer needed to be highly skilled, Ford's plants were staffed by semi-skilled workers.
- When Ray Kroc discovered the McDonald brothers' hamburger stand in Riversdale, California, he quickly recognized the potential for systematizing their operation and fast-service assembly-line meals, not just in a single location but in many McDonald's outlets. McDonald's system is contained in its operating manuals (and videos) which allows McDonald's thousands of

worldwide outlets to produce fast food to exacting standards and produced by a labor force that, for the most part, possess very limited culinary skills.

For management consulting firms, the extent of knowledge systematization is a critical strategic issue. Consulting firms can be classified according to whether they a codification or personalization approach to knowledge management Hansen, Nohria, and Tierney (1999). Accenture is a classic codifier-in its core IT practice; it relies heavily on standardized processes and packaged solution and hires new graduates, which it trains intensively. McKinsey emphasises personalization, it relies on the tacit knowledge of experienced partners typically working in small teams with associates hired mainly for their analytical skills and problem-solving capacity.

....

Knowledge-Based View of the Firm

The emerging knowledge-based view of the firm regards the business enterprise as an institution for generating and applying knowledge. Its basis is a set of ideas about the knowledge processes within the firm. Most importantly, it recognizes that the processes of knowledge generation and knowledge application require different organizational arrangements. Efficiency in creating and storing knowledge requires that individuals specialize in particular types of knowledge. Yet production requires the integration of many different types of knowledge. Hence, the fundamental challenge of business organization it reconcile these two processes (Demsetz 1991; Grant 1996). Despite the emphasis of much of the knowledge management literature on organizational learning, the danger of learning is that it can easily undermine the efficiencies of specialization. When Soichiro Honda and Takeo Fujisawa began their collaboration to form Honda Motor Company at the end of 1949, Honda brought his engineering genius; Fujisawa brought sound business sense and marketing expertise. For Honda and Fujisawa to combine their knowledge by each learning what the other knew would be slow and inefficient. The key was to create a way of collaborating such that each could input their different expertise while avoiding the costs of large-scale knowledge transfer. How can knowledge be integrated in ways that preserve the efficiencies of specialisation? Among the processes that have been suggested are rules whereby specialists translate their knowledge into rules and directives to guide the practices and behavior of others, and routines whereby different specialists establish ways of interacting that allow each to input their knowledge into a combined process. For knowledge integration to work efficiently, there needs to be some degree of common knowledge that permits different specialists to collaborate and interact. Such common knowledge comprises elements such as a common language to support communication and a common culture to support compatible behaviors and cognitive processes. By recognizing the specific features of different knowledge processes, it is possible to recognize the type of organisational structure and systems needed to support each knowledge process. Awareness of these complexities of processing knowledge offers a view of the business enterprise that is richer and more sophisticated than economic theories of the firm that focus upon transaction costs or efficient incentive structures. Thus, Bruce Kogut and Udo Zander (1992: 389) argue that firms are '. . . social communities in which individual and social expertise is transferred into economically-useful products and services by the application of a set of higher-order organizing principles. Firms exist because they provide a social community of voluntaristic action structured by organizing principles that are not reducible to individuals.'

Conclusions

The bursting of the Internet bubble in North America and Europe in 2000 followed by the onset of recession in much of the industrialized world during the latter part of 2001 raises important questions about the nature of the new, knowledge-based economy and the role of knowledge management in steering it. Now that the optimism surrounding the new economy has dissipated, it is useful to return to fundamentals and consider what is distinctive about the technologies that are changing today's business environment. I have pointed to several characteristics of digital technologies and what they mean for the fundamental economics and production and competition. As we have seen, these imply changes in industry structure and the nature and intensity of competition—many of which are not unfavorable to corporate profitability.

Similarly with knowledge management, getting beyond the hype requires that we explore the characteristics of knowledge and the processes through which the firm creates value from knowledge. There is undoubtedly a need to increase the effectiveness and the utilisation of knowledge management techniques. There is a striking contrast between the sophisticated tools of financial and operational analysis used to manage tangible assets (including the full panoply of financial accounting), and the comparative neglect of knowledge and other intangible assets. While plants, equipment, inventories, and financial assets have long been subject to careful scrutiny and detailed valuation, it is only recently that attempts have been made even to value intellectual property while other knowledge assets, including individual competencies and organizational capabilities, have received even less systematic attention. Making progress on this front requires focusing upon the most important issues. Hence, a useful starting point is to identify the linkage between knowledge of the firm and basis upon which it creates value. This can then highlight the key processes through which knowledge is generated and applied, and the key characteristics of the knowledge involved. Consider for example the following examples:

- For Dow Chemical, the core of its value creation is in generating intellectual property—patents and trade secrets—in the form of new chemical products and processes, and exploiting them through worldwide manufacturing, marketing, and sales. If the foundation of value creation is the creation and exploitation of intellectual property, then this is what its knowledge management system should concentrate on. Dow's 'Intellectual Capital Management' places its central emphasis on Dow's patent portfolio, but links its intellectual property to a broad range of intellectual capital variables and processes, and ultimately to the company's total value (Petrash 1996).
- For McKinsey & Company, the key to competitive advantage and creating value for clients is to continually build upon the knowledge it generates from client assignments, and to systematize and conceptualize that knowledge base. Building the knowledge base requires, first, a structure for allowing specialization which was achieved through the creation of practices organized by industry group (e.g. consumer goods, financial institutions, energy, basic materials, and government) and by function (e.g. strategy, organization, IT, and operations) and, second, to ensure that knowledge generated from each project is captured, systematized, and made available for subsequent client projects (Harvard Business School 1996).
- For McDonald's restaurants, knowledge management is primarily concerned with implementing the McDonald's system. This is a detailed set of rules and operating practices that extend from the McDonald's values down to the placing of a pickle on the bun of a Big Mac, and the procedure for servicing a McDonald's mils shake machine. The essence of the McDonald's system is the systematization of knowledge into a detailed set of rules that must be followed in each McDonald's outlet. However, this is not simply a question of converting all experience and tacit knowledge into explicit operating practices but also ensuring that these operating practices are internalised within employees cognition and behaviour through rigorous attention to training—both in formal training programmes at Hamburger University and in training at individual restaurants.

The design of every knowledge process needs also to take account of the characteristics of the knowledge being deployed. As I have already noted, the fundamental distinction is between explicit and tacit knowledge. To take a simple example, the transfer of best practice between the different fabrication plants of a multinational semiconductor plant. If the knowledge is explicit, then such knowledge can be disseminated in the form of reports, videos, or even a directive requiring every plant to adopt a new standard operating practice. If the knowledge is tacit—it is the result of the experience or intuition of a single plant manager—then the task is more difficult. Transferring the best practice is likely to require either visits by other plant managers to the innovating plant, or the innovating plant manager to adopt a consulting role and visit other plants in the group for the purpose of teaching employees there.

It is in the area of managing tacit knowledge (which includes, typically, the major part of the knowledge relevant to organizational capability) that the major challenges and opportunities in knowledge management lie. Information technology has made huge strides in the storage, analysis, and systematization of explicit knowledge. However, the greater part of organizational learning is experienced based and intuitive. Identifying this knowledge and transferring it to other parts of the organization in order to utilize it more effectively remain a fundamental management challenge.

2 Developing a Knowledge Strategy

Michael H. Zack

Business organizations are coming to view knowledge as their most valuable and strategic resource. They are realizing that to remain competitive they must explicitly manage their intellectual resources and capabilities. To this end, many organizations have initiated a range of knowledge management projects and programs.[1] The primary focus of these efforts has been on developing new applications of information technology to support the digital capture, storage, retrieval, and distribution of an organization's explicitly documented knowledge.[2] A smaller number of organizations, on the other hand, believe that the most valuable knowledge is the tacit knowledge existing within people's heads, augmented or shared via interpersonal interaction and social relationships. To build their intellectual capital, these organizations are utilizing the 'social capital' that develops from people interacting repeatedly over time.[3] Many are experimenting with new organizational cultures, forms, and reward systems to enhance those social relationships.[4]

Technical and organizational initiatives, when aligned and integrated, can provide a comprehensive infrastructure to support knowledge management processes. However, while the appropriate infrastructure can enhance an organization's ability to create and exploit knowledge, it does not ensure that the organization is making the best investment of its resources or that it is managing the right knowledge in the right way. How should an organization determine which efforts are appropriate, or which knowledge should be managed and developed?

My research with more than 25 firms has found that the most important context for guiding knowledge management is the firm's strategy. An organization's strategic context helps to identify knowledge management initiatives that support its purpose or mission, strengthen its competitive position, and create shareholder value. Intuitively, it makes sense that the firm that knows more about its customers, products, technologies, markets, and their linkages should perform better. However, the link between knowledge management and business strategy, while often talked about, has been widely ignored in practice.[5]

Many executives are struggling to articulate the relationship between their organization's competitive strategy and its intellectual resources and capabilities. They do not have well-developed strategic models that help them to link knowledge-oriented processes, technologies, and organizational forms to business strategy, and they are unsure of how to translate the goal of making their organizations more intelligent into a strategic course of action. They need a pragmatic, yet theoretically sound model of what I call *knowledge strategy*.

This chapter provides a framework for describing and evaluating an organization's knowledge strategy. The framework is illustrated using examples from five companies representing the spectrum of physical and knowledge-based products and services.[6] 'Image Corp.' is a leading photographic imaging firm manufacturing physical assembled products such as film and photoprocessing equipment. Buckman Labs is a leading manufacturer of specialty chemicals, a physical non-assembled product. Lincoln Re, one of the world's largest life/health reinsurers, provides knowledge-based products and services. 'LeaseCo,' an industrial garment and small equipment-leasing firm, provides a service based on physical products, some requiring assembly. 'Big6' is a leading public accounting and professional services firm, providing knowledge-based services. Together, these companies demonstrate the importance of knowledge strategy regardless of industrial sector.

Business Strategy

The strengths, weaknesses, opportunities, and threats (SWOT) framework is perhaps the most well-known approach to defining strategy, having influenced both practice and research for over 30 years.[7] Performing a SWOT analysis involves describing and analyzing a firm's internal capabilities—its strengths and weaknesses—relative to the opportunities and threats of its competitive environment. Organizations are advised to take strategic actions to preserve or sustain strengths, offset weaknesses, avert or mitigate threats, and capitalize on opportunities. Strategy can be seen as the balancing act between the external environment (opportunities and threats) and the internal capabilities of the firm (strengths and weaknesses).

Michael H. Zack

Application of the SWOT framework has been dominated over the last 20 years by Porter's 'five-forces' model.[8] This model focuses on the external side of strategy, helping firms analyze the forces in an industry that give rise to opportunities and threats. Industries that are structured so as to enable firms to dictate terms to suppliers and customers as well as to provide barriers to new entrants and substitute products are seen as favorable. Strategy becomes a matter of choosing an appropriate industry and positioning the firm within that industry according to a generic strategy of either low cost or product differentiation.

While enjoying much popularity (in no small part because it was perhaps the first attempt to apply solid economic thinking to strategic management in a practical and understandable way), Porter's model has come under criticism[9]. The main argument is that the model addresses the profitability of industries rather than individual firms and therefore does not help particular firms to identify and leverage unique and sustainable advantages. Its underlying economic theory assumes that the characteristics of particular firms per se do not matter with regard to profit performance.[10] Rather it is the overall pattern of relationships among firms in the industry that makes the difference. If the industry as a whole is structured properly (i.e. with sufficient barriers and other impediments to competition), then all firms should realize excess returns.

It turns out, however, that unique characteristics of particular firms within an industry can make a difference in terms of profit performance.[11] To put balance back into the original notion of business strategy, recent work in the area of strategic management and economic theory has begun to focus on the internal side of the equation—the firm's resources and capabilities.[12] This new perspective is referred to as the *resource-based* view of the firm.[13] Strategic management models traditionally have defined the firm's strategy in terms of its product/market positioning—the products it makes and the markets it serves. The resource-based approach suggests, however, that firms should position themselves strategically based on their unique, valuable, and inimitable *resources and capabilities* rather than the products and services derived from those capabilities. Resources and capabilities can be thought of as a platform from which the firm derives various products for various markets.[14] Leveraging resources and capabilities across many markets and products, rather than targeting specific products for specific markets, becomes the strategic driver. While products and markets may come and go, resources and capabilities are more enduring. Therefore, a resource-based strategy provides a more long-term view than the traditional approach, and one that is more robust in uncertain and dynamic competitive environments. Competitive advantage based on resources and capabilities therefore is potentially more sustainable than that based solely on product and market positioning.

Knowledge as a Strategic Resource

While having unique access to valuable resources is one way to create competitive advantage, in some cases either this may not be possible, or competitors may imitate or develop substitutes for those resources. Companies having superior knowledge, however, are able to coordinate and combine their traditional resources and capabilities in new and distinctive ways, providing more value for their customers than can their competitors.[15] That is, by having superior intellectual resources, an organization can understand how to exploit and develop their traditional resources better than competitors, even if some or all of those traditional resources are not unique. Therefore, knowledge can be considered the most important strategic resource; and the ability to acquire, integrate, store, share, and apply it the most important capability for building and sustaining competitive advantage.[16] The broadest value proposition, then, for engaging in knowledge management is that it can enhance the organization's fundamental ability to compete.

What is it about knowledge that makes the advantage sustainable? Knowledge—especially context-specific, tacit knowledge embedded in complex organizational routines and developed from experience—tends to be unique and difficult to imitate. Unlike many traditional resources, it is not easily purchased in the marketplace in a ready-to-use form. To acquire similar knowledge, competitors have to engage in similar experiences. However, acquiring knowledge through experience takes time, and competitors are limited in how much they can accelerate their learning merely through greater investment.

LeaseCo, for example, recognized this opportunity by occasionally bidding aggressively on complex, novel, or unpredictable lease opportunities (e.g. leasing personal computers in 1980) to gain unique and leverageable knowledge from those experiences, while attempting to prevent its competitors from gaining that same knowledge. LeaseCo realized a double benefit over its competitors, first by investing in its strategic knowledge platform and second by learning enough about the particular client to competitively and profitably price leases for future opportunities with the same client. Often, enough mutual learning occurred between LeaseCo and its client that the client contracted with LeaseCo for future leases without going out for competitive bids. In essence, LeaseCo created a sustainable (or renewable) knowledge-based barrier to competition. Lincoln Re, as part of its 'experimental underwriting' process, similarly invested in its learning by insuring strategically selected novel, and difficult classes of risk at favorable rates.

Knowledge-based competitive advantage is also sustainable because the more a firm already knows, the more it can learn.[17] Learning opportunities for an organization that already has a knowledge advantage may be more valuable than for competitors having similar learning opportunities but starting off knowing less.[18] For example, Big6 invested heavily in capturing and sharing knowledge about key engagements across the firm so that it could sustain its areas of advantage by always building on its latest knowledge rather than 'reinventing the wheel' while giving its competitors a chance to catch up.

Sustainability may also come from an organization already knowing something that uniquely complements newly acquired knowledge, which provides an opportunity for knowledge synergy not available to its competitors. New knowledge is integrated with existing knowledge to develop unique insights and create even more valuable knowledge. Organizations should therefore seek areas of learning and experimentation that can potentially add value to their existing knowledge via synergistic combination. For example, Lincoln Re's unique (and patented) capability for capturing and distributing medical risk knowledge via expert systems—above and beyond the knowledge stored in these systems—enabled it to outperform competitors. Combining newly acquired risk management knowledge with its 'meta-knowledge' (of how to document, codify, and structure that knowledge) provided Lincoln Re a greater benefit than either alone. As an additional benefit, by designing its expert system to function as a generic knowledge platform, Lincoln Re was able to apply it to additional knowledge domains at essentially no additional cost (except for that to codify the content knowledge of those new areas), thus providing an economic advantage for entering new markets.

Sustainability of a knowledge advantage, then, comes from knowing more about some things than competitors, combined with the time constraints faced by competitors in acquiring similar knowledge, regardless of how much they invest to catch up. These examples represent what economists call *increasing returns*.[19] Unlike traditional physical goods that are consumed as they are used (providing decreasing returns over time), knowledge provides increasing returns as it is used. The more it is used, the more valuable it becomes, creating a self-reinforcing cycle. If an organization can identify areas where its knowledge leads the competition, and if that unique knowledge can be applied profitably in the marketplace, it can represent a powerful and sustainable competitive advantage.

Organizations should strive to use their learning experiences to build on, or complement, knowledge positions that provide a current or future competitive advantage. Systematically mapping, categorizing, and benchmarking organizational knowledge not only can help make knowledge more accessible throughout an organization, but by using a knowledge map to prioritize and focus its learning experiences, an organization can create greater leverage for its learning efforts. It can combine its learning experiences into a 'critical learning mass' around particular strategic areas of knowledge.

For example, LeaseCo proactively searched for opportunities to build continually on what it knew about leasing formal dress apparel to appearance-conscious organizations. It became one of the most knowledgeable firms in the industry regarding this premium market. Buckman Labs took a similar approach by focusing its learning to maintain and grow its superior knowledge of the pulp and paper industry. Big6 implemented a computer system that tracked its employees' experiences and formal training and matched their capabilities to the knowledge and skills required of its current and future engagements. They focused their training, assignments, and recruiting on continually building the knowledge base to support their most strategically important competitive positions.

While a knowledge advantage may be sustainable, building a defensible competitive knowledge position internally is a long-term effort, requiring foresight and planning as well as luck. For example, as part of its prospective risk management process, Lincoln Re has an 'early-warning' process in place to monitor research in the medical field for anything that eventually may improve its mortality and risk management knowledge. Using its unique expertise for translating commonly available research data into an estimate of actual experience, Lincoln Re is able to effectively learn about and profitably ensure emergent risk management opportunities sooner than its competitors.

Long lead time explains the attraction of strategic alliances and other forms of external ventures as potentially a quicker means for gaining access to knowledge. It also explains why the strategic threat from technological discontinuity tends to come from firms outside of or peripheral to an industry.[20] New entrants often enjoy a knowledge base different from that of incumbents; one which can be applied to the products and services of the industry under attack. This has been especially evident in industries where analog products are giving way to digital equivalents. For example, Image Corp. is experiencing a significant shift from physical film substrates to digital imaging. Its knowledge base is built on the science and technology of a physical consumable packaged good. Digital imaging, on the other hand, requires knowledge of computer systems and peripherals, imaging software, electronic distribution channels, and an economic model entirely different than for consumable physical products. The strategic challenge for the firm is to develop sufficient knowledge to support a shift to those new technologies and markets before nontraditional competitors make significant inroads into those markets. At the same time, it must not abandon its years of experience and knowledge about physical imaging that is supporting its core business.

This long learning lead-time or 'knowledge friction' highlights the importance of benchmarking and evaluating the SWOT of an organization's current knowledge platform and position, as this knowledge provides the primary opportunity (and constraint) from which to compete and grow over the near-to-intermediate term. This must, in turn, be balanced against the organization's long-term plans for developing its knowledge platform.

The Knowledge-Strategy Link

The traditional SWOT framework, updated to reflect today's knowledge-intensive environment, provides a basis for describing a knowledge strategy. In essence, firms need to perform a *knowledge-based* SWOT analysis, mapping their knowledge resources and capabilities against their strategic opportunities and threats to better understand their points of advantage and weakness. They can use this map to strategically guide their knowledge management efforts, bolstering their knowledge advantages and reducing their knowledge weaknesses. Knowledge strategy, then, can be thought of as balancing knowledge-based resources and capabilities to the knowledge required for providing products or services in ways superior to those of competitors. Identifying which knowledge-based resources and capabilities are valuable, unique, and inimitable, as well as how those resources and capabilities support the firm's product and market positions, are essential elements of a knowledge strategy.

To explicate the link between strategy and knowledge, an organization must articulate its strategic intent,[21] identify the knowledge required to execute its intended strategy, and compare that to its actual knowledge, thus revealing its strategic knowledge gaps.

Linking Knowledge to Strategy

Every firm competes in a particular way—operating within some industry and adopting a competitive position within that industry. Competitive strategy may result from an explicit grand decision—the traditional perspective on strategy—or from an accumulation of smaller incremental decisions.[22] It may even be revealed in hindsight, by looking back on actual behaviors and events over time.[23] Regardless of the strategy formation process, organizations have a de facto strategy that must first be articulated.

Every strategic position is linked to some set of intellectual resources and capabilities. That is, given what the firm believes it must do to compete, there are some things it must know and know how to do. The strategic choices that companies make—regarding technologies, products, services, markets, processes—have a profound influence on the knowledge, skills, and core competencies required to compete and excel in an industry. On the other hand, what a firm *does* know and knows how to do limits the ways it can actually compete. The firm, given what it knows, must identify the best product and market opportunities for exploiting that knowledge. For example, Buckman Labs competed on value-added services, requiring it to develop and maintain superior knowledge of how to use its chemicals in various microbiocidal treatment applications to solve its customers' problems. In some markets, Buckman Labs had well-developed knowledge and expertise. In others, it was more limited. Most importantly, it recognized the difference and managed and developed its strategic knowledge accordingly.

Lincoln Re competed directly via the high quality of its knowledge about particular classes of medical risk as well as its knowledge about how to combine ancillary services into an integrated packaged solution for its clients' risk management problems. Lincoln Re, however, knew less about property and casualty risk than some of its competitors and its competitive strategy reflected this. LeaseCo, which specialized in novel and customized leases, had to know more about the economics of pricing a complex lease than its competitors. LeaseCo did not know as much as its competitors about low-cost, high-volume production, or high-volume inventory management. Image Corp. had extensive knowledge and expertise regarding its traditional imaging technologies and products and how they could best be marketed to consumer and industrial customers. Their knowledge regarding digital imaging was much less developed, potentially limiting their ability to compete in that emerging market. Given the strategic importance of the digital imaging market, they were aggressively moving to close this gap.

So-called category killers, such as Circuit City and Toys 'R' Us, focus their retailing knowledge on one product category at the expense of others. In comparison, many broad-line retailers, led by Wal-Mart, have taken a different competitive knowledge position. They have come to realize that while they know some things about retailing tens of thousands of products to the consumer market, their suppliers are able to develop a more focused understanding about the particular products each supplies. Rather than try to be the consumer expert on every product, these retailers have recognized the limits to what they know and can know. They are asking their suppliers to take responsibility for understanding consumption habits, practices, needs, and buying patterns and to share that knowledge with the retailer. The retailer is, in fact, operating as a knowledge integrator, integrating the knowledge of many suppliers to better serve consumers.

In each case, an organization's competitive position created a knowledge requirement, while its existing knowledge created an opportunity and a constraint on selecting viable competitive positions. Success required dynamically aligning those knowledge-based requirements and capabilities.

A Strategic Framework for Mapping Knowledge

Assessing an organization's knowledge position requires cataloging its existing intellectual resources by creating what is commonly called a knowledge map. Knowledge can be characterized in many ways. Popular taxonomies distinguish between tacit and explicit knowledge, general and situated context-specific knowledge, and individual and collective knowledge.[24] Knowledge can also be categorized by type, including declarative (knowledge about), procedural (know-how), causal (know-why), conditional (know when), and relational (know-with). While these distinctions are useful for mapping and managing knowledge at the process level once a knowledge strategy has been formulated, our purpose requires a knowledge taxonomy oriented toward strategy, which reflects the competitive uniqueness of each organization.

Categorizing or describing what a business firm knows and must know about its industry or competitive position is not easy. Although firms within particular industries, firms maintaining similar competitive positions, or those employing similar technologies and other resources often share some common knowledge, there are no simple answers regarding what a firm must know to be competitive—if there were, then there would be no sustainable advantage.

Each company I have worked with has developed an approach to describing and classifying its strategic or competitive knowledge that is in some ways unique. In fact, each firm's general awareness of and orientation to the link between knowledge and strategy tends to be somewhat unique and may, itself, represent an advantage. Regardless of how knowledge is categorized based on content, every firm's strategic knowledge can be categorized by its ability to support a competitive position. Specifically, knowledge can be classified according to whether it is *core, advanced, or innovative.*

Core knowledge is that minimum scope and level of knowledge required just to 'play the game.' Having that level of knowledge and capability will not assure the long-term competitive viability of a firm, but does present a basic industry knowledge barrier to entry. Core knowledge tends to be commonly held by members of an industry and therefore provides little advantage other than over nonmembers.

Advanced knowledge enables a firm to be competitively viable. The firm may have generally the same level, scope, or quality of knowledge as its competitors although the specific knowledge content will often vary among competitors, enabling knowledge differentiation. Firms may choose to compete on knowledge head-on in the same strategic position, hoping to know more than a competitor. They instead may choose to compete for that position by differentiating their knowledge. LeaseCo, for example, competed with others for the custom lease market but used their knowledge of lease pricing and equipment sourcing rather than garment finishing or equipment integration to compete for that position. Buckman Labs competed in certain markets based on its superior knowledge of how to apply its chemicals to solve the process treatment problems of its customers. Big6 knew how to deliver accounting, tax, and consulting solutions of a quality sufficient to enable it to attract and retain high-quality clients.

Innovative knowledge is that knowledge that enables a firm to lead its industry and competitors and to significantly differentiate itself from its competitors. Innovative knowledge often enables a firm to change the rules of the game itself.[25] LeaseCo, based on its extensive knowledge of cost accounting and lease economics, challenged the traditional way leases were priced in its industry. Not only did this confuse the competition to LeaseCo's advantage, but it also allowed LeaseCo to identify many profitable opportunities passed over by competitors while avoiding potentially unprofitable ventures. Lincoln Re developed highly innovative knowledge not only about assessing risk but also about how to codify, structure, distribute, leverage, and market that knowledge using expert systems. Big6 developed expertise in particular industries and services that clearly led its competitors. Buckman Labs developed innovative knowledge for delivering more comprehensive solutions to its customers to help increase their overall processing plant efficiency and quality.

Knowledge is not static and what is innovative knowledge today will ultimately become the core knowledge of tomorrow. Thus defending and growing a competitive position requires continual learning and knowledge acquisition. The ability of an organization to learn, accumulate knowledge from its experiences, and reapply that knowledge is itself a skill or competence that—beyond the core competencies directly related to delivering its product or service—may provide strategic advantage.

Although knowledge is dynamic, this strategic knowledge framework does offer the ability to take a snapshot of where the firm is today vis-à-vis its desired strategic knowledge profile (to assess its internal knowledge gaps) and vis-à-vis its competitors (to assess its external knowledge gaps). Additionally, it can be used to plot the historical path and future trajectory of the firm's knowledge. The framework may be applied by area of competency or, taking a more traditional strategic perspective, by SBU, division, product line, function, or market position. Regardless of the particular way each firm categorizes its knowledge, each category can be further broken down into elements that are core, competitive, or innovative to produce a strategic knowledge map.

Gap Analysis

Having mapped the firm's competitive knowledge position, an organization can perform a gap analysis. The gap between what a firm must do to compete and what it actually is doing represents a *strategic* gap. Addressing this gap is the stuff of traditional strategic management. As suggested by the SWOT framework, strengths and weaknesses represent what the firm can do, opportunities and threats dictate what it must do. Strategy, then, represents how the firm balances its competitive 'cans' and 'musts' to develop and protect its strategic niche.

At the same time, underlying a firm's strategic gap is a potential *knowledge* gap. That is, given a gap between what a firm must do to compete and what it can do, there may also be a gap between what the firm must know to execute its strategy and what it does know. Based on a strategic knowledge and capabilities map, an organization can identify the extent to which its various categories of existing knowledge are in alignment with its strategic requirements. The result is a set of potential knowledge gaps. In some cases, an organization might even know more than is needed to support its competitive position. Nevertheless, a knowledge strategy must address any possible misalignments. The greater the number, variety, or size of the current and future knowledge gaps, and the more volatile the knowledge base because of a dynamic or uncertain competitive environment, the more aggressive the knowledge strategy required. A firm not capable of executing its intended or required strategy must either align its strategy with its capabilities or acquire the capabilities to execute its strategy.

Having performed a strategic evaluation of its knowledge-based resources and capabilities, an organization can determine which knowledge should be developed or acquired. To give knowledge management a strategic focus, the firm's knowledge management initiatives should be directed toward closing this strategic knowledge gap. The important issue is that the knowledge gap is directly derived from and aligned with the strategic gap. This simultaneous alignment of strategy and knowledge is a crucial element of a firm's knowledge strategy. In many firms, knowledge management efforts are divorced from strategic planning and execution. However, having an appropriate knowledge strategy in place is essential for assuring that knowledge management efforts are being driven by and are supporting the firm's competitive strategy. For example, to ensure alignment, Lincoln Re placed responsibility for knowledge management and corporate strategy within the same senior executive position.

A Knowledge Strategy Framework

A knowledge strategy, paralleling the traditional SWOT analysis, describes the overall approach an organization intends to take to align its knowledge resources and capabilities to the intellectual requirements of its strategy. It can be described along two dimensions reflecting its degree of aggressiveness. The first addresses the degree to which an organization needs to increase its knowledge in a particular area versus the opportunity it may have to leverage existing but under-utilized knowledge resources—that is, the extent to which the firm is primarily a creator versus user of knowledge. The second dimension addresses whether the primary sources of knowledge are internal or external. Together these characteristics help a firm to describe and evaluate its current and desired knowledge strategy.[26]

Exploration versus Exploitation

To the extent that an organization finds itself to be at a lower level of knowledge than required to execute its strategy or to defend its position, it requires a high level of knowledge processing to close its internal knowledge gap. To the extent that many competitors in an organization's industry are operating at higher levels of knowledge across many more knowledge positions, a high level of knowledge processing is required to close the external competitive knowledge gap. To the extent that knowledge in the industry is changing rapidly, the organization may need to be creating new knowledge just to keep pace. In these situations, the organization's requirement is to be an explorer, a creator or acquirer of the knowledge required to become and to remain competitive in its strategic position.

On the other hand, when knowledge resources and capabilities significantly exceed the requirements of a competitive position, the organization has the opportunity to further exploit that knowledge platform, possibly within or across other competitive niches. In this situation, the organization's requirement is to be a knowledge *exploiter*. For example, Dow Chemicals screened its portfolio of 29,000 patents to see which should be exploited (and by whom), which could be licensed, and which should be abandoned. This generated $125 million in licensing income and $40 million in savings over ten years.[27] Big6 aggressively sought to sell additional engagements leveraging its experiences, and Lincoln Re aggressively sought reinsurance deals that exploited its existing knowledge regarding insurance risk, service integration, and deal making.

Michael H. Zack

Exploitation and exploration are not mutually exclusive. An organization may need to develop one area of knowledge while simultaneously exploiting another. Ultimately, the ideal for most companies is to maintain a balance between exploration and exploitation within all areas of strategic knowledge. Exploration provides the knowledge capital to propel the company into new niches while maintaining the viability of existing ones. Exploitation of that knowledge provides the financial capital to fuel successive rounds of innovation and exploration. Exploration without exploitation cannot be economically sustained over the long run unless it is subsidized or directly generates a revenue stream (e.g. a research institute). Exploitation without exploration will ultimately result in trying to pump from a dry well. Eventually knowledge becomes stale or obsolete. Those companies that closely integrate knowledge exploration and exploitation I refer to as *innovators*.

Firms that are extremely efficient in exploiting others' knowledge may enjoy some long-term success as an exploiter. However, given the difficulty in transferring knowledge, these cases are rare. Success in those cases usually requires competing against firms whose ability to exploit is not well developed and who make their tacit knowledge accessible to outsiders. For example, recall Apple's exploitation of Xerox's development of the personal computer graphical user interface. The value from knowledge exploitation may be greater when done by the firm creating it or via some form of joint venture between explorer and exploiter firms.

Exploration and exploitation typically occur in different parts of an organization and are often separated temporally and culturally as well as organizationally. Balancing exploitation and exploration requires a well-developed internal knowledge transfer capability between functions such as RSD, sales, marketing, manufacturing, and customer service. This requires a culture, reward systems, and communication networks that support the flow of knowledge and a well-functioning organizational memory (both as embedded in humans and in technology) to transcend the time delays between developing and applying knowledge as well as between applying and developing the next round of knowledge. This knowledge transfer and integration capability is itself strategic.

The creation of unique, strategic knowledge takes time, forcing the firm to balance short- and long-term strategic resource decisions. The firm therefore must determine whether its efforts are best focused on longer-term knowledge exploration, shorter-term exploitation, or both. It must then balance its knowledge-processing resources and efforts accordingly. For example, Image Corp. focused its recruiting and training on the knowledge required to support its future digital products and services. It also implemented computer-based conferencing technologies and created opportunities for face-to-face interaction to support knowledge transfer between its few highly knowledgeable technical, sales, and marketing people in the growing digital products division and their counterparts in traditional products divisions. It did not, however, abandon its existing analog imaging niche but implemented a computer-based knowledge sharing capability among its sales and marketing personnel to exploit as much of their existing knowledge about selling and marketing traditional products as possible.

It is not enough for an organization merely to engage in both exploration and exploitation. More importantly, those activities must be linked and coordinated so that they can reinforce one another. For example, Big6 turned its learning experiences first into semi-structured documents that could be accessed and reused by others immediately and eventually into formal, structured methods for efficiently delivering the service. They established organizational units having explicit responsibility for this function. In this way, they actively managed the exploitation of their exploratory knowledge. New insights gained in the field from reapplying and adapting this knowledge to different contexts were subsequently captured and integrated into existing methods, closing the exploitation/exploration loop. Lincoln Re explored new areas of risk via its prospective R&D process, using the knowledge gained to create new risk management products and services. Those products generated a loss-experience history that could be monitored and analyzed to create additional learning, closing the loop. Image Corp. and Buckman Labs linked their R&D personnel and technical specialists to their field-based marketing, sales, and technical support staffs to ensure that new products were developed with the customers' needs in mind and that customer needs were quickly and accurately communicated to the product development group. New knowledge and insights were therefore more effectively exploited in the marketplace in the form of better products, while interaction with the customers generated knowledge to guide future developments. LeaseCo aggressively attempted to explore knowledge via taking on novel leases and to exploit that learning across its other clients and markets.

Internal versus External Knowledge

A second way to orient a knowledge strategy is to describe the firm's primary sources of knowledge.[28] Knowledge sources may lie within or outside the firm. Internal knowledge may be resident within peoples' heads; embedded in behaviors, procedures, software and equipment; recorded in various documents; or stored in databases and online repositories. Common sources of external knowledge include publications, universities, government agencies, professional associations, personal relations, consultants, vendors, knowledge brokers, and interorganizational alliances. Knowledge generated within the firm is especially valuable because it tends to be unique, specific, and tacitly held. It is therefore more difficult for competitors to imitate, making it strategically valuable. Knowledge from outside the firm—while more abstract, more costly to obtain, and more widely available to competitors—can provide for fresh thinking and a context for benchmarking internal knowledge. Commonly available external knowledge combined with unique internal knowledge can still result in new and unique insights. Buckman labs, for example, maintains close links to universities, taking the generic body of microbiological knowledge and reapplying it within the specific context of its own products and customer applications. Lincoln Re has similarly obtained and reapplied knowledge through its university ties. Joint ventures provide an important means to obtain external knowledge that is tacit, has not been widely distributed, and therefore retains its competitive value.[29] The biotechnology industry, for example, thrives on the collaboration that occurs among firms.[30]

Many externally oriented organizations create opportunities for ongoing dialog with their customers to exchange knowledge. These mechanisms range in formality and include user groups, joint ventures, beta-testing, web sites, e-mail, toll-free numbers, customer care centers, customer advisory boards, conferences, and social gatherings. For example, Lincoln Re maintains strong relationships with its clients through a company-sponsored user group. An advisory council and periodic conferences also provide many opportunities for Lincoln Re to gain access to valuable external customer knowledge and to share its internal knowledge regarding its products and markets. Often, firms use computer-based conferencing systems to supplement face-to-face interaction. They also are creating electronically based repositories to be used for collecting external knowledge, both informal and formal. These materials include papers and presentation slides from conferences, comments, and observations acquired in the field, knowledge picked up at trade shows, and lessons learned from interactions with customers. Buckman Labs is quite well known for their worldwide online conferencing capability and their efforts to build customer-focused knowledge repositories.

Aggressive versus Conservative

Combining the knowledge exploitation versus exploration orientation of the firm with its internally acquired versus externally acquired orientation towards knowledge sources provides a more complete picture of a firm's knowledge strategy. Firms oriented toward exploiting internal knowledge exhibit the most conservative knowledge strategy, while unbounded innovators (those who closely integrate knowledge exploration and exploitation without regard to organizational boundaries) represent the most aggressive strategy. In knowledge-intensive industries, firms that pursue an aggressive knowledge strategy tend to outperform those competitors who pursue less aggressive knowledge strategies over time.[31]

In cases where a firm's knowledge significantly lags its competitors or the firm is defending a knowledge position, an aggressive knowledge strategy will be required to remain viable.[32] Buckman Labs, for example, prioritized its knowledge management efforts by focusing on several markets where its treatment applications knowledge lagged its current or potential competitors, although to maintain existing advantages it continually created and renewed its knowledge of all markets. It took a more aggressive knowledge strategy in those markets than in markets where its knowledge led the industry. LeaseCo claimed the premium, upscale-garment, service-intensive market as a competitive niche and aggressively sought to learn as much as possible about serving that market. Image Corp. found itself needing to aggressively acquire knowledge about digital imaging to ward off both traditional and new competitors. Lincoln Re staked out superior knowledge of risk underwriting and pricing as well as how to integrate multiple services into innovative and comprehensive risk management solutions, and it put in place an aggressive knowledge strategy to maintain this competitive differentiation.

Industry Learning Cycles

Knowledge strategy cannot be formulated in isolation of what competitors are doing. Comparing aggressive and conservative strategies, then, also requires looking at the overall flow of industry knowledge. At the industry level, there is the potential for knowledge to diffuse out from the firm and into the industry at large where it can be absorbed by competitors. At the same time, a similar process may be occurring with other firms in the industry, creating the opportunity for the firm to absorb knowledge from the industry.

Firms taking a conservative strategy view knowledge primarily as proprietary asset to be protected. They attempt to create barriers to its diffusion or transfer outside of the firm. Aggressive firms, however, take a Shumpeterian view of knowledge as an ongoing process of creative destruction. Rather than wait for a competitor to destroy the value of their knowledge, these firms aggressively seek to obsolete their own knowledge, always staying one step ahead of the competition. Aggressive firms are less concerned with erecting barriers to the diffusion or transfer of knowledge, rather they protect their knowledge resources by recruiting and developing intelligent, loyal, and committed employees and support them with a culture of learning, commitment, and collaboration. The firm's advantage comes from being able to absorb external knowledge and integrate it with their internal knowledge to develop new insights faster than the competition. For example, Lincoln Re's competitors were often able to acquire and imitate the underwriting guidelines Lincoln Re provided its clients. However, they were not able to replicate Lincoln Re's skilled medical and actuarial researchers, their deep understanding of how the medical research related to managing and pricing risk, and their unique process for experimenting with that publicly available research to improve and expand their existing knowledge.

The strategic knowledge environment of an industry can be viewed as the sum of the interactions among the knowledge strategies of the individual firms in the industry. In industries with many firms pursuing conservative knowledge strategies, knowledge leaks into the industry slowly and the opportunities to learn from the industry at large may be limited. In industries with many aggressive firms, knowledge flows between individual firms and the industry at large relatively quickly. Only those firms with the best learning capability and the greatest capacity for absorbing external knowledge will survive. Lincoln Re, Buckman, Big6, and Image Corp. were all operating in industries where knowledge was changing rapidly enough that an aggressive strategy was needed just to keep up with the pace of change. Buckman was faced with adding service expertise to its product and manufacturing knowledge. Lincoln Re and Big6 were selling their knowledge directly, transferring it out of the organization at a price. This opened the way for diffusion among competitors and further drove the need to aggressively and continually learn and develop new knowledge.

Positioning

Knowledge can profoundly change the way an organization positions itself in its industry and in doing so, can radically change the organization itself. Buckman Labs exemplified this in their shift from selling chemical products to providing broad microbiocidal treatment solutions. Lincoln Re similarly repositioned themselves from selling reinsurance to selling their knowledge in the form of comprehensive risk management solutions. The case of Bay State Shippers provides an even more profound example. Originally a freight forwarder (a 'travel agent for freight'), Bay State took responsibility for physically routing a shipment from its point of origin to its intended destination, potentially via several modes of transportation (e.g. truck, rail, and ship). Using satellite systems, barcodes, and other information technologies, Bay State created the ability to track a package throughout its multi-modal trip, functioning as 'information central.' While this tracking data was useful to customers, Bay State found a way to add significantly more value while at the same time repositioning themselves from freight handlers to knowledge brokers. Bay State was sitting on a huge amount of transaction data describing point-to-point travel times for various routings and modalities. By analyzing this data and combining it with their employees' experience, they learned how to predict shipment transit times for particular routes and modalities, and they were able to learn about travel patterns in great detail. For example, they might find that particular goods shipped by train through a certain part of Iowa always ran into delays at particular freight yard on Fridays. They combined this knowledge with their ability to track shipments in real time and to create an early warning system for customers. Customers could list their shipments on a computer screen. Shipments highlighted in green indicated expected on time delivery. Yellow indicated the freight was running behind forecasted time. If red, the shipment was expected to arrive late. Customers could now plan and react more intelligently. Beyond this freight control capability, Bay State was able to use their routing knowledge to recommend the most efficient and effective routing for the customers' needs, helping them to avoid delays in the first place. Bay State used its superior knowledge to carve out a significant competitive advantage. In fact, they (like American Airlines and its Sabre reservation system, and Lincoln Re and its Life Underwriting System) eventually saw enough value in the knowledge-based routing system to create a company to sell the system.[33]

Conclusion

Knowledge is the fundamental basis of competition. Competing successfully on knowledge requires either aligning strategy to what the organization knows or developing the knowledge and capabilities needed to support a desired strategy. Organizations must strategically assess their knowledge resources and capabilities, and they need to broadly conceptualize their knowledge strategy to address any gaps. An organization's knowledge strategy must then be translated into an organizational and technical architecture to support knowledge creation, management, and utilization processes for closing those gaps.[34]

If knowledge management is to take hold rather than become merely a passing fad, it will have to be solidly linked to the creation of economic value and competitive advantage. This can be accomplished by grounding knowledge

Michael H. Zack

management within the context of business strategy. Given the state of the art in knowledge management, firms just starting to build a knowledge management infrastructure are not far behind than their more established rivals. By developing the proper strategic grounding, they will be able to focus and prioritize their investments in knowledge management and come out ahead of competitors who have not grounded their efforts in strategy.

Acknowledgement

I wish to thank Nicholas Athanassiou, Dr Arthur DeTore (Director of Strategy and Knowledge Management, Lincoln Re), and William Habeck (CEO, TIE Logistics) for their helpful comments.

Notes and References

1. For a good overview of knowledge management, see T. Davenport and L. Prusak, 'Working Knowledge' (Cambridge, MA: Harvard Business School Press, 1998).
2. For example, see T. Davenport, S. Jarvenpaa, and M. Beers, 'Improving Knowledge Work Processes,' *Sloan Management Review*, 37/4 (Summer 1996): 53–66; P. Goodman and E. Darr, 'Exchanging Best Practices Through Computer-Aided Systems,' *The Academy of Management Executive*, 10/2 (1996): 7–19.
3. J. Nahapiet and S. Ghoshal, 'Social Capital, Intellectual Capital, and the Organizational Advantage,' *Academy of Management Review*, 2312 (1998): 242–67.
4. J. B. Quinn, P. Anderson, and S. Finkelstein, 'Leveraging Intellect,' *Academy of Management Executive*, 10/3 (1996): 7–27.
5. For example, strategy was not identified as a motivating factor or key evaluation criterion regarding knowledge management efforts in a field study of 31 projects in 24 companies [T. Davenport, D. W. De Long, and M. C. Beers, 'Successful Knowledge Management Projects,' *Sloan Management Review*, 39/2 (1998): 43–58], a survey of 431 U.S. and European companies [R. Ruggles, 'The State of the Notion: Knowledge Management in Practice,' *California Management Review*, 40/3 (Spring 1998): 80–9], or a survey of 100 U.S. and European companies [D. E. Leidner, panel presentation, Organization and Information Cultures in Knowledge Management Initiatives, 6th European Conference on Information Systems, Aixen-Provence, June 1998].
6. Image Corp., LeaseCo, and Big6 are pseudonyms.
7. K. R. Andrews, 'The Concept of Corporate Strategy,' (Homewood, IL: Dow-Jones Irwin, 1971), p. 31.
8. M. E. Porter, *Competitive Strategy: Techniques for Analyzing Industries and Competitors* (New York, NY: Free Press, 1980).

9. D. J. Teece, 'Economic Analysis and Strategic Management,' *California Management Review*, 26/3 (Spring 1984): 87–110; J. B. Barney, 'Firm Resources and Sustained Competitive Advantage,' *Journal of Management*, 17 (1991): 99–120.

10. K. R. Connor, 'A Historical Comparison of Resource-based Theory and Five Schools of Thought within Industrial Organization Economics: Do We Have a New Theory of the Firm?' *Journal of Management*, 17 (1991): 121–54.

11. R. Nelson, 'Why Do Firms Differ and Does it Matter?' *Strategic Management Journal*, 12 (Winter 1991, Special Issue): 61–74; A. M. McGahan and M. E. Porter, 'How Much Does Industry Matter, Really?' *Strategic Management Journal*, 18 (1997): 15–30; R. P. Rumelt, 'How Much Does Industry Matter?' *Strategic Management Journal*, 1213 (1991): 167–85.

12. While many authors distinguish (often not consistently) between capabilities and competencies, the term capabilities as used here is meant to include both.

13. J. B. Barney, 'The Resource-Based Theory of the Firm,' *Organization Science*, 7/5 (September/October 1996): 469–76; D. J. Collis and C. A. Montgomery, 'Competing on Resources: Strategy in the 1990s,' *Harvard Business Review*, 73/4 (July/August, 1995): 118–28; R. M. Grant, 'The Resource-Based Theory of Competitive Advantage: Implications for Strategy Formulation,' *California Management Review*, 33/3 (Spring 1991): 114–35; C. K. Prahalad and G. Hamel, 'The Core Competence of the Corporation,' *Harvard Business Review*, 68/3 (May/June 1990): 79–91.

14. B. Kogut and N. Kulatilaka, 'Options Thinking and Platform Investments: Investing in Opportunity,' *California Management Review*, 36/2 (Winter 1994): 52–71.

15. E. T. Penrose, *The Theory of The Growth of the Firm* (White Plains, NY: M. E. Sharpe, Inc., U.S. edition, 1980), pp. 76–80; P. M. Romer, 'Beyond the Knowledge Worker,' *World Link*, Davos '95, January/February 1995; D. J. Teece, G. Pisano, and A. Shuen, 'Dynamic Capabilities and Strategic Management,' *Strategic Management Journal*, 18/7 (1997): 509–33.

16. R. M. Grant, 'Prospering in Dynamically Competitive Environments: Organizational Capability as Knowledge Integration,' *Organization Science*, 7/4 (1996): 375–87; B. Kogut and U. Zander, 'Knowledge of the Firm, Combinative Capabilities, and the Replication of Technology,' *Organization Science*, 3/3 (August 1992): 383–97; Penrose, op. cit.; J.-C. Spender, 'Organizational Knowledge, Collective Practice and Penrose Rents,' *International Business Review*, 3/4 (1994): 353–67; Teece, Pisano, and Shuen, op. cit.; S. G. Winter, 'Knowledge and Competence as Strategic Assets,' in David J. Teece, (ed.), *The Competitive Challenge: Strategies for Industrial Innovation and Renewal* (Cambridge, MA: Ballinger Publishing Company, 1987), Chapter 8, pp. 159–84.

17. W. Cohen, and D. Leventhal, 'Absorptive Capacity: A New Perspective on Learning and Innovation,' *Administrative Science Quarterly*, 35 (1990): 128–52.

18. D. K. Goldstein and M. H. Zack, 'The Impact of Marketing Information Supply on Product Managers: An Organizational Information Processing Perspective,' *Office, Technology and People*, 4/4 (June 1989): 313–36.

19. Romer, op. cit.; D. J. Teece, 'Capturing Value from Knowledge Assets: The New Economy, Markets for Know-how, and Intangible Assets,' *California Management Review*, 40/3 (Spring 1998): 55–79.

20. J. M. Utterback, *Mastering the Dynamics of Innovation: How Companies Can Seize Opportunities in the Face of Technological Change* (Boston, MA: Harvard Business School Press, 1994).

21. G. Hamel and C. K. Prahalad, 'Strategic Intent,' *Harvard Business Review*, 67/3 (May/June 1989): 63–76.

22. J. B. Quinn, *Strategies for Change: Logical Incrementalism* (Homewood, IL: Irwin, 1980).

23. H. Mintzberg, 'The Fall and Rise of Strategic Planning,' *Harvard Business Review*, 72/1 (January/February 1994): 107–14; K. E. Weick, 'Substitutes for Strategy,' in D. J. Teece (ed.), *The Competitive Challenge: Strategies for Industrial Innovation and Renewal* (Cambridge, MA: Ballinger Publishing Co., 1987), pp. 221–33.

24. H. Demsetz, 'The Theory of the Firm Revisited,' *Journal of Law, Economics and Organization*, 4/1 (Spring 1988): 141–61; M. Polyani, *The Tacit Dimension* (Garden City, NY: Doubleday, 1966), J.-C. Spender, 'Organizational Knowledge, Learning and Memory: Three Concepts in Search of a Theory,' *Journal of Organizational Change Management*, 9/1 (1996): 63–78.

25. C. Markides, 'Strategic Innovation in Established Companies,' *Sloan Management Review*, 39/3 (1998): 31–42.

26. P. Bierly, and A. Chakrabarti, 'Generic Knowledge Strategies in the U.S. Pharmaceutical Industry,' *Strategic Management Journal*, 17 (Winter 1996, Special Issue): 123–35; J. G. March, 'Exploration and Exploitation in Organizational Learning,' *Organization Science*, 2/1 (1991): 71–87.

27. D. Cohen, 'Toward a Knowledge Context: Report on the First Annual U.C. Berkeley Forum on Knowledge and the Firm,' *California Management Review*, 40/3 (Spring 1998): 22–39.

28. Bierly and Chakrabarti, op. cit.

29. J. Badaracco, Jr., *The Knowledge Link: How Firms Compete Through Strategic Alliances* (Boston, MA: Harvard Business School Press, 1991).

30. W. W. Powell, 'Learning from Collaboration: Knowledge and Networks in the Biotechnology and Pharmaceutical Industries,' *California Management Review*, 40/3 (Spring 1998): 228–40.

31. Bierly and Chakrabarti, op. cit.

32. L. Kim, 'Crisis Construction and Organizational Learning: Capability Building in Catching-up at Hyundai Motor,' *Organization Science*, 9/4 (1998): 506–21.

33. In 1992, Bay State Shippers spun off their software product, COMMAND, into Tie Logistics, Inc. In 1993, Tie Logistics won the Computerworld Smithsonian Transportation Award for innovative use of information technology in transportation, and COMMAND was made part of the permanent Information Age exhibit at the Smithsonian National Museum of American History. C. H. Robinson Worldwide, Inc acquired Bay State in 1994.

34. For a good discussion, see Davenport and Prusak, op. cit.; M. H. Zack, 'An Architecture for Managing Explicated Knowledge,' *Sloan Management Review* (forthcoming).

II. KNOWLEDGE DEVELOPMENT AND INDIVIDUAL LEARNING

3 The Learning Curve

Atul Gawande

The patient needed a central line. 'Here's your chance,' S., the chief resident, said. I had never done one before. 'Get set up and then page me when you're ready to start.'

It was my fourth week in surgical training. The pockets of my short white coat bulged with patient printouts, laminated cards with instructions for doing CPR and using the dictation system, two surgical handbooks, a stethoscope, wound-dressing supplies, meal tickets, a penlight, scissors, and about a buck in loose change. As I headed up the stairs to the patient's floor, I rattled.

This will be good, I tried to tell myself: my first real procedure. My patient—fiftyish, stout, and taciturn—was recovering from abdominal surgery he'd had about a week before. His bowel function hadn't yet returned, leaving him unable to eat. I explained to him that he needed intravenous nutrition and that this required a 'special line' that would go into his chest. I said that I would put the line in him while he was in his bed and that it would involve my laying him out flat, numbing up a spot on his chest with local anesthetic, and then threading the line in. I did not say that the line was eight inches long and would go into his vena cava, the main blood vessel to his heart. Nor did I say how tricky the procedure would be. There were 'slight risks' involved, I said, such as bleeding or lung collapse; in experienced hands, problems of this sort occur in fewer than one case in a hundred.

But, of course, mine were not experienced hands. And the disasters I knew about weighed on my mind: the woman who had died from massive bleeding when a resident lacerated her vena cava; the man who had had to have his chest opened because a resident lost hold of the wire inside the line which then floated down to the patient's heart; the man who had had a cardiac arrest when the procedure put him into ventricular fibrillation. But I said nothing of such things

53

when I asked my patient's permission to do his line. And he said, 'OK,' I could go ahead.

I had seen S. do two central lines; one was the day before, and I'd attended to every step. I watched how she set out her instruments and laid down her patient and put a rolled towel between his shoulder blades to make his chest arch out. I watched how she swabbed his chest with antiseptic, injected lidocaine, which is a local anesthetic, and then, in full sterile garb, punctured his chest near his clavicle with a fat three-inch needle on a syringe. The patient didn't even flinch. S. told me how to avoid hitting the lung with the needle ('Go in at a steep angle; stay *right* under the clavicle'), and how to find the subclavian vein, a branch to the vena cava lying atop the lung near its apex ('Go in at a steep angle; stay *right* under the clavicle'). She pushed the needle in almost all the way. She drew back on the syringe. And she was in. You knew because the syringe filled with maroon blood. ('If it's bright red, you've hit an artery,' she said. 'That's not good.')

Once you have the tip of this needle poking in the vein, you have to widen the hole in the vein wall, fit the catheter in, and thread it in the right direction—down to the heart rather than up to the brain—all without tearing through vessels, lung, or anything else. To do this, S. explained, you start by getting a guidewire in place. She pulled the syringe off, leaving the needle in place. Blood flowed out. She picked up a two-foot-long twenty-gauge wire that looked like the steel D string of an electric guitar, and passed nearly its full length through the needle's bore, into the vein, and onward toward the vena cava. 'Never force it in,' she warned, 'and never ever let go of it.' A string of rapid heartbeats fired off on the cardiac monitor, and she quickly pulled the wire back an inch. It had poked into the heart, causing momentary fibrillation. 'Guess we're in the right place,' she said to me quietly. Then to the patient: 'You're doing great. Only a couple of minutes now.' She pulled the needle out over the wire and replaced it with a bullet of thick, stiff plastic, which she pushed in tight to widen the vein opening. She then removed this dilator and threaded the central line—a spaghetti-thick, yellow, flexible plastic tube—over the wire until it was all the way in. Now she could remove the wire. She flushed the line with a heparin solution and sutured it to his chest. And that was it.

I had seen the procedure done. Now it was my turn to try. I set about gathering the supplies—a central-line kit, gloves, gown, cap, mask, lidocaine—and that alone took me forever. When I finally had the stuff together, I stopped outside my patient's door and just stood there staring, silently trying to recall the steps. They remained frustratingly hazy. But I couldn't put it off any longer. I had a page-long list of other things to get done: Mrs. A needed to be discharged; Mr. B needed an abdominal ultrasound arranged; Mrs. C needed her skin staples removed. . . . And every fifteen minutes or so I was getting paged with more tasks—Mr. X was nauseated and needed to be seen; Miss Y's family was here and needed 'someone' to talk to them; Mr. Z needed a laxative. I took a deep breath, put on my best don't-worry-I-know-what-I'm-doing look, and went in to do the line.

I placed the supplies on a bedside table, untied the patient's gown behind his neck, and laid him down flat on the mattress, with his chest bare and his arms at his sides. I flipped on a fluorescent overhead light and raised his bed to my height. I paged S. to come. I put on my gown and gloves and, on a sterile tray, laid out the central line, guidewire, and other materials from the kit the way I remembered S. doing it. I drew up five cc's of lidocaine in a syringe, soaked two sponge-sticks in the yellow-brown Betadine antiseptic solution, and opened up the suture packaging. I was good to go.

S. arrived. 'What's his platelet count?'

My stomach knotted. I hadn't checked. That was bad: too low and he could have a serious bleed from the procedure. She went to check a computer. The count was acceptable.

Chastened, I started swabbing his chest with the sponge-sticks. 'Got the shoulder roll underneath him?' S. asked. Well, no. I had forgotten this, too. The patient gave me a look. S., saying nothing, got a towel, rolled it up, and slipped it under his back for me. I finished applying the antiseptic and then draped him so only his right upper chest was exposed. He squirmed a bit beneath the drapes. S. now inspected my tray. I girded myself.

'Where's the extra syringe for flushing the line when it's in?' Damn. She went out and got it.

I felt for landmarks on the patient's chest. *Here?* I asked with my eyes, not wanting to undermine my patient's confidence any further. She nodded. I numbed the spot with lidocaine. ('You'll feel a stick and a burn now, sir.') Next, I took the three-inch needle in hand and poked it through the skin. I advanced it slowly and uncertainly, a few millimeters at a time, afraid to plunge it into something bad. This is a big goddam needle, I kept thinking. I couldn't believe I was sticking it into someone's chest. I concentrated on maintaining a steep angle of entry, but kept spearing his clavicle instead of slipping beneath it.

'Ow!' he shouted.

'Sorry,' I said. S. signaled with a kind of surfing hand gesture to go underneath the clavicle. This time it did. I drew back on the syringe. Nothing. She pointed deeper. I went in deeper. Nothing. I took the needle out, flushed out some bits of tissue clogging it, and tried again.

'*Ow!*'

Too superficial again. I found my way underneath the clavicle once more. I drew the syringe back. Still nothing. He's too obese, I thought to myself. S. slipped on gloves and a gown. 'How about I have a look,' she said. I handed her the needle and stepped aside. She plunged the needle in, drew back on the syringe, and, just like that, she was in. 'We'll be done shortly,' she told the patient. I felt utterly inept.

She let me continue with the next steps, which I bumbled through. I didn't realize how long and floppy the guidewire was until I pulled the coil out of its plastic sleeve, and, putting one end of it into the patient, I very nearly let the other touch his unsterile bedsheet. I forgot about the dilating step until she reminded me. Then, when I put in the dilator, I didn't push quite hard enough, and it was really S. who pushed it all the way in. Finally, we got the line in, flushed it, and sutured it in place.

Outside the room, S. said that I could be less tentative the next time, but that I shouldn't worry too much about how things had gone. 'You'll get it,' she said. 'It just takes practice.' I wasn't so sure. The procedure remained wholly mysterious to me. And I could not get over the idea of jabbing a needle so deeply and blindly into someone's chest. I awaited the X ray afterward with trepidation. But it came back fine: I had not injured the lung and the line was in the right place.

Not everyone appreciates the attractions of surgery. When you are a medical student in the operating room for the first time, and you see the surgeon press the scalpel to someone's body and open it like fruit, you either shudder in horror or gape in awe. I gaped. It was not just the blood and guts that enthralled me. It was the idea that a mere person would have the confidence to wield that scalpel in the first place.

There is a saying about surgeons, meant as a reproof: 'Sometimes wrong; never in doubt.' But this seemed to me their strength. Every day, surgeons are faced with uncertainties. Information is inadequate; the science is ambiguous; one's knowledge and abilities are never perfect. Even with the simplest operation, it cannot be taken for granted that a patient will come through better off—or even alive. Standing at the table my first time, I wondered how the surgeon knew that he would do this patient good, that all the steps would go as planned, that bleeding would be controlled and infection would not take hold and organs would not be injured. He didn't, of course. But still he cut.

Later, while still a student, I was allowed to make an incision myself. The surgeon drew a six-inch dotted line with a marking pen across a sleeping patient's abdomen and then, to my surprise, had the nurse hand me the knife. It was, I remember, still warm from the sterilizing autoclave. The surgeon had me stretch the skin taut with the thumb and forefinger of my free hand. He told me to make one smooth slice down to the fat. I put the belly of the blade to the skin and cut. The experience was odd and addictive, mixing exhilaration from the calculated violence of the act, anxiety about getting it right, and a righteous faith that it was somehow good for the person. There was also the slightly nauseating feeling of finding that it took more force than I'd realized. (Skin is thick and springy, and on my first pass I did not go nearly deep enough; I had to cut twice to get through.) The moment made me want to be a surgeon—not to be an amateur, handed the knife for a brief moment, but someone with the confidence to proceed as if it were routine.

A resident, however, begins with none of this air of mastery—only a still overpowering instinct against doing anything like pressing a knife against flesh or jabbing a needle into someone's chest. On my first day as a surgical resident, I was assigned to the emergency room. Among my first patients was a skinny, dark-haired women in her late twenties who hobbled in, teeth gritted, with a two-and-a-half-foot-long wooden chair-leg somehow nailed into the bottom of her foot. She explained that the leg had collapsed out from under a kitchen chair she had tried to sit upon and, leaping up to keep from falling, she inadvertently stomped her bare foot onto the three-inch screw sticking out of it. I tried very hard to look like someone who had not just got his medical diploma the week before. Instead, I was determined to be nonchalant, world-weary, the kind of guy who had seen this sort of thing a hundred times before. I inspected her foot and could see that the screw was embedded in the bone at the base of her big toe. There was no bleeding, and, so far as I could feel, no fracture.

'Wow, that must hurt,' I blurted out idiotically.

The obvious thing to do was give her a tetanus shot and pull out the screw. I ordered the tetanus shot, but I began to have doubts about pulling out the screw. Suppose she bled? Or suppose I fractured her foot? Or something worse? I excused myself and tracked down Dr. W, the senior surgeon on duty. I found him tending to a car-crash victim. The patient was a mess. People were shouting. Blood was all over the floor. It was not a good time to ask questions.

I ordered an X ray. I figured it would buy time and let me check my amateur impression that she didn't have a fracture. Sure enough, getting one took about an hour and it showed no fracture—just a common screw embedded, the radiologist said, 'in the head of the first metatarsa.' I showed the patient the X ray. 'You see, the screw's imbedded in the head of the first metatarsa,' I said. And the plan? she wanted to know. Ah, yes, the plan.

I went to find Dr. W. He was still tied up with the crash victim, but I was able to interrupt to show him the X ray. He chuckled at the sight of it and asked me what I wanted to do. 'Pull the screw out?' I ventured. 'Yes,' he said, by which he meant 'Duh.' He made sure I'd given a tetanus shot and then shooed me away.

Back in the room, I told her that I would pull the screw out, prepared for her to say something like 'You?' Instead she said, 'OK, Doctor,' and it was time for me to get down to business. At first I had her sitting on the exam table, dangling her leg off the side. But that didn't look as if it would work. Eventually, I had her lie with her foot jutting off the end of the table, the board poking out into the air. With every move, her pain increased. I injected a local anesthetic where the screw went in and that helped a little. Now I grabbed her foot in one hand, the board in the other and then for a moment I froze. Could I really do this? Should I really do this? Who was I to presume?

Finally, I just made myself do it. I gave her a one-two-three and pulled, too gingerly at first and then, forcing myself, hard. She groaned. The screw wasn't budging. I twisted, and abruptly it came free. There was no bleeding. I washed the wound out, as my textbooks said to for puncture wounds. She found she could walk, though the foot was sore. I warned her of the risks of infection and the signs to look for. Her gratitude was immense and flattering, like the lion's for the mouse—and that night I went home elated.

In surgery, as in anything else, skill and confidence are learned through experience—haltingly and humiliatingly. Like the tennis player and the oboist and the guy who fixes hard drives, we need practice to get good at what we do. There is one difference in medicine, though: it is people we practice upon.

My second try at placing a central line went no better than the first. The patient was in intensive care, mortally ill, on a ventilator, and needed the line so that powerful cardiac drugs could be delivered directly to her heart. She was also heavily sedated, and for this I was grateful. She'd be oblivious to my fumbling.

My preparation was better this time. I got the towel roll in place and the syringes of heparin on the tray. I checked her lab results, which were fine. I also made a point of draping more widely, so that if I flopped my guidewire around by mistake again, I could be sure it wouldn't hit anything unsterile.

For all that, the procedure was a bust. I stabbed the needle in too shallow and then too deep. Frustration overcame tentativeness and I tried one angle after another. Nothing worked. Then, for one brief moment, I got a flash of blood in the syringe, indicating I was in the vein. I anchored the needle with one hand and went to pull the syringe off with the other. But the syringe was jammed on too tightly, so that when I pulled it free I dislodged the needle from the vein. The patient began bleeding into her chest wall. I applied pressure the best I could for a solid five minutes, but her chest still turned black and blue around the site. The hematoma made it impossible to put a line through there anymore. I wanted to give up. But she needed a line and the resident supervising me—a second-year this time—was determined that I succeed. After an X ray showed that I had not injured her lung, he had me try again on the other side with a whole new kit. I still missed, however, and before I turned the patient into a pincushion he took over. It took him several minutes and two or three sticks to find the vein himself and that made me feel better. Maybe she was an unusually tough case.

When I failed with a third patient a few days later, however, the doubts really set in. Again, it was stick, stick, stick, and nothing. I stepped aside. The resident watching me got it on the very next try.

Surgeons, as a group, adhere to a curious egalitarianism. They believe in practice, not talent. People often assume that you have to have great hands to become a surgeon, but it's not true. When I interviewed to get into surgery programs, no one made me sew or take a dexterity test or checked if my hands were steady. You do not even need all ten fingers to be accepted. To be sure, talent helps. Professors say every two or three years they'll see someone truly gifted come through a program—someone who picks up complex manual skills unusually quickly, sees the operative field as a whole, notices trouble before it happens. Nonetheless, attending surgeons say that what's most important to them is finding people who are conscientious, industrious, and boneheaded enough to stick at practicing this one difficult thing day and night for years on end. As one professor of surgery put it to me, given a choice between a Ph.D. who had painstakingly cloned a gene and a talented sculptor, he'd pick the Ph.D. every time. Sure, he said, he'd bet on the sculptor being more physically talented; but he'd bet on the Ph.D. being less 'flaky.' And in the end that matters more. Skill, surgeons believe, can be taught; tenacity cannot. It's an odd approach to recruitment, but it continues all the way up the ranks, even in top surgery departments. They take minions with no experience in surgery, spend years training them, and then take most of their faculty from these same homegrown ranks.

And it works. There have now been many studies of elite performers—international violinists, chess grand masters, professional ice-skaters, mathematicians, and so forth—and the biggest difference researchers find between them and lesser performers is the cumulative amount of deliberate practice they've had. Indeed, the most important talent may be the talent for practice itself. K. Anders Ericsson, a cognitive psychologist and expert on performance, notes that the most important way in which innate factors play a role may be in one's *willingness* to engage in sustained training. He's found, for example, that top performers dislike practicing just as much as others do. (That's why, for example, athletes and musicians usually quit practicing when they retire.) But more than others, they have the will to keep at it anyway.

I wasn't sure I did. What good was it, I wondered, to keep doing central lines when I wasn't coming close to getting them in? If I had a clear idea of what I was doing wrong, then maybe I'd have something to focus on. But I didn't. Everyone, of course, had suggestions. Go in with the bevel of the needle up. No, go in with the bevel down. Put a bend in the middle of the needle. No, curve the needle. For a while, I tried to avoid doing another line. Soon enough, however, a new case arose.

The circumstances were miserable. It was late in the day and I'd been up all the night before. The patient was morbidly obese, weighing more than three hundred pounds. He couldn't tolerate lying flat because the weight of his chest and abdomen made it hard for him to breathe. Yet he absolutely needed a central line. He had a badly infected wound and needed intravenous antibiotics, and no one could find veins in his arms for a peripheral IV. I had little hope of succeeding. But a resident does what he is told, and I was told to try the line.

I went to his room. He looked scared and said he didn't think he'd last more than a minute on his back. But he said he understood the situation and was willing to make his best effort. He and I decided that he'd be left sitting propped up in bed until the last possible minute. We'd see how far we got after that.

I went through my preparations: checking the labs, putting out the kit, placing the towel roll, and so on. I swabbed and draped his chest while he was still sitting up. S., the chief resident, was watching me this time, and when everything was ready I had her tip him back, an oxygen mask on his face. His flesh rolled up his chest like a wave. I couldn't find his clavicle with my fingertips to line up the right point of entry. And already he was looking short of breath, his face red. I gave S. a 'Do you want to take over?' look. Keep going, she signaled. I made a rough guess as to where the right spot was, numbed it with lidocaine, then pushed the big needle in. For a second, I thought it wouldn't be long enough to reach through, but then I felt the tip slip underneath his clavicle. I pushed a little deeper and drew back on the syringe. Unbelievably, it filled with blood. *I was in.* I concentrated on anchoring the needle firmly in place, not moving it a millimeter as I pulled the syringe off and threaded the guidewire in. The wire fed in smoothly. He was struggling hard for air now. We sat him up and let him catch his breath. And then with one more lie-down, I got the entry dilated and slid the central line in. 'Nice job,' was all S. said, and then she left.

I still have no idea what I did differently that day. But from then on, my lines went in. Practice is funny that way. For days and days, you make out only the fragments of what to do. And then one day you've got the thing whole. Conscious learning becomes unconscious knowledge, and you cannot say precisely how.

I have now put in more than a hundred central lines. I am by no means infallible. Certainly, I have had my fair share of what we prefer to call 'adverse events'. I punctured a patient's lung, for example—the right lung of a surgeon from another hospital, no less—and, given the odds, I'm sure such things will happen again. I still have the occasional case that should go easily, but doesn't no matter what I do. (We have a term for this. 'How'd it go?' a colleague asks. 'It was a total flog', I reply. I don't have to say anything more.)

But then there are the other times, when everything goes perfectly. You don't think. You don't concentrate. Every move unfolds effortlessly. You take the needle. You stick the chest. You feel the needle travel—a distinct glide through the fat, a slight catch in the dense muscle, then the subtle pop through the vein wall—and you're in. At such moments, it is more than easy; it is beautiful.

Surgical training is the recapitulation of this process—the floundering followed by fragments, followed by knowledge and occasionally a moment of elegance—over and over again, for ever harder tasks with ever greater risks. At first, you work on the basics: how to glove and gown, how to drape patients, how to hold the knife, how to tie a square knot in a length of silk suture (not to mention how to dictate, work the computers, order drugs). But then the tasks become more daunting: how to cut through skin, handle the electrocautery, open the breast, tie off a bleeding vessel, excise the tumor, close up the wound—a breast lumpectomy. By the end of six months, I had done lines, appendectomies, skin grafts, hernia repairs, and mastectomies. At the end of a year, I was doing limb amputations, lymph node biopsies, and hemorrhoidectomies. At the end of two years, I was doing tracheotomies, a few small-bowel operations, and laparoscopic gallbladder operations.

I am in my seventh year of training. Only now has a simple slice through skin begun to seem like nothing, the mere start of a case. When I'm inside, the struggle remains. These days, I'm trying to learn how to fix abdominal aortic aneurysms, remove pancreatic cancers, open blocked carotid arteries. I am, I have found, neither gifted nor maladroit. With practice and more practice, I get the hang of it.

We find it hard, in medicine, to talk about this with patients. The moral burden of practicing on people is always with us, but for the most part unspoken. Before each operation, I go over to the preoperative holding area in my scrubs and introduce myself to the patient. I do it the same way every time. 'Hello, I'm Dr. Gawande. I'm one of the surgical residents, and I'll be assisting your surgeon.' That is pretty much all I say on the subject. I extend my hand and give a smile. I ask the patient if everything is going OK so far. We chat. I answer questions. Very occasionally, patients are taken aback. 'No resident is doing my surgery,' they say. I try to reassure. 'Not to worry. I just assist,' I say. 'The attending surgeon is always in charge.'

None of this is exactly a lie. The attending *is* in charge, and a resident knows better than to forget that. Consider the operation I did recently to remove a seventy-five-year-old woman's colon cancer. The attending stood across from me from the start. And it was he, not I, who decided where to cut, how to isolate the cancer, how much colon to take.

Yet to say I just assisted remains a kind of subterfuge. I wasn't merely an extra pair of hands, after all. Otherwise, why did I hold the knife? Why did I stand on the operator's side of the table? Why was it raised to my six-feet-plus height? I was there to help, yes, but I was there to practice, too. This was clear when it came time to reconnect the colon. There are two ways of putting the ends together—by hand-sewing them or stapling them. Stapling is swifter and easier, but the attending suggested I hand-sew the ends—not because it was better for the patient but because I had done it few times before. When it's performed correctly, the results are similar, but he needed to watch me like a hawk. My stitching was slow and imprecise. At one point, he caught me leaving the stitches too far apart and made me go back and put extras in between so the connection would not leak. At another point, he found I wasn't taking deep enough bites of tissue with the needle to ensure a strong closure. 'Turn your wrist more,' he told me. 'Like this?' I asked. 'Uh, sort of,' he said. I was learning.

In medicine, we have long faced a conflict between the imperative to give patients the best possible care and the need to provide novices with experience. Residencies attempt to mitigate potential harm through supervision and graduated responsibility. And there is reason to think patients actually benefit from teaching. Studies generally find teaching hospitals have better outcomes than nonteaching hospitals. Residents may be amateurs, but having them around checking on patients, asking questions, and keeping faculty on their toes seems to help. But there is still no getting around those first few unsteady times a young physician tries to put in a central line, remove a breast cancer, or sew together two segments of colon. No matter how many protections we put in place, on average these cases go less well with the novice than with someone experienced.

We have no illusions about this. When an attending physician brings a sick family member in for surgery, people at the hospital think hard about how much to let trainees participate. Even when the attending insists that they participate as usual, a resident scrubbing in knows that it will be far from a teaching case. And if a central line must be put in, a first-timer is certainly not going to do it. Conversely, the ward services and clinics where residents have the most responsibility are populated by the poor, the uninsured, the drunk, and the demented. Residents have few opportunities nowadays to operate independently, without the attending docs scrubbed in, but when we do—as we must before graduating and going out to operate on our own—it is generally on these, the humblest of patients.

This is the uncomfortable truth about teaching. By traditional ethics and public insistence (not to mention court rulings), a patient's right to the best care possible must trump the objective of training novices. We want perfection without practice. Yet everyone is harmed if no one is trained for the future. So learning is hidden, behind drapes and anesthesia and the elisions of language. Nor does the dilemma apply just to residents, physicians in training. In fact, the process of learning turns out to extend longer than most people know.

My sister and I grew up in the small town of Athens, Ohio, where our parents are both doctors. Long ago my mother chose to practice pediatrics part-time, only three half-days a week, and she was able to because my father's urology practice became so busy and successful. He has now been at it for more than twenty-five years, and his office is cluttered with the evidence of it: an over-flowing wall of patient files, gifts from people displayed everywhere (books, paintings, ceramics with biblical sayings, hand-painted paperweights, blown glass, and carved boxes, as well as a figurine of a boy who pees on you when you pull down his pants). In an acrylic case behind his oak desk there are a few dozen of the thousands of kidney stones he has removed from these patients.

Only now, as I get glimpses of the end of my training, have I begun to think hard about my father's success. For most of residency, I thought of surgery as a more or less fixed body of knowledge and skill which is acquired in training and perfected in practice. There was, as I envisioned it, a smooth, upward-sloping arc of proficiency at some rarefied set of tasks (for me, taking out gallbladders, colon cancers, bullets, and appendices; for him, taking out kidney stones, testicular cancers, and swollen prostates). The arc would peak at, say, ten or fifteen years, plateau for a long time, and perhaps tail off a little in the final five years before retirement. The reality, however, turns out to be far messier. You do get good at certain things, my father tells me, but no sooner than you do, you find what you know is outmoded. New technologies and operations emerge to supplant the old, and the learning curve starts all over again. 'Three-quarters of what I do today I never learned in residency,' he says. On his own, fifty miles from his nearest colleague—let alone a doctor who could tell him anything like 'You need to turn your wrist more when you do that'— he has had to learn to put in penile prostheses, to perform microsurgery, to reverse vasectomies, to do nerve-sparing prostatectomies, to implant artificial urinary sphincters. He's had to learn to use shock-wave lithotripters, electro-hydraulic lithotripters, and laser lithotripters (all instruments for breaking up kidney stones); to deploy Double J ureteral stents and Silicone Figure Four Coil stents and Retro-Inject Multi-Length stents (don't even ask); to maneuver fiber-optic ureteroscopes. All these technologies and techniques were introduced since he finished training. Some of the procedures built on previous skills. Many did not.

This is, in fact, the experience all surgeons have. The pace of medical innov-ation has been unceasing, and surgeons have no choice but to give the new thing a try. To fail to adopt new techniques would mean denying patients meaningful medical advances. Yet the perils of the learning curve are inescapable—no less in practice than in residency.

For the established surgeon, inevitably, the opportunities for learning are far less structured than for a resident. When an important new device or proced-ure comes along, as they do every year, surgeons start out by taking a course about it—typically a day or two of lectures by some surgical grandees with a few film clips and step-by-step handouts. We take a video home to watch.

Atul Gawande

Perhaps we pay a visit to observe a colleague perform the operation—my father often goes up to Ohio State or the Cleveland Clinic for this. But there's not much by way of hands-on training. Unlike a resident, a visitor cannot scrub in on cases, and opportunities to practice on animals or cadavers are few and far between. (Britain, being Britain, actually bans surgeons from practicing on animals.) When the pulsed-dye laser came out, the manufacturer set up a lab in Columbus where urologists from the area could gain experience. But when my father went, the main experience provided was destroying kidney stones in test tubes filled with a urinelike liquid and trying to penetrate the shell of an egg without hitting the membrane underneath. My surgery department recently purchased a robotic surgery device—a staggeringly sophisticated nine-hundred-and-eighty-thousand-dollar robot, with three arms, two wrists, and a camera, all millimeters in diameter, which, controlled from a console, allows a surgeon to do almost any operation with absolutely no hand tremor and with only tiny incisions. A team of two surgeons and two nurses flew out to the manufacturer's headquarters in San Jose for a full day of training on the machine. And they did get to practice on a pig and on a human cadaver. (The company apparently buys the cadavers from the city of San Francisco.) But even this, which is far more practice than one usually gets, was hardly thorough training. They learned enough to grasp the principles for operating the robot, to start getting a feel for using it, and to understand how to plan an operation. That was about it. Sooner or later, one just has to go home and give the thing a try.

Patients do eventually benefit—often enormously—but the first few patients may not and may even be harmed. Consider the experience reported by the pediatric-surgery unit of the renowned Great Ormond Street Hospital in London, as detailed in the *British Medical Journal* in the spring of 2000. The doctors described their results in operating on 325 consecutive babies with a severe heart defect, known as transposition of the great arteries, over a period (from 1978 to 1998) when its surgeons changed from doing one operation for the condition to another. Such children are born with their heart's outflow vessels transposed: the aorta emerges from the right side of the heart instead of the left and the artery to the lungs emerges from the left instead of the right. As a result, blood coming in is pumped right back out to the body instead of first to the lungs, where it can be oxygenated. This is unsurvivable. The babies died blue, fatigued, never knowing what it was to get enough breath. For years, switching the vessels to their proper positions wasn't technically feasible. Instead, surgeons did something known as the Senning procedure: they created a passage inside the heart to let blood from the lungs cross backward to the right heart. The Senning procedure allowed children to live into adulthood. The weaker right heart, however, cannot sustain the body's entire blood flow as long as the left. Eventually, these patients' hearts failed, and although most made it to adulthood, few lived to old age. Then, by the 1980s, a series of technological advancements made it possible to do a switch operation safely. It rapidly became the favored procedure. In 1986, the Great Ormond Street surgeons made the changeover, and their report shows that it was unquestionably a change for the better. The annual death rate after a successful switch procedure was less than a quarter of that after the Senning, resulting in a life expectancy of sixty-three years instead of forty-seven. But the price of learning to do it was appalling. In their first seventy switch operations, the doctors had a 25 percent surgical death rate, compared with just 6 percent with the Senning procedure. (Eighteen babies died, more than twice the number of the entire Senning era.) Only with time did they master it: in their next hundred switch operations, just five babies died.

As patients, we want both expertise and progress. What nobody wants to face is that these are contradictory desires. In the words of one British public report, 'There should be no learning curve as far as patient safety is concerned.' But that is entirely wishful thinking.

Recently, a group of Harvard Business School researches who have made a specialty of studying learning curves in industry—in making semiconductors, building airplanes, and such—decided to examine learning curves among surgeons. They followed eighteen cardiac surgeons and their teams as they took on the new technique of minimally invasive cardiac surgery. This study, I was surprised to discover, is the first of its kind. Learning is ubiquitous in medicine, and yet no one had ever compared how well different clinicians actually do it.

The new heart operation—involving a small incision between ribs instead of a chest split open down the middle—proved substantially more difficult than the conventional one. Because the incision is too small to admit the usual tubes and clamps for rerouting blood to the heart-bypass machine, surgeons had to learn a trickier method, which involved balloons and catheters placed through groin vessels. They had to learn how to operate in a much reduced space. And the nurses, anesthesiologists, and perfusionists all had new roles to master, too. Everyone had new tasks, new instruments, new ways that things could go wrong, and new ways to fix them. As you'd expect, everyone was found to experience a substantial learning curve. Whereas a fully proficient team takes three to six hours for such operations, these teams took an average of three times longer for their early cases. The researchers could not track rates of morbidity in detail, but it would be foolish to imagine that these rates were not affected.

What's more interesting is that researchers found striking disparities in the speed with which different teams learned. All teams received the same three-day training session and came from highly respected institutions with experience in adopting innovations. Yet, in the course of fifty cases, some teams managed to halve their operating time while others failed to improve at all. Practice, it turned out, did not necessarily make perfect. Whether it did, the researchers found, depended on *how* the surgeons and their teams practiced.

Richard Bohmer, the one physician among the Harvard researchers, made several visits to observe one of the quickest-learning teams and one of the slowest, and he was startled by the contrast. The surgeon on the fast-learning team was actually quite inexperienced compared with the one on the slow-learning team—he was only a couple of years out of training. But he made sure to pick team members with whom he had worked well before and to keep them together through the first fifteen cases before allowing any new members. He had the team go through a dry run before the first case, then deliberately scheduled six operations in the first week, so little would be forgotten in between. He convened the team before each case to discuss it in detail and afterward to debrief. He made sure results were tracked carefully. And as a person, Bohmer noticed, the surgeon was not the stereotypical Napoleon with a knife. Unbidden, he told Bohmer, 'The surgeon needs to be willing to allow himself to become a partner [with the rest of the team] so he can accept input.' It sounded perhaps a little clichéd; but then again, whatever he was doing worked. At the other hospital, the surgeon chose his operating team almost randomly and did not keep it together. In his first seven cases, the team had different members every time, which is to say that it was no team at all. And he had no pre-briefings, no debriefings, no tracking of ongoing results.

The Harvard Business School study offered some hopeful news. We can do things that have a dramatic effect on the learning curve—like being more deliberate about how we train, and about tracking progress, whether with students and residents or senior surgeons and nurses. But the study's other findings are less reassuring. No matter how accomplished, surgeons trying something new got worse before they got better, and the learning curve proved longer, and affected by a far more complicated range of factors, than anyone had realized. It's all stark confirmation that you can't train novices without compromising patient care.

This, I suspect, is the reason for the physician's dodge: the 'I just assist' rap; the 'We have a new procedure for this that you are perfect for' speech; the 'You need a central line' without the 'I am still learning how to do this.' Sometimes we do feel obliged to admit when we're doing something for the first time, but even then we tend to quote the published success rates—which are virtually always from experienced surgeons. Do we ever tell patients that because we are still new at something, their risks will inevitably be higher, and that they'd likely do better with others who are more experienced? Do we ever say that we need them to agree to it anyway? I've never seen it. Given the stakes, who in their right mind would agree to be practiced upon?

Many dispute this presumption. 'Look, most people understand what it is to be a doctor,' a health policy expert insisted, when I visited his office not long ago. 'We have to stop lying to our patients. Can people take on chances for societal benefit?' He paused and then answered his question. 'Yes,' he said firmly.

It would certainly be a graceful and happy solution. We'd ask patients—honestly, openly—and then they'd say yes. Hard to imagine, though. I noticed on the expert's desk a picture of his child, born just a few months before, and a completely unfair question popped into my mind. 'So did you let the resident deliver?' I asked.

There was silence for a moment. 'No,' he admitted. 'We didn't even allow residents in the room.'

One reason I doubt that we could sustain a system of medical training that depended on people saying. 'Yes, you can practice upon me' is that I myself have said no. One Sunday morning, when my eldest child, Walker, was eleven days old, he suddenly went into congestive heart failure from what proved to be a severe cardiac defect. His aorta was not transposed, but a long segment of it had failed to grow at all. My wife and I were beside ourselves with fear—his kidneys and liver began failing, too—but he made it to surgery, the repair was a success, and although his recovery was erratic, after two and a half weeks he was ready to come home.

We were by no means home free, however. He was born a healthy six pounds plus but now, at a month of age, weighed only five, and would need strict monitoring to ensure that he gained weight. He was on two cardiac medications from which he would have to be weaned. And in the longer term, the doctors warned us, his repair would eventually prove inadequate. As Walker grew, his aorta would require either dilation with a balloon or whole-sale replacement in surgery. Precisely when and how many such procedures would be necessary over the years they could not say. A pediatric cardiologist would have to follow him closely and decide.

Nearing discharge, we had not chosen who that cardiologist would be. In the hospital, Walker had been cared for by a full team of cardiologists, ranging from fellows in specialty training to attendings who had practiced for decades. The day before discharge, one of the young fellows approached me, offering his card and a suggested appointment time to bring Walker to see him. Of those on the team, he was the one who had put in the most time caring for Walker. He was the one who saw Walker when we brought him in inexplicably short of breath, the one who made the diagnosis, who got Walker the drugs that stabilized him, who coordinated with the surgeons, and who came to see us each day to answer our questions. Moreover, I knew fellows always got their patients this way. Most families don't know the subtle gradations among players, and after a team has saved their child's life, they take whatever appointment they're handed.

But I knew the differences. 'I'm afraid we're thinking of seeing Dr. Newburger,' I said. She was the hospital's associate cardiologist-in-chief, and a published expert on conditions like Walker's. The young physician looked crestfallen. It was nothing against him, I said. She just had more experience, that was all.

'You know, there is always an attending backing me up,' he said. I shook my head.

I know this was not fair. My son had an unusual problem. The fellow needed the experience. Of all people, I, a resident, should have understood. But I was not torn about the decision. This was *my child*. Given a choice, I will always choose the best care I can for him. How can anybody be expected to do otherwise? Certainly, the future of medicine should not rely on it.

In a sense, then, the physician's dodge is inevitable. Learning must be stolen, taken as a kind of bodily eminent domain. And it was, during Walker's stay—on many occasions, now that I think back on it. A resident intubated him. A surgical trainee scrubbed in for his operation. The cardiology fellow put in one of his central lines. None of them asked me if they could. If offered the option to have someone more experienced, I certainly would have taken it. But that was simply how the system worked—no such choices were offered—and so I went along. What else could I do?

The advantage of this cold-hearted machinery is not merely that it gets the learning done. If learning is necessary but causes harm, then above all it ought to apply to everyone alike. Given a choice, people wriggle out, and those choices are not offered equally. They belong to the connected and the knowledgeable, to insiders over outsiders, to the doctor's child but not the truck driver's. If choice cannot go to everyone, maybe it is better when it is not allowed at all.

It is 2 P.M. I am in the intensive care unit. A nurse tells me Mr. G's central line has clotted off. Mr. G has been with us for more than a month now. He is in his late sixties, from South Boston, emaciated, exhausted, holding on by a thread—or a line, to be precise. He has several holes in his small bowel that surgery has failed to close, and the bilious contents leak out onto his skin through two small reddened openings in the concavity of his abdomen. His only chance is to be fed by vein and wait for these fistulae to heal. He needs a new central line.

I could do it, I suppose. I am the experienced one now. But experience brings a new role: I am expected to teach the procedure instead. 'See one, do one, teach one,' the saying goes, and it is only half in jest.

There is a junior resident on the service. She has done only one or two lines before. I tell her about Mr. G. I ask her if she is free to do a new line. She misinterprets this as a question. She says she still has patients to see and a case coming up later. Could I do the line? I tell her no. She is unable to hide a grimace. She is burdened, as I was burdened, and perhaps frightened, as I was frightened.

She begins to focus when I make her talk through the steps—a kind of dry run, I figure. She hits nearly all the steps, but crucially forgets about checking the labs and about Mr. G's nasty allergy to heparin, which is in the flush for the line. I make sure she registers this, then tell her to get set up and page me.

I am still adjusting to this role. It is painful enough taking responsibility for one's own failures. Being handmaiden to another's is something else entirely. It occurs to me that I could have broken open a kit and had her do an actual dry run. Then again, maybe I can't. The kits must be a couple of hundred dollars each. I'll have to find out for next time.

Half an hour later, I get the page. The patient is draped. The resident is in her gown and gloves. She tells me she has saline to flush the line with and that his labs are fine.

'Have you got the towel roll?' I ask.

She forgot the towel roll. I roll up a towel and slip it beneath Mr. G's back. I look into his face and ask him if he's all right. He nods. I see no fear. After all he's been through, there is only resignation.

The junior resident picks out a spot for the stick. The patient is so hauntingly thin. I see every rib and fear she will puncture his lung. She injects the numbing medication. Then she puts the big needle in, and the angle looks all wrong. I motion for her to reposition. This only makes her more uncertain. She pushes in deeper and I know she does not have it. She draws back on the syringe: no blood. She takes out the needle and tries again. And again, the angle looks wrong. This time Mr. G feels the jab and jerks up in pain. I hold his arm. She gives him more numbing medication. It is all I can do not to take over. But she cannot learn without doing, I tell myself. I decide to let her have one more try.

4

Knowledge-in-the-Making: The 'Construction' of Fiat's Melfi Factory

Gerardo Patriotta

Introduction

The purpose of this chapter, the first part of a double length case study, is to analyse the action-based processes of knowing and organizing surrounding the coming into existence of one of the most advanced car manufacturing plants in the world: Fiat's Melfi assembly plant.[1] This new 'green field' factory features a lean production organization, work flow based on assembly lines and teams, advanced applications of IT (Information Technology) to production management and control, and extensive reliance on total quality management (Ciborra, Patriotta, and Erlicher 1996). Beyond technical specifications, however, the most interesting feature of the plant is that it has been built with the active involvement of the workforce. Indeed, the Fiat management conceived the whole Melfi project as a learning experiment based on a greenfield strategy where the future workers would literally build the factory, including the place and the setting where they would be assembling cars. The experiment had no antecedents in Fiat's history and the whole project relied on a young and inexperienced workforce.

The deliberate strategy of Fiat's management was that a human-centred design would ensure workers' participation and consensus and thereby have a positive impact on the overall performance of the factory; and indeed everything in the present situation of the factory seems to confirm the soundness of such theory. Still, together with intended ones, emergent phenomena were also produced in the course of factory construction which turned out to be crucial for the success of the Melfi project. The distinctive character of the factory was the outcome of an endogenous process of institutionalization of collective action which seems to have been largely invisible to the designers of the Melfi project, and to the workers themselves. Building the factory involved a kind of learning that went beyond resource development, skill acquisition, and workers' participation. In a way, such learning transcended the problems of performance and consensus that were at the core of the HR-based strategy, and more significantly had to do with a knowledge-making endeavour that touched the deeper domains of value and identity. If we take this perspective on the design experiment, the factory becomes different things at the same time: it is an artefact to be assembled, a tool to be used in assembling the car, a medium for knowing and interacting, a formative context (Unger 1987; Blackler 1992; Ciborra and Lanzara 1994).

This chapter is an effort to understand the many facets of the Melfi project. Particularly, I am interested in exploring the foundational and generative mechanisms underlying the making of the factory. Drawing on the time lens, I want to track the process whereby a complex manufacturing machine and the associated institutional order of the factory came into existence in a relatively short period and were encoded into stable organizational structures, procedures, and other artefacts. In the remainder of the chapter I tell the story of the Melfi project as it unfolded over time. Following Latour (1987), the strategy of investigation adopted in the case study will be to follow the characters on the 'construction site' while they are 'busy at work'.[2] A short journey in space and time will take us to the Melfi greenfield at the moment when the construction works of the factory are about to begin. Here, we will follow the phases from the design concept of the factory to its formal opening. The latter marks the technical black boxing of the original nucleus of organizational knowledge developed on the greenfield and, at the same time, provides the 'closure' point for the analysis.

The longitudinal study of the knowledge-creating processes surrounding the making of the factory emphasized the presence of systemic capabilities through which workers and managers were able to connect the details of production to the original experience of building the factory from the greenfield. The progressive appropriation of the factory by its final users resulted in the acquisition of distinctive competencies based on a pervasive identity between the experience of assembling the factory on the construction site and the task of assembling the car on the shop floor. Under these circumstances, the ability to grasp the inner workings of the assembly line seemed to be grounded on the experience of having built it, rather than on a mere technical understanding of the equipment itself.

At the overarching meta-level, the study highlighted a distinctive pattern of knowledge creation and transfer relating to the content and the process of the learning experience. Learning seemed to occur in the form of progressive ownership processes connected to different aspects of work: the role, the task, the product and production process, and most importantly the workplace itself. Rather than a sheer knowledge transmission model, going from a knowledgeable source to a passive recipient, ownership processes imply taking a pro-active role on the part of the learners. As a consequence, knowledge creation appeared as the outcome of interacting forces working according to 'specification–delegation' chains. The latter underscores the interplay between top-down and bottom-up processes, planned and emergent factors involved in the design and implementation of the Melfi project.

This chapter is organized as follows, starting with an elaboration of a conceptual framework for the case study based on a review of two conflicting perspectives on organizational learning. The following section describes the main phases characterizing the unfolding of the Melfi project, identifying knowledge sources and outcomes, learning settings and organizational actors involved in each phase. The last two sections review the chronological advancement of the Melfi project in order to identify both the learning-specific outcomes relating to each phase, and the pervasive patterns of knowledge creation underpinning it. The chapter concludes with some considerations about the sedimentary nature of competence and the importance of approaching knowledge-related phenomena from the point of view of knowledge-in-the-making.

Two Perspectives on Organizational Learning

Conventional learning and training theories are based on a pedagogical perspective which sees learning as the outcome of a knowledge transmission process between a knowledgeable source and a passive recipient. Within this perspective, the details of practice, the communities of practitioners, and the setting in which the learning experience takes place are specifically excluded (Brown and Duguid 1991). Interestingly, training in the work situation seems to fall within this instructional paradigm, as the following definition, quoted from a glossary of training terms, suggests: 'a planned process to modify attitudes, knowledge or skill behaviour through learning experience to achieve effective performance in an activity or range of activities. Its purpose, in the work situation, is to develop the abilities of the individual and to satisfy the current and future manpower needs of the organization' (Jones 1994).

More recent theories have rejected transfer models which isolate knowledge from practice and emphasized the social, situated nature of the learning experience. A chief claim of situated learning theories is that knowledge is embodied in praxis (Pentland 1992) and that learning takes place through participation within 'communities of practice' (Lave and Wenger 1991). Rather than being a passive recipient, the community of learners is constantly engaged in sense-making and interpretation activities whereby knowledge is appropriated out of a wide range of materials. The latter include 'ambient social and physical circumstances and the histories and social relations of the people involved' (Brown and Duguid 1991). Accordingly, what is learned is profoundly connected to the conditions in which it is learned. Importantly, learning is about identity construction through engagement in social practices, including the construction of diverse social bonds with other participants or co-workers. The identity building aspect of the learning experience is captured by the notion of legitimate peripheral participation (Lave and Wenger 1991) according to which learning involves becoming an 'insider', acquiring a particular community's subjective viewpoint and learning to speak its language. Finally, the situated approach is consistent with adult learning theories. In his extensive review of the literature on the topic, Jones (1994) emphasizes the importance of self-directed learning and active participation in the construction of learning events, as opposed to the traditional teacher–learner principle. For example, adults seem to learn most effectively through experience, and by means of actual day-to-day jobs and routines (learning by doing) rather than from formal and structured training programmes. In this regard, meaningful adult learning occurs when it is based on problem-solving and connects with a person's general life events and activities. Accordingly, adult learning is seen as a lifetime process continually shaped by the experience of the past.

The two paradigms described above are characterized by Jones and Hendry (1994) as 'hard' learning, which is pragmatic, formal and brought about through prescribed training, and 'soft' learning, which has a more subtle nature and is concerned with the social context which shapes the learning process. Accordingly, they imply different perspectives on the agents of the knowledge-creation process and the learning path underlying this process. Schematically, the instructional paradigm emphasizes the planned factors of the training process and the fact that knowledge transmission occurs in a top-down manner. Situated learning, by contrast, seems to view the dynamics of knowledge creation through learning as a bottom-up process shaped by those factors emerging along the way.

As we shall see, besides being a physical location, the greenfield site here under study represents a particular situation, a learning setting characterized by distinctive contextual features, where a community of learners is undergoing a peculiar experience. In order to convey the uniqueness of this experience, the case described later adopts a situated perspective, focusing on two important aspects of the appropriation and learning processes surrounding the coming into existence of the new factory. The first emphasizes the holistic character of the learning experience. As Winograd and Flores (1986) have pointed out, any technological artefact is situated or dwells in a heterogeneous network that includes other equipment, materials, institutional arrangements, practices, and conventions. Accordingly, any learning process is shaped by the encounter between heterogeneous sources and multiple outcomes. The second concerns the sense-making and interpretation dynamics underlying the learning experience. The construction of the factory can be compared to the introduction of an 'alien' object which has to be 'metabolized' and placed into context by the community of practitioners in order to represent and understand events related to it.

The Making of a Factory

The SATA plant at Melfi is one of those exceptional plants—like the Toyota-managed NUMMI plant in California (Adler 1993) and Volvo's small scale Udevalla factory (Berggren 1994)—which have recently attracted the attention of the media for their outstanding levels of performance and innovative learning methods (e.g. Fortune 1994; Economist 1998). The plant produces the leading Fiat model, the Punto, today one of the best selling cars in Europe. The factory, situated in the south of Italy between Naples and Bari is a greenfield site set up at the end of 1993 and, after an experimental phase, opened officially in October 1994. Melfi is the world's first car factory capable of running flat-out three shifts, six days a week. With a production capacity of 1,600 cars a day (450,000 per year) employing 6,300 people, the factory holds one of the best productivity records in the world. The Melfi industrial district covers a surface of 2.7 million square metres, including the plants of 16 suppliers. Their location, close to the main assembly plant, makes possible the reduction of suppliers' lead times. Lean production and Just-in-Time (JIT) are applied as a method of organizing the work cycle. The workforce in Melfi belongs to a homogeneous cultural and geographical background. The local identity is quite pronounced: workers, managers, and employees are young and mostly from the south (98 percent), often in their first jobs (the region where the plant is located, like the rest of the south of Italy has a very high level of unemployment).

The factory—what today appears as a ready-made product, a black box—is the main visible outcome of a construction process involving the future workforce. The chronology of the design and implementation of the Melfi project reveals six main phases underlying the construction of the factory and progressively leading to the sedimentation of a core nucleus of organizational knowledge:

1. the design concept;
2. recruitment;
3. formal training;
4. construction work;

5. learning to (dis)assemble;
6. full production.

The following sections portray the chronological advancement of the Melfi project through the phases defined above. In particular, I briefly review the design strategy of the Melfi factory and discuss the premises underlying the coming into existence of the factory. Then, I examine the major building operations through which the factory is constructed. I show how each building step results in an inscription of agency, knowledge, and social interaction into organizational artefacts to which technical, cognitive, and social complexity is delegated.

The Design Concept

The Melfi project is part of a broader strategy formulation process aimed at re-establishing the competitive position of Fiat worldwide. The genesis of the project lies in the increasing attention devoted by the company to the emergence of the lean production paradigm in Japan and to its diffusion in Europe, and especially in the United States. For Fiat the successful experience of the Japanese transplants in the United States was a clear signal of the need to break with the Fordist cultural tradition. Since the mid-1980s Fiat had been carrying out a series of benchmarking activities on Japanese automotive plants and especially an US transplants. These activities gradually led to the elaboration of a new work organization, known as the integrated factory. However, for some years the change process was at a standstill. Only in 1989, when the Punto was conceived, was there a physiological convergence between the above reasoning and the new productive needs.

In an effort to come to terms with chronic problems in production, an industrial relations, and, particularly, in the management of human resources, the design concept of the factory was informed by two fundamental assumptions. The first was the need to break with the cultural tradition of the past, which had led to the crisis of the mid-1980s. This implied the choice of not transferring the 'Headquarters culture' or at least minimizing the transfer. The second was the intention to build a learning organization characterized by high levels of commitment of the workforce. This addressed the need for training a group of knowledge workers and promoting a systemic understanding of the work process:

It is the peculiar quality of work in Melfi that it requires an extended training program, specifically aimed at competence acquisition, one that does not only imply learning how to do things, but also looking at the other segments of the production process. In order to put into practice a form of training that makes one aware of the lateral whereabouts, one needs to know the boundary, that is, what is going on in the upstream and downstream processes; furthermore one needs to know how to work in a team, to control certain variables previously uncontrolled, to develop a financial sensitiveness towards the cost of the product. (Former Fiat Personnel Director, quoted in Donzelli 1994)

As Donzelli (Donzelli 1994) has rightly pointed out, given the complexity of the new work organization, the most challenging task Fiat had to face in the training of the new workforce was to devise specific learning paths. In other words, the challenge did not seem to lie so much in the 'what' of training as in the 'how': how to convey the awareness of the boundary; how to foster a systemic orientation towards work while learning how to do specific things; and how to equip the newly hired workforce with cognitive tools able to support this systemic orientation.

The design of the plant had a major impact on the company's existing culture, since it raised traditional controversies such as the opposition between North and South, novices and experienced, and engineers and Human Resource Management (HRM) managers. Interviews with the former Plant Director and the Personnel Director highlighted four major controversial issues related to the design of the plant. A first point of controversy concerned the governance of the socio-technical system. There was a presumption of conflict related to the history of the company, especially as far as IR practices were concerned. In the past, this problem had been dealt with through massive investments in technology to be used as a defensive strategy against social conflict. However, the technocentric approach was only partially successful. The alternative position was represented by those who believed in the role of HRM policies and the partial involvement of the trade unions as a strategy to gain consensus on such an ambitious project. Secondly, there was a debate about the new production system. The lean production philosophy, the adoption of JIT, the presence of suppliers on site, involved eliminating all those forms of external warehouses which served as the backbone of the traditional mass production systems operating in Fiat's plants. The 'crystal pipeline' concept, that is, the idea of a rigid production flow with no buffers, was more than a technological challenge as it affected the company's traditional culture on production methods. Thirdly, the new team-based organization and the delayering of the traditional organizational model were at odds with the company's deeply hierarchical tradition. Finally, the greenfield concept and the involvement of a green workforce in the realization of the project were a major question mark. Some managers believed that the lack of experienced people would impede the project and that at some point the company would be forced to call back the old 'cavaliers'.[3]

The company board, in charge of the direction of the operations, acted as a sort of tribunal engaged in settling controversies between innovators and the so-called 'cavaliers'. The board assessed the proposals brought forward by the committee in charge of the implementation of the project. It selected between alternative choices by endorsing the entrepreneurial risk behind each option. As mentioned earlier, Melfi certainly represents a breakthrough and a paradigm shift within the Fiat world. It is therefore sensible to imagine that the decision-making process underlying the design of the new factory was characterized by strong negotiation if not open conflict between 'innovators' and 'conservatives'. However, we do not possess any evidence to document the details of this conflict. What can be said here is that the Melfi project was driven from the outset by the idea of radical innovation related to the survival of the company in a fierce competitive environment. The mission, imposed in a top-down manner, set the background against which decisions would be taken within the board.[4]

The Greenfield
The policy decision to go ahead with the Melfi project was made by Fiat senior executives in December 1990. The recruitment of the workforce and construction work commenced almost simultaneously in September 1991. It took twenty-four months to complete the construction work and the first car body rolled off the line in September 1993. The implementation of the project was initially entrusted to a group of fifty young managers, all in possession of a university degree, highly trained, with two to three years of managerial experience within the company's production plants. Their mission, as defined by the company headquarters, was to build one of the most competitive automotive factories in the world, which would be erected on a greenfield site. This high profile group was in charge, among other things, of the recruitment and training of the new workforce. The group of hired employees initially comprised approximately 1,000 workers, engineers, middle managers, and technicians in possession of a high school diploma or university degree. The bulk of the generic workers (approximately 5,000) was hired subsequently and put into training.

Questions of site location, building construction, and plant layout were crucial for the design concept of the Melfi factory. The adoption of a greenfield strategy was a core design specification and a fundamental pre-condition for successful implementation of the whole project.

The rationale behind the choice of Melfi included at least three major reasons. The first was its strategic location within the wide network of Fiat's plants already existing in the south of Italy. Secondly, Basilicata—the region where the plant is located—can be considered a 'green area' in its own right, not contaminated by pre-existing industrial models and yet characterized by the local population's positive attitude towards industry and new work opportunities. Finally, the same region is distinguished by high levels of schooling—a knowledge asset in itself, and therefore offers an ideal recruitment basin.

The strategic implications of greenfield sites for the management of innovation and change have been widely recognized in the literature. A number of authors have emphasized the systemic features of greenfield sites and the holistic character of design connected with the adoption of a greenfield strategy. For Clark (1995), the structural features of greenfield sites allow for the design of systems where all parts of the organization are consistent and the multiple facets of the design concept fit together. Important areas in which greenfield sites offer the opportunity for innovation include building design, internal plant layout, technology, relations with suppliers, customer relations, and distribution and communication networks.

The notion of greenfield stresses the experimental character of a new plant within a network of existing plants (Beaumont and Townley 1985). In turn, the design of innovation processes associated with greenfield sites is made possible by distinctive structural conditions. These include, among others, geographical isolation from a major manufacturing district and cultural distance from industrial communities. Greenfield sites are often located in less-developed regions characterized by high levels of unemployment and by a lack of socially embedded knowledge about industry. Furthermore, those regions are usually eligible for grants from local governments or supranational bodies like the European Union. The presence of new work practices and new employee relations bears crucial implications as far as HRM and industrial relations policies are concerned (Newell 1991). For example, the choice of a greenfield can be instrumental in reducing the potential level of conflict within the new plant and possibly bypassing the unions' control of work organization. As we have seen, a similar strategy had been adopted by Fiat in the past although using different instruments (e.g. automation as a defensive strategy). This time, however, the deal with the unions played a critical role. To a certain extent, the deal was constrained by the very idea of providing a major employment opportunity in a depressed area, which ensured consensus (and major incentives) at the political level, while limiting the bargaining power of the unions. For example, the unions were deliberately excluded from the decision-making process related to the design of the factory. On the other hand, they were crucially involved in the implementation phase through participation in bilateral commissions specifically designed to monitor the advancement of the project. As Rieser (1992) has observed, the main role of the unions in Melfi was to provide feedback in the set-up process and thereby absorb the potential sources of social conflict inherent in the implementation of the new organization model. In other words, they were part of the company's strategy for building consensus around the project (the Melfi workforce is highly unionized, although non-conflictual).

More generally, greenfield sites provide an opportunity for managers to make a philosophical break with the traditional ways of doing things and to experiment with untried systems or practices (Clark 1995). Beaumont and Townley (1985) have clearly explained this point:

The green field site offers the prospect of a *tabula rasa,* . . . the possibility of establishing work organization, job design, personnel and industrial relations policies afresh rather than attempting to tackle these issues on an *ad hoc* basis in existing plants. It provides the opportunity to experiment with the development of a coherent 'green field philosophy'. (Beaumont and Townley 1985: 189)

In its connotation of tabula rasa a greenfield site provides a background for learning and knowledge creation, which is characterized by a low level of knowledge institutionalization. In other words, it provides a context where it is possible to create not only a new factory but also new modes of organizing, and new ways of doing and seeing things. To a certain extent, the structural features of greenfield sites allow a company to keep the learning and know-ledge-creation processes under control. For example, the absence of a sedi-mented industrial tradition associated with greenfield sites may facilitate the 'schooling' of the workforce and the transfer of knowledge in a top-down manner. At the same time, the low degree of institutionalization of the initial stock of knowledge creates the conditions for the emergence of unforeseen facts which may challenge the original design concept, enrich its scope and act as new knowledge-creation forces. The design concept of the Melfi plant embraces many of the ideas connected to the choice of a greenfield strategy. However, the implementation of this strategy, especially as far as training and learning dynamics are concerned, also presents many aspects that are unique and possibly explain the stunning performance of the factory.

Recruitment

The selection process was designed following a benchmarking activity on Japanese automotive plants scattered around the world. A threshold of 10 per cent had been identified as the ideal ratio between selection and recruitment. Consequently, almost 100,000 people were interviewed in order to select 7,000 workers:

We designed a selection system before a training system. We wanted to select people not only in possession of a theoretical background, but also with a positive attitude towards work, in particular towards teamwork; people willing to put themselves at stake, with a sense of challenge; people with whom it would be possible to build a new factory model, far from the traditional one. In sum, people with a strong personality. (Former Personnel Director)

As stated earlier, the original core group of hired workers can be seen as a group of novices. The basic stock of knowledge they possessed came from formal education. What was the nature of this first minimal nucleus of knowledge? It was formal, non-experience-related knowledge; it was explicit knowledge, easily detectable since it coincided with a specific school qualification; more importantly, as we shall see shortly, it was knowledge that could be manipulated and put to use. Another important factor was the homogeneity of the workforce and the cultural values related to the particular area where the plant is located. The workforce embodied the cultural values typical of a rural community, such as the importance of the family, sense of belonging to the territory, honour and accountability, tinkering, and the art of 'managing to get by', inclination towards mutual help, and readiness to 'give each other a hand'. Although those values may seem in sharp contrast with an avant-garde industrial project, the production reality within the Melfi plant offers a different picture. In order to function effectively, a factory like Melfi needs consensus. Hence derives the importance of a healthy cultural environment, where local values can be re-invented and turned into a valuable resource for the company. Today, those values find original applications in key areas such as quality control, teamwork, problem-solving, and organizational learning.[5] On the other hand, in order to be successful, an ambitious project like Melfi had to be contextualized. A number of sociological studies aimed at assessing the core cultural features of the local population, the local subcultures, and the potential impacts of the new plant on the local cultural context were undertaken on behalf of the company as part of the design activity. For example, the presence of a strong local identity and the importance of maintaining close social bonds suggested recruiting people living within a range of 30–60 kilometres (one hour's drive) from the factory, in order to facilitate commuting to work. In this way, workers could keep living in their home towns and carry on their social activities, without having to move closer to the factory. As a consequence the construction of the factory did not produce a dramatic impact on the territory, as had been the case with previous industrial installations in the south of Italy. The contextualization strategy achieved two important results. First, as explained by the former Personnel Director of the plant, it contributed to building consensus and reduced the level of conflict of the workforce:

Melfi represents an innovation even with respect to the other company experiences in the south, characterized by high levels of conflict in the initial two to three years of operations. Many people wonder why Melfi did not have to pay this price. I think that a novice who does not find certain cultural references for his working condition will end up rejecting it. With Melfi, we have tried to understand the needs, the motivations and the experience of the individual and to harness these traits for the benefit of the company's performance.

Second, as we shall see in the following sections, the 'protection' and reception of the local values fostered a crucial process of knowledge creation from the bottom.

Formal Training

Having gone through selection sessions and been tentatively assigned to a role, the freshly recruited workers were subsequently put through intense formal training. One thousand people from southern Italy spent a year at the Fiat headquarters in Turin. There, undergoing a sort of full immersion in Fiat's industrial cosmology, they acquired knowledge about the company, the production process, and the basic principles underlying the new organizational model. Professional profiles, learning programmes, and career advancement tracks were tailored according to their different educational backgrounds, and the individual attitudes that emerged during the selection process. The training period in Turin encompassed both classroom sessions and simulation exercises in laboratories. Knowledge acquired in the classroom would be continually tested and put to work through rotation in other Fiat plants. The latter provided the first contact with the production reality. Here the training consisted of operational simulations where the newcomers would take part in shadow teams working side by side with experienced operators along the assembly lines. In a subsequent phase, while the new plant was still not available, a real simulation of the production process at Melfi was undertaken in the Fiat factories scattered around Italy. The future workforce was organized in virtual teams and assigned to specific UTEs, with each member taking up the position corresponding to his/her future role at Melfi. The training experience in Turin also provided a golden opportunity for socializing the future workforce. For more than a year, the trainees lived as a community in the residences provided by the company. The company also arranged cultural and leisure activities, tours at weekends, and trips back home once a month. Then they were sent back to the greenfield at Melfi, where, at the construction site, they engaged in the construction of the plant in which they would finally end up working.

The Construction Work

On the building site, 3,000 people belonging to the contracting firms in charge of the construction of the plant were at work. The entire operation was supervised by an interdisciplinary group that involved automotive production specialists from Fiat Auto working side by side with the civil and structural engineers from Fiat Engineering. From these combined forces emerged the site plan as well as the architectural and structural design of the factory. In September 1991, large-scale construction began on the site. By September 1992, the Fiat Auto engineers could start installation of the production systems. By May 1993, the energy supply systems were ready for testing. By September 1993, the entire plant was ready for operation. To cite just a few figures, the construction site operation amounted to 12 million working hours, 4 million cubic metres of earth were moved, 16,000 metres of foundation were laid, 500,000 cubic metres of reinforced concrete were used, 90,000 tons of structural steel were erected, 5,000 tons of pipes, 100,000 metres of insulated electrical wiring, 16,000 metres of high and medium tension power lines were used and 16,000 metres of railway track were laid.

The strict deadlines foreseen in the project plan schedule made it necessary to start construction site work concurrently with project development, thus breaking with the traditional procedure of one phase following the other. This innovative methodology required close co-ordination among project partners. More importantly, it allowed for the crucial involvement of the future work-force of the factory in the construction work. As soon as the new hired workers completed the formal training period in Turin, they were sent in small contingents to the greenfield site in Melfi, where an ad hoc training centre had been set up.

The objective of the participatory strategy pursued by the company was twofold: to adapt the new socio-organizational model of the integrated factory to a complex technological system in order to accelerate the operations of debugging the production apparatus; and to create a political and professional avant-garde, highly motivated, integrated in the company culture, carrying deep knowledge of the factory and its inner workings, and able to lead the remaining workforce on the principles of the new production policy. As a result, the building site experience promoted within the workforce the development of a sense of belonging to a community of 'pioneers and constructors' (Cerruti 1994). Working on the greenfield soon assumed the meaning of a founding experience for the novice workforce involved in the construction of their 'own factory'. In the recollections of the core group of hired workers the greenfield site personified the myth of genesis, a tabula rasa where nothing existed before their arrival:

When I arrived here, in May 1992, there were only a few pillars and the roof. One of the first things we did was to involve our work force in issues related to the set-up of the assembly unit. They *assembled* this unit [the Assembly unit], together with the other companies which were here. (Production Engineering Manager, Assembly Unit)

I was one of the first to arrive here in October 1992. Nothing existed here, not even the shell of the building. Although I had been hired as a member of maintenance staff, I did my first work experience as a surveyor (that is my educational background) working with the firms in charge of the construction work. So I was involved in heavy construction jobs before setting up and testing machinery. (Technologist, Body welding unit)

I have been here since May of last year. Now it is difficult to explain. There was nothing here: the plants were here but they were not operational; there was nothing on the (shop) floor, we designed the workstations, we built our boxes: none of this furniture was here, there were no desks, we built them on our own, we cut the iron, painted it, built poles, we did a bit of everything. We could not believe that in a few months all that was going to become operational; and yet it happened. We like to think that it is our achievement too. (Head of UTE, Assembly Unit)

During the first few months, since there was nothing here, we would act as operators of the firms which were supposed to build the plant; therefore we would do nothing that was related to our future work, apart from studying the production cycles on paper. (Head of UTE, Assembly Unit)

For the young workforce the experience of the construction site was a sort of rite of initiation or passage—a ceremony—that might have possibly played the same role that formal co-optation or professional socialization play in more established professional communities (Van Maanen 1984; Beyer and Trice 1987).

Learning to (Dis)Assemble

As a result of Fiat's initial choice, the original 'green field' was transformed into an industrial landscape in a relatively short time. Buildings, equipment, machinery, various implements, and all sorts of industrial paraphernalia were placed and lined up on site according to a predesigned plan. The complete factory materialized as it was simply 'unfolded'. Within the building site, the core group of hired workers was organized into Work Breakdown Structures (WBS) responsible for the development of the multifaceted aspects of the avant-garde factory: monitoring the construction of the plants, testing the machinery, and adapting the new socio-technical system to the specific context of the Melfi factory. Each WBS would act as a start-up team directed by a team leader, and was encouraged to submit written proposals to the newly formed steering committee of the plant. The management structure of the plant was rather loose at the time, with the steering committee comprising a group of twenty-two managers recruited from the original group of fifty. The evolution of the training process was kept fluid, grounded on the solutions proposed by the start-up teams and on the critical issues emerging along the way. Follow-up decisions were kept on stand-by, awaiting new developments. WBS provided the core operational units of an architecture of complexity whereby organizational tasks were 'broken down' into elemental components. The following example illustrates the functioning of a typical start-up team engaged in

Gerardo Patriotta

setting up the presses within the stamping shop, while stressing a crucial learning pattern based on a comparative experience surrounding the appropriation of the machinery:

For assembling the presses, we formed two work teams including both internal personnel and members of the supply companies. As you may know Schuler and Komatsu make the presses we use. The Japanese team was in charge of assembling the large presses, while the German team took care of the medium presses. The Japanese team had managed to rationalize its activities up to a point where, in the face of a sudden disruption, they were able to suspend the job and keep going somewhere else. They had disassembled the press as if it were Lego; they had numbered the containers; in each container there was a set of inferential moves, the so-called 'ifs' of a project, representing variations or possible ramifications within a planned activity. The Japanese never opened more than two containers at the same time, and therefore utilized a minimal amount of space. They were able to complete the assembling job and test the machinery three months before the deadline. On the other side, the Germans had very loose planning, and accordingly each single problem encountered while assembling would disrupt their work. The Germans were just on the deadline, but they occupied the entire shop floor, with parts scattered everywhere. Our engineers were involved in both experiences and clearly they learned something about their own work method. They would not make any move without planning, without assessing the possible consequences of their actions. 'What happens if . . .' and they would start assessing the 'ifs'. (former Plant Director)

The shift of the activity from assembling the plant to assembling the car was a gradual one. It happened through a phase where the car was repeatedly disassembled, laid out on the ground in thousands of separate pieces, and then re-assembled. What in the early stages was the explicit focus of attention and construction later became the implicit background and equipment for the car manufacturing operations on the shop floor. Thus, practical knowledge about assembling learned at the construction site was transposed to the shop floor:

In order to familiarize themselves with the list of components, the young engineers were asked to develop it physically. Basically, they took all the parts of a specific model as listed on the bill of materials, and spread them over a surface of about 800 square metres. Subsequently, they developed all the Punto's product range by separating the common parts from the specific ones. (former Plant Director)

The induction phase that followed the construction work was aimed at making shop floor operators familiar with the details of the product and the intricacies of the production process. In the body welding unit car bodies were dissected and inspected again and again in order to understand the interfaces between the different car parts. In the assembly unit a number of simulations were carried out off the line as a way to convey a practical mode of thinking and knowing:

Later on, the UTE leaders arrived, then the technologists and the line workers, all of them after a training period in Turin. Those people were introduced to the product by working on a stock of cars provided by the Mirafiori plant. On those cars we did some training, by disassembling and re-assembling them again and again. We were asked to come up with a 'disassembling' cycle for the car. Although those people had already gone through operational simulations in other plants, they now had the opportunity to have some 'hands on' experience. (Production Engineering manager, Assembly Unit)

In a subsequent phase, the 'ownership' of the product became a vehicle for transferring a stock of practical knowledge from a core group of knowledge-able workers (namely UTE leaders and technologists) to the newcomers:

Having learned how to disassemble and re-assemble those cars, the UTE leader and the technologist had become 'owners' of the product. They were now in the position to transfer their competence to the line workers. Starting from this training exercise, we moved to the actual production of the car within this plant. Those cars were used to show our people how a car is assembled and produced. Since then we have only built cars that could be sold. (Production Engineering Manager, Assembly Unit)

The previous examples highlight a well-known image, typical of mechanical manufacturing, which portrays the organization as a sort of LEGO-like com-posable and decomposable system. Just like a child exploring the content of a new toy, the act of disassembling becomes a distinctive mode of knowing aimed at understanding the relations between parts and whole. More importantly, through disassembling exercises a work pattern emerged based on the possi-bility of building rules of method 'empirically' by drawing on concrete occur-rences and continuous improvement activities. The resulting patterns of work would be repeatedly tested until they were eventually stabilized at a later stage. Through the endless repetitions of the Disassembling/Assembling (D/A) task, the workers would simulate the functioning of the assembly line. Interestingly, the training provided through this type of simulation was centred around the task (building the car bit by bit), with shop floor operators moving from one work station to the next while the production lines stood still. Only after they had appropriated the practice of manually assembling the car did the workers delegate it to the moving line, which thus inscribed the agency and the task (time and motion, functions and operations). In the process of appropriating the work method, a major anchoring role was played by the car and its physical components. Through the repeated hands-on procedure of breaking down the car into separate pieces and then remaking it by putting the pieces back together, the structure of the task was revealed and the logic of manufacturing was appropriated. Thus the car, in addition to being the thing to be manufac-tured (the product), also became a cognitive tool—a medium—for understand-ing and institutionalizing the method of manufacturing.

A major outcome of the D/A exercise was the production of empirical know-how and rules of thumb which were eventually capitalized and crystallized into explicit rules. A crucial feature of Melfi's generalized work method, at least in that early stage, was the capacity to systematically formalize emerging stocks of empirical knowledge by letting it come to the surface. Under these circumstances, the work method became a virtuous force for generating new knowledge:

Melfi represents a bit of a paradox. Since the start-up phase the Melfi plant has been very successful and today it is one of the most competitive automotive plants in the world. Yet, since the very beginning the factory has been governed by a group of young novices who were on training. Where did such a complex system find the power to sustain itself and become more and more productive? In my opinion the secret of the success of this plant lies in the ability to sustain its growth through method. The major strength of a UTE leader, a technologist or a line conductor was not his/her knowledge. Certainly, a sound knowledge of the integrated factory model was paramount and it had been transferred through the formal training in Turin. On the other hand, that knowledge, albeit important, could not be exhaustive because of the lack of experience. What was crucial was the transfer of a method for handling problematic situations. This has made possible the accumulation of further knowledge about the factory both during the start-up phase and at full production. Method implies very practical questions such as: how to solve a problem? How to organize a job? How to plan? How to take action? How to control? How to question? The methodological capacity of this organization has been a major success factor. (former Plant Director)

The induction phase of the factory came to an end one year later, with the formal opening of the plant in October 1994. This moment represented the closure of the black box as well as the termination point of this part of our analysis. The factory then gradually moved towards its full production capacity and other stages in the knowledge-creation and institutionalization process.

Learning as Appropriation: Building Identity through Ownership Processes

The chronological advancement of the Melfi project and the knowledge sources associated with it highlight knowledge-specific outcomes related to each phase, which have been described in the previous sections. The results are summarized in Table 4.1.

At the outset of the knowledge-creation process lies the encounter between the factory's design concept—laid out in detail by the top management of the company—and a group of young and highly educated novices carrying a stock of core values typical of the area where the greenfield is located. The greenfield strategy is instrumental towards the fulfilment of one of the two

Table 4.1 Phases, sources, and outcomes of the knowledge-creation process

Phase	Knowledge source	Knowledge outcome
1 Design concept	Benchmarking, company values	Integrated factory model
2 Recruitment	School education, local values	Degree-specific knowledge
3 Formal training	Classroom, rotation in other plants	Ownership of the role (e.g. professional profile)
4 Construction work	Building site	Ownership of the factory (e.g. activities, territory, equipment)
5 Learning to (dis)assemble	Simulation exercises on the shop floor	Ownership of the task/product (e.g. work method)
6 Full production	Factory operations	Routines

main assumptions stated in the design concept: to break with the cultural tradition of the past. The second objective specified by the top management, the acquisition of a holistic vision of the work process, relates explicitly to organizational learning, and is to be achieved through an intensive training programme (Phases 3–5). Although the outcomes of the training process are manifold, encompassing both theoretical and practical aspects of work, it is nonetheless possible to identify a pervasive learning strategy underlying the long path preceding the formal opening of the factory. Learning seems to occur as a form of situated appropriation or progressive ownership of different aspects of work: the role, the task, the product and production process, and most importantly the workplace itself. The ownership strategy characterizes the overall organizational learning process in at least two ways. First, it emphasizes the proactive role of the learners: becoming owners does not imply a mere knowledge transfer. Rather, it involves filling a gap on the part of the learners, becoming users and accordingly re-inventing the task at hand. In a sense, even the benchmarking activities performed by the company and leading to the design concept of the new factory can be seen as a process of appropriation and re-invention of concepts invented elsewhere, namely in Japan and filtered by US car manufacturers. Second, the concept of ownership is closely related to identity building. When looking at the larger picture, the learning processes described in the previous section depict an impressive socialization endeavour aimed at the construction of a distinctive identity of the workforce as 'pioneers and constructors'. Entering the work environment implies taking up a role within a community of practice. Accordingly, the training phases described in the previous sections portray the progressive development of individual (role), collective (community), and corporate (product) identities. The evolution of the training process also highlights a move from a narrow focus (the role) to a holistic vision of the production process, with crucial implications for sense-making activities. This is particularly visible in the construction work, where the appropriation of the factory requires the characters involved to relate the task at hand to a broader network of equipment, practices, and institutions. Finally, it is precisely the constitution of a distinctive identity that explains how the workforce came to accept the apparently 'onerous' deal proposed by the company. In fact, a striking characteristic in the evolution of the Melfi project is the considerably low level of conflict and controversy around the knowledge-creation process. For example, how did the company manage to convince the 'green' workforce to spend a large amount of time on training, away from their homes, and even get involved in the building works of the factory?

A major source of identification of the workforce with the objectives of the company and acceptance of the conditions imposed by the implementation process was certainly the conceptualization of the factory as a public good, whose construction required a collective effort. The symbolic value of the involvement of the workforce in the construction work was very strong, stressing the sense of belonging and ownership of the workplace. First of all, the young workforce was asked to work for a 'greater' good, that is to create its own job opportunity in a traditionally depressed area. Secondly, building the workplace was different from just walking into a ready-made one. It emphasized the notion of familiarity as opposed to alienation. Within this conceptualization, the potential sources of conflict were subtly absorbed through a variety of social mechanisms intended to build consensus around the project, maintain the commitement of the workforce, and prevent opportunistic behaviour and free-riding. The deal with the unions, the contextualization strategy, and the socialization of the workforce as part of the training programme, exemplify some of these mechanisms.

Specification-Delegation Chains: Planned and Emergent Factors in the Knowledge-Creation Process

The Fiat Melfi case shows in a straightforward manner what knowledge making entails as a unique, history-dependent mix of purposeful design and unintended, endogenous processes. The chronological advancement of the Melfi project clearly illustrates the previous argument. A first thing to be noted is that the process of knowledge creation and transfer was bidirectional. In the recollection of one of the managers involved in the project, the striking characteristic of the decision-making and implementation processes was the degree of discretion left to the decision-makers at the lower levels:

I would say that the ratio between planned and emergent factors in the design of Melfi was 50–50. Based on benchmarking activities and a feasibility study, the headquarters had defined the rationale for a project aimed at building one of the most competitive automotive factories in the world. We were assigned specific key targets and excellence standards (organizational model, production, ergonomy, working time, etc.). However, we were autonomous as far as how those targets were to be accomplished. The same applied to the start-up teams that were in charge of the set-up of the production system and the training of the generic workers that were eventually hired. (former Personnel Director)

This finding is consistent with the adult learning theories presented earlier for at least two related reasons. On the one hand, the role of the workers' background (including lack of work experience) was a critical feature selected by the company to implement the training process. On the other hand, the learning dynamics observed on the greenfield and during the induction phase, seemed to possess an element of autonomy and self-directedness stressing a learning-by-doing pattern.

The implementation process of the Melfi project seemed to unfold according to a specification–delegation pattern. The original plan was encapsulated in the design concept of the factory. Based on bench-marking activities (a knowledge-creation process in itself) the company defined the strategic mission of the project (to build one of the most competitive factories in the world), outlined the main specifications of the design concept (location of the plant and nature of the workforce) and provided a cutting edge tool kit for the new factory (organizational model, technology, and production system). Also the selection process and the initial training of the workforce, based on pre-existing training modules, was very much under the control of the company headquarters. However, since the early stages, the implementation of the project was characterized by a considerable degree of delegation and consequently by a significant process of knowledge creation from the bottom. As Donzelli put it, 'Melfi has a degree of autonomy, a philosophical independence from the Headquarters, that perhaps escapes even its designers' intentions' (Donzelli 1994: 19). The people chosen to make the project happen were young and highly educated. They can be seen as carriers of 'fresh' knowledge and new values. The more the project moved forward, the more the influence of the company values got diluted. This fact became particularly conspicuous once the operations were transferred to the greenfield site. Here, the Melfi workforce—knowledge builders and construction workers at the same time—was actively involved in 'making the project happen'. The community of 'builders' operating on the greenfield was constantly engaged in a sense-making activity whereby the cognitive and material resources at hand were assembled in original ways. In other words, the construction site provided the locus for the encounter of formal and practical knowledge. The factory itself represented the visible and measurable outcome of this collective effort, the hard product born of a process of social construction. In addition, the advancement of the project was not always smooth: the construction site raised continuous challenges, forcing the different teams at work to adapt existing solutions or to devise new ones. The context shaping the development of the Melfi project was constantly shifting as the multiplicity of implementation phases, training venues, learning settings, and knowledge sources demonstrate. The dynamic character of the knowledge-creation process over the greenfield has been stressed by one of the managers who took part in the Melfi steering committee:

The evolution of the training process in Melfi has been incessant. While the factory was growing, the training programmes and methods were constantly reviewed in accordance with the evolution of the context, the suggestions gathered from the trainees, and the emerging training needs. (former Personnel Director)

Furthermore, the scope of the project required the management of the factory to co-ordinate with the broader network of organizational actors operating in the immediate environment: for example, synchronizing the advancement of the construction work with the suppliers who were constructing their own plants; lobbying political actors at the local and national level in order to get concessions and build infrastructures; and dealing with utility companies to get the necessary connections.

In sum, the construction site embodied the characteristics of a 'formative context' (Ciborra and Lanzara 1994) providing a mixture of opportunity structures and structural constraints. At the same time, the advancement of the construction site described a highly situated process of knowledge creation and accumulation, while emphasizing the provisional character of that knowledge (knowledge in the making). The learning process on the greenfield relied on a collection of multifaceted sources, which were originally combined in the implementation process in order to serve the performance of the newborn factory. Training of the workforce and investment in HRM were critical factors. Teamwork, socialization programmes, respect and protection of the local cultural values, and definition of the project as a collective effort were the multifaceted aspects of a human-centred design concept. However, the expansion of the core stock of knowledge governing the functioning of the new factory was based on a pervasive strategy of delegation: knowledge transfer occurred top-down in the form of guidelines and specifications; bottom-up in the form of finished products that could be capitalized as consolidated knowledge assets. Method played a major role in keeping creativity on course. On the one hand, it made up for the lack of experience of the novice workforce by providing a shared framework. At the same time, method provided a strategy for the capitalization of knowledge, that is, its transformation into a corporate asset: knowledge creation had to be institutionalized in the method in order for successful experiences to be repeatable. Consider the disassembling exercise. The exercise was aimed at transferring knowledge (top-down) about the product and the production process. At the same time, operators were asked to devise a disasembling cycle and suggest the best way for re-assembling the car. In other words, knowledge appropriation was closely linked to practice and institutionalized in the method. The disassembling/assembling exercise also bears important cognitive implications which emerge in the resolution of breakdowns along the assembly line.

Concluding Remarks

What has been the meaning of letting the workers build their own factory from scratch? What have been the knowledge implications of such a move? Why was the greenfield crucial for establishing the technical and institutional order of the factory, from the overall manufacturing system down to the shop floor level? How might such a complex manufacturing system be built?

The construction of the plant from the greenfield represented a unique experience for the original core group of workers. It stood at the heart of a highly situated learning process which carried crucial cultural, organizational, and epistemological implications. Bringing the plant to its full production took two-and-a-half years, which still counts as a significant proportion of time for a young factory like Melfi. Moreover, it consisted of an intense and emotional experience, one which was to remain imprinted in the memory of the participants. Just imagine a group of young people, coming from a rural community to their first work experience, who are actively involved in a major re-engineering process on behalf of the most important Italian company. As we have seen earlier, the interviewees proudly refer to the greenfield as a unique experience, emphasizing the emotional implications of 'being there'.

Certainly, this knowledge-creation process seemed to be characterized by low levels of conflict, thanks to the participatory strategy of implementation promoted by the company. On the other hand, the advancement of the Melfi project was controversial in that it was constantly subject to shifting trajectories and contrasting forces (top-down and bottom-up), albeit within a planned and very structured design concept. In this respect, the 'construction site' became the emblem of knowledge in the making. It provided a competence/identity building space, characterized by the encounter between the avant-garde design concept of the factory, the company culture and the values embodied by the green workforce. The building site was a learning laboratory, a training yard, where experiments and simulation exercises could be tried out without any pressure stemming from production plans. It also conveyed the idea of gradualness of the learning process: as in construction work, competence building took place step by step, gradually moving the workforce towards higher levels of understanding. Yet this learning process was highly situated and never detached from practice. For the previous reasons, I argue that the initial stock of knowledge embedded in the design of the Melfi factory probably represented the most crucial knowledge asset for the company. It can be seen as a distinctive feature of the way the factory operated and therefore regarded as a source of competitive advantage. I have also contended that it is precisely here, in the experience of building the factory from scratch, that a great deal of tacit knowledge lies, and it is here that we need to look in order to explain specific organizational dynamics.

In sum, what emerged from the Melfi building site was a process of social construction of corporate knowledge rather than a mere top-down transfer of knowledge. The factory gradually took shape with the fundamental contribution of the workforce. The development of operators' competence went hand in hand with the physical construction work, highlighting the processual and sedimentary nature of organizational knowledge.

At the methodological level, the strategy adopted in the present case reminds one of the work of an 'archaeologist of knowledge' engaged in a process of discovery and delayering the multiple strata in which knowledge has been sedimented and institutionalized over time. My analysis, based on the use of the time lens, has identified six phases/sources of knowledge creation and institutionalization of core competencies. By the time construction work is completed and the factory runs at full production, knowledge too seems to become fully institutionalized. The factory and the core stock of knowledge underlying its functioning have finally been sealed, transformed into black boxes, and manifold experiences have been concealed in a protected nucleus. From now on, it will be more difficult to access tacit knowledge, except on those occasions when knowledge is displaced and somewhat disclosed.

Notes

1. Melfi is the largest greenfield plant in Europe (Production 1995). In 1998 Melfi ranked third in Europe in terms of productivity, according to a table published yearly by the Economist Intelligence Unit. In 1999 productivity fell slightly—moving the plant into fourth place—owing to the introduction of the new Punto model. In 2000, despite a further drop, Melfi still ranked in the top ten.
2. The analysis focuses on the role of young managers, middle managers and technicians in the process of learning and knowledge acquisition over the greenfield. The choice of the sample is justified by the fact that these profiles were those most closely involved in the training process surrounding the coming into existence of

the factory. In particular, given their connecting function within the new integrated factory model (i.e. 'being in the middle'), middle-managers are considered by the company as a crucial asset in the process of knowledge creation and transfer.

3. Within Fiat, the term 'cavalier' refers to powerful, charismatic figures who have served the company for long periods of time. It also points to a conservative mode of thinking deeply grounded in the old company's tradition.

4. Here it is important to reiterate that the research is not concerned with the paradigm shift per se, which remains in the background providing a context for description. Specifically, in my account I chose the design concept of the factory as a point of departure, without questioning the decision-making process upstream of it. It should be noted that the process under consideration—unfolding according to chronological / thematic phases—is delimited by the presence of black boxes: it starts with a project on paper (a script) and ends with the physical factory. From the above consideration it is possible to derive the following proposition: in a process of social construction, the status of an object or artefact depends on the arbitrary decision to question it or conversely treat it as a final product or black box. It is a matter of where one sets the boundaries of the description. The latter raises an important methodological issue and highlights the role of research design in cutting up the interactionist field.

5. During the interviews some operators described the experience of assembling a Punto as building their own car; others often referred to the team as a family.

5

Generating Creative Options

Dorothy Leonard and Walter Swap

'I don't need to tell you how important this distance learning contract is,' said Hazel as she opened the meeting. 'If we get to design the ad campaign, we'll have a whole new line of business. That's why I've put our very best people on this team—including Fred from Sales and Tom—even though he's moved to our financial services account. I know some of you were a bit surprised at my bringing them in, but we needed a variety of backgrounds and knowledge to be creative. I was really pleased with yesterday's brainstorming session—we came up with a lot of cool ideas. Given our schedule and resource constraints, I've gone ahead and selected one to work on. The parody of university professors concept was funny—but I don't think we know enough about university teaching to pull it off. And I liked the notion of outreach to kids in developing nations, but we could offend some people with that one. So I suggest we go with the puppy training idea. If your dog can be trained to sit up and beg through the Internet, then for sure your kids can be taught calculus the same way. People like animals in ads; it won't offend anyone; we can make it funny and it's a low budget approach. I've divided you up into three subgroups; each group needs to get going on slogans, storyboards, budgets. We'll get together next Friday to see what you've come up with and select the best treatment. Any questions? No? Okay, let's move.''

Hazel's heart is in the right place. She knows about creative abrasion and has convened a group that draws on different kinds of deep knowledge from its members. She knows that she needs divergent thinking among group members in order to generate lots of options—but she thinks she has been there and done that after a single session of brainstorming. Maybe the group knows more about university professors than she thinks. Or maybe they don't need to. Maybe there is a way of making an advertisement about children in developing nations that will not offend. The ideas haven't been explored enough to know. After getting a few options on the table, Hazel is ready to go. The group has hardly paused at the intersection of ideas before she is blowing her horn to move them on.

How would you feel if you had been the one in Hazel's group to suggest the parody on university professors as the basis for an advertisement? Or the ad featuring small children in a developing nation schoolhouse? That not enough energy had gone into kicking the idea around? Even if the ad with the puppies *is* the best idea, it is far from developed. You wish there had been more time for debate, more time for building on each other's ideas, for pulling in knowledge from various people's heads. But you know Hazel. You had better 'climb aboard because the train is leaving the station,' as she is fond of saying.

Premature Convergence: The Urge to Merge

You need only one *super* solution, right? The trouble is, option #1 often seems so appealing that the group closes ranks around it, ignoring options 2, 3, and 4. And options 5 through 50 never arise. To be creative, a group must first be able to generate possibilities—lots of them. Then some of those options have to be elaborated and carefully thought through. Somewhere in this mix of generating and processing options, groups often run afoul of premature consensus, or 'the urge to merge.' What drives the urge? Lots of things, including:

- Perceived time pressures force the group's hand.
- The group's leader is overly directive.
- The group is insulated from outside opinion.
- The group members experience powerful forces to remain in the group.
- The group is guided by norms that defeat divergent thinking.

Time Pressures

A deadline can certainly concentrate the mind. A *real* deadline, such as meeting a Christmas market window, can focus a group's energies and compress the normal creative process. As such, it may serve as a vigorous, necessary spur for convergence. Too often, however, the deadline may be more apparent than real. An impatient manager imposing an *artificial* deadline can short circuit the process of developing options and kill originality.

Hazel, of course, sees the group dynamics through her own distinctive lens. In the trade-off between the highest quality solution and timeliness, she chooses the latter. If the asteroid is going to hit earth tomorrow, the creative plan to knock it off collision course won't help if it can't be activated until next week. And, like most managers, she feels as if she's in a perpetual meteor shower. She knows she has to move quickly as well as creatively.

The tragic destruction of the US space shuttle *Challenger* on January 28, 1986, hurling to their deaths six astronauts and the 'teacher in space,' may be partly attributable to time pressures on the decision-making process. The launch had been delayed once, and the window for another launch was fast closing. As researchers have reconstructed the fatal decision-making process, not a few have noted that the leaders of the decision team were concerned about public and congressional perceptions of the entire space shuttle program and its continued funding. Another delay might damage the chances for future funding. With hindsight, the decision makers wished they had taken time to heed the warnings by a few vocal dissenters. As we will discuss later in this chapter, dissension can usefully keep options open.

Overly Directive Leadership Style

Who in Hazel's group would have the temerity to challenge her conclusion that the puppy ad is the way to go? Hazel has given the *illusion* that the group has a choice in the matter ('I *suggest* that we go with.... Any questions? No?'), but she has clearly signaled how she wants the group to converge. Perhaps the quickest way to close off the pursuit of options is for the leader to express a clear preference at the outset. ('Why should I jeopardize my standing with Hazel and the group by contradicting her?')

Such concerns are not without foundation in reality. When William Niskanen was chief economist at Ford Motor Co. in 1980, his free-trader views came into conflict with his superiors' new protectionism in the face of increasing Japanese competition. Niskanen was fired. CFO Will Caldwell explained to him, 'In this company, Bill ..., the people who do well wait until they hear their superiors express their views. Then they add something in support of those views.' Not exactly the kind of environment to foster divergent thinking! Perhaps you think: 'That was the eighties! Today we empower people.' We agree that the rhetoric has changed—but many leaders still would need their jaws wired shut in order to keep their preferences to themselves.

The urge to merge is reinforced in any organizational decision-making because decisiveness is valued in management. Managers of creativity thus usually have to fight both external pressures to choose something quickly and act, and their own tendency to drive for closure. Hazel's personal thinking style biases her toward immediate action. When the group is considering option A or B, the person who suggests C gets freeze-dried by one of Hazel's famous baleful stares. And her mental gearshift doesn't have 'reverse' on it. 'Never

---

Open and Closed Leadership

Psychologist Matie Flowers composed four-person groups to discuss options on a difficult personnel issue. A financially troubled school district with a powerful teachers' union had a 62-year-old math teacher whose declining mental faculties were apparently preventing her from maintaining discipline in her classes. Each group member was assigned a role: superintendent of schools (the leader of the group, actually a trained confederate), the school principal, a school counselor, and a member of the school board. Each person was provided with a set of 'facts' bearing on the case.

The *open* leader had been instructed not to state a suggested solution until the other three had; to ask for and encourage discussion of each option; and to state twice that the most important thing was to *air all viewpoints*. In contrast, the closed leader gave a preferred solution at the beginning, did not encourage discussion, and stated twice that the most important thing was for the group to *agree* on its decision.

The groups led by an open leader resisted the urge to merge. They generated, on average, more solutions. They also presented more of the supporting facts than the 'closed' leadership groups.

---

revisit a decision' is her motto. So even if she were not under such pressure to deliver the ad campaign ahead of competitors, she would still push for a quick decision so as to move on to implementation.

Well, Hazel, we never promised you *efficient* creativity! Just *effective*. And effective means a balance between exploration and speed. Between opening up options and closing them down. Between divergent thinking and convergent.

In Figure 5.1, the *A* diamond represents a group spending very little time on creating options and most of their effort on implementation issues. This may be appropriate when the problem to be solved or the issue to be resolved is narrowly defined, well understood, or fairly routine. The *B* diamond represents a meeting of a group of people who *love* to discuss, debate, think up options—but who leave very little relative time and resources for homing in on a solution. If time is no issue, this model may be appropriate. However, you see where we are headed— to the *C* diamond in Figure 5.1, which is especially appropriate for creative problem solving. If you don't spend the time and effort to create the requisite variety, you are unlikely to identify a novel solution. If Hazel's deadline is real (i.e. cross the line and the project is dead) then she probably acted appropriately. However, almost certainly she could have allowed more divergent thinking in order to get a more creative solution. Too much time spent on divergence leaves little time to consider implementation, but too much time spent on convergence shortchanges the divergent thinking process.

Insularity and Isolation

Birds that flock together become more of a feather. And the longer they flock together, the more of a feather they become. People who work together over

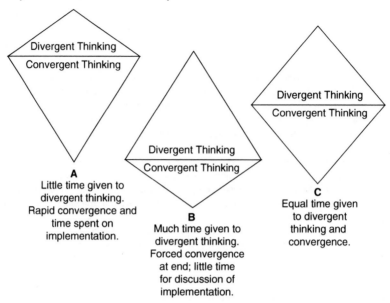

Fig. 5.1 *Balancing divergent and convergent activities*

time may not *look* more alike (as some say long-married couples do) but the deep knowledge possessed by individual members increasingly becomes collective. And we flock together mentally because it is comfortable. Even a talented heterogeneous group is unlikely to explore a full range of alternatives when it isolates itself from those outside the group who have know-how or know-why to contribute. For example, in their study of groups of scientists, Donald Pelz and Frank Andrews found that when membership in the groups turned over frequently, the groups were more creative than were those with stable membership, even when the stable groups were interdisciplinary. Within three years, even interdisciplinary groups had become homogeneous in how they approached problems. Moreover, the more that group members share common information, the more likely that information will weigh heavily in group decisions. Just because we *all* know something doesn't make it important, useful knowledge. We need to figure out what we don't know we don't know—and that means looking outside the flock.

Group Cohesiveness

People have liked being in groups since our conference rooms were caves. We need to feel accepted and valued by others. In fact, a good part of our own identity is tied up with membership in some group or other. Most of us have

---

The Common Knowledge Effect

Daniel Gigone and Reid Hastie devised an experiment in which three-person groups were asked to make judgments about the likely performance of students in a course. Each group member was provided with a set of facts (e.g. the student's high school academic performance, number of classes skipped, standardized test scores). Some of these facts were given to all three members, some were given to two, and some to only one. So the group collectively had all of the information about the student, but some of it was more or less redundant. Gigone and Hastie found that the more *common* knowledge in the group (i.e. the more people who had the same information), the more weight was given to it and the more it influenced the final group judgment, even if it wasn't the most *salient* data. (Interestingly, group members were unaware of the influence of common knowledge on their judgments.) If one wishes a group to think broadly, this study suggests that special efforts will need to be made to encourage the group to consider all of the information at its disposal, not just that which members have in common.

---

belonged to groups in which we have felt good about ourselves, safe, and secure. We like our fellow members and look forward to meeting with them. We would suffer if the group were to disband or if we were somehow forced to leave. The glue that holds group members together has many origins. Initial liking has repeatedly been shown to foster cohesiveness. The more you like your fellow members, the more strongly you are motivated to remain in the group. Second, merely being in extended contact over time can lead to mutual liking and cohesiveness. Familiarity breeds... comfort. A third powerful force drawing people together is an external threat. Combining efforts to combat a rival or enemy unites the group in a common purpose.

So we like clans. However, high cohesiveness—the forces that draw people together and keep them together—is a primary determinant of 'Groupthink.' Irving Janis came up with this Orwellian term to describe 'a mode of thinking that people engage in when they are deeply involved in a cohesive in-group, when the members' strivings for unanimity override their motivation to realistically appraise alternative courses of action.' The Groupthink tendency is really troublesome for creativity. It results from illusions among members that everyone else is in agreement ('The naked emperor is really elegantly dressed today'); self-censorship of any doubts ('Who am I to question all these smart people?'); and pressure from group members on dissenters ('Mustn't be disloyal—I'm part of a team'). The result? The group aborts the divergent thinking process and seizes quickly on one or two options. It is wonderful to have *esprit de corps*. But when these groups are decision-making bodies, we can pay a steep price for group cohesiveness. Janis drew many of his observations about Groupthink from examining some critical decisions at the highest levels of US foreign policymaking—where creativity is often needed.

The invasion of Cuba by 1,400 expatriates in 1961 has been called one of the 'worst fiascoes ever perpetrated by a responsible government.' Within three days, all of the invaders had been killed or captured. All of the major assumptions held by President Kennedy and his National Security Council were completely misguided. They thought the Cuban population would spontaneously rise up to support the small brigade of invading ex-patriots. They underestimated the ability of Castro's large, well-trained army and airforce to respond. And the brigade landed in a swamp. A big one.

Kennedy's advisors were not stupid people. How could the 'best and brightest,' whose different backgrounds clearly positioned the group for creative abrasion, fail so miserably to generate alternatives to the CIA plan presented to them? At least part of the answer lies in the dynamics of cohesive groups. Pulitzer Prize-winning historian Arthur Schlesinger, Jr., a member of Kennedy's group, berated himself for his silence during the deliberations:

though my feelings of guilt were tempered by the knowledge that a course of objection would have accomplished little save to gain me a name as a nuisance. I can only explain my failure to do more than raise a few timid questions by reporting that one's impulse to blow the whistle on this nonsense was simply undone by the circumstances of the discussion.

Cohesive groups present an interesting paradox. On the one hand, members of such groups feel accepted and should be free to say anything they want without fear of antagonizing their fellows. On the other, they don't want to appear ignorant, disruptive, or a spoil-sport. The lesson for managers of creative groups is clearly *not* to reduce the cohesiveness, but rather to harness that cohesiveness in the service of creativity. This can be accomplished by understanding the power of group norms and, if necessary, changing them.

Inappropriate Group Norms

Norms are the rules group members follow, even when no one is watching. They are usually unwritten, often unconscious, almost always powerful. And they can help or inhibit creativity. Consider, for example, these invisible powerful rules:

- Don't interfere with other peoples' jobs. (Mind your own business.)
- Try to keep everyone happy. (Be nice.)
- Don't contradict the boss. (Know your place—and accept it.)
- Conform to the group. (Don't upset the apple cart.)

- Don't presume to know more than your elders. (Defer to more senior members of the group.)

How likely is it that a junior colleague will challenge a fellow group member's plan with one of her own when doing so might make her look like she's not minding her own business, is not being very nice, does not know her place, is being disrespectful, and is trying to upset the apple cart? A group in which these norms are allowed to stand unchallenged is a group that is damned to eternal blandness. You can't expect creative options if group members have all been trained to sit up, roll over, and speak only on command. Creative options will simply not emerge unless the prevailing norms are replaced with those more conducive to creativity. People will either not speak up in the first place; or, doing so, will soon discover how groups treat norm breakers.

Resisting the Urge to Merge: Encouraging Dissent

When Robert Kennedy was asked by his brother to assume the role of devil's advocate in the Cuban Missile Crisis deliberations, he did so with such gusto that only his relationship to the president protected him from the open hostility of other group members. As Oscar Wilde quipped, 'We dislike arguments of any kind; they are always vulgar and often convincing.'

The Group Reacts to Dissenters

Ever been in the following situation? Group members are closing in on the solution to a problem when someone speaks passionately in favor of some other option, maybe even one that has already been discussed and rejected. How do group members react? Eye-rolling? We crave agreement, not dissent. And dissent, even effective dissent, is often unpopular. A dissenter will, first, attract a lot of attention. Other members will attempt to bring him around. Failing that, the group will attempt to ignore or exclude him from group discussions. If that fails, he may be physically expelled from the group or 'reassigned.' Dissenters present a dilemma in group discussions. A person who challenges the emerging consensus may earn a certain grudging admiration for standing up for her principles in the face of group pressure. And she does bring new perspectives—perhaps valuable ones—to the table.

On the other hand, minority views prevent the group from reaching a quick decision and challenge the correctness of each majority member's judgment. 'We all had a pretty good idea of where we should be going, and I was feeling pretty good about myself and the group. Now you're saying we were all wrong?' As a result, the dissenter is generally heartily resented and disliked by the majority.

Wise leaders—or even just competent ones—help a group develop norms that encourage divergent thinking and welcome dissent. At Intel, it is essential to get 'knowledge power' into the organization, and employees learn early on that 'you know more than your boss does' about many things. Open dissent is absolutely encouraged from top management on down, and is repeatedly taught at all levels. Research shows that when the strength of an 'originality norm' is increased, group members not only give more creative responses, but they tolerate and like minority respondents more than when the norm is weak. Creativity flourishes when the unusual is expected and dissent is welcomed.

The Value of Dissent

How do dissenters manage to stimulate creativity if their opinions are so unpopular? It is not because the rest of us necessarily believe they know what they're talking about. Rather, they force us to examine our own positions, search for information on *both* sides of the issue, evaluate the arguments against them—in short, engage in the kind of divergent thinking that is at the heart of creativity. Majorities, on the other hand, move the group in *one* direction—toward consensus and conformity. ('Why should I search for new options? We already have the answer.')

The Power of Minority Dissent

Charlan Jeanne Nemeth and Joel Wachtler devised a laboratory analog of majority and minority influence on creativity. College students were presented with the task of determining whether a standard geometric figure was or was not embedded in a more complex pattern. Experimental confederates were employed to simulate either a *majority influence* (four confederates) or a *minority influence* (two confederates). Nemeth and Wachtler found that majorities caused subjects to converge on their judgments, whether or not they were correct. Minorities, on the other hand, caused subjects to give novel, correct responses (i.e. to correctly identify the standard figure in other complex patterns) that had not previously been identified by the majorities. In short, majority influence served to promote conformity, or a mindless aping of the majority judgments. In the case of minority influence. 'One can be influenced to reanalyze a problem and, in the process, perhaps function more creatively and accurately.'

Managing Divergence: Resisting the Urge to Merge and Creating Options

So it's not just a matter of *tolerating* dissent. We *need* it. If your group is going to be creative, beginning with the ability to generate lots of potentially useful options, members must resist the urge to merge. Dissent can be uncomfortable for everyone, certainly including the dissenter. So it's important to get it into everyone's head that dissent can be vital to the creative process and is normal behavior in your group—not just a hindrance to group consensus. But even if we start with a diverse group and deliberately augment the membership with aliens, and even if we consciously promote a group process encouraging dissent, the urge to converge may seem overpowering. You will be glad to know that resistance is not futile! Let's look at some mental tools and process techniques that can help stave off *premature* convergence.

Techniques for Resisting the Urge to Merge

Harnessing Group Norms: Ground Rules

Rules for creative groups? Sounds stifling. However, one of the reasons that we need to develop conscious, explicit norms is that individuals come into any meeting with a different set of expectations of behavior, born of their personal backgrounds and experience. Some folks grew up in families where lively debate over the dinner table encouraged both argumentation and listening to others. Others grew up in families whose operative rules were: don't ask—and don't tell. And some people continued to be treated as children, with nothing useful to say, even when they were adults. It is small wonder that when we all get together, we often need to talk about how we are going to talk.

Granted, most of us feel a bit foolish creating rules about how we will work together. Surely, we think, we are all adults and have years of experience in dealing with group dynamics. That, of course, is the problem. Many of us have long years of practicing the dysfunctional behaviors we learned from professional or personal experience. If we have come from a very competitive company where information is power, we may unconsciously hold back in order to look brilliant at the right time (and end up missing the moment for our insight). Or we may have worked in an organization where disagreement was impolite. If we are the third or fourth sibling in a large family, we may hesitate to suggest an idea for fear of looking foolish in front of our 'elders.'

Arguments don't have to be personal. Statements like 'That's a ridiculous idea,' or 'The problem with you is . . . ' are just plain abrasive. People who don't understand *creative* abrasion may confuse it with interpersonal conflict, and as a result avoid it. Yet abrasion is essential for creativity. 'Inspiration can come from anyone on the team,' points out Susan Schilling of Lucas Learning. 'By disagreeing, we get the best . . . for the product—but it's not personal disagreement.' So we need group norms—habits of behavior—that make certain kinds of conflict okay or even mandated. In the world of Education meets Entertainment, Schilling found, people from a background in education were more accustomed, to collaboration, whereas in companies producing games, 'Whoever yells the loudest wins!' In order to tap the group's creativity, 'we needed to build a set of internal rules about how we would agree and disagree.'

Many groups take time to compose these ground rules—rules of behavior to which all members agree that encourage creative abrasion. One group we know opted for short but sweet: 'Anyone can disagree with anyone else. No one can disagree without giving a reason. We will actively listen to each other. We will not use the words 'always' and 'never' in referring to each other's behavior.' We know another group whose ground rules originally took up two walls of flip-chart sheets. Not surprisingly, such an abundance of rules is no longer remembered, much less invoked. While we favour pithiness, the important thing is to get agreement on the rules and to enforce them. If disagreement threatens to blossom into anger, team members can point to the principles and remind everyone to listen to each other. It feels a bit like elementary school to post those principles around the meeting room, but the process of agreeing on the principles and then putting them up on the wall where all team members can see them does help everyone keep group interaction in mind. And that's the point of the exercise. We get so caught up in content that we forget process.

Process rules can evolve in surprising ways. Reporter Hal Lancaster recalls 'a dinner meeting where the liberal consumption of after-dinner drinks prompted surprising candor between middle and senior managers. Thereafter, it was understood that a meeting conducted under. 'Armagnac Rules' meant that you could speak freely, without fear of reprisal.'

When 'don't rock the boat' takes precedence over 'generate as many alternatives as possible and evaluate each one carefully,' creativity is likely to suffer. Fewer than two years after the Cuban Bay of Pigs fiasco, when the nation and the world faced the Cuban Missile Crisis, John F. Kennedy proved even presidents can learn. Fidel Castro installed Russian missiles capable of converting major US cities into major craters, and the United States had to decide how to react. This time, Kennedy instituted a new set of 'ground rules' in the foreign policy discussions that included bringing in outside experts, appointing devil's advocates, and deliberately refraining from expressing his private opinion (which was that military action against Cuba would be necessary!). The result was that the initial assumption that the military would have to act against the missile silos was replaced by a decision

---

The Nasa Moon Survival Problem

Your spaceship has crashed, stranding your group on the moon, hundreds of miles from base. Fortunately, no one is seriously injured and much of the cargo can be salvaged. Unfortunately, you can't bring everything, so you must decide which items are most vital for your survival as you make your way to base. Each group member must rank in order of importance all that has been salvaged, including such items as oxygen tanks, water, and food, as well as matches, parachute silk, and a compass. Then the group convenes to arrive at a consensus.

Normally, when compared to the objectively 'correct' answers (as determined by NASA experts), groups are no better than individuals in their final rankings. Some groups, however, are given special norms to follow:

- 'Avoid changing your mind only in order to avoid conflict and to reach agreement and harmony.
- 'Withstand pressures to yield which have no objective or logically sound foundation.
- 'View differences of opinion as both natural and helpful.'

Groups following these instructions were judged more creative and arrived at rankings that were superior to the group's best member 75 percent of the time.

---

to set up a blockade. Time was bought, egos were assuaged, and the crisis was resolved. When US citizens realized later how close we had come to a devastating conflict, we were grateful the president had introduced his advisors to different group norms.

Challenging Unconscious Assumptions
When is a paper clip not a paper clip? When you straighten it out to solve a problem requiring a piece of wire. When is an engineer not an engineer? When she is an anthropologist, visiting a customer's home to understand when, why, and how a product is being used. We think of tools and people in certain roles and have trouble reconceiving those roles. The human mind is extremely susceptible to routine thinking. It is efficient not to question the way we interact with our surroundings. If we stopped to think about it before we sat in a chair, if we did not assume that our medications were uncontaminated, if we did not expect an accountant to give us different information than the house painter—if we did not make hundreds of unconscious assumptions every hour, we would be virtually paralyzed. The trouble is, those assumptions can also keep us from thinking creatively, either individually or as a group. Shared assumptions are a form of convergent thinking. Yet if we can free just a few strands of the mental bonds in our minds connecting persons or objects with their function, we open up new possibilities. Why have you scoured the house for a screwdriver when a dime would do the trick? Well, because a dime is supposed to be used to buy a piece of 'penny' candy—not as a tool. Sometimes

---

Obstacles to Creative Thinking

Consider the following three problems:

1. Given a candle, a box of matches, and some thumbtacks, attach a candle to a bulletin board so it won't drip wax on the floor.
2. Given six toothpicks of equal length, use all six to make exactly four equilateral triangles.
3. What is the rule we're using to develop the number series 5, 10, 15? The objective is to discover the rule by trial. Generate your own sets of three numbers and we'll tell you whether they conform to our rule or not. When you think you know our rule, tell us what it is.

Turn to the last page of this chapter for the answers.

---

simply alerting group members to their own susceptibility helps them develop the ability to question their own assumptions. Asking some basic questions can lead the discussion in new directions:

- What are our assumptions here? Are they the only valid ones?
- Are there different ways of viewing this situation, for example, from some-one else's perspective?

The examples in 'Obstacles to Creative Thinking' illustrate three factors to which we are particularly vulnerable:

1. *Functional fixedness* refers to our inability to free ourselves from the expect-ations of how something (or someone) normally functions. Boxes are containers, not platforms, so we are slow to think of emptying a matchbox to attach to the wall. When we rely on our past experiences of how things are used, we often get stuck, unable to break out of old-thinking habits.
2. *Fixation* is similar: our mental wheels are stuck in the mud of approaching a problem from the 'obvious' direction. (When a problem is presented in two dimensions, we naturally try to solve it in two.)
3. The *confirmation bias* refers to our tendency to seek support for our convictions, and reluctance to either look for or accept contrary evidence. ('I'm such a good judge of character. Almost all the people I've promoted have worked out fine.' Yes, but how about all the people you *didn't* promote? Maybe they worked out fine elsewhere within or outside the organization as well.)

Devil's Advocate

In the Roman Catholic tradition, a devil's advocate is an official of the Congregation of Rites whose duty is to point out defects in the evidence upon which the case for beatification or canonization rests. While we favor instituting a group norm that encourages *everyone* to act as a critical thinker, challenging premature drives to consensus, sometimes a formal devil's

106

advocate role should be assigned. We mentioned earlier how President John F. Kennedy used his brother Robert in that role to good purpose, although the vehemence with which he pursued his role alienated many group members. To be most effective,

- The devil's advocate must, first, have the absolute support of the group leader. When a designated dissenter becomes merely a token (as was the case in President Johnson's councils during the escalation of the Vietnam War) he will not be taken seriously.
- The devil's advocate should be a good role player. It should not be clear what her actual position is. She should be able to argue as though she believed the dissenting viewpoint implicitly.
- The role should rotate among group members from meeting to meeting. This precludes both the danger of 'tokenism' and also the risk that over time group members will begin to confuse the advocate with the devil himself. (Without the support of the leader, this can lead to disaster for the dissenter's future in the organization.)
- The devil's advocate should focus on the issues and refrain from personal attacks.

A top manager who wanted his staff to think creatively about a dilemma, asked two of them to take contrary positions. The issue was how the company should respond to a distributor who both greatly expanded their market for the consumer product (a home appliance) and at the same time inhibited product innovation. One staffer presented the majority opinion that the distributor had the company in a stranglehold and should be challenged, even if the company lost money in the process. The appointed devil's advocate pointed out all the advantages and benefits to be derived from their relationship with the powerful distributor. Interestingly, the group converged on an innovative strategy that incorporated both viewpoints.

Reader's Theatre
At Hewlett-Packard Laboratories, Manager of Worldwide Personnel Barbara Waugh has used 'Reader's Theatres' both in the labs and in the company as a whole to present (and legitimize) divergent views. The 'play' put on by employees takes its script from the actual experiences of the employees, who read their parts before an audience of colleagues. The resulting emotional and visceral experience has effected huge changes in the way the majority feels about an issue. For example, although a liberal company in many ways, Hewlett-Packard initially decided against offering benefits to long-term part-ners of gay and lesbian employees. Confronted with dramatized evidence of discrimination and hardship, senior management reversed its original decision. The drama placed viewers in the uncomfortable position of experiencing first-

---

The Availability Heuristic, or The Vividness Effect

Are you more likely to be killed by a moose or a grizzly bear? Are there more words that begin with the letter *k* or that have *k* as their third letter? It is probably easier to visualize one alternative over the other: the deadly fangs of the world's largest carnivore; lots of words that start with *k*. The tendency to believe that something is more true or more likely to happen if we can vividly imagine it is called the 'availability heuristic.' In many cases, the availability heuristic gives us an accurate representation of reality; in others, however, we are led astray. Far more people are trampled or impaled by moose than are mauled by grizzlies; there are many more words with *k* as their third letter than their first. Yet many, if not most, people would probably overestimate the likelihood of each of these less plausible events. The lesson here? Make something vivid, such as the dramatizations in Reader's Theatre, and observers will be more likely to imagine them, hence find them plausible—a powerful force for generating new, believable, options.

---

hand what their colleagues had told them about in general terms before. Reader's Theatres powerfully compel the audience to view life through the eyes of the minority. The vicarious experience challenges comfortable assumptions and forces attention to dissenting views.

Okay, so we have some techniques for preventing premature convergence. But the manager's job is also to help the group create requisite variety, that is, that big menu of options from which to select potential solutions, market, or service opportunities. The group members undoubtedly *want* to be creative. However, one cannot order creativity like a pint of beer. You may need some tools and techniques to jump-start their imaginations. Some of these techniques are used within the group itself; for others, the group must look beyond its own boundaries.

Creating Options within the Group

Brainstorming

Probably the best-known technique for generating options is brain-storming. Brainstorming sessions range from the intelligent and useful to the banal and unproductive—what one manager interviewed termed 'intellectual masturbation.' The difference, as in so many techniques, is in process and purpose: how the brainstorming session is conducted and what its intent is. Studies in psychological laboratories consistently show that individuals working alone come up with more and better ideas than they do when working in a group and the larger the group, the greater the disparity. Why? Self-consciousness and anxiety about being evaluated by other group members, and the inherent inability to listen simultaneously to others while creating one's own ideas.

Although the experiments generally use college students brain-storming somewhat trivial subjects (e.g. 'What if people had two thumbs on each hand?'), we should not ignore the lessons of the researcher's laboratory. People can believe others will think their ideas are stupid. They can forget their own ideas while others are talking. Unless skillfully managed, brainstorms can merely promote the *illusion* that the group is being creative. For example, people tend to prefer group brainstorming sessions to individual idea generation. They believe they were more creative and prolific in groups, even if there is evidence to the contrary. So—use brainstorms or not?

The lesson we draw is that brainstorming in groups is better than not dedicating any time to generating options. In some cases, *nominal groups*— members working on the same task in isolation—may be the way to go. But when skillfully facilitated and working on substantive issues such as 'How can we survive this crisis?' rather than a superfluity of thumbs, a brainstorming group can often match the nominal groups in number and creativity of ideas. Moreover, proponents of brainstorming can take heart from a study showing that when individuals and groups were instructed to produce a *best* idea, rather than *lots* of ideas, groups performed better than individuals. It is also common to combine the nominal and brainstorming techniques by having individuals generate their ideas on Post-it notes. The facilitator can then either collect the 'yellow stickies' and arrange them according to some category scheme or can let the group develop the scheme. Once the stickies are arranged by category, the group can then elaborate on them as a group, using the same brainstorming rules.

A variant on traditional brainstorming designed to eliminate the blocking of ideas is *electronic brainstorming*. Participants type in their ideas, while the ideas of other members appear in a separate window on the screen. The electronic brainstormers are encouraged to read the others' contributions and elaborate on them. Evidence suggests that because participants are free to focus on their own idea production, more ideas are generated compared to traditional brainstorming.

We find ourselves returning once again to the importance of thinking styles. There certainly are people who would prefer sitting before their computer screens and interacting with their fellow group members electronically. But how well would that work for highly verbal, image-oriented individuals in ad agencies or design firms? Or when an important part of the brainstorming session involves manipulating physical objects?

Take IDEO, one of the top design and engineering firms in the United States, as an example. Almost every project includes some brainstorming. An IDEO 'brainstorm' gathers staff members with diverse skills—human factors, mechanical engineering, industrial design, and often a client—to generate product ideas. A staff member selected for facilitation skills runs the face-to-face meeting. Everyone knows the rules, but they are also stenciled around the top of the walls in the room usually used for this purpose: 'defer judgment; build on the ideas of others; one conversation at a time; stay focused on the topic; encourage wild ideas.' The folks at IDEO have an advantage over most of us in that they can draw. By the end of the session, in addition to the words on the white board, there are sketches on the board and on the paper covering the table around which the participants sit. Note that the rules encourage the kind of free association that people usually think of as brainstorming—but within bounds. A successful brainstorm has to have a clearly understood topic, an experienced facilitator, media for capturing ideas, and accepted rule of conduct.

Role Playing

Most of us gave up role playing when we reached adolescence. However, role playing, like brainstorming, can release floodgates of information. When MTV needed a new game show in 1996, staffers went off-site to 'game-storm.' They spent a day recalling childhood diversions like capture the flag, actually playing children's board games, and analyzing TV game shows. The big hit of 1997, *Figure It Out* came from the game-storm; executive Kevin Kay borrowed ideas from the game 20 Questions and from the TV shows *I've Got a Secret* and *The David Letterman Show.*

One of the nice features of role playing is that it has a fast-forward button as well as reverse. You can try on the future. When Interval Research, a company researching prospects for new media products, wanted to consider how people would use a videophone, they put on an 'informance,' an informational performance by staff members acting out how friends trying to arrange a dinner party over the videophone might interact. In the process, they realized that who controls the video 'eye' was very important. When one participant suggested that the caller wanted to be able to look around the room, an actor at the other end objected. 'I might be sitting here in my skivvies or something,' he said. 'I don't want him to be able to look over here.' Role playing raises issues that might not occur in theoretical discussions.

At times, realistically playing the role of users requires significant adaptation. Imagine Interval Research's challenge in getting a group of twentyish researchers to design interfaces with electronic equipment for elderly people to use. How could Generation X, health club-addicted designers possibly understand the challenges of an aging body? Sure, you could get them to visit some nursing homes or talk with their grandparents. But their observations will still be distant from experience. Far better if the designers *feel* what it is like to inhabit an 80-year-old body, so that their designs will be adequate. The answer? Give them gloves to reduce dexterity, glasses smeared with Vaseline to mimic blurred vision, and weights on their arms and legs to simulate time-worn muscles—and *then* let them role play interactions with the proposed technology.

Some groups even hire actors to simulate the future. At Intel, developers of the next-generation semiconductor chips wanted to peek into the future to see possible future communication appliances. After visiting families in their homes to understand how parents and children in frantic Western civilizations communicate, they hired actors to portray the 'usual' morning rush in an upper-class suburban home, using a futuristic appliance that attached to the refrigerator. This imaginary device (portrayed in the video as a small hand-held computer-cum-videophone) captured video messages among family members, such as Mom's reminders, recorded in the morning for the children to replay when they got home. ('Set the table; finish your homework before you turn on the television,' etc.) It also recorded the grocery list and served as an interface to the Internet. What does Intel learn from such exercises? Employees who see the video have expanded views of the future—where and how their chips might be used. These views in turn lead to speculation about the power and capabilities that such chips would need to accommodate such a variety of communication tasks.

John Kao's Idea Factory in San Francisco keeps an improvisation troupe busy acting out scenarios of the future created by clients. On more than one occasion, an otherwise dignified vice president has suddenly leaped from his spectator seat to join in the improvisation to make a point. The process of role playing pulls the clients into the future through their own imaginations. They never expect themselves to join the players and would have felt silly if you told them they would. Once again, though, they open up options that might never have occurred through sober analytical reflection.

File-drawer Excursions

Picture this: you are sitting in a brainstorming session at award-winning design and engineering firm IDEO. The group has come up with a promising new product idea, but it would require drawing heat away from a surface very quickly—in fact, almost instantly. One of the engineers suddenly jumps up and without a word leaves the room to return with a cup of scalding water and some copper pipes the shape and length of drinking straws. She puts the cup down on the table and hands you the copper piping. 'Stick it in the cup,' she says. You do, and are amazed to find that the pipe is immediately hot. You almost drop it in your surprise. You had expected the pipe to heat up the way a spoon does in hot coffee—taking at least ten seconds. If you worked at IDEO, you would know where she got the pipes—from the 'Technology Box,' a six-drawered filing cabinet in which reside flotsam and jetsam from under the desks of artists and engineers as well as new 'cool things' brought in by employees specifically to add to the collection. The two individuals who serve as 'curators' of the collection decide whether something should be added. The six drawers holding the collection of physical objects and materials are labeled 'Thermo Technologies; Amazing Materials; Cool Mechanisms; Electronic Technologies; Interesting Manufacturing Processes; and Light and Optics.' The labels only hint at the multiplicity of contents: specialty foam that can be almost infinitely compressed and yet spring back into its original volume; strips of metal that retain memory of their original shape when reheated, no matter how distorted during use; superheavy materials; a super-saturated salt solution that discharges heat when it is transformed chemically into a solid; hollow beads smaller than the diameter of a human hair that can be filled with liquids or gases, and dissolve to deliver their contents. The box is like a menu, or artist's palette. During brainstorms, engineers and designers often dash out to retrieve a sample of some material or a component to support an idea or to suggest a possible solution to a problem. Or engineers and designers frequently pull out the drawers and finger the contents just to browse for inspiration. Why keep physical objects instead of pictures or text descriptions? One of the IDEO curators of the Technology Box, Dennis Boyle, explains that 'some of these things are so unobvious, so nonintuitive, that you really have to experience them to believe them.' Adds the other curator Rickson Sun. 'I think there is a mechanism in the brain that helps you recall experiences much more effectively than you recall data.'

Metaphors and Models from Nature

How about using Mother Nature as a supplier of innovative ideas? Interval Research director and cofounder David Liddle argues that nature is a good problem solver because of her 'reckless and random' ways. Whereas humans rely on a narrow range of solutions based on logical processes, nature takes a trial-and-error approach that tests many more potential solutions. Sometimes she helps by giving us a direct functional model—solving the technical problems for us. What would we do if George de Mestral hadn't gotten his jacket covered with cockleburs? We wouldn't have that ubiquitous fastener of everything from shoe tops to teenagers upside down on walls—Velcro. (The name is derived from *vel*vet and *cro*chet.) Of course, people have been removing burs since we were wearing saber-toothed tiger pelts, and no one else had thought to make a virtue (and millions of dollars) out of how tenaciously the burs cling.

Not that we can always figure out nature's recipes. If glue makers can ever fathom how the barnacle manufactures the world's stickiest underwater glue, they will have a winning innovation. Spiders—particularly Florida's golden orb spiders—still hold the world's record for ultrastrong materials. Humans need acids, high temperatures, and carefully controlled factories to make strong fiber, but these spiders spin silk stronger than steel in room-temperature aqueous solutions. Specialists in 'biomimetics' at Cornell University are decoding the structure of the spider's silk, in order to synthesize genes that will yield fiber even stronger than the spiders'.

Even computer nerds will steal from Mother Nature. 'Our view of computer science is rational, mechanistic. But nature winds up doing things in a way we'd never think of,' says David Liddle. The Interval Research creative team working on an antivirus program includes University of New Mexico computer science professor Stephanie Forrest and theoretical immunologist Alan S. Perelson at Los Alamos National Laboratory. The software they designed together attacks unrecognized computer viruses by imitating the body's immune system's ability to identify alien molecules. 'I really believe that our computer systems are so complicated, we can't use them effectively till we make them look more like a biological system,' says Forrest.

Even when Mother Nature doesn't provide the functional recipe, she still offers 'a huge library of design metaphors [and opens] up a wide range of possibilities.' The company Thinking Tools, working with Texas Instruments, took some hints from the navigational skills of salmon finding their way back to a spawning river to design a computerized distribution system. Shipping companies could more efficiently dispatch goods to far-flung areas, they reasoned, if each package could 'seek' the best route.

Along the same lines, Paul Kantor, a professor at Rutgers University, observed that ants leave pheromone trails to help other ants find food. He has parlayed this observation into a $1 million grant from the Defense Advanced Research Projects Agency to develop Ant World Server to help Web browsers find information. Web users seeking particular information would create 'digital pheromone paths' that could be used by others looking for similar information. 'Our metaphor asks, 'Why can't human beings be at least as smart as ants about searching for information?' ' Why not, indeed!

What these people have all done is to dissect their problem into the desired *functions* (e.g. adhesion or repulsion, aggregation or reflection, navigation or identification) and then ask how nature has already performed that task.

Creative groups can use this technique to create options that might not otherwise occur to members.

....

Creating Options: Group Outreach

Managers of creative groups need to be physical as well as mental travel agents. Working within the group is not the only way to create new options. A number of techniques involve wearing out shoe leather.

Visits to Aliens

It is hard to generate creative abrasion when we are isolated or surrounded by people just like us. We can enrich the pool of ideas by visiting people and environments that are 'alien'—outside our normal networks. These aliens may be found almost anywhere—outside our group but elsewhere in the organization, or outside the organization entirely. Visits to aliens can build new knowledge, expose us to approaches to a problem that we would never think of, or even inspire a different definition of a problem. Groups that insulate themselves from those outside the immediate team or from outside the organization run the risk of rapidly running out of new ideas. Research on new product teams in high-technology firms found that those teams with the least amount of contact with those outside the team were the least innovative and productive.

Paul Horn of IBM Research suggests underdefining jobs so that people will move outside of their specified roles. 'We encourage scientists and researchers to venture far outside their realm as experts in semiconductors, physics, mathematics, and computer science. Today, more than 25 percent of researchers' time is taken up by working outside the lab with customers on first-of-a-kind projects.' Such visits will be valuable if we are prepared to observe, absorb, and apply the experience back to the occasion triggering the need for creativity. Stanley Gryskiewicz, vice president of global resources at the Center for Creative Leadership in Greensboro, North Carolina, follows the 'N + 1' plan when scheduling industry conferences. Besides the number of conferences he plans to attend each year, he goes to one on a subject outside his area of expertise.

But you may not need to stray far to identify useful aliens and their ideas; they may lurk down the hall. In their study of innovation in computer industry firms, Brown and Eisenhardt found that innovative companies had extensive cross-project communication. One manager noted, 'It used to be that it was a badge of honor not to use anybody else's ideas or to improve upon them . . . now everybody's borrowing everybody's stuff, the cycle is just so short and the pressure is so intense.' Raychem Corporation actually rewards thievery! Employees who successfully steal ideas from elsewhere in the company earn a 'Not Invented Here' trophy and a certificate that states, 'I stole somebody else's idea, and I'm using it.' But shed no tears for the 'victim,' who also gets a certificate that states, 'I had a great idea, and so and so is using it.'

Empathic Design

Customers, customers' customers, and noncustomers are all informative aliens—but not necessarily if you ask them anything. That probably sounds contradictory. How can you learn anything from clients if you don't do market research? You can. In fact, we argue that you will get more radical ideas from potential and actual clients if you do not conduct traditional market research. It's not that you can't learn from surveys, focus groups, and mall studies.

Searching for Reasons: People can be Clueless

Psychologists Richard Nisbett and Timothy Wilson have analyzed a large number of studies, including some of their own, to determine just how insightful people are about the reasons for their own behavior. Nisbett and Wilson find that people make assertions that 'may bear little resemblance to the actual events' (p. 247). In one of N. R. F. Maier's classic studies of creativity, two cords hung from the ceiling, too far apart for both to be reached simultaneously. Asked to tie the ends together, subjects were unlikely at first to think of the solution: to create a pendulum by tying a heavy object to the end of one rope and swinging it within grasp–until Maier 'accidently' set one cord swinging by brushing up against it. However, few subjects accurately reported that this action stimulated their thought.

In a more dramatic illustration of people's inability to access their own reasoning, Nisbett and Wilson presented subjects with a video of a teacher who spoke English with a European accent. In one version of the video, he was warm and enthusiastic; in the second, he was cold and intolerant of his students. Subjects were asked to rate not only the teacher's likeability but three attributes—his physical appearance, mannerisms, and accent—all three of which were identical in both tapes. Not surprisingly, subjects who saw the warm version liked him better and also rated his attributes more favorably. However, subjects denied that their liking or disliking of the teacher influenced their ratings of his attributes. In fact, subjects who saw the cold version maintained that their reason for disliking him was *because of* their distaste for his appearance, mannerisms, and accent, the *opposite* of what really happened. They were unaware that the teacher's relative warmness or coldness was in fact influencing their assessment of his attributes.

Of course you can. The first impulse many people have when confronted with an opportunity or necessity to innovate is to send out a questionnaire to ask people what they need or to hold focus group meetings to discuss needs in the environment of the triggering occasion. There's nothing inherently wrong with these approaches (although questionnaire construction requires more sophistication than the uninitiated might suspect)—except that they limit the options that will be raised. People cannot tell you about needs they don't know they have, will not tell you about ones that embarrass them for some reason, will say what they think you want to hear, and will blithely prophesy behaviors they will never undertake. In short, for the best of reasons, with the best of motives, and often totally unaware, people can be clueless.

Think of it this way: suppose you are traveling in a familiar country where you speak the language. You know (generally) where you want to go and have some decent although not detailed maps.

You can always start down the right road and stop and ask good questions and get sensible answers that will guide you. Similarly, if a product or service is familiar, you can ask customers about finely drawn preferences. Say you are in the market for a car. How would you like it to sound? Most people can answer that question: 'quiet,' or 'like a purr,' or 'a throaty roar.' And vehicle designers can oblige. They know how to design sound. Harley-Davidson motorcycle aficionados can distinguish the sound of their engines from that of others—and can even describe it. Harley-Davidson sued Honda over imitating the sound of their motorcycle engines! Here is another question people can answer: How would you like your new car to smell? Almost everyone (if you give them a theoretically fat wallet) says: 'like leather.' When Nissan Design International was researching preferences in leather smells for the Infiniti J-30, they stuck ninety pieces of leather under peoples' noses and isolated the three that would sell in the US market. (Turns out, all three were US-made leathers. Evidently even our noses are ethnocentric!) How can potential customers give such sophisticated guidance to the creative process? Think about your knowledge of cars. You have a long history of experience to draw on. You know what cars sound and smell and feel like.

In many cases, however, the group faced with a creativity opportunity wants to identify options that are not already well understood, or for which no current model exists. Instead of being in a familiar country where everyone speaks your language, you are a stranger in a strange land. How then can you *ask* people what they want? One of the most powerful sets of techniques to create options we have dubbed 'empathic design.' *Empathic design* is a set of techniques, a process of developing deep empathy for another's point of view and using that perspective to stimulate novel design concepts. These techniques are most heavily used in new product development, but they are applicable any time you need to create options.

Unobtrusive Measures

Psychologists and sociologists have long been aware of the difficulties in getting information from people by simply asking them. As we saw in the last sidebar, people sometimes think they know what caused their behavior, but are wrong. In other cases, they don't know and can't tell you; in still others, they know but either won't or can't tell you (perhaps because they lack insight into their own preferences or their answers are clouded by a desire to appear 'normal' or otherwise good in the eyes of the interviewer). In a now-classic work, a group of psychologists cataloged various general techniques for extracting information from people without their awareness.

- *'Erosion' measures*. The popularity of museum exhibits is determined by noting the frequency with which the tiles in front of the exhibit are replaced.
- *'Accretion' measures*. During the 'Big Dig' in Boston in the late 1990s, archaeologists were granted prior access to excavation sites for the new highway. They found that privies, and what our ancestors tossed down them, long buried over the centuries, were a treasure trove of old colonial quotidian life.
- *Archival measures*. A sociologist in Philadelphia cataloged the marriage licenses recorded and found that the probability of two people getting married varied directly with how close the two people's families' houses were to one another. Sir Francis Galton even used archives in the nineteenth century to determine the efficacy of prayer! Reasoning that royal families were prayed for most often, he suggested they should therefore be long-lived—if prayer helped. Instead, he found the average life span of royalty to be only 64.04 years, writers and scientists 67.55 years, and gentry 70.22 years.
- *Observational measures*. To determine the popularity of various radio stations, auto mechanics have been instructed to check the radio push-button settings and report them to the investigator. More contrived measures include arming research subjects with pagers, beeping them at random intervals, and asking them what they are doing at that moment.

Here is the central premise underlying empathic design: people often cannot articulate what they want or need in an innovation. Groups undertaking empathic design are like anthropologists exploring a foreign culture. Their objective is to internalize a deep understanding of the environment in which the target population lives, works, and plays—to 'go native.' They take with them their own deep knowledge about what their organization is capable of— the expertise they can bring to the foreign culture. The expertise may be technology or skills or processes. Then the explorers can identify needs that they could creatively meet, innovation options that clients will never request. At the foundation of empathic design, then, is *observation*. Sometimes you don't even have to observe the behavior, only the physical evidence left behind. Other times, however, you will need to watch people in their daily routines— observe the actual behaviour as it occurs.

Why does observation stimulate options that wouldn't arise through questioning? One reason is that people's memories are necessarily selective. Ideas, needs, and desires occur to us while we are in the process of actually using a product or conducting an activity that we may not recall later in reflecting on that activity. You have undoubtedly had hundreds of ideas along the lines of 'Why can't they make this thing...' as you drove your car or made a travel reservation, used a gardening tool or a computer—even tried to open a door the wrong way because the handle clearly signals 'pull' when you have to push to get it open! Colgate-Palmolive researchers had family members videotape people doing chores in their homes to record their stream-of-consciousness observations on what they were doing. What did they see? People commenting on the smell of products, or lack of smell. People combining products in unusual ways—mixing laundry soaps together with dishwashing detergents to get curtains white, or filling the empty bottle of one glass cleaner with another product to take advantage of a superior spray mechanism.

We don't always know our own preferences. When you are reading a map, do you turn it so that up is north or orient it to the direction you are headed? Designers at IDEO working on a car navigational system discovered that people differ in how they read maps. This discovery—never mentioned in interviews—came about because the designers observed pairs of people constantly turning the map as they discussed directions.

Moreover, we develop routines for coping with problems—workarounds. Do it long enough and eventually we become unaware of any need for improvements. Most inexpert computer users (and a surprising number of experts) have primitive rituals to assuage the devils that lurk under the keyboard. ('Turn the machine off twice in a row and the mouse works; count to three before clicking from one application to another or the computer might freeze up.') However, if computer software designers were watching us, assuming they could avoid collapsing in hysterical laughter, they would learn how their programs fail us. We might think to tell them of all the keyboard rain dances we perform, but the likelihood is that we would not remember them all.

When the Sundberg-Ferar product development firm was helping Rubbermaid develop a new walker for adults with limited mobility, they convened in nursing homes focus groups of people using walkers. 'What could we do to improve your walkers?' they asked. 'What don't you like about them?' The participants shook their heads. They liked their walkers as they were. Nope, they couldn't suggest any improvements if the walker could be redesigned from scratch. The researchers gave up and excused the group members. Only as the respondents got up and retrieved their walkers to exit the room did the researchers find that one woman had tied a bicycle basket to her walker with shoe strings; a man had fashioned a holder for his cordless phone out of duct tape; another had hung an aftermarket automotive cupholder on his walker! They had not thought to mention to the researchers these little home-made additions. These observations led Sundberg-Ferar to design a built-in, flexible mesh pouch for walkers, providing what Rubbermaid called a CCA, a compelling competitive advantage.

Activities often have an emotional or psychological content that remains untapped by questionnaires or surveys. Kimberly-Clark launched a very successful new diaper line after in-home visits by design firm GVO. The designers recognized that both toddlers and their parents were embarrassed by diapers—yet small children still needed them. As a step toward 'grown-up' clothes, the design team developed Huggies Pull-Ups which satisfied the ego requirements of customers—and kept the children dry. MTV sends researchers into the field to dig through the dormitory rooms, closets, and CD collections of 18–24-year-olds, because younger teenagers aspire to be like these older role models. The younger consumers often won't admit or don't understand themselves the psychological impact of the others on their tastes, but MTV can foresee what users are going to want.

People also fail to identify options in interviews simply because they don't know what is possible—what your group can do. You may have a technical solution to a problem that would not occur to anyone with less expertise. The lumber products company Weyer-haeuser was in danger of losing a lot of business because one of their customers, a major furniture maker, was laminating together thin boards produced by Weyerhaeuser competitors to create inexpensive table legs. Weyerhaeuser was unable either to match the competitors' prices or to convince the customer to pay more for superior quality. After a visit to the customer's plant, Weyerhaeuser engineers came up with a whole new way to make table legs—a new, much thicker particleboard that did not have to be laminated. The consequent savings to customers in tooling and labor costs put Weyerhaeuser back in the competitive running.

Cool-Hunting

Related to empathic design is the hunt for what is 'cool'—the bizarre, the different, the norm breaking. The term cool-hunting comes from the fashion industry—locating what people are doing individually that may be adopted by a larger segment of the market. The underlying concept is to stretch the boundaries of your options by seeking nontraditional, possibly idiosyncratic and extreme examples of solutions before they become popular. So, for instance, when cool-hunters saw kids wearing baggy pants or dressed all in black or painting their nails green, they thought, Hey! such outlandish garb could become a trend if supported and promoted by the industry. When Converse's cool-hunter DeeDee Gordon was in Los Angeles, she saw white teenage girls dressing like *cholos*, or Mexican gangsters, wearing tight white tank tops known as 'wife beaters,' a bra strap hanging out, long shorts, tube socks, and shower sandals. As she recalls, she came back to tell fellow cool-hunter Baysie Wightman, 'I'm telling you, Baysie, this is going to hit. There are just too many people wearing it. We have to make a shower sandal.' They did, retrofitting the hugely popular Converse One Star by cutting off the back and putting a thick outsole on it. The sandal was an immediate and long-lasting hit. On the advice of cool-hunters, Sony designed their Walkman for athletic users, the Freq, with heavy-duty clips, like chains, since they had noticed the emergence of chains as decoration among the ultracool. When Youth Intelligence, a New York firm, suggested to telecommunications giant Sprint that tattoos would become popular, Sprint used temporary tattoos as part of a calling-card promotion targeting students. The program produced twice as many sign-ups as expected.

Cool-hunters, like empathic design teams, use up a lot of film, and go where the knowledge is—where cool kids hang out. Gordon spent hours in the then-cool area of New York, SoHo, snapping pictures of everyone walking by. Wightman watches the skateboarders or snowboarders for ideas. It is definitely difficult to pin down how cool-hunters get their ideas, but after following some around for a while, one writer concluded that

the key to coolhunting . . . is to look for cool people first and cool things later, and not the other way around. Since cool things are always changing, you can't look for them, because the very fact they are cool means you have no idea what to look for. What you would be doing is thinking back on what was cool before and extrapolating, which is about as useful as presuming that because the Dow rose ten points yesterday it will rise another ten points today. Cool people, on the other hand, are a constant.

Most cool-hunting is done among the young and uninhibited as well as possibly inexperienced. So, for instance, if you were designing a new magazine, what could you learn from visiting some of the tiny web sites set up by start-up publications? Although cool-hunting trips are mostly conducted by fashion-driven organizations in search of new product ideas, the process of generating options by seeking the far-out behaviors of possible trendsetters applies more broadly.

Attribute Benchmarking

Almost everyone knows about benchmarking—at least the usual kind. You send out a task force to compare your performance or process with that of other organizations. It is a win-win activity. If the other group does it better than yours, you can imitate. If they do it worse, you can crow (once you are back home). There are whole books on how to benchmark—but we are suggesting a somewhat different kind here. First, you don't want to go to performers within your own industry. Oh, sure, you can learn a lot, but you are likely to get more creative ideas if you: (1) go outside your known competitors and (2) isolate attributes, characteristics, or functions that are especially critical to the innovation opportunity you are addressing. When 3M was designing hearing aids, the engineers pondered how to make the instrument as invisible as possible. Expert in electronics, miniaturization, and the function of the auditory nerve, they nevertheless had little knowledge about aesthetics. The options they could generate were limited. Who knows the most about matching skin tones with various materials? Cosmetic dentistry, they decided—and they found a wealth of information by visiting firms in that business.

Solutions to one problem can be transferred to another, but if you don't stretch to think in terms of functionality instead of product or service category, you are unlikely to identify them. After World War II, Heathkit came up with a novel idea for commercializing Sonar technology. What use could the technology be put to besides locating submarines? Consider its function: Sonar identifies under-water objects and allows a visual display of their shape. Hmm, what might Sonar reveal underwater that would be useful to consumers; consumers such as . . . fishermen! Hence was born the predecessor to today's fish-locators, purchased by many sportsmen for their boats. The fish-locator's performance is limited, of course, to the functions provided by Sonar technology. As one purchaser ruefully noted of his new equipment, 'It doesn't really work. It shows me where the fish are—but it doesn't make them bite!'

When Ceramics Process Systems Corporation was founded, the MIT professors who started the company understood from the beginning that, internationally known experts though they were, they were unlikely to possess all the knowledge they needed to apply their technological breakthrough to various problem arenas. Counteracting the temptation to build on only the scientific foundations the founders were most familiar with, the first president had a framed statement on his wall: 'Our most important technical breakthroughs will come from disciplines and literature outside our industry and scientific field.' When they subsequently experienced difficulties in separating ceramics pieces from the mold and realized that temperature differentials could help, they sought the best expertise on fast freezing they could—the frozen foods industry. When they needed to figure out options for producing a smooth, thin layer of an emulsion, they brought in a Sherwin Williams paint expert.

A government postal service trying to improve the customer experience had a major breakthrough in their thinking when the members of the task force began visiting retailers known for personalized, friendly service. An option that they had never considered was to have postal clerks come out from behind their counters to ask 'may I help you?' just as a salesperson at the Nordstrom clothing store would. When this approach was implemented in the Washington, D.C. area, customers were initially puzzled both because the context was so different for this kind of service and because they did not expect innovation from a quasi-government agency.

We've now considered a pretty wide range of techniques designed to avoid the urge to merge and to promote a wider exploration of options. While these techniques all help generate options, they don't help select one. All those possibilities! Now to narrow down to the one that will work in your context.

....

Back to Hazel . . .

Friday arrived, and Hazel was disappointed. The troops were uninspired—the storyboards were bland, devoid of the humor and the spark she had hoped for. She decided to gather the group members for another round of brainstorming. 'Any suggestions?' she asked, with faint hope. 'At this point I'm really open to suggestions.' Despite Hazel's apparent new openness, Geraldine was clearly skeptical about Hazel's willingness to revisit the original decision to go with the puppies. 'I was thinking,' she said hesitantly. 'My brother was a Peace Corps volunteer in West Africa. Maybe we could invite him in if we are going to talk about picturing children in a developing nation.' A quick glance at Hazel. She was nodding! Geraldine was encouraged enough to continue. 'We don't know that we couldn't do something inoffensive. I think he could give us some perspective.'

Jose wanted to start even further back in the process. 'I think we should go visit some distance learning centres,' he said. 'Frankly, I don't have the slightest idea how it all works. The trainers from the center didn't give me a real feel for what message we should be putting across. I'll bet we would come back with all sorts of ideas.'

'I know it sounds weird,' Hank offered. 'But we could sort of try out what it would be like to do distance learning, you know—role play the teacher and the students—if it's too expensive for us all to go to the center. Linda knows a lot about Greek mythology, for instance. She could be the instructor and some of us could be the students over the company closed TV network. And the rest of us could observe. Just a few minutes worth, Linda,' he added, seeing her start to object. 'Just to get an idea of what it might feel like and how it's different from regular school.'

'Why not have the center include us in their next regular session tomorrow evening instead?' Linda said. 'Then we'd have real instructors and real topics—see what it is

like as a consumer. We might see a way to do the university professor lampoon. And I'd much rather give up my dinner time than try to simulate it ourselves.'

David chimed in: 'Then we could get together tomorrow morning and brainstorm the message again. I get some of my best ideas at night.'

'Any chance we could get your brother in to talk with us tomorrow morning, Geraldine?' Jose asked. 'Then we could brainstorm in the afternoon.'

Hazel sat back in amazement. There was so much more energy in the room than when they had come in. Given this level of enthusiasm, the group would surely come up with more options. Then, could she get them to agree on one in time to make the deadline?

Key Points

Generating lots of options, while only part of the overall creative process, is often equated with 'creativity.' Particular care must be taken to maximize the group's ability to think divergently.

- Give the group the maximum allowable time to generate options; use brainstorming, but be aware of its limitations.
- Group leaders should frame the problem as clearly as possible, but refrain from indicating a preferred solution.
- Except when strict security is required, keep the group's boundaries as permeable as possible. Encourage members to discuss options—and solicit new ones—from spouses, friends, and colleagues. Visit aliens whose expertise may be tangential to your primary concerns.
- Recognize that a group can sometimes be a little too cozy. Rotate membership and bring in 'new blood' as projects change.
- Develop a simple set of ground rules designed to promote divergent thinking, welcome dissent, and depersonalize conflict.
- Protect dissenters by publicly supporting them.
- Be alert to implict norms (e.g. 'don't rock the boat') that inhibit creativity.
- As the group approaches a consensus, appoint a member as devil's advocate, instructed to challenge the group forcefully and persuasively.
- Seemingly implausible or impractical options are often the most creative. Help make them more plausible by having members vividly imagine their success or through role-playing techniques.
- Tap the natural and social world for ideas. Encourage the use of metaphors from nature and other worlds of knowledge.
- Empathic design can help identify the unarticulated needs of customers, customers' customers, and noncustomers.

Answers and interpretation

1. A matchbox is supposed to hold matches, right? Not be emptied of its contents and tacked to the wall to support a candle. When people are presented with this problem with the contents of the matchbox already emptied, they are much better at solving it.

2. Hey, who said the solution was limited to two dimensions? Yet most people who approach this problem *assume* that they are so limited. We must stretch our thinking to encompass a third dimension if we are to avoid being fixated on our false assumptions.

3. What did you try? 15, 20, 25? 100, 105, 110? For each of these, we would answer yes, they fit our rule. You might then conclude from this feedback that our rule is to count by 5. If so, you would be wrong. The rule is simply to name three ascending numbers. If you're like most folks, you will only give number sequences that you think *confirm* the rule, not those you think might *disconfirm* it (say, 15, 20, 30 or 1, 2, 3, both of which, you would be told, fit the rule).

6

Partnerships for Knowledge Creation

Salvatore Parise and Laurence Prusak

> Successful alliances are more critical than ever to our strategy. We are working hard to be recognized as the pharmaceutical industry's premier partner by consistently creating value for our partners and for Lilly.
>
> *Sidney Taurel, Chairman of the Board, President, CEO, Eli Lilly and*
> *Company*

Strategic Alliances in the Knowledge Economy

There is little doubt that alliances and partnerships among companies will be a critical component of strategic management in the 21st century, including playing a major role in the transfer and management of knowledge resources. If done successfully, alliances can contribute significantly to a company's growth potential. The numbers are very impressive. In a recent study, highly successful alliance companies expect 35 percent of their revenues by 2003 to come from alliances, up from 21 percent in 1998 and 15 percent in 1995.[1] Also, from the same study, the most active alliance participants achieved a 17.2 percent return on equity, which is much higher than the average return on equity for both Fortune 500 companies as well as companies least active with alliances.

However, we argue that alliances do more than just contribute to a firm's bottom line. Alliances are a critical mechanism for a company to learn and acquire knowledge resources to complement its own internal capabilities and resources. Recent research seems to validate the view that alliances are a means

125

to acquire know-how and to learn from other firms.[2,3,4] The types of knowledge resources exchanged in alliances can include such things as employee expertise, technological know-how, and customer knowledge, in addition to more tangible, physical resources such as equipment, property, or products. The management of these resources for joint value creation, however, is very difficult to do. An alliance learning capability, therefore, is both an important component of partnership success and a differentiating factor among partnering companies. In this paper, we attempt to draw some insights around this issue and ultimately provide success factors for the creation of knowledge through partnerships.

There has been a dramatic increase in the number of alliances formed over the past decade, with annual growth rates of roughly 25 percent cited from many sources. It is no coincidence that alliances and partnerships became popular when the term 'knowledge economy' became a household phrase. Knowledge, and more accurately, capabilities tend to become specialized and 'sticky' over time, and it is very difficult for an individual company to possess all the capabilities needed to develop, manufacture, and market products and services on its own. In the industrial economy where the focus was on producing a physical product, the emphasis was on *vertical integration*, in which the goal was to own or control as much of the linear value chain as possible. This resulted in economies of scale. In the knowledge economy where the focus is on the knowledge surrounding the product (e.g. services), the emphasis now is on *virtual integration*, in which the goal is to assemble a network of partners each having unique capabilities to deliver a customer solution. The key level of analysis is the network, and management's attention is now focused on building relational and social capital, in addition to the more traditional physical, technological, and commercial capital.

Motivations for Forming Alliances

Just as there are many different structures an alliance or partnership can take (e.g. joint venture, marketing agreement, and license), there are just as many motivations for companies to form an alliance. Thompson[5] distinguished between pooled, sequential, and reciprocal interdependence, and we can use these distinctions to better understand alliance motivations. Pooled interdependence exists when partners pool their resources to achieve a shared goal. Usually, the motivation is to improve operations by sharing high costs or substituting more expensive internal resources with more efficient partner resources. An example is a joint venture between two semiconductor firms to share the costs of building a $2 billion fabrication plant.

Sequential interdependence describes alliances in which a particular product or resource is transferred linearly from one partner to another. The motivation for these alliances is to gain access to the partner's knowledge resources, such as technology, customer expertise, or employee know-how. For example, software vendors often partner with system integrators or consulting companies to gain access to their corporate markets. Sequential alliances are also used to manage risk and to hedge bets. Large technology companies will partner simultaneously with several smaller companies working on competing technologies, not because of short-term benefits, but to hedge their bets on which technology will become the next standard or win out in the market place.

The potential for the most value and knowledge creation, we believe, involves alliances with reciprocal interdependence. These alliances involve both partners sharing their respective knowledge resources, resulting in innovation and joint product development. These alliances involve a high degree of integration and coordination between partners. The multi-year alliance between Intel and Hewlett-Packard, started in the mid-1990s to develop a 64-bit chip, is an example of a very complex alliance in which both companies contributed their own capabilities to develop a new product. The reciprocal alliance also provides the partner with the greatest opportunity to learn. Corning Glass began forming alliances in the 1970s with both telecommunication companies and research firms with the goal of developing a commercial fiber optic solution. They found that one of the benefits from these initial alliances was the collection of new and innovative information. As a result, Corning entered into a second series of alliances with manufacturers and early adopters.[6] Launching these series of alliances has helped Corning not only develop commercial products, but to learn from their partners.

However, with all the attention being paid to alliances and partnerships, it is alarming to see success rates falling well short of expectations. Success rates of less than 50 percent have often been cited in the literature.[7,8] Often, poor alliance design gets the blame. Unrealistic expectations at the onset results in failed objectives. Or, benefits may be weighted too heavily in favor of one partner, which leads to the other partner being dissatisfied. Also, changes and disruptions in the market place will cause the partner to re-think its purpose and objectives for the alliance, which may cause the partnership to end prematurely.

Relational and Social Aspects of Alliances

Increasingly, however, it is the relationship management aspect of partnering that is seen as the critical component. A recent study indicates that the high incidence of alliance failure is indeed due to the poor working relationship among partners.[9] Another recent study analyzed the social connections in an alliance and concluded that close attention to personal relationships accelerates learning and leads to a more effective alliance.[10] Frequently, the relationship aspect of the alliance gets neglected after the deal has been struck. The person working with the partner to structure the deal leaves after the contracts are signed, and a new person unfamiliar with the partner takes over to manage the relationship. Also, the process of how information and knowledge is shared and communicated between partners is critical. This is especially true of partnerships involving innovation and knowledge creation, which require an effective working relationship to be successful. Finally, studies suggest that the way partners manage the collective learning process plays a central role in the success or failure of an alliance.[11]

We strongly believe that knowledge creation is very much a social activity, and to see how knowledge is created effectively in alliances requires an understanding of the social relationship among the individuals and organizations involved in the partnership. This is not to say that alliance design principles are not important to alliance success, but rather the alliance design and structure should be created with the social context in mind. For example, an R&D alliance between long-time competitors will require a different design and structure than an R&D alliance between companies who have worked together in the past. Perhaps the biggest lesson from recent alliance findings is to not ignore the social aspects of the partnership.

In the next section, we provide several success factors that we believe to be important for alliance knowledge creation. (See Table 6.1 for a summary.) We have emphasized the relational or social factors in building knowledge-based alliances. These factors are based on a synthesis of the research conducted at the IBM Institute for Knowledge Management and other recent research on the topic.

Develop a Working Relationship with the Partner that Fosters and Maintains Trust

Trust is perhaps the most critical aspect of building an effective partnership for knowledge creation. Trust essentially performs two functions: (1) reduces transaction costs by eliminating the need to constantly monitor the partner or write everything in contracts and (2) creates an effective working environment which produces a 'spirit' of collaboration and sharing.

Of course, an alliance can still be effective without the element of trust. However, without trust, there is an opportunity cost. Every contingency must be documented in a contract, which consumes valuable time that the partners

Table 6.1 Alliance success factors and associated actions

Success factor	Action
Foster and maintain trust	• Target companies with reputation as a preferred partner • Start to build trust during negotiations • Staff alliance teams with personnel familiar with partner and who possess effective interpersonal skills
Build awareness and transparency	• Document information requirements early in alliance process • Have frequent alliance review meetings with partner • Introduce the role of knowledge intermediary • Understand partner language and culture
Develop and communicate alliance learning objectives	• Define alliance learning objectives in addition to financial measures of success • Communicate learning objectives both internally and with partner • Create structures and processes to capture and disseminate alliance knowledge • Understand similarity with partner's knowledge domain
Manage partnerships holistically	• Understand partner's role (e.g. supplier, competitor, customer, complementor) • Assess the interdependencies among all partners • Ensure alignment between business strategy and alliance strategy

could spend working with each other. Trust enables the partners to collaborate, share critical knowledge, and debate without fear of opportunism or misappropriation. Ideas and insights can be shared quickly, without the need to formally plan every exchange of information and knowledge. All of this leads to a greater likelihood of achieving innovation in the partnership.

What can we do to build trust with a partner? Trust usually grows from interacting with the same partner over time. In other words, trust builds trust.[12] Research has shown that both trust and previous ties with a partner predict alliance formation.[13,14] However, even though trust may take a long time to build, it can quickly be served. Companies with a reputation as an effective and trustworthy partner realize that their position as a 'preferred partner' disappears by behaving opportunistically for even just one instance. Therefore, all other things being equal, it is better to target companies with reputations as a preferred partner.

An important question that remains, however, is how to build trust when working with a new partner. Actually, first impressions are critical, and the way two companies interact during the negotiating phase of the alliance goes a long way in building (or not building) a trusting relationship. Negotiations, in which both partners act in good faith and strive for a 'win-win' outcome will result in quick trust, versus very competitive negotiations where every point is debated and which ultimately leads to resentment. Who is selected to participate on the alliance team must also be carefully considered. Select alliance members who are familiar with the partner (e.g. their products, culture, and values) and have very good interpersonal skills. An electronic alliance profiler could be used to capture information about the employee's previous alliance experience, and this could help staff alliance teams. Finally, effective dialog and communication among alliance members result in clear objectives, purpose, and commitment, which often lead to trust.

Build Awareness and Transparency with the Partner

Awareness and transparency are two key components of partnerships involving knowledge sharing. *Awareness* is the ability of one partner to understand or be cognizant of the goals, values, and resources of the other partner. Too often, the alliance objectives formally documented in the contract are not effectively communicated to the alliance team. Our study of R&D alliances found that one of the major obstacles during the implementation phase is not knowing who to turn to (both internally and in the partner organization) for certain information or expertise. Many research participants stated that they wished they had known about a certain group or department before they started working on the alliance. This problem stems from the fact that the alliance team is not aware of parallel research work going on in their own company or in the partner organization.

One solution for building awareness is for each partner to document information and knowledge requirements at the beginning stages of implementation and to review what internal groups might complement the alliance work. Also, frequent review meetings, especially at the beginning of the partnership, should be a venue to discuss any awareness issues. Another solution is to introduce the role of a knowledge intermediary who could serve as a bridge between the two organizations. This person would be responsible for connecting alliance team members with the information and knowledge they require. For example, the knowledge intermediary can collect and disseminate information about the partner or technologies involved in the alliance, manage critical alliance documents such as the Statement of Work, and connect alliance team members with other people residing both internally and in the partner firm. An alliance portal could also be used as a repository for alliance documents.

Another critical component of the alliance process is called *transparency*, which is the firm's opportunity to learn from its partner.[15] Transparency is a measure of how easy it is to obtain information, knowledge, and skills from a partner. You might be aware that the partner has certain capabilities, but if transparency is low, then it will be very difficult to assess the partner's knowledge.

Social aspects of the relationship enable transparency. Having compatible language and culture between the companies is important. Each partner may be using different terms or language to describe the same technology or product, and this often results in confusion and poor communication. Trust also affects transparency by making partners more willing to share their information and knowledge. In fact, long-standing partnerships based on trust enable partners to make their respective business strategies transparent to each other, to the point of actually shaping each other's strategy. Of course, there is a limit to the degree you want to make things transparent to the partner. But, in order for collaboration and innovation to take place, both awareness and transparency must exist in some form.

Develop and Communicate Alliance Learning Objectives

Another key finding from our research is the importance placed on clearly defining and communicating *alliance learning objectives*, in addition to the more financial measures of alliance success such as revenue and market share. Intent to learn refers to the firm's propensity to view partnerships as an opportunity to learn. Doz and Hamel[15] point out that the key difference between US and Japanese companies regarding alliances has been intent to learn. In US–Japanese alliances for example, Japanese firms have often viewed collaboration as a way to learn, while US firms have used alliances as a way to substitute for more competitive skills, resulting in an erosion of internal skills and ultimately competitive disadvantage.

Alliance learning can take many different forms. There is content learning, which involves acquiring the skills and know-how of the partner. There is also learning about the alliance process. In other words, understanding what went right and what went wrong with the current alliance process, and documenting and sharing these lessons with the alliance team. Finally, there is also partner-specific learning that involves building social capital with the partner. This involves understanding the partner's values, culture, and work routines, and using this knowledge to continuously build an effective relationship with that company.

Once defined, alliance learning objectives should be communicated both internally and to the partner. Internal alliance team members should be cognizant of the different skills and know-how they should acquire from the partner, and both a structure and a process should be established to internalize and disseminate this knowledge. The learning objectives should be discussed during the negotiations phase of the alliance in case more formal cross-training between partners is required. It is also important to understand that an alliance where learning is heavily one-sided will probably not succeed in the long run. Partners who are perceived as entering into an alliance for the sole purpose of learning as much as they can without regard for a 'win-win' objective run the risk of developing a poor reputation as an alliance partner.

A company's ability to learn from its partner is actually dependent on its *absorptive capacity*. Absorptive capacity refers to the firm's ability to recognize the value of new, external information, assimilate it, and apply it to commercial ends.[16] Therefore, absorptive capacity is a function of how closely related the partners are with respect to their knowledge domains. For example, if a firm collaborates with a partner outside its industry, absorptive capacity might be an issue since the firm might not have the level of understanding needed to internalize a new knowledge domain. Alliances with competitors, meanwhile, often present an ideal situation to learn since the knowledge domains of the partners are similar.[17]

Manage Partnerships Holistically as well as Individually

A final critical area involves a holistic approach to alliance management. Most companies are involved with many partners simultaneously. Just as product managers must use a portfolio approach when developing, pricing, and marketing their products, alliance managers must understand the interdependencies among alliance partners when pursuing and developing partnerships. In other words, the partnering company should have an overall relationship portfolio strategy, in addition to a strategy for each individual alliance.

Organizations also find that they have several alliances with the same partner. This is often the case in large organizations when there are several alliance groups across different departments and business units. Being aware of current partnerships is important since they can affect how a company behaves toward that same partner. We were often told by alliance managers that if they had known that their company already had an existing alliance with a certain partner, they would have behaved differently toward that partner during both the design and implementation stages.

How should the portfolio of partners be designed? One approach is to understand the role of the partner relative to the markets the company serves. Partners could be competitors, complementors, suppliers, customers, or 'others' from different industries. Alliances with competitors could be used to learn or reduce risk, alliances with complementors and customers to help develop products, alliances with suppliers to improve efficiency and integration, and partnerships with companies in different industries to help create new markets. A recent study analyzed the alliance portfolios of Dell Computer and Sun Microsystems and concluded that Dell's strategy centered around its supplier partners while Sun's strategy focused on partners with complementors.[17] By understanding the role of each partner, the relationship manager could now start to think holistically about different business objectives from a portfolio of partners.

When assessing the portfolio, the relationship manager must understand the interdependencies among partners. An alliance with Partner A can have a positive, negative, or no effect on an alliance with Partner B. The key, especially when the objective is to learn and create new knowledge, is to try to build a complementary or synergistic portfolio, and understand how partnerships will be affected by other partnerships. For example, a portfolio of alliances that consists of competitors promoting competing standards might result in a 'negative' portfolio, even if the objective of the company is to learn from its competitors or to reduce risk. The alliance manager must understand the ramifications of a competitive portfolio: partners might be protective and reluctant to share important knowledge with the company when they realize the company is also partnering with their competitor. However, a portfolio consisting of partners promoting similar solutions, standards, or innovations might be considered a complementary portfolio since partners are more likely to share their knowledge resources.

Using a holistic or portfolio approach to alliance design and management allows for better alignment between alliance and business strategy. Usually, capabilities and competencies are obtained from a group of partners working together and not just from one individual partner. On the basis of recent research, the alignment between business and alliance strategy remains a huge challenge. 'I wish we had a better sense of what our business strategy is' is a common refrain among alliance managers we interviewed. Often, the alliance functions are localized with no formal structure or process to communicate with the business strategy group. Or a separate group is established to generate new business for the company. Alliances play a major role in business development for this group. The problem is that this new group is, in a sense, isolated from the main company, and as a result, there are major challenges when it comes to allocating resources and staffing the alliance teams.

Building an Alliance Capability

Today, firms are quickly trying to build their alliance capability, so they can be viewed as preferred partners in the marketplace. Recent findings suggest that companies that use best practice capture and implement effective alliance processes have high-alliance success rates and are viewed as preferred partners.[1] IBM, for example, has established their Partner World program for software partners, which includes co-marketing, education and certification, technical support, incentives, and relationship management. Eli Lilly, a leading pharmaceutical firm, has created a dedicated organization responsible for alliance management. Lilly's Office of Alliance Management is responsible for developing and implementing best partnering practices, training Lilly's staff to work with partners, and assessing cross-cultural differences with the partner.

Knowledge management techniques could also be used to build an alliance capability. We have made brief mentions of such techniques when discussing the success factors: knowledge intermediaries, alliance portals, and alliance profilers will all help in satisfying the alliance team's information requirements. Also, a social network analysis can help in understanding the social connections among alliance partners and alliance team members.

To summarize, alliances and partnerships will remain an important source of learning and innovation in the 'knowledge economy'. We have emphasized the relational or social aspects in developing collaborative partnerships: building trust, awareness, and transparency with the partner, articulating and communicating alliance learning objectives; and managing partners holistically, as well as individually. Alliances are much more than 'closing the deal', a series of 'one-offs', or a list of generic steps for alliance managers to follow. Of course, there are some basic alliance design rules that all companies should follow. But ultimately, successful collaborative relationships are about building social capital with the partner.

Notes and References

1. Harbison, J. R. and Pekar, P. (1998). *Smart Alliances: A Practical Guide to Repeatable Success*. San Francisco: Jossey-Bass.
2. Hamel, G. (1991). 'Competition for Competence and Interpartner Learning within International Strategic Alliances,' *Strategic Management Journal*, 12: 83–104.

3. Hagedoorn, J. and Schakenraad, J. (1994). 'The Effects of Strategic Technology Alliances on Company Performance', *Strategic Management Journal*, 15: 291–309.

4. Stuart, X. (2000). 'Interorganizational Alliances and the Performance of Firms: A Study of Growth and Innovation Rates in a High-Technology Industry', *Strategic Management Journal*, 21: 791–811.

5. Thompson, J. D. (1967). *Organizations in Action: Social Science Bases of Administration*. New York: McGraw-Hill.

6. Gomes-Casseres, B. (May 2000). 'Alliances and Risk: Securing a Place in the Victory Parade', *Financial Times*, 6–7.

7. Harrigan, K. R. (1988). 'Strategic Alliances and Partner Asymmetries', In *Cooperative Strategies in International Business*. Lexington, MA: Lexington Books, pp. 205–26.

8. Bleeke, J. and Ernst, D. (1995). 'Is Your Strategic Alliance really a Sale?' *Harvard Business Review*, 73: 97–105.

9. Ertel, D., Weiss, J., and Visioni, L. J. (2001). 'Managing Alliance Relationships', Study by Vantage Partners.

10. Hutt, M., Stafford, E., Walker, B., and Reingen, P. (2000). 'Case Study Defining the Social Network of a Strategic Alliance', *Sloan Management Review*, 41(2): 51–62.

11. Larsson, R., Bengtsson, L., Henriksson, K., and Sparks, J. (1998). 'The Interorganizational Learning Dilemma: Collective Knowledge Development in Strategic Alliances', *Organization Science*, 9(3): 285–305.

12. Cohen, D. and Prusak, L. (2001). *In Good Company*. Boston, MA: Harvard Business School Press.

13. Garcia-Pont, C. and Nohria, N. (1997). 'Local versus Global Mimetism: The Dynamics of Alliance Formation in the Automobile Industry', *Academy of Management Conference*.

14. Gulati, R. (1995). 'Social Structure and Alliance Formation Patterns: A Longitudinal Analysis', *Administrative Science Quarterly*, 40(4): 619–52.

15. Doz, Y. L. and Hamel, G. (1998). *Alliance Advantage*. Boston, MA: Harvard Business School Press.

16. Cohen, W. M. and Levinthal, D. A. (1990). 'Absorptive Capacity: A New Perspective on Learning and Innovation', *Administrative Science Quarterly*, 35: 128–52.

17. Parise, S. and Henderson, J. Forthcoming in *IBM Systems Journal*, 40(4).

III. KNOWLEDGE RETENTION AND ORGANIZATIONAL LEARNING

7

Swing Doors and Musical Chairs

Arnold Kransdorff and Russell Williams

The notion that there has been a trend away from physical work toward intellectual work is not particularly new. Back in 1993, Peter Drucker pointed out that we exist in an 'information age,' a 'knowledge society.' But whatever the point of origin of this idea, acceptance of the trend toward intellectual work and the issues it raises has now gained considerable momentum—not least, for example, Hebeler and Van Doren (1997), Nurmi (1998). The significance of this trend is that it has revised the idea of what creates competitive advantage.

The old competitive strategy notion typified by Porter (1980) reasons that competitive advantage is derived from the firm's environment—the industry in which it operates. Thus, the job of the strategist is to scrutinize the structure of the industry (suppliers, buyers, potential new entrants, rivalry-substitutes, and so on) and obtain from this a position from which the firm can best defend itself from competitive forces as well as influence them to best advantage. In essence, industrial conditions determine the options available to firms, and a competitive advantage stems from optimally relating the business to its environment.

By way of contrast, the new competitive strategy notion is one whereby competitive advantage is created from a complementary perspective of managing its own resources. Appending a resource-based perspective for competitive advantage in the Information Age has, however, tended to shift attention away from the traditional resource categorization of land, capital, and labor, or at least skewed the relevance attributed to each of these. Thus, in a postindustrial era increasingly characterized by knowledge-intensive firms, attention has shifted toward labor, in which the resource of knowledge and intellect ultimately side. Use of the term 'labor,' however, often obscures the fact that it is something more than the mere physical effort of a human that is important as the key driver of wealth creation. As such, the more specific term 'intellectual capital' (IC) is preferred, with investigation and analysis of the issues this throws up categorized under the banner of 'knowledge management' and 'The Learning Organization.' However, labeled knowledge is still an asset that needs to be managed in terms of its recollection, capture, codification, dissemination, and use.

The management aspect of any one of these processes warrants an article in its own right, and it would be a disservice to attempt coverage of all of them here. Rather, the management of one particular facet of IC is highlighted here—the retention of Organizational Memory (OM) and its significance for organizations alongside the flexible labor model increasingly adopted in Western society over the last three decades.

Intellectual Capital and Organizational Memory

IC can be defined as the intellectual material—the data, information, knowledge/experience, and intellectual property—that can be put to use to create wealth. OM is the experience component of this, although a more exacting distinction between data, information, and knowledge helps clarify its exact nature. Data are facts, depicted as figures or statistics. In a comparative format (say, in a historical framework), data become information. In contrast, knowledge is interpretive and predictive, with its deductive character allowing its 'owner' to understand the implications of data and information and act accordingly. Within this definition, knowledge may be either explicit or tacit, the former being of the formal type normally codified in text books and manuals, and the latter being a 'coping skill' that allows a person to use explicit knowledge more effectively. All accountants have the explicit knowledge to produce a profit and loss account, but the actual ability to carry it out within a particular firm is tacit knowledge.

This application of knowledge is closely allied to memory or retained experiences, a fact that would hold true for both an individual and an organization. Such recollections comprise the experience of both success and failure and are the basis for applied actions. Thus, on the notion that progress is mostly organic (companies generally owe their success to building one experience on another), we are drawn to the conclusion that in the business arena—as in life—decisions are better made with the benefit of hindsight. Thus, OM for a private-sector firm marks in part its capability and, in the ultimate, its durability. In the public sector, OM is a constituent ingredient of the organization's effectiveness, its durability being typically protected by the 'essential' nature of the (public) service being provided.

OM is more concerned with tacit knowledge, though not exclusively. It has not so much to do with retaining a skill as with understanding its application—the 'how' of 'know-how.' It is the type of knowledge that, say, allows an individual to operate more effectively in an organization. Among a range of different elements, this would comprise an awareness of the particular nuances that make the firm tick, such as an understanding and accommodation of the shared value and belief system, knowledge of the communication and decision-making style, and a comprehension of the relationships among colleagues as well as with customers, collaborating firms, and competitors. Ultimately, OM consists of the memory of tried and tested formulas as they relate to the firm.

The Flexible Labor Market Model

The last three decades have seen a considerable and growing change in the way work is undertaken. Some of this change—what we call the flexible labor market model—reflects the transition to a 'knowledge society' described earlier. Among other things, organizations are delayering tiers of hierarchy in response to the belief that professional intellect does not necessarily need the center as a directional force through line managers. Moreover, the traditional horizontal boundaries that once circumscribed functions are also decomposing as broader interpersonal interaction (a characteristic of the knowledge-intensive firm) crosses old functional boundaries. As a result, the once functionally demarcated tasks are now increasingly being merged.

Yet the adoption of the flexible labor market model is more than a reaction to a trend for knowledge-intensive firms; it is being used as a tool to accommodate new work structures. Ideology, too, has played its part in the adoption of the flexible labor market model. The public sector illustrates this well, for a while it has always been human capital-intensive and therefore a perfect stomping ground for knowledge management, it now finds itself reorganized largely for other reasons, including an embrace of 'fiscal prudence' and a greater confidence in the market forces model espousing that competition generates efficiency.

Evidence of the trend toward a flexible labor market model is not hard to find. In the UK, recent survey evidence has reported that the rise in the use of nonpermanent contracts for professional occupations increased from 10 percent in 1992 to 13 percent in 1995. This is just one of the types of flexibility being employed, another example being job rotation. In this vein, OECD (1994) figures show that one in five jobs are being created or destroyed each year, with about 80 percent of this job turnover not related to the business cycle.

Such figures provide a vivid picture of the flux and flexibility currently being witnessed in the marketplace. Against this background, there is unlikely to be an imminent retreat from such 'flexibility' practices. The arguments in its favor continue to be somewhat compelling: flexible work enables management to bear down on costs both by eliminating labor (downsizing, delayering, and so on) and by the increased pressure that can be bought to bear on employees from such flexible practices, at least in the short term. Nonstandard contracts also allow management to focus more closely on the work as opposed to the job. As a result, it can establish more reliable performance targets, which in turn enables greater efficiency. Moves to a flexible labor market model, therefore, follow both the shifts to an information era and some ideological belief in the relative efficiency of an idea of market-type relations.

Nevertheless, hidden within this coherent case for flexibility is an almost invisible downside that is threatening to offset the advantages. Every time an employee resigns, leaves to join another firm, retires, is rotated, dismissed, rationalized, or comes to the end of his contract, the firm's momentum is disrupted and some of its hard-won and expensively acquired know-how/experience/knowledge leaves with him. To put a bottom-line figure on what this costs, the Washington-based Corporate Leadership Council, representing more than 700 *Fortune* 2000 companies, calculates that the turnover charge of, say, a middle manager is equal to 241 percent of his annual pay. Given that many companies are turning over their staff at the rate of up to 25 percent a year, and sometimes more, businesses need to manage this resource if relearning—a time-consuming and expensive process—is to be avoided.

Managing OM

In the face of the widespread adoption of the flexible labor market model, the legitimacy of several relatively inexpensive knowledge-capture methods, collectively called *oral debriefings,* is forwarded here. Oral debriefing—more graphically called 'brain dumping' in the computer industry—is a method most commonly confused with the unsophisticated exit interview, which is usually employed as a formulaic, 20-question means of trying to uncover reasons why employees leave. The technique requires expert debriefing skills to extract the valuable OM component of IC.

Carefully constructed, oral debriefings are a powerful means of capturing OM. Circumscribed around rigorous research into the company, individuals, and their jobs, the key to this method is to ask the right questions, with the debriefer using judgment to inquire further when answers are otherwise unclear, fudged, or avoided.

The reason for the oral approach is that individuals are generally better speakers than writers. Moreover, the spoken word—prompted by a skilled debriefer—is a more efficient way of conveying the abstract and complex nature of such elements as the nuances of corporate culture, management style, and the often obscure issues surrounding decision-making within groups. As such, it can effectively fill the gaps that otherwise exist in the written record.

As a means of capturing know-how and experience, debriefings, which necessarily have to be constructed according to organizational circumstances, have a variety of corporate applications. At one level, they can be used to capture relevant OM from departing employees that can be used to induct new appointees quickly and efficiently. In essence, the outgoing individual's OM provides the foundation on which new placements can operate efficiently in their new jobs without having to start from scratch. Such a process can otherwise take up to twelve months and sometimes longer.

Pharmaceutical company Glaxo Wellcome has used this technique to overcome the problem of both knowledge loss and induction. In one period in 1996–7, eight departures and 15 arrivals occurred over a period of just 18 months in a key, 20-man planning department that was dependent on a detailed understanding of the clinical and commercial aspects of all group compounds and their markets. In addition to the routine settling-in period, new employees had to acquire the knowledge that departing individuals took with them—a time-consuming and expensive operation.

Much of this know-how, which existed only in the minds of individuals, was typically held informally and, in theory, passed along orally to newer appointees when they joined the company and at appropriate junctures thereafter. Because of time pressures, the short and selective memory recall of departees, and the fact that the knowledge was normally so difficult to characterize and document in conventional ways, little was actually being conveyed. The problem was compounded by the fact that the managers worked independently from each other, so there was little shared knowledge of the detailed issues each was addressing from day to day.

To manage the transitions more effectively, the oral debriefing techniques developed by Pencorp, a London-based consultancy specializing in knowledge management applications, were chosen. Pre-project research included both detailed discussions with department heads to define the project's objectives and provide specific guidance on important areas to be covered in the debriefing, and the scrutiny of such departmental documents as monthly reports and periodic briefings. A skilled knowledge manager with an expert comprehension of management issues, human resources, and corporate culture undertook the assignments, which typically took two days to research and half a day to record.

In transcript format, the debriefings typically ran to about one-fifth the length of an average novel. These transcripts were then edited and indexed to ensure clarity, continuity, and readability. For Glen Slade, the project's commissioner:

The results were considered very successful, concluding that the handover reports would not only be useful when people left, but were worth the expense even for internal moves. This finding is now departmental policy and the service continues to be used as the department undergoes another reorganization. The method proved very easy to integrate into the department since we were quickly able to minimize the management overhead associated with each debriefing [the time to brief the interviewer and collate the background documentation] to less than half an hour. Furthermore, use of this technique has been demonstrated to be fully applicable to middle managers, as opposed to senior executives who may be the more common target for such debriefings. We even used the tool successfully on a junior member of staff who left the company shortly after her department was integrated into ours. (Kransdorff 1998)

Designed slightly differently, oral debriefings can also be applied among the more stable echelons of staff to overcome people's inherent short memory recall. To ensure that the detail of corporate knowledge and experience is not forgotten, debriefings are undertaken with designated knowledge owners at regular intervals, usually on an annual basis. They can be designed around particular events or projects and applied both functionally and cross-functionally.

At Kraft Foods, the company's oral archive was used to fashion a new marketing approach to an old product. Toward the end of the 1980s, one of the company's brands. Cracker Barrel cheese, was experiencing a slowdown in growth. The brand's manager, Linda Crowder, used the oral tapes to delve into the brand's origins in 1953 in an effort to shape a new marketing strategy. By reading the transcripts of interviews, she was able to gain the time-undistorted insights of retiree Med Connelly, national sales manager of cheese products from 1959 to 1962, the period when the brand's sales began to take off. As she concluded from the reading. 'He gave us a perspective we just couldn't get anywhere else—our research gave us a sense of what the theory was when Cracker Barrel was first introduced, and what we told consumers about the brand in the beginning' (Kransdorff 1998).

Oral debriefing is not just applicable to firms in which the knowledge is seen to have a commercial profit imperative. When the US government decided to stop testing nuclear weapons, officials were concerned that if some kind of knowledge preservation project was not conducted, its expensively acquired know-how would fade away as the key individuals retired, died, and dispersed. As part of the program, retired weaponeers are being brought back to Los Alamos for videotaped interviews to supplement the explicit knowledge already recorded in blue-prints and archived documentation. So far, approximately 2,000 videotapes have been made. Behind the need to guarantee that the expertise to build atomic bombs is retained is the imperative to ensure that the wheel does not have to be reinvented. For John D. Immele, director of nuclear weapons technology at Los Alamos, the imperative was clear. 'We don't want to press the erase button on our memory and go back to where we were 50 years ago' (Kransdorff 1998).

Constructed somewhat differently, oral debriefing can also be used more specifically in project management. It helps companies learn better from prior experiences, a discipline that is overlooked by many firms and is also affected by the mobile labor force.

In a method called 'learning history,' the oral accounts of key project participants are collected after the event. Recording staff members' experiences of change programs to ensure that mistakes are not repeated has been used to impressive effect at companies such as Ford and British Petroleum (BP) in the United States. In these debriefings, interviewees recalled their experiences anonymously, in their own words, in a way that reflected their collective learning experience. The transcripts have been used to extract insights, and the result is a best practice manual that managers and staff read before starting another project of a similar nature. Personnel specialists are also using the manual to design training courses.

Ford, which has debriefed 1,200 employees this way in tracking the progress of teams in the US, Hungary, Ireland, and Brazil, has learning histories under way in its car parts division, at an assembly plant, and in product design and development. The benefit, according to Vic Leo, a system dynamics and organizational learning manager at Ford in Detroit, is that the assembly plant factory has achieved quality improvements of 25 percent per year since 1995, compared with less than 10 percent achieved for two comparable factories. 'The plant was ranked third out of the three when we started,' explains Leo. 'When we stopped our learning history, it was number one' (Kransdorff 1998). Among its benefits, Leo adds, is the fact that the learning history has helped expose such unexpected problems as culture clashes and the 'knock-on effects' a new working practice can have when spread throughout a (Ford) 380,000-strong workforce.

At BP, where learning histories are calculated to have saved $22.5 million in a three-year trial at one of its refineries, the company plans to introduce the technique to its overseas subsidiaries. Learning histories came to BP when a group of Ohio employees solved a dangerous butane leakage problem that had gone unnoticed by managers for eight years. Since then, dozens of other efficiency projects and two learning histories have been launched at the refinery, helping staff increase productivity by an estimated 35 percent in the last two years. Paul Monus, who launched BP's first learning history at Ohio, is now advising other refineries how to introduce the techniques of oral debriefing.

Ford's and BP's approaches are imaginative adaptations of the traditional post-project review, in which a manager or a consultant comes in after a project is completed and reviews the evidence, usually through existing documentation and oral discussions with the key decision-makers involved. A report, sometimes in the form of a case study, is usually prepared containing recommendations for future action. In this report, it is hoped, lie the fruits of experiential learning.

This method is often flawed because many individual managers cannot be accurate and unprejudiced in their recall, or neutral in their assessments. Their input into any review is invariably susceptible to inherent short and selective memory recall and what Argyris (1991) has identified as the defensive reasoning process: when individuals screen out criticism and put the blame on anyone and everyone but themselves. If the input data/information/knowledge are incomplete or flawed in any way, conclusions will also be less than efficacious.

By changing the focus of oral debriefings, it is possible to overcome such traditional obstacles. With a technique called the 'learning audit' (developed by Pencorp), the debriefings are undertaken at regular intervals with the project's main decision-makers during its life cycle. At the end of the project, a suitably edited verbatim transcript contains unequivocal—and thus indisputable—sequential and philosophical evidence of how and why individuals made their decisions at the time. These are then subjected to the scrutiny of independent functional experts who—alongside the verbatim record and exactly as a manager, academic, or management consultant might do—jointly produce a list of recommendations for the company that specifically identifies lessons to be applied in the future.

Crucially, OM needs to be captured immediately in retrospect. The important feature is to ensure that a record is made while events are still fresh in the mind and, ideally, before the project's conclusion. In effect, this allows access to accurate hindsight, as opposed to hindsight that has been tempered by poor memory recall and defensive reasoning. Events can be assessed in real time as opposed to hindsight—and without the emotive fog and factual disputes that come with conventional post-project reviews.

As with all the debriefing techniques, the use of independent and expert researchers imposes the necessary discipline, the requisite nonpartisan attachment, and the employment of professional oral debriefing techniques. At a stroke, it improves the qualitative character of the evidential input and its learning potential. Managers can more efficiently learn specifically and directly from their—and each other's—experiences while providing a workable method of arresting the costly cycle of unlearned successes, repeated mistakes, and reinvented wheels.

Decisions are invariably made better with the benefit of hindsight. Knowledge workers are a storehouse for a multitude of experiences (memories) that allows them to leverage added value for their employer. Not only can they engage formal skills in similar settings (reflexive action, single-loop learning), but also, via reflection on both previous successes and failures, they can adopt cogent action in unfamiliar settings (double-loop learning). With knowledge retention now a major issue for organizations, the use of oral debriefings in their various applications offers management a powerful and cost-effective tool to capture the valuable know-how that is susceptible to both inherent short-memory recall and the flexibility of the labor market.

Underlying this concept is the fact that firms have little experiential advantage without the ability to efficiently build on their own tried and tested usage, a condition that cedes a greater disposition toward repeating mistakes, reinventing the wheel, and not learning properly from successes. Ultimately, learning from experience is the most efficient way of improving productivity and competitiveness.

....

References

Argyris, C. (1991 May–June). 'Teaching Smart People How to Learn,' *Harvard Business Review*, 99–109.

Demarest, M. (1997). 'Understanding Knowledge Management', *Long Range Planning*, 30(3): 374–84.

Drucker, P. F. (1965). *Post-Capitalist Society*. Oxford: Butterworth-Heinemann.

Heather, P., Rick, J., Atkinson, J. and Morris, S. (1996 September). 'Employers' Use of Temporary Workers', *Labour Market Trends*, 403–12.

Hebeler, J. W. and Van Doren, D. C. (1997 July–August). 'Unfettered Leverage: The Ascendancy of Knowledge-Rich Products and Processes', *Business Horizons*, 2–9.

Kleiner, A. and Roth, G. (1997 September–October). 'How to Make Experience Your Company's Best Teacher', *Harvard Business Review*, 172–8.

Kransdorff, A. (1998). *Corporate Amnesia*. Oxford: Butterworth-Heinemann.

Lee, T. W. and Maurer, S. D. (1997). 'The Retention of Knowledge Workers with the Unfolding Model of Voluntary Turnover', *Human Resources Management Review*, 7(3): 274–5.

Mayrhofer, W. (1997). 'Warning: Flexibility Can Damage Your Organizational Health!' *Employee Relations*, 19(6): 519–34.

Nurmi, R. (1998 May–June). 'Knowledge-Intensive Firms', *Business Horizons*, 26–32.

OECD (Organization for Economic and Cooperative Development), (1994). *Employment Outlook, Enterprise Tenure*. Paris: OECD.

Porter, M. E. (1980). *Competitive Strategy*. New York: Free Press.

Quinn, J. B., Anderson, P., and Finkelstein, S. (1996 March–April). 'Managing Professional Intellect: Making the Most of the Best', *Harvard Business Review*, 71–80.

Stewart, T. A. (1997). *Intellectual Capital: The New Wealth of Organizations*. New York: Doubleday/Currency.

8

Organizational Memory

Linda Argote

Introduction

What do organizations learn as they gain experience in production? Where is this knowledge embedded within organizations? What are the consequences of where knowledge is embedded for organizational performance? This chapter begins with a discussion of what is learned as groups and organizations gain experience in production. A more general discussion of organizational memory and various 'retention bins' or 'repositories' of organizational knowledge follows. Examples of knowledge embedded in various repositories drawn from our studies of manufacturing and service industries are provided. Empirical evidence on the extent to which organizational knowledge is embedded in these various repositories is described. The chapter concludes with a discussion of the implications of where knowledge is embedded for important aspects of organizational functioning and effectiveness.

Sources of Productivity Gains

Many researchers have speculated about factors responsible for the productivity gains observed in organizations with increasing experience. For example, Joskow and Rosanski (1979) discussed the following factors as contributors to the productivity gains observed with increasing experience: routinization of tasks, more efficient production control, improved equipment design, and improved routing and material handling. Thus, these researchers emphasize changes in the task and technology as contributors to productivity gains associated with experience. Hayes and Wheelwright (1984) listed a broader set of factors as facilitators of organizational learning. According to Hayes and Wheelwright (1984), organizational learning curves are due to: individual learning, better selection and training, improved methods, enhanced equipment and technology, more appropriate division of labor and specialization, improved product design, substitution of capital for labor, incentives, and leadership. Similarly, Porter (1979) noted that with more experience, firms learn to make methods more productive, to design layout and workflow more efficiently, to coax more production out of machinery, to develop specialized new processes and product design modifications that improve manufacturability, and to institute better management control. In our interviews with managers at manufacturing plants about their views of the most important determinants of organizational learning curves, our respondents emphasized the following: increased proficiency of individual workers; improvements in the organization's technology, tooling, and layout; improvements in its structure, organization, and methods of coordination; and better understanding of who in the organization is good at what (Argote 1993). Better understanding of each individual's skills enables the organization to assign tasks more appropriately so as to take better advantage of each individual's unique capabilities. Knowledge of each member's special expertise is also beneficial because members of the organization know whom to go to for help or advice about specific issues.

These myriad factors believed to affect learning can be classified into three general categories: improvements in the performance of individual employees, including direct production workers, managers, and technical support staff; improvements in the organization's structure and routines; and improvements in the organization's technology. Examples of improvements in each of these categories will now be discussed. These examples are drawn from our field studies of learning in manufacturing and service organizations.

Increased Individual Proficiency

Most discussions of factors responsible for organizational learning curves cite learning by individual workers as a key factor (e.g. see Hayes and Wheelwright 1984; Yelle 1979). A long stream of research in psychology has documented that individual performance improves as individuals acquire more experience with a task (Graham and Gagne 1940; Thorndike 1898; Thurstone 1919). Reviews of the large body of research on individual learning can be found in Anzai and Simon (1979), Newell and Rosenbloom (1981), and Mazur and Hastie (1978).

Our interest is in individuals working in organized settings. What qualify as examples of improvements in individual performance that occur in ongoing groups and organizations as individuals gain experience in production? Many examples of individuals becoming more skilled at their particular tasks can be found in our study of fast food franchises. For example, pizza makers typically became more proficient at hand-tossing pizza dough and transforming it into a pizza shell as they acquired experience. Much of the knowledge about how to hand-toss pizza was tacit and therefore difficult to articulate to others (Nonaka 1991; Polanyi 1966). This knowledge remained primarily embedded in the individual workers who had acquired experience with the pizza-tossing task.

We also observed improvements in the performance of individual workers in manufacturing plants. At one plant we studied, a second shift was introduced almost two years after the plant had been in operation with one shift. Workers on the new shift worked side by side with workers on the first shift to learn their jobs. Workers on the new shift were gradually 'weaned' from their experienced counterparts until the new employees were working independently on the second shift. Through observing workers on the first shift and gaining experience with the task, workers on the new shift learned their individual jobs and became very proficient at them.

Modifications in Technology

Modifications in technology are another major contributor to the productivity gains observed in organizations with increasing experience. By technology, we mean equipment, including hardware and software (cf. Amber and Amber 1962; Barley 1986; Blau et al. 1976) used in production. An example of modification in technology that derived from experience in production can be found in the paint shop at one of the truck assembly plants we studied. The plant experienced problems in its new highly automated paint shop. When light-colored products followed dark-colored ones, vestiges of the dark color could be found on the subsequent, light-colored product. This was clearly unacceptable. Plant managers and engineers tried various approaches to remedy the problem. The most effective solution that was developed involved dedicating particular paint booths to particular dark colors. Thus, only products of the same dark color would be processed through each booth. If any residue paint remained in the system, it would not be harmful since all the products going through the booth were the same color. While dedicating a paint booth to a particular color resulted in some loss in flexibility for the system, the lost flexibility was more than offset by the improved product quality and the reduced waste. This manufacturing example illustrates how knowledge acquired via learning by doing can lead to modifications in an organization's technology. Knowledge was embedded in the 'software' and the 'hardware' of the paint shop that enabled the organization to produce a higher quality, less costly product.

We also observed several examples of improvements in technology in our study of fast food franchises (Argote and Darr 2000). Technology in the context of these pizza stores includes the equipment, such as ovens, and tools used to make pizzas, as well as the physical layout of the stores. The 'cheese spreader' is an example of an innovation developed through production experience that became embedded in the organization's technology. Achieving an even distribution of cheese across a pizza is a desired goal. Too much cheese decreases profit margins, whereas too little cheese decreases customer satisfaction. A manager at one of the stores we studied decided that spreading cheese by hand was not the best method. The manager believed that the problem was analogous to spreading fertilizer on a lawn and that some type of 'spreader' was needed. The manager experimented with various configurations of plastic dishes and metal screens to develop a tool that would help pizza makers use a consistent amount of cheese and achieve an even distribution of the topping. The final version of the 'cheese spreader' tool was a plastic cone with holes that sat on feet several inches above the pizza. A pizza maker would pour grated cheese into the cone and the cheese would fall in a consistent pattern over the pizza. This example illustrates—in a very different organizational context—how knowledge acquired via experience can be embedded in an organization's technology.

Elaborations in Structure and Routines

Elaborations in structure and routines made as organizations gain experience in production also contribute to organizational learning. One such elaboration we saw at a manufacturing plant involved changing the structure of the industrial engineering group. A decision was made to deploy the industrial engineering group that had previously been centralized in one area of the plant to various areas on the plant floor so that the engineers could be more responsive to production problems. Thus, the industrial engineers were shifted from a functional-type organization where they were centralized in one area to a product-type organization where they were decentralized to various areas on the plant floor. The decentralized organization enabled the engineers to respond more quickly to issues on the plant floor. In this example, knowledge about how to be more responsive was embedded in the manufacturing plant's structure.

Another example of knowledge embedded in routines occurred in a manufacturing plant we studied. The particular routine involved preparing the products (trucks) for painting: painting two-tone trucks was challenging since workers had to mask the areas of the truck that were not to be painted a particular color by taping large sheets of protective paper over the appropriate areas. As experience was gained with the task, a better method for placing the protective paper was discovered. Initially, workers masked the area of the truck that was not to be painted a particular color to protect those areas and then painted the rest of the truck the desired color (e.g. white). They then reversed the masking by placing protective paper over the area that had already been painted the desired color (e.g. white) and painted the remainder of the truck the second color (e.g. red). This process required two stages of carefully masking the truck with protective paper. A new method of masking was discovered that required only one round of masking. All of the truck was painted one background color (e.g. white). The parts of the truck that were to remain the background color were then masked and the truck was painted the second color (e.g. red). The new process saved considerable time since the trucks only had to be masked with protective paper once. The new method, which required fewer labor hours and less material to achieve the desired two-tone paint job, ultimately became embedded in a routine that all workers used.

We also observed knowledge embedded in an organization's routines in our study of fast food franchises (Argote and Darr 2000). When deep-dish pizza was introduced at the pizza stores, all stores experienced a persistent problem with the new product. The usual method of distributing pepperoni on pizzas was to distribute it evenly over the pizza before the pizza was cooked. Although this method worked for regular pizzas, it did not work well for deep-dish ones. When pepperoni was distributed evenly on deep-dish pizzas, the pieces of pepperoni would all move into the center in one 'clump' as the pizza cooked and the cheese flowed. Various methods of dealing with the problem were implemented. The most successful one involved distributing the pepperoni on the pizza before it was cooked in a pattern that resembled spokes on a wheel. As the pizza was cooked, the flow of the cheese distributed the pepperoni pieces (more or less) evenly over the pizza. Thus, knowledge about how to distribute pepperoni evenly became embedded in a routine. This routine proved to be very effective at achieving an even distribution of pepperoni. The routine is now used by virtually every store in the corporation.

Repositories of Organizational Knowledge

How do these examples of sources of productivity gains relate to more theoretical discussions of organizational memory or of where knowledge is embedded in organizations? Stein (1995) defined organizational memory as the means by which knowledge from the past is brought to bear on present organizational activities. According to Stein (1995), 'memory is a persistent record not dependent on a tight coupling between sender and receiver' (p. 22). Similarly, Walsh and Ungson (1991) defined organizational memory as stored information from an organization's past and Casey (1997) defined it as shared interpretations of the past.

Where is this knowledge from the past embedded within an organization? Levitt and March (1988) indicated that knowledge is embedded in an organization's routines and standard operating procedures, in its products and processes, in its technologies and equipment, in its layout and structures, and in its culture and norms about how things are generally done. Similarly, Walsh and Ungson (1991) conceptualized five 'retention bins' for organizational memory: individual employees, the organization's culture, its standard operating procedures and practices, roles and organizational structures, and the physical structure of the workplace. According to Starbuck (1992), in knowledge-intensive firms, knowledge is embedded in individuals, in physical capital (including hardware and software), in the organization's routines, and in its culture.

These theoretical discussions of organizational memory or retention bins share much in common. The key point on which they differ is whether or not individuals are seen as a repository for organizational knowledge. Walsh and Ungson (1991) and Starbuck (1992) took the position that they are, whereas Levitt and March (1988) argued that the memory does not become organizational until it is captured in a repository that is not dependent on the vagaries of individual membership.

Yates (1990) provided a fascinating account of the evolution of organizational memory from knowledge that resided primarily in individuals to knowledge that resided in supra-individual form. In the early 1800s, organizational memory was primarily embedded in individuals. According to Yates (1990), the growth of the railroads changed that. The changes were brought about by the need to coordinate a geographically dispersed business where lapses of coordination could result in serious accidents. For these firms, timetables, and detailed operational procedures became part of their way of doing business— part of their organizational memory.

An elaboration of organizational memory occurred on a more widespread basis with the advent of scientific management at the turn of the century (Taylor 1911). One of the principles of this movement was to capture the knowledge of individuals so that organizations would not be dependent on them or vulnerable to their turnover. Written records were elaborated; manuals were developed that described an organization's rules and procedures. Reporting systems were also established to transmit information up the hierarchy. Thus, the late 1800s and early 1900s witnessed a shift from organizational memory being embodied primarily in individuals to its embodiment in records, rules, and procedures that did not depend on individuals.

Nelson and Winter (1982) focused on routines as repositories of organizational knowledge (see Cyert and March 1963; March and Simon 1958 for earlier discussions of organizational routines). Gersick and Hackman (1990) described routines at the group level of analysis. Carley (1996) provided evidence from a simulation study that the use of routines or standard operating procedures (SOPs) can enhance the accuracy of organizational decision making.

According to Nelson and Winter (1982), routines are programs or repetitive patterns of activity. In order for organizations to function effectively in routine conditions, individuals must be familiar with the procedures their jobs require and know when particular routines are appropriate. While each individual must know his or her particular job, the individual does not need to know the jobs of others or the routines that guide the organizations as a whole. Indeed, the scale and complexity of many organizations make it difficult to achieve coordination through centralized information or control systems that describe all the routines used by the organization and the interrelationships among them.

Theraulaz and Bonabeau (1995) described a fascinating example of the implementation of routines in a wasp colony. The researchers noted that while individual insects possess a limited repertoire of routines; insects are collectively capable of performing complex tasks such as nest building. Theraulaz and Bonabeau cited an early study by Grasse showing that coordination of nest-building activity in termites does not depend on interactions among the workers themselves but rather depends on the structure of the nest. The inputs of one worker are cued by the outputs of another. Actions taken by one worker modify the nest configuration, which in turn automatically triggers new actions by other workers.

This example is similar to Nelson and Winter's discussion of routines in organizations in that individual members of the collectivity must know their own routines and the triggering conditions for them but do not need to know others' routines. The nest-building example is analogous to how work is structured on many assembly lines. Employees know their own routines. They identify which routine to implement by observing the product—either its physical condition or information cues attached to it describing its requirements. For example, an employee might observe that the next truck she is to work on requires an air conditioning system—either by observing that there already are parts of the air conditioning system installed or by reading a list of product specifications attached to the truck. This knowledge then cues particular activities by the employee that involve installing an air conditioner. This example illustrates how an individual's activities can be cued by the product and its specification sheet. Direct interaction among individual employees may not be required.

Although these discussions of organizational memory differ concerning the exact number of repositories of knowledge, the discussions have much in common. Researchers generally agree that organizational knowledge resides in: individuals, including managers, technical support staff, and direct production workers; the organization's technology, including its layout, hardware, and software; the organization's structure, routines, and methods of coordination; and the organization's culture.

The first three factors (individuals, technology, and structure) have consistently been cited by other researchers who study manufacturing organizations as contributing to the productivity gains observed with increasing experience (e.g. Hayes and Wheelwright 1984). These three factors were also mentioned by respondents at the organizations we studied as contributors to organizational learning curves. By contrast, culture did not emerge as being particularly important in these settings, although it may be more important in organizations that produce less tangible products. Culture is certainly a repository for some knowledge in these manufacturing organizations. In order for culture to explain the changes in productivity associated with experience, however, it would have to change as the organizations gained experience. We did not see examples of significant changes in culture in our studies and apparently neither did other researchers who study learning curves in manufacturing organizations. Thus, knowledge about productivity improvements in manufacturing organizations is primarily embedded in individuals or in the organizations' technology or structure. Empirical evidence about the extent to which knowledge is embedded in these repositories will now be presented.

Knowledge Embedded in Individuals

We turn now to evaluating empirical evidence on the extent to which knowledge acquired through learning by doing is embedded in individual employees. As noted previously, most discussions about factors responsible for organizational learning curves include learning by individual employees as a key factor. Similarly, most discussions of organizational memory cite individuals as a key repository of organizational knowledge. If knowledge is embedded in individuals, then their turnover should affect organizational memory.

Engeström et al. (1990) described an example of knowledge being embedded in an individual. The researchers analyzed a Urology Clinic where virtually all of the knowledge was embedded in one administrator. Few documents existed, and other individuals who were knowledgeable about the clinic had either retired or moved to a different organization. The administrator hoarded knowledge by protecting his network of personal contacts and by solving problems without explaining the rationale to his subordinates. Engeström et al. (1990) suggested that when the administrator retired, he would take all the knowledge with him. In this example, knowledge was embedded primarily in one individual. The researchers argued that his departure would hurt the clinic's performance.

Studies of the effect of turnover provide a gauge of the extent to which knowledge is embedded in individuals. What does the evidence say about the relationship between turnover and organizational learning? Our analysis of the effect of turnover of direct production workers in World War II shipyards did not reveal any evidence that turnover affected the productivity of the yards. The shipyards were large organizations with formalized and specialized structures. Jobs were generally designed to be low in skill requirements (Lane 1951) so that a worker without previous experience could be brought up to speed quickly. We speculated that perhaps these conditions mitigated the effect of turnover and that one would find more of an effect of turnover for highly skilled workers or for workers who performed less structured tasks.

The Argote et al. (1997) study investigated one of these factors—whether the effect of turnover depended on the performance of departing members. We collected data that contained information on the reason employees left a manufacturing plant (e.g. whether employees were discharged for poor performance, promoted for good performance, retired, deceased, quit, 'bumped' due to contractual agreements, and so on). Our results indicated that the variable representing the number of employees who were promoted out of the plant to participate in competitive apprenticeship programs on the basis of their good performance was generally negatively related to the truck plant's productivity. This study suggests that the effect of turnover on productivity depends on the performance level of departing employees: the departure of high-performing employees appeared to hurt the truck plant's productivity.

We examined whether the effect of turnover depended on how organizations were structured in another study (Devadas and Argote 1995). Past work had suggested that how an organization was structured might moderate the effects of turnover. For example, Grusky (1961) found that managerial succession was less disruptive in large than in small firms. Grusky suggested that the greater use of written rules and hierarchies in the larger companies buffered them from the potential negative effects of managerial turnover.

To investigate whether structure affected the consequences of turnover, we simulated varying degrees of structure in the laboratory and contrasted the effect of turnover in highly structured groups to the effect in less structured groups. The central hypothesis was an interaction between turnover and work group structure—that turnover would affect the performance of groups that were high in structure less than that of groups low in structure and that the performance of high and low structure groups would not differ when turnover did not occur. Thus, high structure was hypothesized to mitigate the effect of turnover.

The hypothesis was tested through a laboratory study in which three-person groups performed five trials of a production-type task (building origami products). The level of turnover and the structuring of activities were varied. In the no-turnover condition, the same three members worked together for the five experimental periods. In the turnover condition, one member was replaced by a new member who had received the same training as the initial three members at the end of each trial. In the low structure condition, group members were not given any special instructions about how to organize themselves, whereas in the high structure condition, group members were required to perform specialized roles and follow certain procedures.

Results indicated that there was a significant interaction between turnover and structure: groups in the low structure turnover condition performed significantly more poorly than groups in the other three conditions. Videotapes of the groups performing the tasks were analyzed to shed light on the processes underlying group performance. These analyses suggested that one factor contributing to the poor performance of groups in the low structure turnover condition was their continual need to reorganize around the skills of new members. For example, the group might organize around the idiosyncratic skills of one member who was good at a particular set of tasks (e.g. building crowns). When that person departed, not only was the group deprived of his or her individual skills, the group also found that its division of labor was obsolete since it was unlikely the new member possessed the exceptional skills of the old. This required a revision in the organization of work and assignment of tasks. Groups in the low structure turnover condition showed more evidence of continual reorganizing than groups in any of the other conditions. The continual need to reorganize hurt their performance.

Other factors contributing to the poor performance of groups in the low structure turnover condition included the difficulty the groups had accessing knowledge and the loss of critical knowledge when members left the group. The former occurred typically when one group member asked a question and another group member had to stop what he or she was doing to aid the person asking the question. This variable was negatively correlated with performance and its incidence was higher in the low structure turnover condition. Knowledge was coded as 'lost' when a group member asked a question that no other group member could answer. This occurred only in the low structure turnover condition. The results of this study suggest that embedding knowledge in an organization's structure is an effective way to mitigate the effects of turnover.

Linda Argote

Groups in the high structure condition were not as adversely affected by turnover as groups in the low structure condition.

The results of this laboratory study are generally consistent with simulation results Carley (1992) obtained in her analysis of personnel turnover and organizational learning. Carley (1992) compared the effect of turnover on hierarchies and teams. A hierarchy was modeled as a three-tier organization composed of a chief executive officer, a set of assistant executive officers, and a set of analysts. Analysts made recommendations to their assistant executive officer, who in turn forwarded his or her recommendation to the chief executive officer making the final organizational decision. A team was modeled as a single-tier organization comprised of analysts. Each analyst made a decision independent of the decision of the other analysts. The final organizational decision was the decision of a majority of the analysts. Carley (1992) found that while teams learned better and faster than hierarchies, hierarchies were less affected by turnover than teams.

Argote et al. (1995) analyzed whether the effect of turnover on group learning depended on the complexity of the task. We simulated varying levels of task complexity in the laboratory and contrasted the effect of turnover on groups performing complex versus simple tasks over several time periods. One theoretical argument would predict that turnover would have a more negative effect on complex than on simple tasks. Complex tasks require more distinct acts or skills (Wood 1986). Thus, groups performing complex tasks that experience turnover would be even more disadvantaged than those performing simple tasks, because the gap between the skills necessary to perform the task, and those possessed by new members, is greater for complex than for simple tasks. This line of reasoning leads one to predict that turnover would have a more negative effect for complex than for simple tasks.

Another theoretical argument, however, would predict that turnover would have a less negative effect on the performance of complex than of simple tasks. Several studies have found a positive effect of turnover on group or organizational performance (Guest 1962; Virany, Tushman and Romanelli 1992; Wells and Pelz 1966; Ziller, Behringer and Goodchilds 1962). These studies have all used complex tasks or studied work that involved innovation. For example, Wells and Pelz (1966) analyzed the performance of groups of scientists and engineers while Virany, Tushman and Romanelli (1992) studied executives in the computer industry. The work of scientists, engineers, and executives is more complex and more subject to innovation than, for example, work performed by direct production workers in bureaucratic organizations. Due to innovations that occur in the performance of complex tasks, knowledge of incumbents may become obsolete. Thus, their departures may not be costly since much of their knowledge may no longer be relevant for task performance. By contrast, newcomers may be more up-to-date and possess expertise

158

relevant to the task. This theoretical argument leads one to predict that turnover would have a less negative (or even positive) effect on the performance of complex than of simple tasks.

Results indicated that group performance improved significantly as experience was gained with the task. Groups that did not experience turnover produced significantly more products than groups that experienced turnover, and this difference was amplified over time. That is, the gap between the performance of groups that experienced turnover and those that did not widened over time. Groups produced more of the simple than the complex product, and this difference was also amplified over time. The gap in the performance of no-turnover versus turnover groups increased over time, and the increase in the gap was greater for the simple than for the complex task. Thus, while all groups were hurt by turnover, it had less impact on the complex than on the simple task. Based on analyses of innovations generated in the experiment, we suggested that the lesser impact of turnover on the complex tasks was due to the greater frequency of innovations that occurred on the complex task. The departure of experienced group members appeared less costly on the complex tasks since some of their knowledge was no longer relevant due to technological innovations.

The effect of turnover has also been found to depend on the quality of replacements and on the extent to which turnover is anticipated. Trow (1960) investigated the effect of turnover on performance in a laboratory study that employed the common symbol task. Trow found that turnover was not disruptive when replacements had experience with the task, were at least as competent as their predecessors, and the group had previous experience with the same rate of turnover.

Although these studies of the effect of turnover have primarily focused on turnover of workers engaged in direct production activities, a few studies have examined the effect of executive turnover on organizational learning. Virany, Tushman, and Romanelli (1992) examined turnover of executives as a mechanism for organizational learning and adaptation in a study of mini-computer firms. The researchers suggested that executive change facilitates learning and adaptation by changing the knowledge base and communication processes of the executive team. Their results indicated that turnover of the chief executive officer and turnover in the executive team were positively associated with organizational performance. Thus, in the turbulent mini-computer industry, executive change may have served as a means for bringing in new knowledge and relevant expertise.

Similarly, in their study of the cement industry, Tushman and Rosenkopf (1996) found that executive succession alone was positively associated with subsequent firm performance in stable contexts and negatively associated in turbulent contexts. A more complex picture emerged for executive team change. Departures of executive team members (exits) had different effects than arrivals of new members (entries). In turbulent contexts, executive team entries were more positively associated with subsequent performance, whereas executive team exits were more negatively associated with subsequent performance. The researchers suggested that when environments shift and the locus of the crisis is outside the firm, organizational performance is strengthened by bringing in new executive team expertise while retaining existing expertise. By contrast, when the source of the crisis is within the firm, executive team exits were more positively associated with organizational performance.

These results are more complex than those of the Virany, Tushman, and Romanelli (1992) study in the mini-computer industry. The results suggest that turnover in the executive team may have different effects than turnover of the top executive and further that entries and exits of executive team members may have differential effects on performance. Comparing the two studies, it is interesting to note that it is in the more stable cement industry that one finds some benefits of retaining existing knowledge and expertise, while in the more turbulent computer industry, turnover at the executive level was more uniformly associated with performance improvements. These results are generally consistent with the Argote et al. (1995) study. Turnover is less harmful—and may even be beneficial—on complex tasks that involve change and innovation.

Taken together, these studies of turnover and organizational learning begin to suggest the conditions under which turnover is most likely to have a significant effect on organizational learning. Results indicate that turnover affects performance gains when: (a) departing members are exceptional performers (e.g. see Argote et al. 1997); and (b) when the organizations, or the positions departing members occupy, are low in structure and constraints (e.g. Carley 1992; Devadas and Argote, 1995; Virany, Tushman and Romanelli 1992). While turnover of high-performing direct production workers in a manufacturing plant negatively affected the plant's productivity, turnover of executives in the mini-computer industry had a positive effect on performance. The former effect may have reflected the cost of the loss of individuals who had critical knowledge embedded in them while the latter may have reflected the benefit of incorporating individuals with new knowledge into the organizations.

Knowledge Embedded in Organizations

We turn now to evaluating empirical evidence on the extent to which knowledge is embedded in organizations. Knowledge embedded in an organization is harder to measure and analyze than in individuals, since assessing the effect of individual turnover provides an indicator of the extent to which knowledge was embedded in individuals. An interesting naturally occurring experiment provided an opportunity for us to analyze the extent to which knowledge acquired through learning by doing became embedded in the organization versus in individual employees (Epple, Argote and Murphy 1996). While the natural experiment did not enable us to further disentangle whether the knowledge was embedded in the organization's technology or its structure, it was informative about whether knowledge was embedded in individuals versus in the organization.

A manufacturing plant added a second shift almost two years after the first shift had been in operation (Epple, Argote and Murphy 1996). The second shift used the same technology and was embedded in the same structure as the first shift but was composed of predominantly new employees. Thus, comparing the performance of the second to the first shift provides an indicator of the extent to which knowledge was embedded in the organization's structure and technology versus in individual workers. If the learning curve on the second shift followed the same pattern as the first shift's curve had, it suggests that knowledge is embedded primarily in individual workers since workers on each shift went through the same learning process. Alternatively, if the second shift learns faster than the first, it suggests that knowledge acquired from the start of production by the first shift was embedded in the organization and led to improvements in the performance of the second shift. To investigate this issue, we analyzed the transfer of knowledge that occurred from the period of operating with one shift to the period of operating with two shifts and the ongoing transfer of knowledge between the two shifts once they were both in operation (see Epple, Argote and Devadas 1991 for development of the method).

Our results indicated that knowledge acquired during the period of operating with one shift carried forward quite rapidly to both shifts of the two-shift period. The second shift was composed predominantly of new employees, and achieved a level of productivity in two weeks that it had taken the first shift many months to achieve. This suggests that knowledge acquired during the period of one-shift operation had been embedded in the organization's structure or technology. The second shift did not have to go through the long-learning period that the first shift had. The second shift benefited from knowledge acquired by the first shift that had been embedded in the organization (i.e. its technology, structure, or layout). This knowledge improved the second shift's performance.

As noted previously, this study did not enable us to disentangle the effect of knowledge embedded in the organization's technology from knowledge embedded in its structure. Both contributed to the ability of the second shift to achieve a high level of productivity so rapidly. Our sense from observing the plant and the interviews we conducted there was that more of the action occurred on the technological than on the structural dimension. While some structural modifications were made, enormous changes occurred in the plant's layout and its technology as it gained experience in production. The studies described in the following two sections enable one to determine somewhat more clearly whether knowledge was embedded in the organization's technology or its structure.

Knowledge Embedded in Technology

Studies of technology transfer provide a more direct window on the extent to which knowledge is embedded in technology. These studies typically examine how technology developed at one site transfers to another and the conditions that facilitate or impede such transfer (e.g. Allen 1977; Ounjian and Carne 1987; Szulanski 1996). Much of this work is based on surveys of the conditions that facilitate or impede the transfer of knowledge from one site to another.

A relevant study that is particularly compelling for the goals of this book is one that included productivity as the dependent measure, and analyzed the effects of various factors on how long it took a 'recipient' site to reach the level of productivity a 'donor' site had achieved (Galbraith 1990). Galbraith (1990) studied 32 attempts to transfer technology internally from one site to another within the same organization. The results of the Galbraith study illustrate both the difficulty of transferring technology and the savings in productivity that can occur from successful technology transfer attempts. For the 32 technology transfer attempts, the initial productivity at the recipient site after the technology was transferred averaged 34 percent less than what the donor site had achieved at the time of transfer. The productivity loss ranged from a low of 4 percent to a high of 150 percent. Thus, some of the recipient organizations almost instantaneously achieved a level of productivity that it had taken the donor sites months or even years to achieve whereas other recipient sites did not even approach the productivity of the donor sites after the transfer. Indeed, 10 of the 32 technology transfer attempts were considered failures because they never reached the level of productivity of the donor site prior to the transfer.

The Galbraith results tell a story that is both 'half-full' and 'half-empty' from the perspective of knowledge embedded in technology. On the positive side, the results illustrate that some organizations can achieve remarkable productivity gains by transferring technology. These organizations are able to embed knowledge in technology and successfully transfer the knowledge to a new site. For other organizations, however, the results are less satisfying. Their attempts to embed knowledge in technology and transfer it to another site do not result in large productivity gains at the recipient organization. Some organizations are able to embed knowledge in technology and use it to transfer knowledge effectively to a new site.

Knowledge Embedded in Structure and Routines

Researchers have also analyzed the extent to which knowledge acquired through learning by doing is embedded in routines. Cohen and Bacdayan (1994) demonstrated that knowledge acquired through task performance can be embedded in supra-individual routines. Based on empirical evidence from a laboratory study of dyads playing a card game, the researchers concluded that the behavior of the dyads was indicative of the operation of routines. In particular, the performance of the dyads became faster and more reliable over time. Different dyads evolved different routines that were stable over time (see also Weick and Gilfallen 1971). And dyads persisted in using their idiosyncratic routines, even when more effective routines existed.

Further, Cohen and Bacdayan (1994) found that task performance slowed down significantly with the introduction of novelty in the experiment but not with an increase in time delay. The researchers argued that this pattern provided further evidence of the operation of routines. Delay should not affect routinized task performance since routines are stored as procedural memory which exhibits little decay, whereas novelty should affect routinized task performance since novelty causes subjects to switch to slower, declarative processing (Singley and Anderson 1989).

Moorman and Miner (1998) developed propositions about the effects of procedural and declarative knowledge on organizational improvisation. Improvisation was defined as the convergence of composition and execution in time. The researchers argued that procedural memory would increase the speed but reduce the novelty of improvisational activity. By contrast, declarative memory was hypothesized to reduce the speed but increase the novelty of improvization.

Research on 'transactive memory' (Wegner 1986, 1995) is also relevant for understanding whether knowledge is embedded in social structures versus in individuals. This research emphasizes that as social systems gain experience, members acquire knowledge about the system as well as about their individual tasks. In particular, members acquire knowledge about who is good at what, about how to coordinate and communicate effectively, and about whom to trust. This knowledge in turn improves their performance.

Let us consider an example of how a transactive memory system might work. A group of research collaborators might learn that one member of the team is particularly good at experimental design, while another excels at data analysis and a third is a very strong writer. As the group gains experience and learns who is good at what, it specializes and assigns tasks to the individual with the most skill and expertise. That is, as group members work together, they learn who has a deeper understanding of statistics and rely more on that person for dealing with statistical concerns. As group members read each other's writing, members also learn who the most gifted writer is. That person is likely to take on more of the group's writing tasks. Furthermore, as group members see the consequences of various design choices, members acquire information about who has the best instincts about the design of research studies. This knowledge of who knows what facilitates matching of tasks to individuals' skills and expertise. Individuals' meta knowledge of who knows what in the group allows them access to a much larger knowledge base than their own. Individuals learn whom to go to if they have a question or need advice. Group members also learn how to communicate and coordinate effectively with one another, perhaps by developing special terms and customs. Members also learn whom they can trust. The transactive memory system the group develops facilitates its performance.

My colleagues and I used Wegner's concept of transactive memory to investigate the effects of training methods on group performance (Liang, Moreland, and Argote 1995). In an initial study, we compared the performance of groups whose members were trained individually to that of groups whose members were trained together on a production task, assembling a radio. Groups whose members were trained together recalled more about the task and made fewer errors than groups whose members were trained apart. The superior performance of groups in the group training condition seemed to stem from the operation of a transactive memory system. Groups whose members were trained together exhibited greater specialization or memory differentiation, seemed to trust one another to a greater extent, and were better coordinated than groups whose members were trained individually. Further, the transactive memory system mediated the relationship between training and group performance (Baron and Kenny 1986): when the degree to which the groups developed transactive memory systems was taken into account, training methods no longer mattered. Thus, the superior performance of groups who received training together was due to the operation of transactive memory systems.

A subsequent study replicated the first and included two additional conditions (see Moreland, Argote, and Krishnan 1996). One condition in which participants were trained as individuals and then given a team-building exercise was added to investigate further whether the superior performance of participants trained as a group was due to enhanced group development. The performance of participants in this individual training plus team-building condition was inferior to that of participants trained as a group, and comparable to that of participants who only received individual training. This finding enabled us to rule out the hypothesis that enhanced group development led to the superior performance of participants who were trained together.

Providing groups an opportunity to interact was not sufficient to improve their performance.

Another condition was added to the second study in which participants were trained in one group and performed in another. The performance of participants who were trained in this condition was comparable to the performance of participants in the individual training condition and the individual training plus team-building condition, and inferior to that of participants who trained and performed in the same group. Thus, it is not experience in working with any group that leads to superior performance, but experience in working with particular group members that allows for the development of knowledge of who is good at what and leads to the creation of a transactive memory system. It is the transactive memory system that drives group performance.

A third study measured more directly what members of a group learned as they gained experience (Moreland, Argote, and Krishnan 1998). To assess whether group members who trained together would know more about one another than those trained apart, participants were asked to complete a questionnaire after they received training and before they took part in the second experimental session. The questionnaire measured what the members of each group knew about each other's expertise. Participants who were trained together wrote more complex analyses of each others' strengths and weaknesses. To assess the accuracy of these perceptions of each others' strengths and weaknesses, the questionnaire data were compared to objective information about performance on the radio assembly task. Results indicated that participants who were trained together had more accurate perceptions of each others' expertise than participants who were trained individually. Further, members of groups who were trained together agreed more about each others' strengths and weaknesses than members trained apart.

Another goal of the third experiment was to see if social loafing and free-riding (see Karau and Williams 1993) affected performance in the various training conditions. Training members of a group together could lead to social loafing: some group members may not learn the task very well because they expect to be able to rely on others. During the first experimental session of this study, participants were trained either individually or in a group, as in previous studies. When they returned for the second experimental session, however, all participants were asked to perform the task *individually.* This enabled us to determine whether participants who were trained in a group learned the task as well as subjects who received individual training. Results indicated that there were no significant differences in *individual* performance between participants who were trained individually and those who were trained as a group. While further research is needed to rule out the possibility of social loafing in group training, our results suggest that individual learning occurs to about the same

Linda Argote

degree whether participants are trained individually or in a group. Thus, social loafing does not seem to be a serious problem here.

Hollingshead (1998) also compared the effect of group and individual training on group and individual performance for a different task: collective induction. Results indicated that group performance was facilitated by previous practice as a group and not by practice as individuals. Individual performance, however, was not affected by either individual or group practice. These results obtained on collective induction tasks are very similar to those already described for the radio production task.

Hollenbeck et al. (1995) also found that experience improved group performance in a study of hierarchical teams. Much (albeit not all) of the effect of experience on performance was mediated by its effect on three core variables: (1) the degree to which the team was informed about the decision; (2) the extent to which members' judgments were accurate, and (3) the degree to which the leader gave appropriate weights to group members' judgments. This last factor is similar to a dimension of transactive memory—knowing who is good at what and weighting their contributions accordingly. In a second study, Hollenbeck et al. (1995) found that teams that had an incompetent member and those low in cohesiveness performed more poorly than their counterparts. Similar to the previous results, much (but not all) of the effect of cohesion and competence on decision accuracy was mediated by the three core variables.

These laboratory studies of small groups relate to information we obtained from interviewing and observing managers at manufacturing facilities. As noted previously, when we interviewed managers about what accounts for organizational learning curve, they emphasized the importance of learning who was good at what and assigning tasks accordingly. Thus, these organizations were developing transactive memory systems—knowledge of who was good at what—and using this knowledge in task distribution and performance.

The concept of transactive memory has been extended to the organizational level and expanded to include knowledge of the capabilities of other organizations as well as knowledge of the capabilities of one's own organization. Rulke, Zaheer, and Anderson (1998) developed and collected fine-grained measures of the knowledge retail food organizations possessed about their own capabilities and the capabilities of other firms. The researchers examined the relationship between these two types of knowledge (self-knowledge and knowledge of others) and objective measures of performance, such as sales per square foot. Results indicated that both types of knowledge contributed significantly to firm performance. Further, a significant interaction was found between the two knowledge variables that indicated that firms with high self-knowledge did not benefit as much from knowledge of the capabilities of others as those with low self-knowledge. The Rulke, Zaheer, and Anderson (1998) study is particularly exciting because it demonstrates the importance of transactive memory in a field setting and shows the link between transactive memory and objective indicators of firm performance.

Consequences of Where Knowledge is Embedded

Although empirical work on organizational learning and memory has increased in recent years (Miner and Mezias 1996), there is little empirical evidence about the consequences of where knowledge is embedded for aspects of organizational performance. In this section, I draw on related literature and qualitative work we have done in franchise organizations (Argote and Darr 2000) to suggest how where knowledge is embedded affects its persistence and transfer in organizations. The following sections suggest how embedding knowledge in individuals, in technology, or in structure affects its persistence over time and its transfer to other organizational units.

Knowledge Embedded in Individuals

Individuals provide both a sensitive and a precarious way of storing, maintaining and transferring knowledge. Individuals are capable of capturing subtle nuances that other repositories are not able to store as readily. For example, in a series of ingenuous experiments, Berry and Broadbent (1984, 1987) showed that although individuals improved their performance as they gained experience with a task, they were not able to articulate what strategies they had used to perform the task or why their performance had improved. Thus, as they gained experience with the task, individuals acquired tacit knowledge that they were not able to articulate to others. Individuals were able, however, to transfer their tacit knowledge to another similar task. When participants in the experiments performed a second task, the performance of those with previous experience on a similar task was significantly better than that of participants without any previous experience. Thus, even though participants could not articulate why their performance improved, they were able to transfer the knowledge that enabled them to improve their performance to a similar task.

These results suggest that moving personnel is a very effective way to transfer knowledge in organizations since individuals can transfer their tacit knowledge to other tasks and contexts. Thus, by transferring personnel, one transfers the tacit knowledge that individuals carry with them. Most studies of technology transfer find that moving personnel is a powerful facilitator of knowledge transfer (e.g. see Galbraith 1990; Rothwell 1978). A benefit of personnel movement is that it allows individuals to transfer their tacit knowledge to new contexts.

An alternative way of transferring tacit knowledge is to convert it to explicit knowledge. Nonaka (1991) described a fascinating example of how an engineer apprenticed herself to a bread maker to acquire the bread maker's tacit knowledge. Through a long period of observation of the bread maker, the engineer captured the bread maker's tacit knowledge and converted it to explicit knowledge. This explicit knowledge served as the base for Matsushita's bread-making machine.

Individuals are the most effective media for acquiring and storing tacit knowledge. They are also an effective media for transferring tacit knowledge. Individuals can apply their tacit knowledge to a new task or a new context without converting their tacit knowledge to explicit knowledge. Alternatively, through a lengthy period of observation and apprenticeship others may be able to capture an expert's tacit knowledge and convert it to explicit knowledge that others can access.

Without moving personnel or explicitly attempting to capture their knowledge, knowledge embedded in individuals will generally not transfer. Qualitative results from our study of fast food franchises illustrate how knowledge embedded in individuals generally does not transfer to new sites. In our study of fast food franchises, we observed 14 innovations at the stores (Argote and Darr 2000). Of the 14 innovations that occurred in the fast food franchises, six were embedded in individuals. For example, knowledge about how to hand toss pizza remained embedded in individual workers. Knowledge about how to prioritize pizzas so as to take advantage of cooking time differences across pizza types and sizes and, thus, make better use of the oven, also remained embedded in a few individual order-takers. Of the six innovations that were embedded in individuals, only two transferred outside the store of origin. By contrast, both of the innovations embedded in technology transferred outside the store of origin and five of the six innovations embedded in routines transferred outside the store of origin. Thus, knowledge embedded in individuals does not transfer as readily outside the organization of origin as knowledge embedded in technology or routines does.

Several pitfalls are associated with relying on individuals as a knowledge repository for organizations. Knowledge embedded in individuals may decay or depreciate faster than knowledge embedded in social systems. The results of an interesting laboratory study that compared individual and group recall suggest that knowledge embedded in groups is more stable than knowledge embedded in individuals (Weldon and Bellinger 1997). The researchers found a tendency for groups to exhibit less forgetting than individuals. Further, the organization of group recall was more consistent over trials than the organization of individual recall. Thus, an important difference between collective and individual memories may be the relative stability of collective memories. Knowledge embedded in the group or social system seems to be more stable than knowledge embedded in individuals, even when there is no turnover of those individuals.

Another downside of relying on individuals as a knowledge repository is that individuals may not be motivated to share their knowledge. The Engeström et al. (1990) example discussed earlier in which an individual hoarded knowledge and did not share it with others is an example of this phenomenon. Many studies have shown that individuals typically do not share information that they uniquely hold (e.g. see Stasser and Titus 1985). This line of work is discussed in depth in the next chapter.

A third downside of relying on individuals as a knowledge repository for organizations is that individuals can leave and take their knowledge with them. Conditions under which individual turnover will be especially harmful for organizations were discussed earlier in this chapter. Organizations can use a variety of strategies for capturing individual knowledge. Embedding individual knowledge in organizational structures and routines is a productive way to mitigate the effect of individual turnover (Devadas and Argote 1995). Similarly, organizations may try to capture the knowledge of individuals and embed it in technology such as information systems and knowledge networks (cf. Moreland in press; Stewart 1995a, 1995b). A significant component of individual knowledge, however, such as tacit knowledge, may be less amenable to being embedded in organizational structures and technologies. For organizations with a large component of tacit knowledge, attempts to bond the individual to the organization may be more fruitful than attempts to embed the knowledge in structures and technologies. Starbuck (1992) described the strategies organizations such as law firms and consulting firms use to prevent individuals from leaving. In these organizations, where much of the knowledge is embedded in individuals, their turnover would be very harmful for the organization's performance. Hence, contracts are written and incentives are developed to motivate key individuals to remain with the firm.

A fourth disadvantage of relying on individuals to transfer knowledge is that it is hard for individuals to reach a large number of people without some degradation in the communication. Thus, for large organizations where reliability is important, it will not be efficient or effective to rely on individuals as the primary means for transferring knowledge. Individuals can be used effectively to complement other repositories, but relying solely on individuals to transfer knowledge in these settings will not be effective.

Knowledge Embedded in Technology

Technology is a very effective repository for retaining explicit knowledge. The least depreciation of knowledge can be observed in technologically sophisticated organizations. While more research is needed to determine whether it is technological sophistication that drives these organizations' ability to retain knowledge, the depreciation rates observed across a variety of settings are consistent with the hypothesis that embedding knowledge in technology is an effective way to mitigate its depreciation. Similarly, Smunt (1987) suggested that embedding knowledge in technology is an effective way to prevent organizational forgetting. While embedding knowledge in technology does not guarantee its persistence (cf. the 'Star Wars' example), it makes persistence more likely.

Embedding knowledge in technology is also an effective way of transferring knowledge to other sites. Two of the innovations we observed in our study of fast food franchises were embedded in technology. The 'cheese spreader' example discussed earlier in this chapter is an example of one of these innovations. Both of the innovations embedded in technology transferred outside the store of origin. While the number of innovations embedded in technology was, of course, too small to permit firm conclusions, the results are suggestive of the effectiveness of technology as a medium for transferring knowledge.

The results of our study of knowledge transfer across shifts in a manufacturing facility also illustrate the effectiveness of technology as a mechanism for transferring organizational knowledge. The technology-transfer literature provides further evidence that embedding knowledge in technology and transferring it to another site can result in substantial savings for the recipient organization.

Interestingly, transferring knowledge by embedding it in technology is often most successful when it is accompanied by transferring a few individuals as well (e.g. see Galbraith 1990; Rothwell 1978). The advantages of individuals as knowledge repositories complement those of technology. Individuals capture the tacit knowledge, the subtlety, and the understanding behind the technology. By contrast, technology provides consistency and reliability and reaches a large scale.

A cost of embedding knowledge in technology is that the knowledge may become obsolete yet be more resistant to change because it is embedded in 'hard' form. Abernathy and Wayne's (1974) analysis of Ford's production of the Model T suggested that Ford's investment in 'hard' automation to produce the Model T made it more difficult for Ford to change to meet customer preferences and offer a more varied product line. This example illustrates potential disadvantages of embedding knowledge in technology: increased rigidity and resistance to change. Today's technologies are generally more flexible than they were in the 1920s, so the downside potential of embedding knowledge in technology may now be somewhat less. Nonetheless, rigidity associated with embedding knowledge in hard form is an important potential cost of embedding knowledge in technology that should be considered.

Knowledge Embedded in Structure and Routines

Structure may be defined in this case as recurring patterns of activity (Katz and Kahn 1978). Routines and standard operating procedures are important examples of structure. Routines are softer than technology because they are more dependent on people enacting them. While people still have to use the technology, more of the knowledge is typically embedded in the technology than in the routine. Thus, routines share many of the benefits (and costs) of embedding knowledge in technology—but to a somewhat lesser degree.

Routines are very efficient mechanisms for storing and maintaining knowledge. For example, in our study of fast food franchises, we saw an example of a very efficient and effective routine for placing pepperoni on pizza. As described previously, it was discovered that placing pepperoni in a pattern that resembled spokes on a wheel before deep-dish pizza was cooked resulted in an even distribution of pepperoni on the cooked pizza. The discovery was embodied in a routine that could be used easily by all pizza makers. Embedding the knowledge in a routine made it more resistant to employee turnover. If the individual who made the discovery of how to achieve an even distribution departed from the store, the knowledge would remain in the organization. Embedding knowledge in a routine enhances persistence.

Routines are also an effective mechanism for transferring knowledge to other organizations. The routine for placing pepperoni was discovered in a store in southwestern Pennsylvania. The routine transferred very quickly to other stores in the same franchise. A consultant from the parent corporation who saw the routine on a visit to one of the stores was impressed by the routine's effectiveness and diffused it widely to stores throughout the corporation. The routine is now used in virtually all of the stores of the parent corporation.

Indeed, other routines we observed in the fast food franchise study also transferred outside the store of origin. Of the 14 innovations we identified in our fast food franchise study, six were embedded in routines. Of these six, five transferred outside the store of origin. And three of those transferred to stores in different franchises. Thus, embedding knowledge in a routine is an effective way to facilitate knowledge transfer.

The results of a study by Zander and Kogut (1995) are consistent with our qualitative results regarding knowledge transfer. Zander and Kogut (1995) examined factors affecting the speed of transfer of manufacturing capabilities. The researchers found that capabilities that could be codified (e.g. in documents or software) transferred more readily than capabilities not easily codified. In order to be embedded in a routine, capabilities must be codified.

A downside of relying on routines is that they may be used inappropriately. Researchers have written about the importance of 'unlearning' in organizations—forgetting the old and developing a better, more appropriate routine as a way of adapting to changed circumstances (e.g. Hedberg 1981). Unlearning is arguably an example of learning—of developing a more elaborate response repertoire that specifies the conditions under which various responses are appropriate. So rather than 'forget' a routine used in the past, it would be preferable to remember the routine, the conditions under which it worked, and why it is no longer successful. Thus, lessons of the past can be applied to the present to facilitate organizational performance.

We are just beginning to understand the effect of organizational memory on organizational outcomes. An empirical study that directly examined the effect of memory on dimensions of organizational performance found that organizational memory affected the new product development process by influencing both the interpretation of new information and the performance of new product action routines (Moorman and Miner 1997). Results indicated that higher organizational memory levels enhanced the short-term financial performance of new products, while greater memory dispersion increased both the performance and creativity of new products. Results also indicated that high-memory dispersion could detract from creativity under conditions of environmental turbulence.

Conclusion

The chapter began with a discussion of examples of productivity-enhancing improvements that occurred as organizations gained experience in production. These improvements were mapped onto theoretical discussions of organizational memory. For organizations that make things, productivity improvements are generally embedded in three repositories: individual workers, an organization's technology, and its structure and routines. Empirical evidence on the effect of embedding knowledge in these three repositories was reviewed. The chapter concluded with a discussion of the implications of where knowledge was embedded for organizational performance. Individuals are capable of capturing and transferring subtle nuances and tacit knowledge. By contrast, organizational structures and technologies are less 'sensitive' repositories. Knowledge embedded in organizational structures and technologies, however, is more resistant to depreciation and more readily transferred than knowledge embedded in individuals. Organizations can use the strengths of one knowledge repository to offset the weaknesses of another.

9

Balancing Act: How to Capture Knowledge without Killing It

John Seely Brown and Paul Duguid

History will pity the managers of the 1990s. The Internet touched down in their midst like a tornado, tearing up the old game book, disrupting every aspect of business, and compelling them to manage for a new economy. When managers sought help, they found the experts were offering two radically different theories about what such management should look like. The first approach—re-engineering—focused on process. Organizations that re-engineered their business processes would gain sustainable competitive advantage, according to an army of highly paid consultants. Major corporations spent millions of dollars and man-hours trying to do exactly that. But just as scores of reengineering VPs took their seats at *Fortune* 500 companies, word came down that process was stale. The *new* new thing was knowledge management—businesses that could capture the knowledge embedded in their organizations would own the future.

Re-engineering and knowledge management are profoundly different approaches—as all those business people who got whiplash from the turnaround soon realized. Re-engineering is about the structured co-ordination of people and information. It is top-down. It assumes that it is easy to codify value creation. And it assumes that organizations compete in a predictable environment. Knowledge management focuses on effectiveness more than efficiency. It's bottom-up. It assumes that managers can best foster knowledge by responding to the inventive, improvisational ways people actually get things done. It assumes that value-creating activities are not easy to pin down. And it assumes that organizations compete in an unpredictable environment.

Of course, management fads shift all the time. (How else could consultants stay in business?) But we think this shift from process engineering to

173

knowledge management represents something more substantial than a change of fashion. It suggests a dilemma that all managers grapple with: the organizational tension between process, the way matters are formally organized, and practice, the way things actually get done.

Managers find this tension difficult to handle. They are paid to resolve or overcome tensions, but this is one they have to live with. Successful companies are not those that work around the problem; they are those that turn it to their advantage. For in the delicate art of balancing practice and process lies the means both to *foster* invention—by allowing new ideas to spark—and to *further* it—by implementing those same ideas.

It is undoubtedly a hard balancing act. Lean too much toward practice, and you may get new ideas bubbling up all over the place, but you'll lack the structure to harness them. (And in the modern business world, worthwhile ideas that you don't harness end up in your competitors' hands.) Lean too much toward process, and you get lots of structure but too little freedom of movement to strike that initial spark. Finding the right balance is a central task for managers everywhere. It is embodied in a million business fads, and it transcends them all.

It is possible to strike the right balance. In this article, we'll look closely at an example drawn from a company we know well because we work there. This is the story of how Xerox Corporation learned to foster best practice among a particular group of employees and then to circulate their expertise using the organizational support that process can provide.

The Limits of Process-Based Thinking

One way managers attempt to resolve the tension between process and practice is by compartmentalizing. They do everything possible to foster invention and creativity among highly paid, elite workers (designers and scientists, for example). At the same time, they try to make everyone else's work completely predictable and to hold the majority of workers tight within the clamps of process. As a result, searches for under-utilized knowledge round up the usual suspects—the output of the obviously inventive—and ignore everyone else whose work practices are thought of as purely routine.

But this compartmentalization doesn't reflect the way most businesses currently operate. Today even the people involved in seemingly routine work practices have to be inventive because the world they're working in changes so quickly. Their routines are always a little out of kilter. They must improvise to make up the difference between the conditions their routines were designed for and the actual conditions thrown up by a mutable world.

Consider an ordinary business form. Even the most recently printed (or Web-posted) form usually has boxes that are no longer used, categories that no longer apply. These redundant boxes are signposts of change. Employees quickly devise ways to fix the slightly out-of-date process. 'Oh, leave that box,' they'll tell customers, 'but make sure to check under "c." That will ring a bell in the marketing department, and they'll take care of you.'

This particular example is insignificant. But such conversations—which happen all the time—are evidence of practical inventiveness used to get around the limits of process. These small fixes may be part of a company's best practice—where local inventiveness has enabled practices on the ground to outstrip processes on paper. All the small, individually insignificant best practices scattered around a company add up to an enormous amount of knowledge.

For a company to make the most of that knowledge—to 'know what it knows,' in the famous phrase of former Hewlett-Packard CEO Lew Platt—it needs to take practice, practitioners, and the communities that practitioners form seriously. That requires two steps. First, managers need to learn what local knowledge exists. Then if the knowledge looks valuable, they need to put it into wider circulation. Let's take those tasks one at a time. They lie at the heart of knowledge management, of course, and they also show us a lot about the tension between process and practice.

Knowing What You Know

Identifying a company's best practices is not easy, for a couple of reasons. First, there's a large gap between what a task looks like in a process manual and what it looks like in reality. Secondly, there's a gap between what people think they do and what they really do. Actual work practices are full of tacit improvisations that the employees who carry them out would have trouble articulating. The manager who wishes to understand the company's best practices must bridge both of those gaps.

To illustrate the difficulty of identifying best practices, we'll look at the customer service representatives who fix Xerox machines. From the process perspective, a rep's work can be described quickly. Customers having difficulty call the Customer Service Center. The center, in turn, notifies a rep. He or she then goes to the customer's site. With the help of error codes, which report the machine's state, and documentation, which says what those codes mean, the rep diagnoses the problem and follows instructions for fixing it. Practice here would seem to involve little more than following the map you are given and doing whatever it tells you to do.

It would seem that way, if someone had not bothered to look more closely. Julian Orr, formerly an anthropologist at Xerox's Palo Alto Research Center (PARC), studied what reps actually did, not what they were assumed to do. And what they actually did turned out to be quite different from the process we've just described. The reps' work is organized by business processes, without a doubt. But they succeed primarily by departing from formal processes; those processes followed to the letter would soon bring their work (and their clients' work) to a halt.

For example, the company's documented repair processes assume that machines work predictably. Yet large machines, made up of multiple subsystems, are not so predictable. Each reflects the age and condition of its parts, the particular way it is used, and the environment in which it sits, which may be hot, cold, damp, dry, clean, dusty, secluded, in traffic, or otherwise. Any single machine may have profound idiosyncrasies. Reps know the machines they work with, Orr suggests, as shepherds know their sheep. While everyone else assumes one machine is like the next, a rep knows each by its peculiarities and sorts out general failings from particular ones.

Consequently, although the documentation gives the reps a map, the critical question for them is what to do when they fall off the map—which they do all the time. Orr found a simple answer to that question. When the path leads off the map, the reps go . . . to breakfast.

When the Going Gets Tough

Orr began his account of the reps' day not where the process view begins—at nine o'clock, when the first call comes in—but at breakfast beforehand, where the reps share and even generate new insights into these difficult machines. Orr found that a quick breakfast can be worth hours of training. While eating, playing cribbage, and gossiping, the reps talked work, and talked it continually. They posed questions, raised problems, offered solutions, constructed answers, laughed at mistakes, and discussed changes in their work, the machines, and customer relations. Both directly and indirectly, they kept one another up-to-date about what they knew, what they had learned, and what they were doing.

The reps' group breakfast shows that work goes on that formal processes don't capture. But it shows more. It demonstrates that a job that seems highly independent on paper is in reality remarkably social. Reps get together not only at the parts drop and the customer service center but also on their own time for breakfast, at lunch, for coffee, or at the end of the day—and sometimes at all of those times. This sociability is not just a retreat from the loneliness of an isolating job. The constant chatting is similar to the background updating that goes on all the time in any ordinary work site.

There, too, chatting usually passes unnoticed unless someone objects to it as a waste of time. But it's not. Orr showed that the reps use one another as their most critical resources. In the course of socializing, the reps develop a collective pool of practical knowledge that any one of them can draw upon. That pool transcends any individual member's knowledge, and it certainly transcends the corporation's documentation. Each rep contributes to the pool, drawing from his or her own particular strengths, which the others recognize and rely on. Collectively, the local groups constitute a community of practice. (For a detailed description, see 'Communities of Practice: The Organizational Frontier,' HBR January–February 2000.)

Storytelling

Much of the knowledge that exists within working groups like the one formed by our Xerox reps comes from their war stories. The constant storytelling about problems and solutions, about disasters and triumphs over breakfast, lunch, and coffee serves a number of overlapping purposes. Stories are good at presenting things sequentially (this happened, then that). Stories also present things causally (this happened because of that). Thus stories are a powerful way to understand what happened (the sequence of events) and why (the causes and effects of those events). Storytelling is particularly useful for the reps, for whom 'what' and 'why' are critical but often hard matters to discern.

We all tell stories this way. Economists tell stories in their models. Scientists tell stories in their experiments. Executives tell stories in their business plans (see 'Strategic Stories: How 3M Is Rewriting Business Planning,' HBR May–June 1998). Storytelling helps us discover something new about the world. It allows us to pass that discovery on to others. And finally, it helps the people who share the story develop a common outlook. Orr found that war stories give the reps a shared framework for interpretation that allows them to collaborate even though the formal processes assume they are working independently.

Improvisation

Not all of the reps' problems can be solved over breakfast or by storytelling alone. Experimentation and improvisation are essential, too. One day, Orr observed a rep working with a particularly difficult machine. It had been installed recently, but it had never worked satisfactorily. Each time it failed, it produced a different error message. Following the established process for each particular message—replacing or adjusting parts—didn't fix the overall problem. And collectively the message made no sense.

Having reached his limits, the rep summoned a specialist. The specialist could not understand what was going on, either. So the two spent the afternoon cycling the machine again and again, waiting for its intermittent crashes and recording its state when it did. At the same time, they cycled stories about similar-looking problems round and round until they, too, crashed up against this particular machine. The afternoon resembled a series of alternating improvisational jazz solos, as each man took the lead, ran with it for a little while, then handed it off to the other, this all against the bass-line continuo of the rumbling machine.

In the course of this practice, the two gradually brought their separate ideas closer together toward a shared understanding of the machine. Eventually, late in the day, everything clicked. The machine's erratic behavior, the experience of the two technicians, and the stories they told finally formed a single, coherent account. They made sense of the machine and worked out how to fix it. And the solution quickly became part of the community lore, passed around for others in their group to use if they encountered the same problem.

As Orr's study shows, executives who want to identify and foster best practices must pay very close attention to the practices as they occur in reality rather than as they are represented in documentation or process designs. Otherwise, they will miss the tacit knowledge produced in improvisation, shared through storytelling, and embedded in the communities that form around those activities. Does that mean process has no importance in this context? Of course not. But the processes that support how people work should be deeply informed by how they already work—not imposed from above by process designers who imagine they understand the work better than they actually do. Armed with a sense of what really happens on the ground, it's possible to design processes that prompt improvisation rather than ones that are blindly prescriptive.

Spreading What You Know

People working in small groups develop very rich knowledge in practice, as we've seen. Assuming a company has correctly identified those practices and the tacit knowledge embedded within them, the question becomes: How can we spread that useful knowledge around? This is the point at which process becomes useful. Process—in the form of organizational coordination—can get that local knowledge into wider circulation.

Let's return to the Xerox reps. The group Orr studied included about a dozen people; the rep force worldwide currently numbers some 25,000. Locally generated fixes and insights circulated pretty efficiently within the small group but rarely made it beyond. So people in different groups spent time grappling with problems that had already been solved elsewhere. The reps as a whole still did not know what some reps, as a group, knew.

The far-flung communities that made up the entire network of reps needed some organizational support to help them share local knowledge around the world. So Xerox initiated the Eureka project to oversee the knowledge dissemination. The project set out to create a database to preserve resourceful ideas over time and deliver them over space.

Do we hear a yawn? Databases are the most basic of knowledge management tools. They're also among the most ignored. Organizations fill their databases with useful tips and data, and nobody uses them. Why should another be any different? The answer in this case is that it is different because of how the data are judged to be useful.

Most such databases, like most business processes, are top-down creations. Managers fill them with what they think will be useful for the people they manage. And—surprise, surprise—the people usually don't find them so. Yet even when individuals fill databases with their own ideas of what's useful, they aren't much help either, Often what one person thinks useful others find flaky, idiosyncratic, incoherent, redundant, or just plain stupid. The more a database contains everyone's favorite idea, the more unusable it becomes.

The Eureka database was designed to get past that problem by establishing a process to help capture best practices. Reps, not the organization, supply the tips. But reps also vet the tips. A reps submits a suggestion first to a local expert on the topic. Together, they refine the tip. It is then submitted to a centralized review process, organized according to business units. Here reps and engineers again vet the tips, accepting some, rejecting others, eliminating duplicates, and calling in experts on the particular product line to resolve doubts and disputes. If a tip survives this process, it becomes available to reps around the world, who have access to the tips database over the Web. So reps using the system know that the tips—and the database as a whole—are relevant, reliable, and probably not redundant.

It's interesting to compare this method of circulating knowledge with the established practices and formal processes of the scientific community. The two methods are quite similar. Scientists, too, work in small, local groups. To circulate their ideas more widely, they also put those ideas through a well-established process of peer review. If accepted, the ideas are then published for others to see.

Most scientists don't get paid for scientific articles. Good articles do, however, earn them status among their peers. They become known and respected for careful work, reliable results, and important insights. The reps have followed a similar course. The corporation offered to pay for the tips, but the pilot group of reps who helped design the system thought that would be a mistake, worrying, among other things, that payment for submissions would lead people to focus on quantity rather than quality in making submissions. Instead, the reps chose to have their names attached to tips. Those who submit good tips earn positive recognition. Because even good tips vary in quality, reps, like scientists, build social capital through the quality of their input. At a recent meeting of Xerox reps in Canada, one individual was surprised by a spontaneous standing ovation from co-workers who were expressing their respect for his tips. Of course, as in the scientific community, such recognition may also lead to career advancement. But it is important not to underestimate the value of social and intellectual capital within work-place communities—particularly those not usually recognized for their knowledge production.

The current Eureka database holds about 30,000 records. And its value is growing as it grows. In one case, an engineer in Brazil was about to replace a problematic high-end color machine (at a cost of about $40,000) for a disgruntled customer. Experimenting with a prototype of Eureka, he found a tip from a Montreal technician that led him to replace a defective 50 cent fuse instead. In all, Eureka is estimated to have saved the corporation $100 million.

Process and practice, then, do not represent rival views of the organization. Rather, they reflect the creative tension at the center of innovative organizations. In this, organizations resemble the well-known picture that, looked at once, appears to show a vase, but looked at once again, turns into two people, face-to-face. The vase resembles well-defined and precisely structured process—easy to understand though hard to change. The faces reflect practice—always unfolding in unpredictable ways, full of promise and problems, just like a conversation. The manager's challenge is to keep both images in view simultaneously.

So, to come back to where we began, the swing from business process reengineering to knowledge management did represent a radical shift in focus. But the goal for managers is not to choose between the two. Rather, the goal is to find the right balance between them—one that can grow only more important as knowledge becomes the factor that distinguishes the successful companies from the failures. Indeed, as dot-com companies mature, they're starting to search for seasoned managers who can provide their inventive, explosive communities of practice with the structure of process—but who won't suffocate practice while they are at it.

IV. KNOWLEDGE TRANSFER AND DISSEMINATION

10

Managing Knowledge the Chevron Way

Kenneth T. Derr

Of all the initiatives we've undertaken at Chevron during the 1990s, few have been as important or as rewarding as our efforts to build a learning organization by sharing and managing knowledge throughout our company.

In fact, I believe this priority was one of the keys to reducing our operating costs by more than $2 billion per year—from about $9.4 billion to $7.4 billion—over the last seven years.

Oil prices—adjusted for inflation—are now at their lowest levels since Woodrow Wilson was in the White House. Nevertheless, the long-term forecast for the global energy business is one of growth and opportunity. So Chevron has to further reduce its operating costs and at the same time, we have to sustain an aggressive capital-investment program.

That means we have to keep finding new and better ways to do things, and we have to apply new knowledge in all areas of our business, because both of these will be even more important for us in the years ahead. Sharing knowledge is no longer merely a performance issue. Today it's a reputation issue as well. And it directly affects every major company's ability to win new business and attract and keep top employees. The fact is, finding and applying new knowledge makes everyone's work more interesting and more challenging. Because of that, it also has the potential to make people's jobs more fulfilling and personally rewarding.

I want to talk more later about motivation. But first I would like to reflect briefly on a speech I gave in 1995 at a forum organized by the American Productivity and Quality Center. It was my first address on 'knowledge management,' which I think was just as hard to define back then as it is today.

At Chevron we emphasize instead the concept of 'the learning organization.' And let me read some words here from my last talk that say what this means for our company: 'We will create an organization that learns faster and better than competitors through benchmarking... through sharing and implementing best practices... by learning from experience... and through continuous individual learning and personal growth.'

Those words come from 'The Chevron Way,' which is a guiding set of objectives, principles, and values that define who we are, where we're going and how we need to interact and work with each other to get there. In one sense, 'The Chevron Way' is a learning tool to communicate and reinforce our values and goals as well as our years of experience in our business for all our employees, and especially those new to Chevron. It's a reference for what's essential to success—and again, building a learning organization is one of the most important.

The other thing I wanted to retain from my 1995 talk was some of our success stories. One is energy efficiency. Our six-year effort in this area has reduced energy costs by about $200 million a year compared to when we started. A big part of the savings has come from the systematic application—throughout our operations—of best practices for managing energy use.

We track that progress through an energy-efficiency index that's based on reports from each of our business units. And we have a network of practitioners who meet and hold regular conferences and who network through e-mail, an internal web site and a newsletter.

Another success story is how we manage our major capital projects. The oil and gas industry is very capital intensive just in 1999, we plan to invest over $5 billion. In 1991, a benchmarking study told us we were spending more than some of our competitors on big projects. So we combined best practices and internal know-how to create the Chevron Project Development & Execution Process, which in U.S. industry today is considered to be a world-class tool.

We've since identified hundreds of millions of dollars in project-cost savings since we started tracking the results of this process—in fact, it's probably higher—and that translates into a 10–15 percent improvement in capital efficiency. We've continued to improve that process and we've formed a central Project Resources group to help people use this tool companywide. They also support our community of project-management people all over the world.

The other story I've told before is the 'process masters' program in our network of U.S. oil refineries. These are seven full-time experts who support Best Practice Teams covering the major, high-cost functions common to all six plants—ranging from catalytic cracking to plant maintenance. The refineries have a lot of other networks called 'natural teams'—that is, employees who work in best-practice groups as part of their regular jobs. And the mix of these and the process masters program has distinguished our U.S. refining operations for the systematic sharing of both internal and external best practices.

In those three cases, the impact on business results has been both measurable and significant. And during the 1990s, these kinds of efforts have been essential to reducing our costs, to achieving a productivity gain of over 30 percent (in terms of barrels of output per employee) and to improving employee safety performance more than 50 percent.

Protecting people and the environment has always been a priority, for obvious reasons—and we spell that out extensively in 'The Chevron Way.' But a safer workplace also boosts morale, and that pays off in productivity. Also, because incidents cost the oil industry billions of dollars each year, safety has become recognized as a financial issue as well. Every gain not only protects people and the natural world, it helps the bottom line in a very real sense.

I'd like now to give you a little better idea of the range of things we're doing at Chevron—and I hope these examples will be useful in your own pursuit of best practices.

In gasoline, we're transforming a traditional area of our company by applying new retail concepts supported by the tools of e-commerce. We call it the Chevron Retailer Alliance, and it shows what can happen when a business starts to evolve into a true learning organization. Gasoline and convenience retailing are extremely competitive, with a rapid rate of change and innovation. You can't survive if you don't use best practices. Thirty years ago it was car washes. Now it's pump-card readers.

But it's not enough to keep up. You have to use knowledge as a platform for continuous innovation. So we asked ourselves how we could get the greatest value from our network of 8,000 retail sites. Ultimately, we combined experience, creativity, and ideas from all kinds of businesses and people to invent a superior way to manage brand image, gasoline supplies, and convenience-store retailing. Among other things, we plan to leverage the full buying power of our network, and streamline the ordering and distribution system. Internet technology is making a lot of this possible, and tracking these online exchanges will give us a steady flow of new knowledge to help redefine our relationships with our retailers throughout the country.

At the other end of our business—in international oil and gas—we've been benchmarking our costs for drilling oil and gas wells internally, every year, for more than 10 years, and we started external benchmarking in 1992. We've used the data between locations—West Africa, Australia, Kazakhstan, China and the rest—to improve drilling performance around the globe. Last year's external study showed we were an industry leader on the basis of cost-per-foot drilled.

However, the most exciting new example in oil-and-gas has been our adoption of an 'organizational learning system' or 'O.L.S.' Basically, it provides a map for planning, execution, and evaluation of ongoing work. In drilling, it uses a simple software tool to capture lessons from the first wells in a new area, and then it helps you use that knowledge to drill the rest of the wells faster and cheaper. We've seen well costs drop by 12–20 percent and cycle time reduced as much as 40 percent in some cases—and that really adds up with big offshore drilling vessels that cost up to $250,000 a day.

But we didn't invent the O.L.S. It came from Oil & Gas Consultants International who developed it with Amoco and later verified a model by working with the Gas Research Institute. Chevron didn't fully appreciate the potential of the O.L.S. until after we learned more about it from a group we formed in 1996 with Mobil, BP, and Texaco to share best practices in technology. That group eventually funded a special study of the O.L.S.—and later, the group proved the value of the O.L.S. by conducting a pilot project on Chevron's oil development in Papua New Guinea. Now Chevron uses O.L.S. to manage key elements of our deep-water exploration and development in the Gulf of Mexico. And, as of January first, we've added an O.L.S. specialist to our Project Resources group to help other Chevron organizations make use of this new tool.

Earlier, I mentioned best-practice sharing in our refineries. Hurricane Georges damaged our Mississippi refinery so badly that we had to shut it down for more than two months. To keep customers supplied, we had to go out and buy replacement fuels—and that cost us a great deal of money. As crews worked to restart the refinery, they found a blockage in a sulfur unit. Using their best-practice network, they got solid advice based on both inside and outside expertise. Within days, they had a cost-effective way to fix the problem—and they updated the unit with new technology at the same time. The point is, if you add up all the small things we do better today because of sharing, what you get is a big impact.

Not far away, offshore in the Gulf of Mexico, another group has combined the process-masters concept from our refineries with some best practices from Union Pacific Resources to create a new program they call 'technology brokers.' And now six employees work full time in these new jobs, searching for best practices in offshore oil and gas operations.

This is already paying off—again—in the area of drilling. The typical oil or gas well is about as wide as a dinner plate and thousands of feet deep. Just getting in and out of the hole takes a great deal of time and money. Now we've found a one-step way to do two separate but essential operations at the bottom of the wells. What once took five days and two trips down the well now takes a day and a half and a single trip. After just 10 wells, we've logged over $2 million in savings compared to the old method.

We used to emphasize large, in-house R&D organizations and internal invention of tools and methods. But we decided several years ago that it's more cost effective to invest less in that approach—and invest more in finding and integrating technology from a diverse set of suppliers from the larger world, particularly the networked world.

I have more Chevron stories than I can tell all at once, but I'd like to add a few more. I was very pleased, for example, when our human resources organization adapted best practices from companies like Bechtel and TRW to set up a new process to reduce conflict in disputes between individual employees and the company. Among other benefits, we hope it will help us find fair solutions before things get to the lawsuit stage.

Meanwhile, in community relations, the Chevron Best Classroom Practices program has captured innovative ways to teach math, science, and technology from a dozen great teachers. And we've put their lesson plans on our Internet site—*www.chevron.com*—so than any teacher can take advantage of them.

Also last year, we created the Chevron Environmental Management Company. Our environmental remediation work used to be done by separate groups scattered around different locations. But this new unit will share the know-how and experience of the whole company, with a goal to reduce remediation costs by at least 15 percent.

Also, I mentioned in my 1995 talk that we use in-house conferences as a knowledge-sharing tool. We still hold these, for example, to energize our project-management network and our supplier quality improvement network.

Also last year, we held our first conference to exchange ideas on valuing and promoting diversity. It was a great event, and a very satisfying outgrowth of our efforts to stress the importance of diversity to our business.

In many ways, diversity is a learning-organization issue. It teaches us to seek the full range of skills, ideas, and perspectives in our workforce, and it helps us make sure we try to build a workforce that will improve that range.

But the standout conference over the years has been the Chevron Chemical Quality Conference, now supported by its own intranet site. We often describe our chemical company as the birthplace of quality at Chevron, so they've set a high standard for sharing knowledge.

Right now, for example, they're managing four Vision Objective Teams based on sharing best practices and promoting standard work processes in the areas of plant management, marketing, technology planning, and supply-chain management.

I can't cover all those here, but our best-practices newsletter recently reported that the plant-management team had achieved a plant-reliability level of 100 percent in 1998, compared to about 85 percent in the prior year.

One last point on events. In January 1999, we'll hold our first conference on cogeneration facilities. We operate seven of these energy plants at a cost of about $100 million a year, so we want to take a closer look at them. But what's most important about this example is that we probably never would have thought to hold this conference if we hadn't first created our larger energy network six years ago to swap ideas on reducing energy costs.

I hope those additional stories give you a better idea of the breadth of our efforts in managing knowledge. However, probably nothing we've done recently can compare to the rollout of our new Global Information Link (GIL). In 1998, we replaced every PC in the company with a common machine, software and connective system, creating a single desktop and operating environment, worldwide. This was a huge undertaking—about 30,000 computers, with full intranet capability and Internet access for those who need it, advanced e-mail, scheduling and presentation tools—the whole works.

And I think it's worth mentioning here that we used our own Chevron project-management process—which I described earlier—to implement this massive change. We did it in just one year, where similar overhauls have taken as long as four years. And in addition to the networking benefits, we believe GIL is going to save us about $40 million a year in system-management costs.

These information technology tools weren't new to us, of course. What's new is having them all standardized, compatible, and connected. What's new is that now, essentially every employee has an identical—and very friendly—'sharing machine' on their desktop.

GIL has also supercharged the already rapid growth in the scope and usage of our intranet. We now have a wide range of internal sites, from best practices, to environmental, to the company home page and the individual sites of the subsidiaries and departments.

Of course, employees need to have good reasons to share knowledge, so let me turn now to the issue of motivation. Obviously, the CEO has a major responsibility here. So I talk about sharing best practices when I speak to employees. I ask top people from companies like HP, Motorola, and G.E. to speak at our monthly Management Committee meetings. And those meetings are also a forum for Chevron teams to tell their success stories in using knowledge to improve operations and results.

Beyond that, I think the formula for continuous improvement is fairly simple. You need clear objectives, the opportunity to share rewards and an empowered workforce.

An objective can be a financial goal, or a production target—whatever is important. In our case, providing data on the business performance of our closest competitors—and then setting a goal to do better—has been a simple but powerful tool for improving performance. People really seem to respond to the simple fact that somebody else is doing things better.

Goals aren't a new concept. But they work because they give people a compelling reason to find better solutions. Recently, I challenged our project management specialists to shave an additional 10 percent off our project costs in 1999. And last month—because of oil prices—we launched a $500 million cost-reduction plan to advance beyond the $2 billion in savings we've already achieved in the 1990s. A lot of the new gains will have to come from finding better ways to do our business.

As for sharing rewards, our Success Sharing bonus program is based partly on corporate earnings, partly on competitors' earnings, and partly on safety and operating costs. The bonus can be as much as 8 percent of pay. More recently, we started giving stock options to all of our people to connect them more directly to our financial performance. Of course, sharing rewards isn't managing knowledge—it just gives everyone another good reason to do it, and I don't think you can have one without the other.

Lastly—on empowerment—again, it's not rocket science. Delegating authority helps people feel ownership for their work and give their best to the organization. Of course, this is hard to measure, but not impossible. In our annual Worldwide Employee Survey, for example, we try to track feelings of commitment to the company. The latest results show a 15 percent improvement in recent years, partly because people are feeling more empowered in their work. That's the kind of thing you want to hear, of course. But there are some related issues here that I'd like next to discuss briefly.

My talk to the APQC in 1996 was titled 'Managing Knowledge in a Decentralized Learning Environment.' At the time, we felt that our focus on delegation, decentralization—and our shift to strategic business units—might create new barriers to sharing. I raise this because I suspect other companies probably struggle with this same issue.

Like others, we're sold on the merits of the decentralized model of management. It's really the only way you can manage a global company the size of Chevron. So we just have to work harder to make sure the right people connect and share knowledge across the geographic and organizational boundaries of our company.

Decentralized companies—especially global companies—will always be challenged to achieve uniform performance in sharing knowledge just as they are in other areas. We see this in our performance metrics, with differences of 20–30 percent between organizations in many key areas. Of course, the comparisons are useful. But the key is to view the differences as opportunities rather than deficiencies. Replacing less-effective ways to work with better ways is what people in a learning organization are supposed to do, and frankly, I think you gain more from encouraging those behaviors than you do by trying to correct differences in performance.

The other point about decentralized companies is that instead of one good way of working, we have dozens. Instead of one incubator for new ideas, we have hundreds. Of course, you still want to standardize the most important work processes. But at the same time, you don't want uniformity to undermine the potential for creativity. The fact is, you can have both—as long as you recognize that company structure can sometimes raise some pretty significant barriers to sharing knowledge.

Recently, we asked Jerry Moffitt—who coordinates our energy-efficiency network—to reflect on his program. Even though it has been a great success, it wasn't surprising to learn that he believes there's still some low-hanging fruit out there that we haven't taken advantage of—and I'm sure he's right. Jerry also said that we need to start stretching higher and looking harder so we can harvest the opportunities that we haven't seen yet. And after that, we're going to have to get ourselves a ladder and reach even higher.

But Jerry also said we should remember that looking for better ideas is only one of many jobs that command the attention of employees. This is a critical issue. Most of us are working in downsized situations, trying to do more with fewer resources. Still, the only way to know if we're performing at a bench-mark level is to test that assumption by looking inside and outside for new solutions. This is why we're going to need our knowledge-sharing advocates to generate enthusiasm. We're going to need the process masters and technology brokers and cross-pollinators—like Jerry—to help people embrace this priority.

There are some other basic things we can do at Chevron to make sure we keep the momentum going. We can keep working on our culture to promote individual and organizational learning, because we're convinced this can help give us a competitive advantage. After all, that's what it's all about. This is especially important for management. We need more of our leaders to model and reinforce the right cultural behaviors. And I might mention here that one way to help achieve that is to promote people who excel at learning-organization behaviors.

We can also make better use of our supplement to 'The Chevron Way,' which spells out specific behaviors for leading a learning organization, such as networking... and investing in training. We can try to emphasize learning from mistakes rather than laying blame. And to help drive out the 'not-invented-here' syndrome, we can recognize and reward people more for using best practices from the outside.

We can keep telling our story in our town-hall meetings, in company publications, and through our intranet. That should stimulate more grassroots activity, where employees with similar jobs—no matter where they work—will use our Global Information Link to take the initiative and start networking and sharing best practices. And to help make that happen, we're going to expand the availability and use of web-based tools for sharing and managing knowledge.

At the same time, we're going to keep the emphasis on the strategic and capital-intensive areas of our businesslike project management, energy efficiency, and deep-water oil development, because that's where the biggest payoffs are waiting to be found.

I mentioned earlier the talk I gave in 1995, and one of the things I did was hold up a copy of our Chevron Best Practice Resource Map. It was kind of like a snapshot of that point in our development, showing dozens of networks such as maintenance, safety, and strategic planning—all kinds of functional areas—with contact names and numbers, and how often they meet, and all color-coded according to the Baldrige categories.

The map is out of print now. It has become sort of a collector's item around the company, and in fact I keep one on my desk, even though we've since replaced it with an online version that's easier to update and more easily available to employees worldwide. But I bring up the map because it was one of the first things that got Chevron noticed in the area of managing knowledge—it made us more aware of ourselves in this area.

More recently, Carla O'Dell—the APQC's president, who will speak here tomorrow—was kind enough to mention our company in her new book on knowledge management. And last fall, in a study cosponsored by the *Journal of Knowledge Management*, we were named one of the Top 20 'most admired knowledge enterprises.'

Certainly, we're proud that others have noticed our past progress. But the real value of that recognition is that it helps make us want to *remain* an admired knowledge enterprise—and that's not going to be easy. Yesterday's learning curve has become today's race track and that means building a superior learning organization is now a necessity for any company that wants to be a top competitor.

11 Getting It Right the Second Time

Gabriel Szulanski and Sidney Winter

Once a business is doing a good job performing a complex activity—managing a branch bank, say, or selling a new product—the parent organization naturally wants to replicate that initial success. Indeed, one of the main reasons for being a big company rather than a small one is to capture on a grand scale the gains that come with applying smart processes and routines.

Yet getting it right the second time is surprisingly difficult. Whole industries are trying to replicate best practices and manage organizational knowledge— but even so, the overwhelming majority of attempts to replicate excellence fail. A slew of studies has confirmed this uncomfortable fact. One found that only 12 percent of senior executives are happy with how their organizations share knowledge internally. Another found that companies invariably have more trouble than they anticipate transferring capabilities between units.[1] Anecdotal evidence suggests that chief knowledge officers and chief information officers—the senior executives charged with exploiting knowledge assets—are also failing to get the job done. From all reports, these executives come and go extraordinarily quickly.

The reason for this dismal state of affairs? In reality, the underlying problem has more to do with attitude than it does with the inherent difficulty of the task (although the task is not easy). People approach best-practice replication with the optimism and overconfidence of a neophyte stock trader out to beat the market. They try, for example, to go one better than an operation that's up and running nearly flawlessly. Or they try to piece together the best parts of a number of different practices, in hopes of creating the perfect hybrid. They assume, usually incorrectly, that the people running best-practice operations fully understand what makes them successful. As a result of this general overoptimism, people attempting to replicate a best practice are nowhere nearly as disciplined as they need to be.

There's a better way to get it right the second time (and the third, and the fourth, and the fifth). It involves adjusting attitudes, first of all, and then imposing strict discipline on the process and the organization. In this article, we'll describe in detail what goes wrong with best-practice replication and then we'll suggest principles to help managers harvest the knowledge developed so painstakingly in their organizations.

What Goes Wrong

Before we plunge in, we should note that we're talking about a particular kind of knowledge transfer: the kind that happens when one group is engaged in a complex, systematized activity that produces good results and another group attempts to reproduce those results. The goal is to capture and leverage existing knowledge and *not* to generate new knowledge. This kind of activity is less glamorous than pure innovation—and it's also far more common in every kind of business. In the course of researching this subject, we studied a wide range of business settings: branch banks, retail stores, real estate franchises, factories, and call centers, to name a few. Such enterprises all need to be able to reproduce successful organizational routines in new settings. In fact, we'd be hard pressed to name a medium- to large-sized business that doesn't need to replicate its own best practices.

Managers who want to leverage knowledge in this way typically start by doing one of two things. Sometimes they go straight to an expert source—say, the person who designed and runs a best-practice call center—and pick her brain. They ask what she did at the start, why she did it, what problems have cropped up along the way, why the operation works as well as it does now, and so forth. Alternatively, managers consult documentation covering the same territory that has been put together by one or more expert sources. This information is often available on intranets. Both approaches can be used to gain a rough understanding of a particular system or to obtain insight into smaller, isolated problems. But if you use only these methods to try to gain a deep, rich understanding of the knowledge implicit in a complex organizational system, you'll run into real problems. When it comes to complex system, we found that no single expert fully grasps, and no set of documents fully captures, the subtle ways in which individual components are interwoven with one another.

The expert source's ignorance—of which she's generally unaware—can take a number of forms. Many details of the system are inevitably invisible to her.

Some may be known to individual workers but not shared with higher-ups. Others may be tacit—learned on the job and well known but impossible to describe in a way that is helpful. Some may be secrets undisclosed because they make individual workers' jobs easier or because they run counter to an organization's formal work rules. Some represent 'learning without awareness,' adjustments that people make without being aware that they've made them. For example, hearing fluid moving through pipes may be a cue, not consciously recognized, that a process is operating correctly. Other unacknowledged characteristics may be hidden contextual factors related to, say, the design of equipment or even prevailing weather conditions.

Documents suffer from similar shortcomings. Information can be incomplete, fragmented, distorted in subtle ways, and insufficiently attuned to the nuances and inter-dependencies of complex processes. In addition, when many documents are involved, the information is frequently contradictory. Individual sources contain unique perspectives that reflect differing jobs, responsibilities, and assumptions.

Placing too much trust in experts and documents is the first big mistake organizations can make when trying to replicate best practices. The second can occur when a manager actually starts to set up the new process: He turns into a cowboy. He forgets that he's trying to replicate something and immediately starts trying to improve upon it. These 'improvements' can take many forms. The manager might cherry-pick parts of a process: The folks in our Singapore plant do a terrific job controlling mask placement, for example, but the US factories have radically improved stepper alignment, so why not combine these improvements to have the best of both worlds? Or maybe he tinkers with the process: He came from a doughnut franchise, perhaps, and he's pretty sure that bagels can sell faster if customers wait for service in several lines rather than just one. Or he might try to customize the process prematurely; managers can only rarely predict correctly which aspects of retail operations will need to be adjusted in new locales—but they usually go right ahead and try anyway.

These attempts to improve the process usually turn out to be misguided. The perceived advantages may be illusory because they are based on inaccurate information or an imperfect analogy between two business settings. More typically, the advantages are real enough, but attendant disadvantages have been overlooked: The changes may compromise safety, for example, or they may create nonobvious interactions within the system. Very commonly, the effects of disadvantages spread out through various parts of the system and go unnoticed because they are small individually but significant in the aggregate.

The people who are trying to get it right the second time—like the expert sources they consult—overestimate how much they know and are

---

A Little Knowledge Is a Dangerous Thing

Behavioral researchers studying decision-making have documented a general tendency for human beings to be both overoptimistic (expecting things to turn out better than they actually do, on average) and overconfident (overestimating the quality of their own knowledge and skills). If you ask students how well they'll do on an exam, for example, most guess that their own performance will be above average. Researchers obtain similar results when they ask about the likelihood that people will contract a disease, earn high salaries in the future, and so forth.

There is analogous evidence relating specifically to overconfidence about causal understanding. As long as things work, people tend to style themselves as experts on *why* they work. And when something goes wrong, they tend to seize on the first plausible contextual explanation that presents itself—even though other explanations no less reasonable than the first may exist. When people try to explain a disaster after the fact (an accident in a nuclear power plant, for example), they are typically under pressure to name a relatively simple cause so that existing policies can be revised to prevent similar events in the future.

Much of what we've observed seems to fall into the pattern of these research findings. People running a successful practice overestimate their understanding of it, so they unintentionally provide misinformation to managers trying to replicate the practice. When something in the process goes wrong, a diagnosis can occur too quickly and a variety of factors in play may get overlooked. And when people are trying to replicate success, they may rely too much on their own understanding of its causes and cheerfully expect that a system modified according to that understanding will deliver results that are as good as or better than the original.

For a review of overconfidence in decision-making, see R. Nisbett and L. Ross, *Human Inference: Strategies and Shortcomings of Social Judgment* (Prentice Hall 1980). About the tendency to simplify causation, see Charles Perrow, *Normal Accidents: Living with High-Risk Technologies* (Princeton University Press 1999), and J. S. Carroll, 'Organizational Learning Activities in High-Hazard Industries: The Logics Underlying Self-Analysis,' *Journal of Management Studies*, 1998. Studies about optimism include F. P. McKenna, 'It Won't Happen to Me: Unrealistic Optimism or Illusion of Control?' *British Journal of Psychology*, 1993, and N. D. Weinstein, 'Unrealistic Optimism About Future Life Events,' *Journal of Personality and Social Psychology*, 1980.

over-optimistic about their chances for success. (See the sidebar 'A Little Knowledge Is a Dangerous Thing' for more about this phenomenon.) In some managerial contexts, of course, overconfidence and overoptimism are great things. But in the context of best-practice replication, they're big trouble.

Recasting Best Practice

To surmount these difficulties, we propose that you do two things differently. First, don't look to experts or documentation for a complete understanding of any complex activity. Instead, look to the ongoing activity itself. That's not to say you shouldn't consult experts—you should and you must. But don't fool yourself into thinking they hold the keys to the kingdom. You're much better off looking to a working template; it's the only thing that will provide a coherent, comprehensive illustration of the knowledge you're trying to leverage. Secondly, when you look directly at that activity, don't assume that you'll fully understand what makes it work any better than the experts. Adjust for your own overconfidence.

Practically speaking, these suggestions have one implication: You should copy the template as closely as you can. In reality, perfect replication can never be expected, but closely copying a template gives you three advantages. First, you know it's possible to succeed, because there's a successful example in front of you. Second, you have a clear objective: to create a replica. Importantly, that replica includes performance measures that will tell you if you've succeeded. Third, you have a built-in tactical approach: Copy the working example *in detail*. This means not merely duplicating the physical characteristics of plant and equipment but also duplicating the skill sets of employees and the practices they follow. Reliance on a template offers the huge advantage of built-in coherence; the replica will be coherent because the template itself already is. This approach allows you to copy quite complex organizations: Close copying of pieces that fit together will produce pieces—and ultimately subsystems— that can be fitted together with minimal troubleshooting.

Banc One (now Bank One) is a good example of the approach we recommend. During the 1980s and early 1990s, the bank became extraordinarily good at converting acquired banks and their branches over to its own systems. (Indeed, it was this capability that drove its unprecedented success in this period.) To operate within the Banc One family, branches and back offices needed common operating procedures. One tool the bank used to disseminate operating knowledge was traditional documentation, such as procedural guidelines and flowcharts that gave certain employees instructions for handling commercial loans, installment loans, money orders, and food stamps. Similarly, it provided other employees with instructions about how to open new savings accounts, make loans, and sell stocks and treasury notes. These codified procedures supported and complemented the in-depth training given to personnel in the acquired banks and remained in place until the staff could comfortably operate the new systems on their own. Trainers were experienced in the actual use of the systems in other bank branches. Thus, Banc One extensively used both people and documents to transfer knowledge.

But it did much more. It also selected a sister bank to provide staff in the new bank or branch with a model for the postconversion operating environment. Typically, a sister bank had recently converted to a similar set of products and systems and served similar types of customers. The new staff could visit the sister bank to see how it operated. Having a living template helped the new bank make conversion-related decisions with more confidence. There were still plenty of judgment calls about how to realign operating units, for example, despite the many operating procedures provided. A sister bank that had already

---

Copying Starbucks

As he tells the story in his autobiography,[1] Starbucks chairman Howard Schultz founded Il Giornale, the store that eventually morphed into Starbucks, because he wanted to recreate the Italian espresso-bar experience. Schultz was paranoid about any detail that would undermine the authenticity of the experience. Only Italian opera could play over the loudspeakers. The servers had to wear bow ties. There were no chairs—just a stand-up bar. Schultz vowed that he would never offer nonfat milk; the mere mention of it was tantamount to treason. Menus were sprinkled with Italian words. The decor was as Italian as he could make it. In short, Schultz transplanted all the details he deemed essential to the Italian coffee-bar experience.

He and his colleagues gradually realized that many of the coffee bar details didn't work well in Seattle. Customers complained about the opera. Employees complained about the bow ties. People wanted chairs so that they could sit and read newspapers. So the entrepreneurs started to adapt the store to their customers' needs. They fixed some things easily—they added chairs and changed the music. Nonfat milk even found its way onto the menu. But Schultz was careful, even early on, not to make too many compromises or changes. Gradually, a US version of the Italian-style coffee bar emerged. It was substantially different from the original store, but it retained some Italian flair and developed a unique flavor all its own.

Now Starbucks is expanding internationally. As an exercise in knowledge transfer, we ask our students: How would you advise Schultz to proceed with the expansion? We get them to list everything they can remember about Starbucks stores and fill several pages on a flip chart with their responses. Then we ask, Which details are fundamental to the concept of Starbucks? Which can be safely adjusted? We don't know the answers to these questions; probably Schultz doesn't, either. But he'd do well to remember his own early approach—copy exactly. When McDonald's first attempted to adapt itself to foreign markets, the results were disastrous. The company concluded that it would be easier to change a country than to change the McDonald's system. So it faithfully copied all the processes and then just made small modifications to the menus.

Our students, like many managers, start out thinking they know exactly what's essential and what isn't. Eventually, they recognize the truth: They can never know for sure precisely what makes a Starbucks a Starbucks.

[1] Howard Schultz and Dori Jones Yang, *Pour Your Heart into It: How Starbucks Built a Company One Cup at a Time* (Hyperion 1997).

---

made these calls could point the acquired bank's managers in the right direction. The sister bank relationship also reduced the likelihood that the new bank would repeat avoidable errors. If the sister bank's employees had resisted the shift from in-house to centralized processing, for example, the acquired bank's managers could use that information to anticipate the problem and circumvent it through superior internal communication.

In addition, Banc One developed a different sort of template in the form of a 'model' bank located close to its headquarters. The model was a functioning laboratory that replicated a retail bank's front and back offices, with all the latest corporate standards, operating procedures, and work flows implemented just as in the branches and sister banks. Every new system was incorporated into the model bank. The model bank complemented the sister banks before, during, and after conversions occurred.

Close copying isn't simply the best way to reproduce good results. It can also create a competitive advantage. For example, franchises, more than any other type of business, pretend to be very good at exact replication of successful models. Not all of them actually are, but the ones that do deliver on that promise generally gain a competitive edge. As the CEO of Re/Max Israel's real estate franchise network reflects: 'Our competitors charge half what we do, and we sell more franchises than all our competitors put together. I attribute a good part of our success to the fact that I was wise enough to understand that I was purchasing a lot of wisdom.' When the CEO first opened franchise offices in Israel, he didn't fully comprehend the reason for many of Re/Max's processes—but he followed them to the letter nonetheless, figuring that as he learned the business, their purpose would become clearer.

Guidelines for Success

Defining the activity itself as the authoritative source of knowledge, and then copying it closely, works best if several guidelines are followed.

Make Sure You Have Got Something that Can be Copied and that Is Worth Copying

Some processes work for idiosyncratic reasons and cannot be copied. The most common of these: a great manager or a group that's worked together well for years. Obviously, the person or group can't be broken down into component parts and cloned, so it's always worth asking, Is this something we can copy? We should note, however, that successful people often believe that their unique gifts are what make something work; a close observer might come to a different conclusion.

Some processes can be copied but maybe shouldn't be. Think about whether an activity or process might have a better reputation than it deserves. Perhaps it has a charismatic champion, or perhaps the group performing the activity delivered great results one year due mostly to luck. Before an activity is held up as an exemplar, someone with a clear head needs to answer a few basic questions: Does this activity have a track record? Is it really important enough to copy? Is it a detailed example of what we're trying to achieve? If we merely replicate its results, will that be good enough for us?

Work from a Single, Active Template

Having a living template is important for a number of reasons already noted: It provides managers with proof that success is possible, performance measurements that define success, a tactical approach to achieve success, and something to refer back to when the copy falls short. Having a *single* template matters just as much. Indeed, there's really no such thing as a best-of-the-best template.

Rank Xerox, previously the European arm of Xerox Corporation, learned the importance of having a single, active template several years ago. In 1994, Rank Xerox selected nine best sales practices. It designated 'benchmark country business units,' country operations that provided working examples and served as concrete illustrations. If you wanted to know how to sell DocuTech color copiers, for example, you went to Switzerland and learned. If you wanted to know how to retain major accounts, you went to Spain or Portugal. Taken as a whole, this initiative—referred to as Wave I—was a resounding success. It contributed $200 million in incremental revenue to the bottom line of this $4 billion company and achieved 133% of the established goal, at the nominal cost of $1 million.

Based on this extraordinary performance, Rank Xerox launched an even more ambitious initiative—known as Wave II—to leverage a computer-assisted sales management process. In this case, the two units that could have served as templates were located in countries from which best practices were not easily accepted. To work around potential skepticism, the practices were presented as if they had resulted from a combination of modules, taken from different countries, that added up to the desired activity. The hope was that this best-of-the-best approach would forestall political opposition. It did, but at a high cost. Country units did pay attention, but they had no working example that demonstrated feasibility or provided guidance. They had a poorly defined sense of what was expected and how to proceed. The absence of a template was fatal to Wave II; implementation efforts were universally abandoned before they had seriously begun.

Copy as Closely as You Can

Eventually, many complex activities that are copied need to be adapted. If you anticipate some of these changes, why not adapt immediately? The short answer is that the wisdom embedded in complex practices—that is, the complexity of the many problems already faced and addressed by those who developed the template—may not be apparent right away. Thus, it makes sense to demonstrate that you can obtain decent results before you introduce changes.

Intel, working with that philosophy, developed its 'Copy Exactly!' method to transfer semiconductor manufacturing know-how from the first factory that produces a particular device to subsequent ones.[2] This method was introduced because the company hoped that the effectiveness of its knowledge transfer could be improved by an order of magnitude. It replaced the then prevailing approach called 'Process Output Matching,' which had allowed engineers to selectively copy what they thought would be useful and simultaneously to introduce changes, like incorporating the latest-model equipment, for example.

Simply put, the Copy Exactly! philosophy means that any potential contributing factor to the process, in all its specificity, must be copied in minute detail, unless it's not physically possible to do so or unless the competitive benefits of introducing a change override the imperative for precise replication. For example, a request to use a differently configured pump, which also produces the desired pressure, is met with a stern reply that it's crucial to use the same components and that changes are not allowed. Occasional adaptations do occur, to be sure—but there's a strong bias against adaptation, and they occur far less frequently than they did in the days of Process Output Matching.

Implementing Copy Exactly! is a complex, multilevel process. First, physical inputs to production must be shown to have been correctly copied; next, process outcomes are matched; and finally, the product itself is proven to be up to standard. Tests at each level must be passed before moving on to the next level. If a test fails, the root cause must be found and eliminated before moving to the next step. If the root cause can't be located, troubleshooting occurs to determine which of the previous inputs is responsible. Managers must resist the temptation to solve problems by making adjustments not found in the tem-

---

Barriers to Success

An organization can employ people or create a climate that facilitates best-practice replication—or that does the reverse. Typical barriers include the following.

Uncooperative sources. If the people responsible for an existing best practice don't want to help others, it's unlikely that their success will be repeated.

Strained personal relationships. If the manager attempting to replicate the practice has a difficult relationship with expert sources, successful transfer is unlikely to occur.

Internal competition If an organization actively discourages cooperation by pitting units against one another, no one has an incentive to copy or to be copied from.

Overemphasis on innovation. If an organization idealizes innovation and scoffs at copying, replication won't happen.

Cranky copiers. If the managers charged with replicating a best practice are temperamentally unsuited to absorbing new knowledge, afraid to change, or excessively focused on preserving their own status, they'll probably fail.

If several of these barriers exist, a person who's supposed to copy a best practice is practically pushed into being a cowboy and trying to improve on the template. Of course he'll make it up as he goes along—the organization's making it too hard to act any other way.

---

plate. Yielding to such temptation usually creates more difficult problems down the road. Exact replication facilitates rapid diagnosis and problem solving because employees have previously attended so carefully to the detailed implementation of individual activities or components.

The importance of preserving each element in its given form increases when there is uncertainty about how a departure from the original form will affect performance. When skills are complex, a small departure from an established way of doing things may have dire consequences. Such departures are typically mistakes, often already encountered by the original developers, that may yield valuable lessons but are not worth repeating. Occasionally, a small departure can be devastating.

The Copy Exactly! policy has been a resounding success and has brought about dramatic improvements in transfer effectiveness. Intel is now able to open new factories with yield, quality, reliability, and efficiency comparable to those of the template—beginning on the first day of production. In the past, each new facility had to repeat much of the same learning curve independently and usually took several months to catch up.

Adapt Only after You Achieve Acceptable Results

At Intel, once a new product meets acceptable performance standards, the production line engineers earn the right to make improvements. At Rank Xerox, as the UK director explained in 1997, 'We now only allow a business to adapt a model process if and when it has raised its performance to the same level of the benchmark unit.' Reflecting the thinking of a company whose main business is seen as the management of documents, he continued, 'We lost a lot of best practices because people edited them before implementing them.' Similarly, the Great Harvest Bread Company explains to new franchisees that there are no acceptable reasons for diverging from the operating manual—and makes them agree to adhere to the 'tiniest letter' of its instructions—for a year. Then, they've earned their freedom. A lot of adaptation and incremental innovation can be built on a platform of existing knowledge; the key is to be sure the platform is solid.

Keep the Template in Mind even after You Create the Replica

There is no such thing as a perfect copy of a complex organizational activity. Communication gaps between the original process and its replica are almost guaranteed to occur, so being able to refer to the template will serve you well when problems arise. The quality of a specific performance also depends on the nature and quality of the people involved. Demographic and cultural differences often challenge the effort to achieve a close match. Finally, you may miss some aspects of the template activity altogether, at least at first.

Other changes are deliberate and necessary. For example, it's nearly impossible to take a complicated process across country borders without making some changes, and companies that try set themselves up to fail. Wal-Mart's decision to enter Argentina with the same basic US store model, disregarding local idiosyncrasies (a decision since reversed), is a dramatic example of such a situation. The new enterprise didn't stock the kinds of meat Argentineans eat, the kinds of cosmetics they like to wear, or even appliances wired with the 220-volt power that's standard in Argentina. Slavish copying of the home-market model probably won't work across borders.

Since imperfections in attempted copying are inevitable and judgment calls about what to copy may at times be inescapable, there's a fair possibility that the replica will not work well—or perhaps at all—on the first try. That's why it's important to have the working example to return to. The template can be used to identify existing problems and to debug the replica. Thus, at least for part of the knowledge leveraging process, there is a time when the working example is needed as a reference, before it can be dispensed with.

A note of caution. When an attempt to leverage knowledge that appeared to be going well fails, it's usually because the working template is no longer being referred to, or adaptations were introduced too early, or both. When something goes wrong—as it often does—you need to be able to retrace your steps and figure out what happened. 'Look for discrepancies' is the guiding principle for problem solving. If you can't identify discrepancies—either because the template is no longer available or because you've introduced adaptations promiscuously—then you'll have to make larger efforts to solve the problem. Other potential causes for failure may reside within your organizational climate; some of these are highlighted in the sidebar 'Barriers to Success.'

Far more often than they realize, managers have to decide whether they want to leverage existing knowledge or create new knowledge. If they choose to leverage knowledge, exact replication is the way to go; there is limited leeway for modification. If they choose to innovate, they modify, they adapt—maybe they even invent a whole process. It is impossible to do both simultaneously to the extent that most people seem to imagine, particularly in the context of a single project.

Leveraging knowledge means using what others have already learned, with effort and sometimes with pain, through experience and mistakes. When managers leverage knowledge, they stand on the shoulders of giants. The poor track record of knowledge reuse—and the importance that replication plays in most companies' bottom lines—suggests that effective copying is not a trivial achievement but rather a challenging, admirable accomplishment. In suggesting that managers approach institutional knowledge with humility and respect, we're hoping that they acknowledge the careful creation done by their predecessors and that they be realistic about their own efforts. Indeed, managing to get up on the shoulders of giants appears to be an achievement all by itself.

Notes

1. For knowledge sharing, see R. Ruggles, 'The State of the Notion: Knowledge Management in Practice,' *California Management Review,* 1998. Regarding transfer capabilities, see C. S. Galbraith, 'Transferring Core Manufacturing Technologies in High-Technology Firms,' *California Management Review,* 1990.
2. Our discussion of the Copy Exactly! process draws on C. J. McDonald, 'The Evolution of Intel's Copy Exactly! Technology Transfer Method,' *Intel Technology Journal,* 4th quarter (1998).

Making a Market in Knowledge

Lowell L. Bryan

Just like people, companies in today's economy find that their primary source of competitive advantage increasingly lies in the unique proprietary knowledge they possess. Companies and individuals may have equal talent and access to public knowledge, but the special value that comes with unique understanding provides a real edge. The bond trader who is the first to understand an opportunity to arbitrage securities across two different markets can earn extraordinary returns until other traders figure out the secret. A company thoroughly familiar with how to compete in a particular geographic market—China, say—has huge advantages over competitors lacking that familiarity.

Put simply, there is great value in sharing, across a whole company, proprietary insights into customers, competitors, products, production techniques, emerging research, and the like. In practice, of course, companies find it far more difficult than do individuals to take advantage of all this knowledge. An individual's knowledge is self-contained, always available. But in companies—including small ones—it can be hard to exploit the valuable knowledge in the heads of even a few hundred employees, particularly if they are scattered in different locations. In a large, diverse company, the task expands to cover thousands of highly educated professionals and managers spread across a variety of specialties, locations, even countries. But difficult as it may be to profit from this diffused knowledge, the power that such large-scale interaction yields can dwarf what individuals or small teams, however brilliant or effective, can accomplish.

Misguided Management

Many companies have long been reasonably proficient at distributing knowledge by using technology no more advanced than the telephone and the fax machine. In the past decade, as advances in communications, software, and computers opened entirely new possibilities for sharing knowledge rapidly and efficiently, many leading companies, academics, and management consultants came to believe that the future belonged to large companies that could manage knowledge. The promise of bringing all of a company's proprietary knowledge to bear on every problem or issue it faces led executives to invest billions of dollars in what came to be called knowledge management.

Of course, there was progress. But if the goal was to use a company's best proprietary knowledge to solve every problem it faced, knowledge management, as generally applied, has barely begun to fill the bill. Most companies have tried one of three approaches to managing knowledge, with mixed success. Indeed, many companies have tried all three.

1. Build it—they will use it: Some companies have relied exclusively on big investments in document-management systems, shared servers, and other technology solutions, believing this approach to be enough to let employees unlock knowledge. The result, simply, brings inefficiency. The sheer volume of documents at large companies today is overwhelming, and many such documents are out of date, poorly written, or otherwise difficult to parse. Even a diligent search by a determined knowledge seeker is likely to produce only a few valuable, easy-to-access insights.

2. Take it from the top: Companies with large corporate staffs try to push knowledge to users, often via internal web sites. The effort can be worthwhile when the idea is, for example, to distribute top-down messages about best-practice approaches or new product features. Still, the limitations of any central-planning approach apply. Do the people writing the documents know what knowledge seekers really want, or are they guessing? Are the content producers the real experts? Do most corporate staffs even know who the experts are? The typical result: knowledge pushed out in this way is not very valuable to most frontline employees and certainly not to those with the best skills and knowledge.

3. Let a thousand Web sites bloom: A third approach has been somewhat more successful, particularly for those companies that accept decentralized technology spending. It is to let organizational units solve their own knowledge problems. What large company doesn't have pockets of a few hundred people with common interests—such as employees working in a particular

product group or on a common design problem or sales professionals serving the same industry? The knowledge creators and seekers in these units usually know one another and exchange ideas easily. The units in turn use whatever technology solutions they favor in order to develop small, specialized approaches to managing knowledge. Authors earn peer recognition, motivating them to produce and share more content. Usually, a senior person in the group cares enough about the exchange to invest in the technology and staff needed to build an effective, high-quality internal web site or portal that gives knowledge seekers easy access.

This decentralized approach works because it facilitates exchange among small groups of workers with common interests. Still, as a solution to the exchange of knowledge across a broad organization, it often produces mixed results. For every example of a small organization unit with terrific success in sharing specialized knowledge among a narrow group of people, there are usually large numbers of outright, and often expensive, failures. The obvious flaw is that the proliferating approaches and technological tools have few common protocols or standards and typically remain useful only to small groups of workers interested in very specialized topics. For most companies, this approach will provide just a fraction of the potential benefits of exchanging knowledge on a company-wide scale.

A Market Problem

The truth is that the real value comes less from managing knowledge and more—a lot more—from creating and exchanging it. And the key to achieving this goal is understanding that a company's really valuable knowledge resides largely in the heads of the most talented employees. Moreover, they will be unlikely to exchange their knowledge without a fair return for the time and energy they expend in putting it into a form in which it can be exchanged. Then it must also be worth the price of seeking it.

In short, effectively exchanging knowledge on a company-wide basis is much less a technological problem than an organizational one: encouraging people who do not know each other to work together for their mutual self-interest. There is, of course, a well-known, well-tested solution to making it possible to exchange items of value among parties who don't know each other. We call it a market.

Large public markets for knowledge have long existed, of course, through books and articles and through public services such as libraries. More recently, companies such as Amazon.com, America Online, and Yahoo! have served as external markets for public knowledge. But there are no equivalent internal markets for the valuable proprietary knowledge lodged within a company's own frontline employees.

So how does a company create effective internal markets when the product is something as intangible as the valuable knowledge gained from experience and personal thinking? Working markets need, among other things, valuable objects for trading, prices, exchange mechanisms, and competition among suppliers. Often, there are also standards, protocols and regulations, and market facilitators to make markets work better.

Knowledge or Information?

Effective knowledge management begins with drawing a distinction between information and knowledge, because these terms are often used interchangeably. If information is the raw material—the input—used to make decisions, knowledge is what provides the context for how people think. As people approach a traffic light that has turned red, they take in that *information* and decide to stop. They do so because they have a *knowledge* of what red, green, and yellow mean.

Companies gain a competitive advantage from information by providing the right information to the right managers at the right time. If information isn't timely, it is often useless. For most of the past several decades, corporate investments in IT provided employees with information useful to their jobs. These investments paid off, for the most part. Not so for knowledge-management investments.

In a large company, a competitive advantage from knowledge is gained through the productive internal exchange of insights that help employees think differently as they make decisions and take actions. This is a far higher bar than the one for exchanging information, because people must be persuaded by the quality of the thought, the facts, and the logic presented that the knowledge they are being asked to acquire is superior to what they already know.

Beyond personal experience, people acquire knowledge through formal training, dialogue with others, or reading, viewing, and listening to codified knowledge content. 'Knowledge management' usually refers to a company's investment to improve the internal exchange of proprietary knowledge, through dialogue or codified content. McKinsey's work in building knowledge markets focuses on this latter form of knowledge exchange—particularly the electronic exchange of knowledge through codified content among managers and professional staff.[1]

Knowledge by nature has a much longer shelf life than information does. Knowledge about how a competitor acts in the marketplace, for example, can be valuable to a company for years. But even the most distinctive and proprietary knowledge, such as that held by a company's best professionals, undergoes an eventual decay curve that terminates at the point where it becomes common knowledge. A professional possessing secret information on a key business issue may initially have no incentive to dilute its value by sharing it. But as others learn what once was secret, there eventually comes a point in the half-life of proprietary knowledge when it has greatest value to a company if its insights become easily and broadly available across the organization.

[1] A subject closely related to knowledge management is distance learning, which focuses on electronically assisted education and training.

Lowell L. Bryan

A Valuable Object to Trade

Markets will form only around items valuable enough to justify the time and effort of buyers and sellers. Common knowledge, by definition, hardly needs trading. The opportunity lies in trading distinctive knowledge (see sidebar, 'Knowledge or information?').

From a buyer's perspective, the knowledge to be acquired from the market must be more insightful and relevant—as well as easier to find, gain access to, and assimilate—than alternative sources. Usually, knowledge available through most internal knowledge-management systems fails this test.

The trick is motivating authors to produce content that meets this standard. Almost all content produced by most companies—whether short internal memos or documents packed with charts—needs to be backed up with oral discussion. Companies must give the reader, who has no opportunity to talk with the expert, more insightful, more relevant, more accessible knowledge. The answer is a new internal equivalent of a signed article, in which the author is motivated to produce a high-quality document that is easily accessible to any user. Once knowledge is in this form, it can be traded in the market. This 'knowledge object' allows a 'buyer' of knowledge to understand an author's thinking without the parties having to talk to each other. The bad news for most companies is that documents generally fail to meet this standard.

Pricing Knowledge

Defining the item being traded creates the conditions for pricing the exchange. Authors, who are the suppliers to the market, need something that justifies their 'costs,' or effort, in return for creating the knowledge object. In internal knowledge markets, the price that authors receive is usually the enhancement of their own personal, internal reputation. Providing knowledge that catches the eye of peers and superiors and helps the author build a reputation can provide plenty of incentive. Buyers—those who seek knowledge—will have the motivation to go to the market if they believe that they will find valuable knowledge at a price, in time and effort, that is lower than, say, making numerous phone calls to locate an expert.

An Exchange Mechanism

The company's role now is to provide an exchange mechanism so that authors and knowledge seekers come to the market out of mutual self-interest. Meeting this goal requires investments in a technology infrastructure and in the staff to maintain it, in order to make the exchange possible.

An internal knowledge market has special characteristics. For starters, the company is the ultimate beneficiary of the effort to form and maintain a knowledge marketplace. Therefore the company, rather than the knowledge-seeking buyer, is responsible for rewarding authors to ensure that they are motivated to produce valuable knowledge objects.

Ensuring that authors are paid appropriately for their knowledge is often the hardest part of this equation. Internal knowledge can provide an employee with a performance advantage over his or her peers. But once that knowledge is codified, others can assimilate it, thereby negating the author's advantage. The trick, therefore, is to provide incentives so that individuals who contribute their distinctive, valuable knowledge enjoy greater internal recognition and success than they would have experienced if they had kept their knowledge to themselves. Thus, the company must create a culture in which smart people are expected to contribute valuable codified knowledge. Part of this culture is a reward structure—recognition, pay, and promotion—in which distinctive performers who contribute knowledge earn more than their noncontributing peers.

This requirement also means that companies must protect individual intellectual property rights. Those who develop knowledge—not the people they report to or those who borrow the knowledge to make presentations—must be identified and credited as the authors. This provision is important not just for equity's sake but also to provide incentives for the best thinkers, whatever their seniority or position, to produce further high-value content in the future. There is nothing more demotivating to young people seeking recognition than for some senior figure to take credit for their thinking.

Keeping up Competition

Inside companies, dialog is the preferred method for exchanging valuable proprietary knowledge. If knowledge seekers find a willing expert, they can quickly pinpoint and acquire the knowledge they need. Whether meeting with them one-on-one or in a group, the knowledge provider usually has a sense that payment will come in the form of appropriate recognition from peers and superiors.

So why can't companies rely just on dialog? Often the expert doesn't think through the problem rigorously or convert knowledge into a form that sufficiently helps the knowledge seeker. An even larger problem is that knowledge seekers may not know how to find the right person. But the biggest problem with relying solely on dialog is that it takes time, particularly on the part of the person with the knowledge. If topics generate great interest, experts in a large company simply don't have the time to both do their jobs and talk to everyone interested in discussions about knowledge. By producing a knowledge object available to everyone, however, an expert is freed from that time burden. A knowledge object can at least provide a basic grounding before higher-level discussions take place.

Dialog will always be a primary source of the knowledge exchanged in companies. But the promise of the knowledge marketplace lies in its potential to increase vastly the reach of distinctive knowledge, to the benefit of the entire company rather than just a few individuals. Since knowledge buyers can get what they need from several sources, however, a knowledge marketplace will work only if it can deliver a satisfying product. This requirement in turn means keeping authors motivated to produce high-quality content. In practice, that stimulus will take the form of competition among authors for recognition.

All markets, including knowledge markets, thrive on competition. As with any kind of intellectual property, knowledge objects compete for attention at the level of quality and popularity. Experience shows that companies providing recognition for those who produce the highest-quality knowledge objects (as judged by experts and senior management) or the most popular ones (as measured by download volume) ensure that internal authors will be motivated to compete with each other on both dimensions.

A Set of Standards

The market's transaction costs—the time and effort involved in creating and seeking knowledge—must be bearable. For internal knowledge markets to pass this test, companies need to develop standards, protocols, and regulations to lower costs that act as a deterrent to both buyers and sellers. Standards can include everything from the templates used to define the content that goes into a knowledge object to the taxonomy used to define how documents are categorized so that a search process will turn up relevant content. Protocols include everything from rules determining which kinds of knowledge will be traded in the marketplace to what kind of document qualifies as a knowledge object that can be traded there. Regulations include whatever internal compliance mechanisms are put in place to reinforce these standards and protocols.

Market Facilitators

To date, the bulk of corporate investment in knowledge management has gone into providing the staff to build and maintain the technology platform. But that is not enough. In a true knowledge market, people are needed to apply standards and protocols and to exercise judgment in enforcing the regulations. These people become marketplace insiders, like brokers and specialists in a stock exchange, who facilitate the market's operation through familiarity with its mechanics. They don't have to constitute a large bureaucracy; no more than two dozen facilitators are needed to run and regulate an internal knowledge market at, say, a large investment bank. The alternative—relying on authors and knowledge seekers to follow protocols and standards and to regulate them-selves—simply does not work: they lack the familiarity, the interest, or the time.

One group of market facilitators comprises the knowledge-service employ-ees at the center of the marketplace. They can, for example, ensure that each document traded there has an attached tag to provide the information enabling the search process to be effective, as well as enough context to let readers preview a document before they download or read it. It is also helpful to have editors who, through a little dialog with authors, are efficient at adding text to a set of exhibits in order to convert them into a knowledge object of sufficient quality.

Another group of market facilitators consists of 'knowledge-domain owners.' In a large company, there can be hundreds of these domains, each representing different subsets of users with common knowledge interests. These are the kinds of decentralized units whose efforts to serve their common interests have pro-duced the limited successes in knowledge sharing discussed earlier. Defining knowledge domains is a way of trying to replicate the conditions that have led to these decentralized successes but through an approach that utilizes the com-mon standards and protocols of a company-wide marketplace. The 'owner' of a knowledge domain is usually a senior executive who might make specific workers from the unit responsible for content listed in the knowledge market. They determine what meets the standard as a knowledge object or what if upgraded could meet the standard. They are also responsible for stimulating the creation and codification of new content by experts who have an interest in that knowledge arena. And they usually maintain and remove obsolete content and identify any knowledge gaps that need filling.

....

Knowledge Markets at Work

The idea of rigorously applying market principles to knowledge-management activities is relatively new. As a result, there are few examples of companies that have fully adopted the concept. Among those that have, however, the potential appears to be great.

Consider the case of J. M. Huber, a large privately owned US company with three diversified business sectors. In 1995, its top management introduced an 'after-action review process to capture the lessons learned from projects and events and thus to improve its future performance. Lessons may be specific to a particular business sector when they pertain to areas such as manufacturing processes and procedures. Other lessons—for instance, those pertaining to strategy, safety, or marketing—may be useful across all three business sectors. Members of project teams conduct post-project meetings to answer three basic questions: What happened? Why did it happen? What can we do about it? At the end of the meeting, the team emerges with an action plan and a list of lessons learned to improve future performance. These findings are submitted to a common electronic-document library accessible to all employees through a portal.

Today the process has become part of Huber's culture, and the database contains more than 8,000 reports. Why? Because managers can reach knowledge seekers interested in the same subjects while simultaneously building a reputation with colleagues in other divisions and with top management. Once the market formed, the self-interest of the knowledge creators and knowledge seekers took over. Huber's management says that this exchange of knowledge was instrumental in improving company performance.

There is another type of situation that illustrates the appeal of knowledge markets for groups of high-talent professionals whose work is almost completely knowledge based. This type of situation can be found, for example, in the R&D units of pharmaceutical companies, in the exploration and production units of petroleum companies, in investment banks, and in professional-services organizations such as law and accounting firms.

One such firm had long used a system to share knowledge among its professional staff. As the firm undertook a rigorous effort to apply market principles to this system, content was improved and old material culled, knowledge-domain owners were named, market facilitators were introduced, and the technology platform was upgraded. Signs of productivity gains began appearing almost immediately. Within a few months, the average number of monthly downloads of documents per professional more than doubled, from three to seven. The average number of searches per document downloaded, however, dropped from 5 to 1.2, meaning that users were now finding what they wanted with nearly every search.

A Large Potential

Anecdotal as this account of some of these early efforts may be, the potential for knowledge sharing and productivity gains is plainly there. Some 48 million of the 137 million workers in the United States alone can be classified as knowledge workers; a single company can employ 100,000 or more. Even small companies employing no more than a few hundred knowledge workers have the potential to create company-wide markets to facilitate the creation and exchange of knowledge. Logically, though, the largest opportunities would appear to reside in the largest, most diverse, most geographically far-flung companies that employ significant numbers of professionals who are unlikely ever to meet—let alone to exchange relevant knowledge.

That said, the challenge of creating an effective company-wide knowledge market is daunting. It may take $20 million to $30 million in annual incremental spending to launch an initial-prototype knowledge market in a large company. Most of this sum would go to creating the knowledge-services staff whose members would act as market facilitators. The cost–benefit analysis for this kind of expense would face the same subjective measurement problems that executives have with efforts to assess the impact of IT expenditures. But with US companies spending trillions of dollars annually on the salaries of knowledge workers, not to mention the technology that supports them, anything that would boost their productivity by even 1 percent would justify the investment.

In practical terms, taking the first steps toward building a knowledge market requires the formation of an initial company-wide market in at least one knowledge arena. It could be strategic knowledge about the behavior of competitors, for example, or proprietary functional knowledge concerning marketing or human-resources issues.

Next comes establishing a library that has at least some high-quality knowledge objects. Without that minimum, users will not find it worth their time to go to the knowledge marketplace to search for content. The value of a knowledge marketplace depends primarily on the quantity and quality of the content available to attract demand. Who makes use of a library with only ten poorly written books on the shelf? However, experience indicates that even as few as 750–1,000 high-quality documents can attract enough demand to start an effective marketplace. Usually, getting one started will involve a systemic effort to find and upgrade the best existing content in the knowledge arena, plus an effort to supply fresh content that meets the quality standard and shows the potential of scaling up. This endeavor requires top management—through visible recognition, a mandate, or both—to motivate employees with distinctive knowledge and the best communications skills to produce highly valuable showcase content voluntarily. Happily, once a vibrant knowledge market is created, it takes on a life of its own even if it starts small.

The proprietary knowledge that resides in the minds of a company's top professionals is a source of competitive advantage. An effective, efficient, company-wide knowledge market can deliver this power in ways that past efforts at knowledge management have failed to do. By creating a market mechanism for knowledge and a culture that encourages employees to share valuable knowledge with peers, companies can aggregate internal supply and demand from the many small, subscale knowledge-management systems that already exist within them.

13 The Performance Variability Dilemma

Eric Matson and Laurence Prusak

Performance variability frustrates managers everywhere. It takes a variety of forms: vastly different sales figures for similar retail stores in similar neighborhoods; significantly varying productivity rates at factories producing the same products; major differences in insurance payments for similar auto accidents. Companies make strenuous efforts to reduce such differences as the financial benefits that result when laggards imitate leaders are often immense. For example, Ford Motor Co. claims to have saved $886 million after four years of sharing best practices throughout its manufacturing sites.[1]

In their quest to reduce performance variability, however, managers often go too far. By forcing workers to 'copy exactly' or 'follow instructions exactly' in every situation, they make it far more difficult for people to use their own judgment and knowledge to solve problems that would benefit from a new approach. Hence the dilemma: How can companies reduce performance variability without stifling their employees' discretion and ability to innovate?

The answer lies in the distinction between processes and practices. Many efforts to reduce variability focus on refining processes as the primary intervention—the enormous success of Six Sigma at General Electric Co. and Motorola Inc., for example, results from the use of established statistical process controls to eliminate deviations in quality. Despite such process change, however, variability often persists because of differences in practice.[2] While a process outlines how tasks are to be organized, practice refers to the way those tasks are understood and actually performed. And practice is rarely based on narrow definitions that show how to complete a job from A to Z; more often, it stems from stories, principles, heuristics (rules of thumb) and expertise that emerge over time and combine to create a basis for action.[3] The

215

fluid nature of practice, then, generates *new* approaches to work, while process refinements make *existing* work approaches more efficient. To get the best of both, managers must find a balance between streamlining processes and allowing employees the freedom to improve practices.

Such balance is difficult to achieve. It has been argued, in fact, that managers have to choose between innovation and replication—they can't have both— because effective replication does not allow for adaptation.[4] According to this argument, the invisible complexities of most systems prohibit successful attempts to cherry-pick parts of a process or to customize processes on the basis of local conditions. Managers should instead copy a template as closely as possible.

Similarly, it has been suggested that companies should create 'ambidextrous' or dual organizational forms in order to isolate process from practice.[5] According to this view, process management leads to a diffusion of techniques that favor 'exploitative' activities—those in which innovation occurs along an existing technological trajectory and within an established customer or market segment—over purely exploratory activities. The two types of work need to be kept in separate units, by this logic, with strategic integration achieved by the senior team.

In suggesting such a drastic separation of approaches at the corporate or division level, this argument misses a fundamental point: Individual managers already make trade-offs between process and practice every day. Having studied this issue in-depth, we found that the appropriate intervention to reduce differences in performance is not a matter of organizational change; rather, it depends on individual work practices—their frequency and predictability. (See 'About the Research.') Practices that are more frequent and predictable tend to be more conducive to rigid duplication, while those that are rare and unpredictable have greater need for flexibility and innovation. That's why it's not enough to have a balance between uniformity and discretion at the company level: Each group of practitioners within an organization must also have it.

When a balance exists, employees are able to resolve problems with the greatest efficiency. To achieve it, companies must categorize work practices by frequency and predictability. Next, they should create an integrated program so that employees can take different approaches as circumstances dictate. But before they embark on these activities, managers should identify which variations in performance are most important to the organization.

Identifying Key Areas of Variability

Not all variations in performance are equally important to companies, so it is necessary to decide which areas merit the greatest attention. To do that, managers should identify variation in key metrics: Where are differences in performance causing the most competitive damage? For a retail outlet, it may be the average purchase size or labor costs; for a sales operation, it may be the close rate of its salespeople.

Some variations can be traced to things beyond managerial control such as inflation or an industry downturn. To carry out proper comparisons, executives should look at peers within the organization. A bank's senior managers, for example, should compare branches in similar competitive environments, and the leaders of a manufacturing company should compare factories producing similar products.

The next step is to clarify targets—that is, to decide on the outcome that should apply across the board. A target is typically based on the top perform-ance for a given metric; a retail outlet, for example, boasting the highest average purchase size in its group is likely to have its labor-cost targets determined by the store with the lowest costs. Finally, managers focused on this issue must estimate the cost of reducing a given variation; the change must be significant enough to warrant the expenditure.

The exploration and production business of British Petroleum (now known as BP Plc) divided its 40 business units into four peer groups on the basis of stages in the exploration and production process—finding a new field, devel-oping a new field, maintaining production in a mature field or ramping down a late-stage field.[6] The units within each group face similar challenges and have clear performance metrics. For example, the group that develops new fields focuses on the time it takes to drill a deepwater well. Over the course of two years, it reduced the average time from 100 to 42 days, taking a large chunk out of the $2 billion BP spends on drilling each year. Like most peer groups, they aren't static—units shift into new peer groups when they enter new phases of the business life cycle.

Of course, in addition to measuring variability against other units within the company, it is also critical to use competitive benchmarks to measure perform-ance variation.[7] If an organization's best unit is equal to the average unit of a competitor, sharing internal best practices will not be a winning strategy.

Categorizing Practices

Once the metrics and benchmarks are clear, managers can analyze the fre-quency and predictability of the practices that affect outcomes. The frequency of a practice is important because it determines the value of codification; the higher the frequency, the more it makes sense to codify rules or analogous

---

Three Steps to Reducing Variability

Companies can reduce major differences in performance outcomes by following a logical sequence of tasks. Understanding that a practice's frequency and predictability dictate the use of different tools is the key to success. Not all practices warrant intervention. An organization should take no action when the cost of introducing changes outweighs the benefits—as indicated by the smaller, randomly placed circles in the quadrants below. A whole category of practices, in fact—those that are low in frequency and high in predictability—typically lacks enough financial impact to justify intervention, which is why one quadrant is blank.

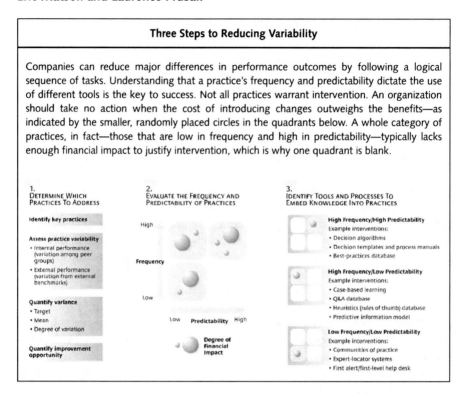

---

cases. The degree of predictability is important because it determines the need for judgment to override guidelines: the less predictable the situation, the greater the need for flexibility within interventions. (Employee experience is another important factor. Less experienced people are often likely to value rules, while more experienced people are more likely to want—and deserve—flexibility to experiment. The most experienced practitioners, 'wise old bulls,' usually drive innovative problem solving and informally govern the evolution of a given practice.)

Once managers categorize the practices, they can reduce variation in ways that are appropriate to specific practices. (For a graphic representation of the process, see 'Three Steps to Reducing Variability.') The results will vary along with the methods: Although it is possible to virtually eliminate variability within predictable practices, it is more difficult (and less desirable) to eliminate variability completely within unpredictable practices. But the financial rewards of even moderate reductions in differences can still be significant. On the other hand, practices that are both low in frequency and highly predictable typically don't have enough financial impact to justify intervention.

High Frequency/High Predictability

When practices are high in frequency and predictability, variability can be reduced by standardizing the practices with such established methods as rules, templates, decision algorithms, and process manuals.

Ford's Best Practice Replication Process, for example, is an intranet-based process for collecting, distributing and tracking the value of practices at 38 manufacturing plants.[8] Ford found dozens of performance differences between plants, such as the time it takes to install wheels on a car: It took 1.4 minutes in Atlanta but up to 4 minutes in other plants, so the Atlanta plant manager submitted detailed instructions on how to replicate that location's speed. For each of 150 process chunks like wheel installation, plant managers described the practices at their factory for completing the process, and Ford identified a benchmark that each plant should strive to meet. There is room for innovation as older practices are replaced by new techniques, but at any given time, the system recommends one best way to perform each practice. Participation is optional but strongly encouraged through incentives: The formal performance-ranking system used to evaluate plant managers includes an assessment of whether they are using the tools.

Intel Corp. has a stricter approach. It makes the cloning of its plants in every detail mandatory.[9] When variations between plants in the early 1980s hurt productivity and product quality, Intel created the Copy Exactly program. In order to discourage experimentation at individual factories, hundreds of rotating technicians, called 'seeds,' transfer manufacturing techniques from plant to plant. The techniques include not only major process steps but also background details such as the color of workers' gloves and the paint on the wall. This isn't micromanagement; small variations really matter in chip production. In one case, for example, technicians found that identical tools were producing different defect rates because of the way in which the workers were wiping the tool (circular versus back and forth). The technicians determined which direction worked better and made it the rule.

In both of these cases, the relatively high level of predictability allows practitioners to reduce variability by removing much of the judgment from the process. Using this kind of intervention means that while change is possible, it is not done lightly. At Intel, any new ideas must be submitted to a committee called the 'Process Change Control Board' and must have demonstrated value. More flexible interventions, however, are required for less predictable practices.

High Frequency/Low Predictability

When practices are frequent but unpredictable, variability can't be reduced through strict rules. Instead, practitioners should be given the option of following suggestions based on case examples, a Q&A database or a set of heuristics.

Managers face many recurrent tasks whose outcome is far from assured— preparing employees to outgrow their current jobs, for example, or trying to turn a team into a meritocracy. Those were two important aspects of the manager's role discussed during ManagerJam, a 48-hour online event hosted in 2002 by IBM Corp. for 32,000 of its managers.[10] As the participants contributed their ideas in a process of culling best practices, event moderators selected ideas that appeared suitable for immediate implementation. The managers then rated each one as 'ready now' or 'almost ready' (requiring further analysis or debate). The key is that adoption of the ideas was not mandatory; although 60 percent of managers claimed they would apply the best practices in their work, they could choose which practices seemed most relevant and adapt them to their own situations.

Partners HealthCare System Inc. developed a more systematic approach to common problems that still allows room for judgment.[11] Partners, a health- care provider made up of multiple institutions and based in Boston, noticed that its physicians ordered lab tests and prescribed drugs inconsistently. It determined that more than half of the lab tests being ordered were clinically unnecessary and that inappropriate prescriptions were the cause of more than half of the adverse drug reactions experienced by patients under the care of a Partners doctor. The company then created an online system to synthesize ordering guidelines, which reduced serious medication errors by 55 percent and saved money spent on unnecessary care. Individual doctors are relieved of the responsibility for staying informed about the latest facts on 3,000 medica- tions and 1,100 laboratory tests. The system provides them with suggestions for appropriate prescriptions and lab tests that have been generated by com- mittees of physicians focused on particular domains such as radiology.

Unlike the Ford and Intel systems, this one lets practitioners use their own judgment. Physicians can reject suggestions because of mitigating circum- stances. The sheer number and unpredictability of potential mitigating cir- cumstances make it impossible to turn the guidelines into iron laws of practice, but the high number of orders entered—13,000 per day at one hospital alone— and the savings that result from fewer tests and better prescriptions mean that the system is well worth the expense of developing it.

Low Frequency/Low Predictability

When practices are unpredictable and infrequent, it is rarely worth the effort to provide guidelines indicating alternative responses. In this case, the most effective way to reduce variability is by providing access to expert advice.

That can be done by establishing communities of practice, creating expert-locator systems and setting up help desks. Practitioners may also want to complete after-action reviews or simulate hypothetical recurrences to retain the lessons learned from a particularly important practice.[12]

In the Partners system, physicians sometimes use videoconferencing to consult with experts in real time. For example, if a patient in a remote area needs to be diagnosed rapidly, specialists can interview and observe the patient on a video screen, and then recommend the appropriate treatment.

Similarly, BP's virtual team network has been used for several years to reduce variability in such metrics as the time required to solve problems on offshore rigs.[13] The network of computers allows people to use electronic yellow pages in order to find functional experts and get their advice in real time using videoconferencing and electronic blackboards. Problems get solved faster and fewer helicopter trips to offshore rigs are needed. For example, when a mobile drilling ship experienced equipment failure in 1995, an expert analyzed the hardware by video over a satellite link and quickly diagnosed the problem; the operations were up and running in a few hours instead of the days it would have taken to fly out the expert by helicopter or send the ship back to port.[14]

The challenge, of course, is to use experts' time wisely. In order to save experts the trouble of offering advice repeatedly on similar problems, it's important to document their knowledge in process steps and case examples and to use this intervention only for truly uncommon situations.

Creating an Integrated Program

As the Partners case suggests, practitioners often need to combine different types of interventions in order to deal with different types of practice. Partners could broaden its repertoire even further if it wished to focus on highly predictable practices. Children's Hospital and Health Center in San Diego, for example, has recently created 'pathways' that standardize medical care for certain conditions like asthma attacks.[15]

In many cases, use of the full range of interventions will have the greatest impact on the effectiveness of a group of practitioners—and that will become increasingly true for employees focused on services at companies like GE and IBM, where the historical emphasis on standardized processes in aid of manufacturing will no longer be suitable. Consider how practitioners employ a range of options in three examples. (For an overview, see 'Taking a Balanced Approach.')

			Clarica Life
Taking a Balanced Approach			

To solve problems most effectively, groups must have a range of tools at their disposal—from templates that dictate solutions to expert advice on unusual situations. A balanced approach can be developed in a wide variety of settings, as shown below.

	Royal Dutch/Shell Group 'Turbodudes' (geoscientists)	World Bank Urban Services Thematic Group (urban planners)	Clarica Life Insurance Co. The Advisor Network (financial advisors)
High Frequency/High Predictability: Standardize with rules and templates	Standardized methods for estimating oil volume in reservoirs	Created electronic toolkit for basic steps in programs to upgrade slums	Created a business-letter template to help find prospective clients
High Frequency/Low Predictability: Suggest a range of alternatives	Created rules of thumb for analyzing geological formations	Organized workshop to capture innovations in street-addressing systems	Documented cases illustrating common challenges of approaching affluent clients
Low Frequency/Low Predictability: Provide access to expert advice	Provided advice to group members deciding whether to drill at a specific site	Provided advice to help country director respond to a government's proposal to clear slums	Provided advice to agent deciding which products to recommend to a young couple that received cash gift

Geoscientists at Shell

A group of about 125 geoscientists at Royal Dutch/Shell Group, dubbed the 'Turbodudes' after a type of geological structure that they analyze, handles similar technical problems, but as individual members of project teams working at different locations.[16] Together they work to reduce the variability of site-development costs, primarily by focusing upon one critical low-frequency/low-predictability decision—that is, whether or not to drill at a specific site. They seek each others' advice on a weekly basis and collaboratively interpret data to determine the likelihood of successful drilling. By means of such team interactions, they have reduced variability in the drilling success rate at Shell sites, which—by avoiding unnecessary drilling and testing at three sites per year—has resulted in an estimated savings of $120 million annually.

On the basis of their frequent analyses, these scientists also began to create categories of structures to facilitate their rapid identification. Because these categories are not entirely predictive of drilling outcomes, they serve mainly as guidelines for action rather than as strict templates. However, the group did create templates for frequently occurring activities that exhibit greater predictability. For example, they routinely assess the volume of oil in reservoirs, and in the past such estimates varied wildly. By creating a standard methodology that is now used by all the Turbodudes, they have greatly reduced the variability of these estimates.

Urban Planners at the World Bank

The Urban Services Thematic Group of the World Bank comprises about 100 urban planners whose main focus is undertaking projects to upgrade slums.[17] This group has worked to reduce regional variability in the outcome of its efforts—as indicated by the quality of basic services like water, sanitation, waste collection, and street lighting.

Like the Shell geoscientists, the urban planners spend a lot of time helping each other solve infrequent and highly unpredictable problems. In one case, the bank's country director for Bangladesh encountered political opposition to the bank's proposal to upgrade slums; opponents advocated razing the slums instead of upgrading them. In response, government representatives posed questions about the alternatives to the World Bank director, the bank's local urban specialist and to Urban Services members worldwide. From the latter group, they soon received input corroborating the value of upgrading slums. Urban Services respondents asserted that clearing slums and resettling the inhabitants had never worked on a sustainable basis in any of the world's developing economies and typically had cost 10–15 times as much as upgrading. In contrast, upgrading slums had been successful in dozens of locations.

The urban planners are also codifying their collective knowledge of more-routine practices. To prepare for a highly unpredictable practice like designing street-addressing systems (slums typically grow haphazardly, resulting in a maze of unpaved footpaths), the group held a workshop to glean valuable knowledge from the experience of 10 African countries; the group then documented the innovations and created a 'how-to' manual in four languages. For a more predictable activity, such as designing and implementing a large-scale upgrading program, topics like how to appropriately staff a team are outlined in video and text in an electronic toolkit on compact disc.

Eric Matson and Laurence Prusak

Financial Advisors at Clarica

Working for Waterloo, Ontario-based Clarica Life Insurance Co., a group of 200 independent advisors is part of 'The Advisor Network.' The main objective of this group is to reduce the variability in close rates and the value per sale among the advisors in order to serve more customers and increase the revenue per customer. Less experienced members gain knowledge that can help advance their careers, and seasoned advisors are able to test themselves with innovative thinking.

In infrequent and unpredictable situations, an advisor may start an online dialogue to elicit advice from peers. In one example, an advisor posted a case to the discussion database, outlining the financial situation and goals of a young couple that had received a substantial cash gift. Other advisors commented, debating the pros and cons of whole life insurance, term life insurance, mortgage insurance and money market options, as well as their tax implications. The advisor then met with his clients, discussed options generated by the dialogue and reported the result to the advisor community: two new life policies, an increase in an existing policy, two retirement fund contributions, a term deposit and a financial plan. His value per sale was much higher than it would have been had he dealt with the situation alone.

To prepare for situations that happen more often, the advisors read and discuss case examples. In one instance, the group documented half a dozen cases illustrating the common challenges of approaching affluent clients. Workshop discussions have led to consensus on the establishment of some rules of thumb for overcoming common barriers to making certain types of sales. In addition, advisors also have created templates and tools for the routine parts of their job, including a target-market checklist to help find potential clients, a business-letter template to help find prospective customers and a PowerPoint presentation template to help with introductory interviews. Such aids help newer agents find the right prospects and improve their value per sale.

As these examples show, groups of practitioners trying to reduce variability don't need to decide between rigidly codifying processes and exercising individual judgment. Depending on the frequency and predictability of the practices they're trying to improve, they can use a combination of interventions that, taken together, allow the group to take advantage of what they've learned yet continue to innovate. For executives focused on reducing performance variability in all its varied forms within their organizations, the flexibility provided by a practice-based approach offers the best combination of uniformity and discretion.

Notes and References

1. S. Kwiecien and D. Wolford, 'Gaining Real Value Through Best-Practice Replication: How Ford Motor Company Counts the Returns on Knowledge Efforts,' *Knowledge Management Review,* 4, March–April 2001: 12–15.

2. J. S. Brown and P. Duguid, 'Balancing Act: How To Capture Knowledge Without Killing It,' *Harvard Business Review,* 78, May–June 2000: 73–80; and J. S. Brown and P. Duguid, 'Creativity Versus Structure: A Useful Tension,' *MIT Sloan Management Review,* 42, Summer 2001: 93–4.

3. E. Wegner, R. McDermott and W. M. Snyder, 'Cultivating Communities of Practice'. Boston: Harvard Business School Press, 2002, 38.

4. G. Szulanski and S. Winter, 'Getting It Right the Second Time,' *Harvard Business Review,* 80. January 2002: 62–9. For more details, see G. Szulanski, 'Sticky Knowledge: Barriers to Knowing in the Firm'. Thousand Oaks, California: Sage Publications, 2003.

5. M. J. Benner and M. Tushman, 'Exploitation, Exploration and Process Management: The Productivity Dilemma Revisited.' *Academy of Management Review,* 28, April 2003: 238–56; and M. Benner and M. Tushman, 'Process Management and Technological Innovation: A Longitudinal Study of the Photography and Paint Industries,' *Administrative Science Quarterly,* 47, December 2002: 676–706.

6. S. E. Prokesch, 'Unleashing the Power of Learning: An Interview With British Petroleum's John Browne,' *Harvard Business Review,* 75, September–October 1997: 146–68.

7. It is beyond the scope of this article to discuss the process of benchmarking, but many others have explored that topic in detail. See, for example, F. G. Tucker, S. M. Zivan and R. C. Camp, 'How To Measure Yourself Against the Best,' *Harvard Business Review,* 65, January–February 1987: 8–10; and R. H. Hayes and G. P. Pisano, 'Beyond World-Class: The New Manufacturing Strategy,' *Harvard Business Review,* 72, January–February 1994: 77–86.

8. Kwiecien and Wolford, 'Gaining Real Value.'

9. D. Clark, 'Inside Intel, It's All Copying—In Setting Up Its New Plants, Chip Maker Clones Older Ones Down to the Paint on the Wall,' *Wall Street Journal,* Oct. 28, 2002, p. B1.

10. L. Dorsett, T. O'Driscoll and M. A. Fontaine, 'Redefining Manager Interaction at IBM: Leveraging Massive Conversations To Exchange Knowledge,' *Knowledge Management Review,* 5, September–October 2002: 24–8.

11. T. Davenport and J. Glaser, 'Just-in-Time Delivery Comes to Knowledge Management,' *Harvard Business Review,* 80, July 2002: 107–11.

12. J. March, 'Learning from Samples of One or Fewer,' in 'The Pursuit of Organizational Intelligence' Malden, Massachusetts: Blackwell Publishers, 1999: 137–55.

13. Prokesch, 'Unleashing the Power of Learning.'

14. T. H. Davenport and L. Prusak, 'Working Knowledge' Boston: Harvard Business School Press, 1997, 21.

Eric Matson and Laurence Prusak

15. B. Wysocki, Jr., 'Follow the Recipe: Children's Hospital in San Diego Has Taken the Standardization of Medical Care to an Extreme,' *Wall Street Journal*, April 22, 2003, p. R4.
16. Wenger, et al., 'Cultivating Communities,' 94–5.
17. W. E. Fulmer, 'The World Bank and Knowledge Management: The Case of the Urban Services Thematic Group,' *Harvard Business School*, case no. 9-801-157, Boston: Harvard Business School Publishing, 2001.

V. SOCIAL PERSPECTIVES

14

Knowledge Management's Social Dimension: Lessons from Nucor Steel

Anil K. Gupta and Vijay Govindarajan

To sustain competitive advantage, a company must give people incentives to transfer their knowledge. A look at the innovative steel company Nucor and others suggests how to build a knowledge-sharing environment.

A gap exists between the rhetoric of knowledge management and how knowledge is actually managed in organizations. There is widespread awareness of the economic value that creating and mobilizing intellectual capital can unleash. Yet, for most companies, the reality rarely matches the potential. As the CEO of a commercial-services company lamented in an interview, 'We provide pretty much the same services in every location. But my regional managers would rather die than learn from each other.' Our research suggests the CEO's experience is not an isolated one. In fact, too often, actual knowledge sharing does not just fall below executives' expectations; it does not even match their perceptions about the extent to which knowledge is being shared within their organizations.

Building an effective social ecology—that is, the social environment within which people operate—is a crucial requirement for effective knowledge management. Nucor Corp., the world's most innovative and fastest-growing steel company for the past three decades, is a case in point. The company's phenomenal success cannot be explained without examining the exemplary social ecology that Nucor has created for accumulating and mobilizing knowledge. By adopting a similar framework, any company can convert itself into an effective knowledge machine.

The Central Role of Social Ecology in Knowledge Management

Because all knowledge starts as information, many companies regard knowledge management as synonymous with information management. Carried to an extreme, such a perspective can result in the profoundly mistaken belief that the installation of a sophisticated information-technology infrastructure is the be-all and end-all of knowledge management. Effective knowledge management depends not merely on information-technology platforms but more broadly on the social ecology of an organization. Social ecology refers to the social system in which people operate. It drives an organization's formal and informal expectations of individuals, defines the types of people who will fit into the organization, shapes individuals' freedom to pursue actions without prior approval, and affects how people interact with others both inside and outside the organization. The determinants of social ecology are culture, structure, information systems, reward systems, processes, people, and leadership. The word ecology suggests that the social system should be viewed not as a random collection of disparate elements but as a comprehensive whole in which the various elements interact with one another.

Information technology (IT) certainly plays a central role in knowledge management. IT is the only viable mechanism to connect efficiently large numbers of geographically dispersed people. IT can be used effectively, or it can be misused. Technology providers (such as Lotus, Microsoft, Oracle, and SAP) strive to disperse the technology to as wide a customer base as possible. Thus, for most companies, IT platforms are neither proprietary nor unique and therefore provide at best a temporary advantage. Sustainable advantage depends on how smart the company is at using the technology. And that depends fundamentally on the social ecology of the organization. Senior executives echo that perspective.

Penetrating the Knowledge Management Agenda

In a world in which the half-life of new knowledge is becoming ever shorter, an effective knowledge machine must excel at two central tasks: creating and acquiring new knowledge, and sharing and mobilizing that knowledge throughout the corporate network. Unless an enterprise continuously generates new knowledge, it will soon be playing tomorrow's game with yesterday's tools. And unless knowledge is pumped efficiently throughout the network, the enterprise will not only pay the price of reinventing the same wheel but will also risk becoming prey to competitors that are able to replicate its ideas rapidly. So the intellectual capital of an enterprise is a function of the stock of knowledge accumulated by individuals and units—and the extent to which such knowledge is mobilized across the enterprise. An analogy may be found in the concept of money supply. Economists measure money supply as a product of two factors: the stock of notes in circulation multiplied by the velocity of circulation. Similarly, an enterprise's intellectual capital consists of the stock of knowledge held by individuals and corporate units multiplied by the velocity at which such knowledge is shared throughout the organization.

The task of accumulating knowledge can be further disaggregated into three subtasks: knowledge creation (learning by doing), knowledge acquisition (internalizing external knowledge), and knowledge retention (minimizing the loss of proprietary knowledge). The task of mobilizing knowledge can also be disaggregated into a set of subtasks: knowledge identification (uncovering opportunities for knowledge sharing), knowledge outflow (motivating potential senders of knowledge to share it), knowledge transmission (building effective and efficient channels for the transfer of knowledge), and knowledge inflow (motivating potential receivers to accept and use the incoming knowledge). Myriad pathologies and pitfalls can (and often do) bedevil every element of the knowledge-management process in many organizations.[1]

A common pathology is the 'knowledge is power' syndrome, which plagued one European global engineering company. At the time of our interviews, the company had three business areas (BAs). Each BA president had complete responsibility for his business globally—except in North America. There, all operations reported to the president of Market Area (MA) North America, who in turn reported directly to the CEO. The three BA presidents objected to the arrangement, advocating that the company abolish the MA-North America position and that they directly control activities in the region. The result was an extremely limited transfer of technological know-how from Europe to North America. As one BA president explained, 'People know that it is the BAs who create the technology and control it. They also realize that, in the middle of the technology pipeline between BA headquarters and MA-North America, there exists a control valve. The hands on that control valve belong to us. We can open that valve, or we can keep it shut. Sooner or later, people are going to realize where the power in this company lies. Of course, we want to share our know-how with North America; but we will do so only after we obtain complete control over them.' After a frustrating three years, the CEO concluded that he had little choice but to accept the BA presidents' power and abolish the MA-North America position.

Virtually all the pathologies that companies exhibit emanate from some type of dysfunction in the social ecology of the enterprise. But companies can avoid such pathologies and create an exemplary social ecology for effective knowledge management as Nucor Corporation did.

The Social Ecology of a Knowledge Machine: The Case of Nucor

Nucor Corporation has been the most innovative and fastest-growing steel company for the past 30 years. Nucor's success can be explained only by analyzing its social ecology. As an example of how a knowledge machine works, Nucor is far more interesting than, say, professional-services firms such as Andersen Consulting or McKinsey & Co., whose only output is knowledge. Even though Nucor's end product is steel—a tangible, nondifferentiable commodity—the company has been a knowledge machine par excellence for decades. Since the late 1960s, the U.S. steel industry has faced numerous problems—such as declining demand, substitution from other materials, foreign competition, and strained labor relations—and has reported one of the poorest profit-and-growth records in the U.S. economy. Despite operating in such a fundamentally troubled industry for more than three decades, Nucor has enjoyed an annual compounded sales growth rate of 17 percent, all generated internally without Nucor making any acquisitions. Furthermore, between 1968 and 1998, the company's profit margins were consistently well above industry medians, and average annual return to shareholders exceeded 20 percent. Starting from virtually ground zero in 1968, Nucor had become one of the largest steel producers in the United States by 1999.

Nucor's phenomenal success cannot be explained by its industry structure, access to raw materials or other external factors. (See p. 234 'Nucor's Performance Cannot Be Explained by External Factors.') Nucor achieved its success by excelling at a single task: becoming and remaining the most efficient steel producer in the world. It did so by developing and constantly upgrading three competencies that were both strategic and proprietary: plant construction and start-up know-how, manufacturing-process expertise and the ability to adopt breakthrough technologies earlier and more effectively than competitors.[2]

How Nucor Accumulates Knowledge

Nucor's social ecology allowed the company to excel at the three subtasks associated with accumulating knowledge: creating knowledge from direct experimentation, acquiring external knowledge, and retaining internally created or externally acquired knowledge.

Knowledge Creation

Nucor's success at knowledge creation sprang from three elements of its social ecology: superior human capital, high-powered incentives, and a high degree of empowerment (which included both a high tolerance for failure and a high degree of accountability).

Nucor was able to gain access to superior human capital by locating plants in rural areas that had an abundance of hardworking, mechanically inclined people. The company became a leading employer in those locations and offered a top-of-the-line compensation package, enabling it to attract an unusually large pool of applicants for every job opening. For instance, 1,200 applicants applied for eight job openings at Nucor's Darlington, South Carolina, plant. As a result, the company was able to use stringent selection criteria to hire conscientious, dedicated, goal-oriented, self-reliant people.

Nucor built on that foundation by investing in continuous, on-the-job, multifunctional training. Furthermore, it cultivated hunger for new knowledge through a high-powered incentive system for every employee—from the production worker to the corporate CEO. There was no upper cap on the incentive payouts. In the 1990s, for example, payouts for production employees averaged 80–150 percent of base wage, making those workers the best paid in the steel industry. The incentive structure for department managers and senior officers was even steeper.

There were several ways that incentives motivated Nucor's employees to push the boundaries of manufacturing-process know-how. First, because the incentives were a function of production output, employees could earn higher bonuses only by discovering new ways to boost productivity. Second, because the incentive payouts depended only on output that met quality standards, employees were motivated to develop innovations that would help them do things right the first time. Finally, because the magnitude of the bonus payouts was not limited and employees' discovery of new process innovations did not lead to a resetting of the standards, people were challenged to expand the frontiers of process know-how.

Whenever employees are encouraged to experiment, there is always the possibility of failure. A company that does not tolerate failure will severely inhibit experimentation, whereas a company that experiences nothing but failures will not survive. The following observation by Ken Iverson, Nucor's architect and, until recently, its chairman, illustrates how Nucor fostered experimentation within a context of accountability: 'We try to impress upon our employees that we are not King Solomon. We use an expression that I really like, 'Good managers make bad decisions.' We believe that if you take an average person and put him in a management position, he'll make 50 percent good decisions and 50 percent bad decisions. A good manager makes 60 percent good decisions. That means 40 percent of those decisions could have been better. The only other point I'd like to make about decision making is, 'Don't keep making the same bad decisions.'...Every Nucor plant has its little storehouse of equipment that was bought, tried and discarded.'[3]

Knowledge Acquisition
Being a first mover in adopting breakthrough process technologies is always risky, particularly in a capital-intensive industry such as steel. Despite such risks, Nucor was not only the first U.S. company to adopt minimill technology, it was also the first company in the world to make flat-rolled steel in a minimill and to commercialize thin-slab casting. The company's extraordinary success in technology acquisition over three decades can be traced back to various aspects of its abilities, mindset, and behavior.

Nucor's Performance Cannot Be Explained by External Factors

Because Nucor's social ecology drove every employee to search for better and more efficient ways to make steel and steel-related products, its operating personnel had a deeper mastery of the industry's manufacturing processes than personnel at other steel companies. Other steel companies sent senior executives and staff engineers to analyze emerging technologies, but teams of Nucor managers, engineers, and operators made decisions about technology adoption. Thus, Nucor's technology-assessment teams went to equipment suppliers with a deep knowledge of both technological and operational issues. Given their mastery of manufacturing-process know-how, members of Nucor's technology-assessment teams also had greater confidence in the company's ability to resolve unknown bugs that would inevitably appear during implementation of the new technology. Nucor's leading role in the adoption of thin-slab casting technology is only one example of the company's ability to excel at acquiring knowledge. Until the mid-1980s, minimills could not produce high-end flat-steel products for automotive and appliance customers. Nucor made history in 1987 by building in Crawfordsville, Indiana, the first minimill that could make flat steel—an innovation that moved the company into the premium segment of the steel industry. By 1997, Nucor had built two more minimills using the process. Despite the fact that the company had obtained the technology from an equipment supplier on a nonexclusive basis, the first plant built by a competitor using the same technology did not appear until 1995.

Knowledge Retention
Companies often lose sizeable chunks of their knowledge through the departure of employees. Nucor protected itself from such losses by successfully

implementing a policy of no layoffs during recessions and by cultivating a high degree of loyalty and commitment among its personnel.

When hit by a recession, the company reduced the workweek rather than the workforce. Employees regarded a reduced workweek and the correspondingly lower wages as a relatively attractive option when compared with the prospect of being laid off in a rural area where Nucor was the leading employer. Of course, reductions in the workweek did reduce wages and could have weakened the fabric of loyalty and commitment between the company and its employees. To counter that threat, Nucor's workweek reductions were always accompanied by a 'share the pain' program: any reduction in a worker's compensation was accompanied by a greater reduction in managers' compensation and a still greater cut in the CEO's pay (by as much as 70 percent). Nucor's response to recessions ended up strengthening the spirit of trust and respect within the company. Not surprisingly, Nucor enjoyed the lowest turnover rate of any company in its industry.

How Nucor Mobilizes and Shares Knowledge

Nucor's social ecology also allowed the company to excel at the four subtasks associated with sharing and mobilizing knowledge: identifying opportunities to share knowledge, encouraging individuals to share their knowledge, building effective and efficient transmission channels, and convincing individuals to accept and use the knowledge they receive.

Identifying Opportunities to Share Knowledge
Nucor was systematic in measuring the performance of every work group, department, and plant and in making the performance data visible within the company. The routine measurement and distribution of performance data allowed individual units and corporate headquarters to uncover myriad opportunities to share best practices.

Encouraging Individuals to Share Knowledge
Nucor's social ecology was also fashioned to encourage eagerness on the part of every work unit to share best practices proactively. Nucor relied on group-based incentives at every level of the organization. Such incentives ensured that one individual's superior performance would have a minimal impact on his or her bonus if the performance of the other individuals in the group remained below par. The incentives motivated individuals to share their own best practices with peer units in order to boost the performance of the entire bonus group. For example, the bonus of shop-floor workers depended not on their own performance but on the performance of their entire 25- to 40-person

work group. Similarly, department managers earned an annual incentive bonus tied to the performance of the entire plant rather than that of their own department. In addition, the incentive bonuses of plant general managers depended on the performance of the entire company rather than just their individual plants.

Building Effective and Efficient Transmission Channels
A company's knowledge base encompasses a wide spectrum of different types of knowledge from highly structured, codified and thus mobile forms of knowledge (for instance, monthly financial data) to highly unstructured, tacit, and embedded forms of knowledge (for instance, plant start-up know-how). Information technology is a highly effective and efficient mechanism for the transfer of codified knowledge, and Nucor, like many organizations, exploited the power of IT. Unlike many organizations, however, Nucor also excelled at the sharing of unstructured knowledge—a key driver for building and leveraging core competencies. The ability to transfer unstructured knowledge requires rich transmission channels, such as face-to-face communication and the transfer of people.

Intraplant Knowledge Transfers
Nucor's goal within each plant was to build a social community promoting trust and open communication, in which each person knew everyone else personally and had ample opportunity to interact. Achieving that goal began with the company's policy of keeping the number of employees in each plant between 250 and 300. The small number, coupled with employees' long tenure, fostered a high degree of interpersonal familiarity. In addition, each plant's general manager routinely held dinner meetings for groups of 25–100, inviting every employee once a year. The format was free and open but included some ground rules. All comments were to remain business-related and were not to be aimed at specific individuals. In turn, managers guaranteed that they would carefully consider and respond to every criticism and suggestion.

Interplant Knowledge Transfers
Nucor used several transmission channels when it transferred knowledge among plants. First, detailed performance data on each mill were regularly distributed to all plant managers. Second, all plant general managers met as a group three times a year to review each facility's performance and to develop formal plans for the transfer of best practices. Third, plant general managers, supervisors, and machine operators periodically visited each other's mills. Such visits enabled operations personnel, the true possessors of process knowledge, to go beyond performance data and to understand firsthand the factors that

make particular practices superior or inferior. Fourth, recognizing the special difficulties inherent in the transfer of complex knowledge, Nucor selectively reassigned people from one plant to another on the basis of their expertise. In addition to sharing best practices across existing plants, Nucor systematically recycled process innovations from existing plants to start-up plants. The company built or rebuilt one or more mills every year. Rather than rely on outside contractors to build the mills, Nucor put together a group of engineers from existing mills. The internal group was responsible for designing and managing the construction of any new building or rebuilding project. Moreover, Nucor hired local workers to construct the mills and informed them that they were likely to be recruited later to operate the mills.

Nucor's unique approach to building and rebuilding mills yielded various benefits. First, existing process knowledge was recycled into new-plant design and construction. Second, construction workers knew that they were building the plant for themselves and had a natural incentive to build it well. Third, knowledge of the underlying process technology embedded in the plant design was carried over in the workers' minds from the construction phase to the operations phase. Fourth, plant start-up expertise emerged as yet another of Nucor's core competencies.

Convincing Individuals to Accept and Use the Knowledge They Receive
Nucor's social ecology countered the 'not invented here' syndrome in two ways. First, the structure of the company's incentives signaled strongly to employees that relying solely on their own efforts at knowledge creation could be costly—literally. Second, by making every unit's performance visible to other units in the company, Nucor made the workplace into something of a fishbowl. Strong performers were showcased before their peers; weak ones were exposed to the intense heat of peer pressure.

A Framework for Building an Effective Knowledge Machine

Nucor Corporation avoided the pathologies that plague many companies and built an exemplary social ecology for accumulating and sharing knowledge. By following a general framework, other companies can transform themselves, like Nucor, into effective and efficient knowledge machines. The guidelines for companies fall into two categories: those for maximizing the creation and acquisition of knowledge and those for maximizing the sharing of knowledge.

Anil K. Gupta and Vijay Govindarajan

Maximizing Knowledge Creation and Acquisition

To maximize knowledge creation and acquisition, companies need to set stretch goals, provide incentives, empower people, encourage experimentation, and cultivate within the company a market for ideas.

Set Stretch Goals
The easier the target, the less a company needs to create new approaches. Therefore, the starting point for developing a culture of knowledge creation is to set targets that cannot be achieved without some innovation. As Jack Welch, the CEO of General Electric, has observed, 'If you do know how to get there, it's not a stretch target. … The CEO of Yokogawa, our Japanese partner in the medical systems business, calls this concept 'bullet-train thinking'; that is, if you want a 10-mile-per-hour increase in train speed, you tinker with horsepower, but if you want to double its speed, you have to break out of both conventional thinking and conventional performance expectations.'[4]

Provide High-Powered Incentives
By definition, stretch goals increase a person's level of risk in performing a task. Unless the potential reward matches the increased level of risk, competent employees simply won't stay with the company. Stretch goals without high-powered incentives are likely to end up as lofty exhortations lacking power to stir people to seek new approaches.

Cultivate Empowerment and Provide 'Slack' Resources
Stretch goals and high-powered incentives stimulate a demand for new ideas. By contrast, empowerment and so-called slack resources—for example, time given to employees for playful experimentation—are supply-side tools that play a critical role in increasing the creative capacity of subunits. Companies that require employees to justify in advance how they allocate their time and other resources stifle experimentation. The '15% Rule' at 3M Corporation is a good example of how empowerment and slack resources foster innovation. According to the 15% Rule, scientists at 3M are allowed, indeed expected, to use 15 percent of their working time on projects of their own choosing that don't require advanced approval by superiors.

Equip Every Unit With a Well-Defined 'Sandbox' for Play
Creating a culture that values experimentation means encouraging a willingness to take risks. Senior executives, in concert with the board of directors, must undertake 'bet the company' types of moves from time to time. But it would be suicidal to have a culture in which the power to make such moves is

238

widely distributed throughout the firm. One way to encourage experimentation without subjecting the organization to undue risk is to give people or units well-defined 'sandboxes' for experimentation and play. If an experiment fails in such a context, the risks are likely to be acceptable. For example, a large hotel chain could specify that each hotel general manager has the freedom to experiment with 10 percent of the rooms on its properties. Or a retail chain could give each store manager the freedom to design and create one new merchandise department.

Cultivate a Market for Ideas within the Company
Every company must have a screening mechanism to determine which of the many ideas emerging from the various subunits deserve support and which should be abandoned. When senior managers stifle good ideas, the problem usually is not that the company has screening mechanisms but that those mechanisms are inadequate. Companies must accept the fact that no single individual has a monopoly on wisdom. They should create a culture in which an idea that is rejected by one's immediate superior can still be 'shopped around' within the company without creating a perception of insubordination.

Maximizing Knowledge Sharing

The best ways to maximize knowledge sharing are: ban knowledge hoarding, use group-based incentives, codify tacit knowledge, and match knowledge-transfer mechanisms to types of knowledge.

Ban 'Knowledge Hoarding' and Turn 'Knowledge Givers' Into Heroes
Every company must decide, implicitly or explicitly, which resources are to be treated as if they were corporate resources—and therefore 'leased' to the business units—and which resources are to be treated as if they were 'owned' by the business units. Consider, for example, brand names such as Nokia, Honda, or IBM. Business units use those corporate brand names as a critical resource, but the brand name does not belong to any single business unit or subsidiary. To maximize knowledge sharing, companies must treat knowledge in a similar way; that is, as a corporate resource that cannot be hoarded by any particular subsidiary or business unit. It is also important to recognize, honor, and even reward proactive 'knowledge givers.' In an effective knowledge machine, heroes do not merely invent leading-edge practices but also facilitate their adoption by other individuals and units within the corporation.

Anil K. Gupta and Vijay Govindarajan

Rely on Group-Based Incentives

Group-based incentives reinforce knowledge sharing as a cultural norm. In companies such as Nucor, incentives take the form of cash compensation. In other companies, such as Cisco, they take the form of sizeable stock options. The power of group-based incentives stems from the fact that they direct attention to maximizing the performance of the entire system rather than that of an individual unit. Minimize problems with underperformers by ensuring that incentives are large enough to be meaningful, by making individual behavior visible within the group and by empowering the group to expel the chronic underperformer.

Invest in Codifying Tacit Knowledge

Investing in codifying tacit knowledge—or complex, unstructured knowledge that resides in the minds and behaviors of individuals and groups—can have high payoffs. Consider Marriott International. In 1998, Marriott expanded from 1,500 to about 1,700 properties. Given an average of more than 300 rooms per hotel and 1.3 employees per room, Marriott's growth meant the addition of about 80,000 new employees in that year alone. With that level of growth, Marriott has been compelled to convert virtually everything that its people know about the operation of a hotel into codified, standard operating procedures. Without codification, the outcome would have been either highly inconsistent service or a dramatic decrease in the rate at which the company could grow. Of course, there is a limit to how much knowledge can be codified. Nevertheless, a company can reap many rewards from codification in terms of a broader sharing of knowledge throughout the enterprise and an increased development of new knowledge. Often, an explicit mapping of what a company knows is the basis for discovering what it does not know.

Match Transmission Mechanisms to Type of Knowledge

The transfer of all knowledge occurs through one or more of the following transmission mechanisms: the exchange of documents, conversations and coaching and the transfer of people and teams. To be both effective and efficient, transmission mechanisms must be tailored to the type of knowledge being transferred. When it comes to transmission mechanisms, 'effectiveness' refers to whether the receiver actually receives what the sender has sent; 'efficiency' refers to the cost and speed of the transmission channels. Document exchange is a highly effective and efficient mechanism for sharing codified knowledge. It is often highly ineffective, however, for transmitting tacit knowledge. Conversations and the transfer of people, by contrast, are relatively inefficient mechanisms for sharing codified knowledge. But, for transferring tacit knowledge, they may be the only effective mechanisms.

240

Recreating Competitive Advantage Every Day

That intellectual capital is central to creating competitive advantage is widely recognized. But in an era of relentless technological revolutions and ubiquitous benchmarking, intellectual capital alone is but an ephemeral advantage. In the emerging economic landscape, competitive advantage must be recreated every day. To do so, companies must focus on creating and mobilizing new knowledge faster and more efficiently than competitors—and not get stuck in the mechanics of measuring the worth of what they already know. A company's ability to function as a knowledge machine depends not merely on the sophistication of its IT infrastructure but more critically on the social ecology that drives the behavior of its people and teams. It is relatively easy for a company to adopt a sophisticated IT architecture, but it is even easier for competitors to neutralize or even leapfrog that architecture. Creating a social ecology that is free of pathologies, as Nucor did, is a much more difficult challenge. It requires building a whole ecosystem of complementary and mutually reinforcing organizational mechanisms. The bad news for companies is that this is a tough challenge. Any company can acquire a new piece of hardware, but not every company can overcome the difficulties and build an effective social ecology. There is good news, however, for the companies that succeed: precisely because they have tackled such a difficult challenge, they will enjoy a competitive advantage that their rivals will find hard to beat.

Acknowledgements

Our chapter benefited from the comments of Edwin A. Locke.

Additional Resources

For a scholarly development of some of the ideas in the chapter, see: A. K. Gupta and V. Govindarajan, 'Knowledge Flows and the Structure of Control Within Multinational Corporations,' *Academy of Management Review* 16, no. 4 (October 1991): 768–92; A. K. Gupta and V. Govindarajan, 'Knowledge Flows Within Multinational Corporations,' *Strategic Management Journal*, 21 (April 2000): 473–96; N. Nohria and S. Ghoshal, 'The Differentiated Network: Organizing Multinational Corporations for Value Creation' (New York: Jossey-Bass, 1997); J. Birkinshaw, N. Hood and S. Jonsson, 'Building Firm-Specific Advantages in Multinational Corporations: The Role of Subsidiary Initiative,' *Strategic Management Journal* 19, no. 3 (March 1998): 221–42; B. Kogut and U. Zander,

Anil K. Gupta and Vijay Govindarajan

'Knowledge of the Firm, Combinative Capabilities, and the Replication of Technology,' *Organization Science* 3, no. 2 (August 1992): 383–97; M. Cohen and D. A. Levinthal, 'Absorptive Capacity: A New Perspective on Learning and Innovation,' *Administrative Science Quarterly* 35 (March 1990): 128–52; R. L. Daft and R. H. Lengel, 'Organizational Information Requirements, Media Richness, and Structural Design,' *Management Science* 32 (May 1986): 554–71; M. Polanyi, 'The Tacit Dimension' (London: Routledge & Kegan Paul, 1966); T. H. Davenport and L. Prusak, 'Working Knowledge' (Boston: Harvard Business School Press, 2000); I. Nonaka and H. Takeuchi, 'The Knowledge Creating Company' (New York: Oxford University Press, 1995); T. A. Stewart, 'Intellectual Capital: The New Wealth of Organizations' (New York: Doubleday, 1997).

....

Notes and References

1. For an extensive discussion of the pathologies that bedevil companies in utilizing knowledge within or outside their corporate boundaries, see also: J. Pfeffer and R. I. Sutton, 'The Knowing-Doing Gap: How Smart Companies Turn Knowledge Into Action' (Boston, Massachusetts: Harvard Business School Press, 2000).
2. Data on Nucor are drawn primarily from V. Govindarajan and A. K. Gupta, 'Nucor Corporation: A Case Study,' unpublished case study (Hanover, New Hampshire: Amos Tuck School of Business Administration, Dartmouth College, 1998).
3. P. Ghemawat and H. J. Stander III, 'Nucor at a Crossroads,' case no. 9-793-039 (Boston: Harvard Business School Publishing Corp., 1992): 8; and K. Iverson and T. Varian, 'Plain Talk' (New York: John Wiley & Sons, 1997): 96.
4. Letter to shareholders, 1993 Annual Report, General Electric Co.

15

Fair Process: Managing in the Knowledge Economy

W. Chan Kim and Renée Mauborgne

A London policeman gave a woman a ticket for making an illegal turn. When the woman protested that there was no sign prohibiting the turn, the policeman pointed to one that was bent out of shape and difficult to see from the road. Furious, the woman decided to appeal by going to court. Finally, the day of her hearing arrived, and she could hardly wait to speak her piece. But she had just begun to tell her side of the story when the magistrate stopped her and summarily ruled in her favor.

How did the woman feel? Vindicated? Victorious? Satisfied?

No, she was frustrated and deeply unhappy. 'I came for justice,' she complained, 'but the magistrate never let me explain what happened.' In other words, although she liked the outcome, she didn't like the process that had created it.

For the purposes of their theories, economists assume that people are maximizers of utility, driven mainly by rational calculations of their own self-interest. That is, economists assume people focus solely on outcomes. That assumption has migrated into much of management theory and practice. It has, for instance, become embedded in the tools managers traditionally use to control and motivate employees' behavior—from incentive systems to organizational structures. But it is an assumption that managers would do well to reexamine because we all know that in real life it does not always hold true. People do care about outcomes, but—like the woman in London—they also care about the processes that produce those outcomes. They want to know that they had their say—that their point of view was considered even if it was rejected. Outcomes matter, but no more than the fairness of the processes that produce them.

Never has the idea of fair process been more important for managers than it is today. Fair process turns out to be a powerful management tool for companies struggling to make the transition from a production-based to a knowledge-based economy, in which value creation depends increasingly on ideas and innovation. Fair process profoundly influences attitudes and behaviors critical to high performance. It builds trust and unlocks ideas. With it, managers can achieve even the most painful and difficult goals while gaining the voluntary cooperation of the employees affected. Without fair process, even outcomes that employees might favor can be difficult to achieve—as the experience of an elevator manufacturer we will call Elco illustrates.

Good Outcome, Unfair Process

In the late 1980s, sales in the elevator industry headed south as overconstruction of office space left some large U.S. cities with vacancy rates as high as 20 percent. Faced with diminished domestic demand for its product, Elco knew it had to improve its operations. The company made the decision to replace its batch-manufacturing system with a cellular approach that would allow self-directed teams to achieve superior performance. Given the industry's collapse, top management felt the transformation had to be made in record time.

In the absence of expertise in cellular manufacturing, Elco retained a consulting firm to design a master plan for the conversion. Elco asked the consultants to work quickly and with minimal disturbance to employees. The new manufacturing system would be installed first at Elco's Chester plant, where employee relations were so good that in 1983 workers had decertified their own union. Subsequently, Elco would roll the process out to its High Park plant, where a strong union would probably resist that, or any other, change.

Under the leadership of a much beloved plant manager, Chester was in all respects a model operation. Visiting customers were always impressed by the knowledge and enthusiasm of Chester's employees, so much so that the vice president of marketing saw the plant as one of Elco's best marketing tools. 'Just let customers talk with Chester employees,' he observed, 'and they walk away convinced that buying an Elco elevator is the smart choice.'

But one day in January of 1991, Chester's employees arrived at work to discover strangers at the plant. Who were these people wearing dark suits, white dress shirts, and ties? They weren't customers. They showed up daily and spoke in low tones to one another. They didn't interact with employees. They hovered behind people's backs, taking notes and drawing fancy diagrams. The rumor circulated that after employees went home in the afternoon, these people would swarm across the plant floor, snoop around people's work-stations, and have heated discussions.

During this period, the plant manager was increasingly absent. He was spending more time at Elco's head office in meetings with the consultants—sessions deliberately scheduled away from the plant so as not to distract the employees. But the plant manager's absence produced the opposite effect. As people grew anxious, wondering why the captain of their ship seemed to be deserting them, the rumor mill moved into high gear. Everyone became convinced that the consultants would downsize the plant. They were sure they were about to lose their jobs. The fact that the plant manager was always gone—obviously, he was avoiding them—and that no explanation was given, could only mean that management was, they thought, 'trying to pull one over on us.' Trust and commitment at the Chester plant quickly deteriorated. Soon, people were bringing in newspaper clippings about other plants around the country that had been shut down with the help of consultants. Employees saw themselves as imminent victims of yet another management fad and resented it.

In fact, Elco managers had no intention of closing the plant. They wanted to cut out waste, freeing people to enhance quality and produce elevators for new international markets. But plant employees could not have known that.

The Master Plan

In March 1991, management gathered the Chester employees in a large room. Three months after the consultants had first appeared, they were formally introduced. At the same time, management unveiled to employees the master plan for change at the Chester plant. In a meeting that lasted only 30 minutes, employees heard how their time-honored way of working would be abolished and replaced by something called 'cellular manufacturing.' No one explained why the change was needed, nor did anyone say exactly what would be expected of employees under the new approach. The managers didn't mean to skirt the issues; they just didn't feel they had the time to go into details.

The employees sat in stunned silence, which the managers mistook for acceptance, forgetting how many months it had taken them as leaders to get comfortable with the idea of cellular manufacturing and the changes it entailed. The managers felt good when the meeting was over, believing the employees were on board. With such a terrific staff, they thought, implementation of the new system was bound to go well.

Master plan in hand, management quickly began rearranging the plant. When employees asked what the new layout aimed to achieve, the response was 'efficiency gains.' The managers didn't have time to explain why efficiency needed to be improved and didn't want to worry employees. But lacking an intellectual understanding of what was happening to them, some employees literally began feeling sick when they came to work.

Managers informed employees that they would no longer be judged on individual performance but rather on the performance of the cell. They said quicker or more experienced employees would have to pick up the slack for slower or less experienced colleagues. But they didn't elaborate. How the new system was supposed to work, management didn't make clear.

In fact, the new cell design offered tremendous benefits to employees, making vacations easier to schedule, for example, and giving them the opportunity to broaden their skills and engage in a greater variety of work. But lacking trust in the change process, employees could see only its negative side. They began taking out their fears and anger on one another. Fights erupted on the plant floor as employees refused to help those they called 'lazy people who can't finish their own jobs' or interpreted offers of help as meddling, responding with, 'This is my job. You keep to your own workstation.'

Chester's model workforce was falling apart. For the first time in the plant manager's career, employees refused to do as they were asked, turning down assignments 'even if you fire me.' They felt they could no longer trust the once popular plant manager, so they began to go around him, taking their complaints directly to his boss at the head office.

The plant manager then announced that the new cell design would allow employees to act as self-directed teams and that the role of the supervisor would be abolished. He expected people to react with excitement to his vision of Chester as the epitome of the factory of the future, where employees are empowered as entrepreneurial agents. Instead, they were simply confused. They had no idea how to succeed in this new environment. Without supervisors, what would they do if stock ran short or machines broke down? Did empowerment mean that the teams could self-authorize overtime, address quality problems such as rework, or purchase new machine tools? Unclear about how to succeed, employees felt set up to fail.

Time Out

By the summer of 1991, both cost and quality performance were in a free fall. Employees were talking about bringing the union back. Finally, in despair, the plant manager phoned Elco's industrial psychologist. 'I need your help,' he said. 'I have lost control.'

The psychologist conducted an employee opinion survey to learn what had gone wrong. Employees complained, 'Management doesn't care about our ideas or our input.' They felt that the company had scant respect for them as individuals, treating them as if they were not worthy of knowing about business conditions: 'They don't bother to tell us where we are going and what this means to us.' And they were deeply confused and mistrustful: 'We don't know exactly what management expects of us in this new cell.'

What Is Fair Process?

The theme of justice has preoccupied writers and philosophers throughout the ages, but the systematic study of fair process emerged only in the mid-1970s, when two social scientists, John W. Thibaut and Laurens Walker, combined their interest in the psychology of justice with the study of process. Focusing their attention on legal settings, they sought to understand what makes people trust a legal system so that they will comply with laws without being coerced into doing so. Their research established that people care as much about the fairness of the process through which an outcome is produced as they do about the outcome itself. Subsequent researchers such as Tom R. Tyler and E. Allan Lind demonstrated the power of fair process across diverse cultures and social settings.

We discovered the managerial relevance of fair process more than a decade ago, during a study of strategic decision-making in multinational corporations. Many top executives in those corporations were frustrated—and baffled—by the way the senior managers of their local subsidiaries behaved. Why did those managers so often fail to share information and ideas with the executives? Why did they sabotage the execution of plans they had agreed to carry out? In the 19 companies we studied, we found a direct link between processes, attitudes, and behavior. Managers who believed the company's processes were fair displayed a high level of trust and commitment, which, in turn, engendered active cooperation. Conversely, when managers felt fair process was absent, they hoarded ideas and dragged their feet.

In subsequent field research, we explored the relevance of fair process in other business contexts—for example, in companies in the midst of transformations, in teams engaged in product innovation, and in company-supplier partnerships. (See the sidebar 'Making Sense of Irrational Behavior at VW and Siemens-Nixdorf.') For companies seeking to harness the energy and creativity of committed managers and employees, the central idea that emerges from our fair process research is this: individuals are most likely to trust and cooperate freely with systems—whether they themselves win or lose by those systems—when fair process is observed.

Fair process responds to a basic human need. All of us, whatever our role in a company, want to be valued as human begins and not as 'personnel'

W. Chan Kim and Renée Mauborgne

Making Sense of Irrational Behavior at VW and Siemens-Nixdorf

Economic theories do a good job of explaining the rational side of human behavior, but they fall short in explaining why people can act negatively in the face of positive outcomes. Fair process offers managers a theory of behavior that explains—or might help predict—what would otherwise appear to be bewilderingly noneconomic, or irrational, behavior.

Consider what happened to Volkswagen. In 1992, the German carmaker was in the midst of expanding its manufacturing facility in Puebla, Mexico, its only production site in North America. The appreciation of the deutsche mark against the U.S. dollar was pricing Volkswagen out of the U.S. market. But after the North American Free Trade Agreement (NAFTA) became law in 1992, Volkswagen's cost-efficient Mexican facility was well positioned to reconquer the large North American market.

In the summer of 1992, a new labor agreement had to be hammered out. The accord VW signed with the union's secretary-general included a generous 20% pay raise for employees. VW thought the workers would be pleased.

But the union's leaders had not involved the employees in discussions about the contract's terms; they did a poor job of communicating what the new agreement would mean to employees and why a number of work-rule changes were necessary. Workers did not understand the basis for the decisions their leaders had taken. They felt betrayed.

VW's management was completely caught off guard when, on July 21, the employees started a massive walkout that cost the company as much as an estimated $10 million per day. On August 21, about 300 protesters were attacked by police dogs. The government was forced to step in to end the violence. Volkswagen's plans for the U.S. market were in disarray, and its performance was devastated.

In contrast, consider the turnaround of Siemens-Nixdorf Informationssysteme (SNI), the largest European supplier of information technology. Created in 1990 when Siemens acquired the troubled Nixdorf Computer Company, SNI had cut head count from 52,000 to 35,000 by 1994. Anxiety and fear were rampant at the company.

In 1994, Gerhard Schulmeyer, the newly appointed CEO, went out to talk to as many employees as he could. In a series of meetings large and small with a total of more than 11,000 people, Schulmeyer shared his crusading mission to engage everyone in turning the company around. He began by painting a bleakly honest picture of SNI's situation: the company was losing money despite recent efforts to slash costs. Deeper cuts were needed, and every business would have to demonstrate its viability or be eliminated. Schulmeyer set clear but tough rules about how decisions would be made. He then asked for volunteers to come up with ideas.

Within three months, the initial group of 30 volunteers grew to encompass an additional 75 SNI executives and 300 employees. These 405 change agents soon turned into 1,000, then 3,000, then 9,000, as they progressively recruited others to help save the company. Throughout the process, ideas were solicited from managers and employees alike concerning decisions that affected them, and they all understood how decisions would be made. Ideas would be auctioned off to executives willing to champion and finance them. If no executive bought a proposal on its merits, the idea would not be pursued. Although 20–30% of their proposals were rejected, employees thought the process was fair.

People voluntarily pitched in—mostly after business hours, often until midnight. In just over two years, SNI has achieved a transformation notable in European corporate history. Despite accumulated losses of DM 2 billion, by 1995 SNI was already operating in the black. In the same period, employee satisfaction almost doubled, despite the radical and difficult changes under way.

248

Why did employees of Volkswagen revolt, despite their upbeat economic circumstances? How, in the face of such demoralizing economic conditions, could SNI turn around its performance? What is at issue is not *what* the two companies did but *how* they did it. The cases illustrate the tremendous power of fair process—fairness in the process of making and executing decisions. Fair process profoundly influences attitudes and behavior critical to high performance.

or 'human assets.' We want others to respect our intelligence. We want our ideas to be taken seriously. And we want to understand the rationale behind specific decisions. People are sensitive to the signals conveyed through a company's decision-making processes. Such processes can reveal a company's willingness to trust people and seek their ideas—or they can signal the opposite.

The Three Principles

In all the diverse management contexts we have studied, we have asked people to identify the bedrock elements of fair process. And whether we were working with senior executives or shop-floor employees, the same three mutually reinforcing principles consistently emerged: engagement, explanation, and expectation clarity.

Engagement means involving individuals in the decisions that affect them by asking for their input and allowing them to refute the merits of one another's ideas and assumptions. Engagement communicates management's respect for individuals and their ideas. Encouraging refutation sharpens everyone's thinking and builds collective wisdom. Engagement results in better decisions by management and greater commitment from all involved in executing those decisions.

Explanation means that everyone involved and affected should understand why final decisions are made as they are. An explanation of the thinking that underlies decisions makes people confident that managers have considered their opinions and have made those decisions impartially in the overall interests of the company. An explanation allows employees to trust managers' intentions even if their own ideas have been rejected. It also serves as a powerful feedback loop that enhances learning.

Expectation clarity requires that once a decision is made, managers state clearly the new rules of the game. Although the expectations may be demanding, employees should know up front by what standards they will be judged and the penalties for failure. What are the new targets and milestones? Who is responsible for what? To achieve fair process, it matters less what the new rules and policies are and more that they are clearly understood. When people

W. Chan Kim and Renée Mauborgne

clearly understand what is expected of them, political jockeying and favoritism are minimized, and they can focus on the job at hand.

Notice that fair process is not decision by consensus. Fair process does not set out to achieve harmony or to win people's support through compromises that accommodate every individual's opinions, needs, or interests. While fair process gives every idea a chance, the merit of the ideas—and not consensus— is what drives the decision-making.

Nor is fair process the same as democracy in the workplace. Achieving fair process does not mean that managers forfeit their prerogative to make decisions and establish policies and procedures. Fair process pursues the best ideas whether they are put forth by one or many.

'We Really Screwed Up'

Elco managers violated all three basic principles of fair process at the Chester plant. They failed to engage employees in decisions that directly affected them. They didn't explain why decisions were being made the way they were and what those decisions meant to employees' careers and work methods. And they neglected to make clear what would be expected of employees under cellular manufacturing. In the absence of fair process, the employees at Chester rejected the transformation.

A week after the psychologist's survey was completed, management invited employees to meetings in groups of 20. Employees surmised that management was either going to pretend that the survey had never happened or accuse employees of disloyalty for having voiced their complaints. But to their amazement, managers kicked off the meeting by presenting the undiluted survey results and declaring, 'We were wrong. We really screwed up. In our haste and ignorance, we did not go through the proper process.' Employees couldn't believe their ears. There were whispers in the back of the room, 'What the devil did they say?' At more than 20 meetings over the next few weeks, managers repeated their confession. 'No one was prepared to believe us at first,' one manager said. 'We had screwed up too badly.'

At subsequent meetings, management shared with employees the company's dismal business forecast and the limited options available. Without cost reduction, Elco would have to raise its prices, and higher prices would further depress sales. That would mean cutting production even more, perhaps even moving manufacturing offshore. Heads nodded. Employees saw the bind the company was in. The business problem was becoming theirs, not just management's.

But still there were concerns: 'If we help to cut costs and learn to produce elevators that are twice as good in half the time, will we work ourselves out of a job?' In response, the managers described their strategy to increase sales

250

outside the United States. They also announced a new policy called *proaction time*: no-one would be laid off because of any improvements made by an employee. Instead, employees could use their newly free time to attend cross-training programs designed to give them the skills they would need to work in any area of operations. Or employees could act as consultants addressing quality issues. In addition, management agreed not to replace any departing employees with new hires until business conditions improved. At the same time, however, management made it clear that it retained the right to let people go if business conditions grew worse.

The Price of Unfairness

Historically, policies designed to establish fair process in organizations arise mainly in reaction to employees' complaints and uprisings. But by then it is too late. When individuals have been so angered by the violation of fair process that they have been driven to organized protest, their demands often stretch well beyond the reasonable to a desire for what theorists call *retributive justice*: not only do they want fair process restored, they also seek to visit punishment and vengeance upon those who have violated it in compensation for the disrespect the unfair process signals.

Lacking trust in management, employees push for policies that are laboriously detailed, inflexible, and often administratively constricting. They want to ensure that managers will never have the discretion to act unjustly again. In their indignation, they may try to roll back decisions imposed unfairly even when the decisions themselves were good ones—even when they were critical to the company's competitiveness or beneficial to the workers themselves. Such is the emotional power that unfair process can provoke.

Managers who view fair process as a nuisance or as a limit on their freedom to manage must understand that it is the violation of fair process that will wreak the most serious damage on corporate performance. Retribution can be very expensive.

Employees may not have liked what they heard, but they understood it. They began to see that they shared responsibility with management for Elco's success. If they could improve quality and productivity, Elco could bring more value to the market and prevent further sales erosion. To give employees confidence that they were not being misled, management pledged to regularly share data on sales, costs, and market trends—a first step toward rebuilding trust and commitment.

Elco's managers could not undo past mistakes, but they could involve employees in making future decisions. Managers asked employees why they thought the new manufacturing cells weren't working and how to fix them. Employees suggested making changes in the location of materials, in the placement of machines, and in the way tasks were performed. They began to share their knowledge; as they did so, the cells were redesigned and performance steadily improved, often far exceeding the expectations originally set by the consultants. As trust and commitment were restored, talk of bringing the union back died out.

High Park's Turn

Meanwhile, management worried about introducing the new work methods at Elco's High Park plant, which, unlike the Chester plant, had a history of resisting change. The union was strong at High Park, and some employees there had as much as 25 years' service. Moreover, the plant manager, a young engineer new to High Park, had never run a plant before. The odds seemed to be against him. If change had created animosity at Chester, one could only imagine how much worse the situation could become at High Park.

But management's fears went unrealized. When the consultants came to the plant, the young manager introduced them to all employees. At a series of plantwide meetings, corporate executives openly discussed business conditions and the company's declining sales and profits. They explained that they had visited other companies' plants and had seen the productivity improvements that cellular manufacturing could bring. They announced the proaction-time policy to calm employees' justifiable fears of layoffs. At the High Park plant, managers encouraged employees to help the consultants design the new manufacturing cells, and they encouraged active debate. Then, as the old performance measures were discarded, managers worked with employees to develop new ones and to establish the cell teams' new responsibilities.

Every day, the High Park plant manager waited for the anticipated meltdown, but it never came. Of course, there were some gripes, but even when people didn't like the decisions, they felt they had been treated fairly and, so, willingly participated in the plant's eventual performance turnaround.

Three years later, we revisited a popular local eatery to talk with people from both plants. Employees from both Chester and High Park now believe that the cellular approach is a better way to work. High Park employees spoke about their plant manager with admiration, and they commiserated with the difficulties Elco's managers had in making the changeover to cellular manufacturing. They concluded that it had been a necessary, worthwhile, and positive experience. But Chester employees spoke with anger and indignation as they described their treatment by Elco's managers. For them, as for the London woman who had been unfairly ticketed, fair process was as important as—if not more important than—the outcome.

....

Fair Process in the Knowledge Economy

Fair process may sound like a soft issue, but understanding its value is crucial for managers trying to adapt their companies to the demands of the knowledge-based economy. Unlike the traditional factors of production—land, labor, and capital—knowledge is a resource locked in the human mind. Creating and sharing knowledge are intangible activities that can neither be supervised nor forced out of people. They happen only when people cooperate voluntarily. As the Nobel laureate economist Friedrich Hayek has argued, 'Practically every individual . . . possesses unique information' that can be put to use only with 'his active cooperation.' Getting that cooperation may well turn out to be one of the key managerial issues of the next few decades. (See the sidebar 'Fair Process Is Critical in Knowledge Work', p. 254)

Voluntary cooperation was not what Frederick Winslow Taylor had in mind when at the turn of the century he began to develop an arsenal of tools to promote efficiency and consistency by controlling individuals' behavior and compelling employees to comply with management dictates. Traditional management science, which is rooted in Taylor's time-and-motion studies, encouraged a managerial preoccupation with allocating resources, creating economic incentives and rewards, monitoring and measuring performance, and manipulating organizational structures to set lines of authority. These conventional management levers still have their role to play, but they have little to do with encouraging active cooperation. Instead, they operate in the realm of outcome fairness or what social scientists call *distributive justice*, where the psychology works like this: When people get the compensation (or the resources, or the place in the organizational hierarchy) they deserve, they feel satisfied with that outcome. They will reciprocate by fulfilling to the letter their obligation to the company. The psychology of fair process, or *procedural justice*, is quite different. Fair process builds trust and commitment, trust and commitment produce voluntary cooperation, and voluntary cooperation drives performance, leading people to go beyond the call of duty by sharing their knowledge and applying their creativity. In all the management contexts we've studied, whatever the task, we have consistently observed this dynamic at work. (See the exhibit 'Two Complementary Paths to Performance.' on p. 255)

Consider the transformation of Bethlehem Steel Corporation's Sparrows Point, Maryland, division, a business unit responsible for marketing, sales,

W. Chan Kim and Renée Mauborgne

Fair Process Is Critical in Knowledge Work

It is easy to see fair process at work on the plant floor, where its violation can produce such highly visible manifestations as strikes, slowdowns, and high-defect rates. But fair process can have an even greater impact on the quality of professional and managerial work. That is because innovation is the key challenge of the knowledge-based economy, and innovation requires the exchange of ideas, which in turn depends on trust.

Executives and professionals rarely walk the picket line, but when their trust has not been won, they frequently withhold their full cooperation—and their ideas. In knowledge work, then, ignoring fair process creates high-opportunity costs in the form of ideas that never see daylight and initiatives that are never seized. For example:

A multifunctional team is created to develop an important new product. Because it contains representatives from every major functional area of the company, the team *should* produce more innovative products, with less internal fighting, shortened lead times, and lower costs. The team meets, but people drag their feet. Executives at a computer maker developing a new workstation, for example, thoughtfully deploy the traditional management levers. They hammer out a good incentive scheme. They define the project scope and structure. And they allocate the right resources. Yet the trust, idea sharing, and commitment that everyone wants never materialize. Why? Early in the project, manufacturing and marketing representatives on the team propose building a prototype, but the strong design-engineering group driving the project ignores them. Subsequently, problems surface because the design is difficult to manufacture and the application software is inadequate. The team members from manufacturing and marketing are aware of these issues all along but remain passive in sharing their concerns with the powerful design engineers. Instead, they wait until the problems reveal themselves—at which time they are very expensive to fix.

Two companies create a joint venture that offers clear benefits to both parties. But they then hold their cards so close to their chests that they ensure the alliance will create limited value for either partner. The Chinese joint-venture partner of a European engineering group, for example, withholds critical information from the field, failing to report that customers are having problems installing the partner's products and sitting on requests for new product features. Why do the Chinese fail to cooperate fully, even if it means hurting their own business?

Early in the partnership, the Chinese felt they had been shut out of key product and operating decisions. To make matters worse, the Europeans never explained the logic guiding their decisions. As the Chinese withhold critical information, the increasingly frustrated European partner responds in kind by slowing the transfer of managerial know-how, which the Chinese need badly.

Two companies create a supplier partnership to achieve improved value at lower cost. They agree to act in a seamless fashion, as one company. But the supplier seems to spend more energy on developing other customers than deepening the partnership. One consumer goods manufacturer, for example, keeps delaying the installation of a joint electronic consumer-response data system with a major food retailer. The system will substantially improve inventory management for both partners. But the supplier remains too wary to invest. Why? The retailer has a history of dropping some of the supplier's products without explanation. And the consumer company can't understand the retailer's ambiguous criteria for designating 'preferred suppliers.'

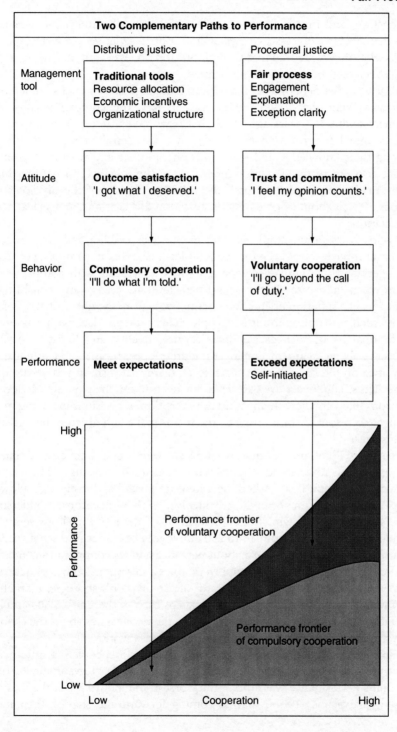

Two Complementary Paths to Performance

	Distributive justice	Procedural justice
Management tool	**Traditional tools** Resource allocation Economic incentives Organizational structure	**Fair process** Engagement Explanation Exception clarity
Attitude	**Outcome satisfaction** 'I got what I deserved.'	**Trust and commitment** 'I feel my opinion counts.'
Behavior	**Compulsory cooperation** 'I'll do what I'm told.'	**Voluntary cooperation** 'I'll go beyond the call of duty.'
Performance	**Meet expectations**	**Exceed expectations** Self-initiated

Performance frontier of voluntary cooperation

Performance frontier of compulsory cooperation

High

Performance

Low

Low   Cooperation   High

production, and financial performance. Until 1993, the 106-year-old division was managed in the classic command-and-control style. People were expected to do what they were told to do—no more and no less—and management and employees saw themselves as adversaries.

That year, Bethlehem Steel introduced a management model so different at Sparrows Point that Taylor—who was, in fact, the company's consulting engineer about 100 years ago—wouldn't have recognized it. The new model was designed to invoke in employees an active sense of responsibility for sharing their knowledge and ideas with one another and with management. It was also meant to encourage them to take the initiative for getting things done. In the words of Joe Rosel, the president of one of the division's five unions, 'It's all about involvement, justification for decisions, and a clear set of expectations.'

At Sparrows Point, employees are involved in making and executing decisions at three levels. At the top is a joint-leadership team, composed of senior managers and five employee representatives, that deals with company-wide issues when they arise. At the department level are area teams, consisting of managers like superintendents and of employees from the different areas of the plant, such as zone committee people. Those teams deal with day-to-day operational issues such as customer service, quality, and logistics. Ad hoc problem-solving teams of employees address opportunities and obstacles as they arise on the shop floor. At each level, team mates share and debate their ideas. Thus, employees are assured a fair hearing for their points of view on decisions likely to affect them. With the exception of decisions involving major changes or resource commitments, the teams make and execute the decisions themselves.

Sparrows Point uses numerous processes and devices to ensure that all employees can understand why decisions need to be executed. There is, for example, a bulletin board where decisions are posted and explained, allowing employees who haven't been directly involved in those decisions to understand what's going on and why. In addition, in more than 70 four-hour seminars, groups ranging in size from 50 to 250 employees have met to discuss changes occurring at the division, learn about new ideas under consideration, and find out how changes might affect employees' roles and responsibilities. A quarterly newsletter and a monthly 'report card' of the division's strategic, marketing, operational, and financial performance keeps each of the unit's 5,300 employees informed. And the teams report back to their colleagues about the changes they are making, seeking help in making the ideas work.

Fair process has produced significant changes in people's attitudes and behavior. Consider, for example, the tin mill unit at Sparrows Point. In 1992, the unit's performance was among the worst in the industry. But then, as one employee explains, 'People started coming forward and sharing their ideas.

They started caring about doing great work, not just getting by. Take the success we've had in light-gauge cable sheathing. We had let this high value-added product slip because the long throughput time required for production held up the other mills in the unit. But after we started getting everyone involved and explained why we needed to improve throughput, ideas started to flow. At first, the company was doubtful: if the product had created a bottleneck before, why should it be different now? But people came up with the idea of using two sequential mills instead of one to eliminate the bottleneck. Did people suddenly get smarter? No. I'd say they started to care.'

The object in creating this new way of working at Sparrows Point was to improve the intellectual buy-in and emotional commitment of employees. It has apparently been successful. Since 1993, Sparrows Point has turned a profit three years in a row, the first time that has happened since the late 1970s. The division is becoming a showcase demonstrating how a declining industry can be revitalized in today's knowledge economy. In the words of one Sparrows Point employee, 'Since we know now everything that's going on in the company, we have more trust in management and are more committed to making things happen. People have started doing things beyond the normal call of duty.'

Overcoming Mental Barriers

If fair process is such a simple idea and yet so powerful, why do so few companies practice it? Most people think of themselves as fair, and managers are no exception. But if you ask them what it means to be a fair manager, most will describe how they give people the authority they deserve, or the resources they need, or the rewards they have earned. In other words, they will confuse fair process with fair outcomes. The few managers who focus on process might identify only one of the three fair-process principles (the most widely understood is engagement), and they would stop there.

But there are two more fundamental reasons, beyond this simple lack of understanding, that explain why fair process is so rare. The first involves power. Some managers continue to believe that knowledge is power and that they retain power only by keeping what they know to themselves. Their implicit strategy is to preserve their managerial discretion by deliberately leaving the rules for success and failure vague. Other managers maintain control by keeping employees at arm's length, substituting memos and forms for direct, two-way communication, thus avoiding challenges to their ideas or authority. Such styles can reflect deeply ingrained patterns of behavior, and rarely are managers conscious of how they exercise power. For them, fair process would represent a threat.

The second reason is also largely unconscious because it resides in an economic assumption that most of us have grown up taking at face value, the belief that people are concerned only with what's best for themselves. But, as we have seen, there is ample evidence to show that when the process is perceived to be fair, most people will accept outcomes that are not wholly in their favor. People realize that compromises and sacrifices are necessary on the job. They accept the need for short-term personal sacrifices in order to advance the long-term interests of the corporation. Acceptance is conditional, however, hinged as it is on fair process.

Fair process reaches into a dimension of human psychology that hasn't been fully explored in conventional management practice. Yet every company can tap into the voluntary cooperation of its people by building trust through fair processes.

16 Communities of Practice: The Organizational Frontier

Etienne C. Wenger and William M. Snyder

Today's economy runs on knowledge, and most companies work assiduously to capitalize on that fact. They use cross-functional teams, customer-or product-focused business units, and work groups—to name just a few organizational forms—to capture and spread ideas and know-how. In many cases, these ways of organizing are very effective, and no one would argue for their demise. But a new organizational form is emerging that promises to complement existing structures and radically galvanize knowledge sharing, learning, and change. It's called the community of practice.

What are communities of practice? In brief, they are groups of people informally bound together by shared expertise and passion for a joint enterprise—engineers engaged in deep-water drilling, for example, consultants who specialize in strategic marketing, or frontline managers in charge of check processing at a large commercial bank. Some communities of practice meet regularly—for lunch on Thursdays, say. Others are connected primarily by e-mail networks. A community of practice may or may not have an explicit agenda on a given week, and even if it does, it may not follow the agenda closely. Inevitably, however, people in communities of practice share their experiences and knowledge in free-flowing, creative ways that foster new approaches to problems.

Because its primary 'output'—knowledge—is intangible, the community of practice might sound like another 'soft' management fad. But that is not the case. During the past five years, we have seen communities of practice improve organizational performance at companies as diverse as an international bank, a major car manufacturer, and a U.S. government agency. Communities of practice can drive strategy, generate new lines of business, solve problems, promote the spread of best practices, develop people's professional skills, and help companies recruit and retain talent. (For examples of how communities of practice have helped companies, see the sidebar 'Communities in Action.')

If communities of practice are so effective, why aren't they more prevalent? There are three reasons. The first is that although communities of practice have been around for a long time—for centuries, in fact—the term has just recently entered the business vernacular. The second is that only several dozen forward-thinking companies have taken the leap of 'installing' or nurturing them. The third reason is that it is not particularly easy to build and sustain communities of practice or to integrate them with the rest of an organization. The organic, spontaneous, and informal nature of communities of practice makes them resistant to supervision and interference.

But we have observed a number of companies that have overcome the managerial paradox inherent in communities of practice and successfully nurtured them. In general, we have found that managers cannot mandate communities of practice. Instead, successful managers bring the right people together, provide an infrastructure in which communities can thrive, and measure the communities' value in non-traditional ways. These tasks of cultivation aren't easy, but the harvest they yield makes them well worth the effort.

....

The Hallmarks of Communities of Practice

Communities of practice were common as far back as ancient times. In classical Greece, for instance, 'corporations' of metalworkers, potters, masons, and other craftsmen had both a social purpose (members worshipped the same deities and celebrated holidays together) and a business function (members trained apprentices and spread innovations). In the Middle Ages, guilds played similar roles for artisans throughout Europe. Today's communities of practice are different in one important respect: instead of being composed primarily of people working on their own, they often exist within large organizations.

Communities of practice are as diverse as the situations that give rise to them. People in companies form them for a variety of reasons. For example, when a company reorganizes into a team-based structure, employees with functional expertise may create communities of practice as a way of maintaining connections with peers. Elsewhere, people may form communities in response to changes originating outside the organization, such as the rise of e-commerce, or inside, such as new company strategies—think of auto manufacturers going into the financing business or computer makers offering consulting services.

A community of practice can exist entirely within a business unit or stretch across divisional boundaries. A community can even thrive with members from

Communities in Action

Communities of practice add value to organizations in several important ways:

They help drive strategy. Communities of practice are the heart and soul of the World Bank's knowledge management strategy. Some communities of practice have existed for years at the bank, but they were mostly small and fragmented. That has changed now that the bank has made knowledge management the key to its goal of becoming the 'knowledge bank'—providing high-quality information and know-how about economic development.

The bank's decision to fund communities of practice, for example, led to a significant increase in the number of organizationwide communities—it's now over 100—and in the intensity of participation. As the bank supplements its emphasis on lending money with providing development expertise, these communities will increasingly contribute to the bank's strategic direction.

They start new lines of business. Consider how a group of consultants from one firm created a community that eventually generated an entirely new line of business. The group met regularly at O'Hare airport between engagements with clients. Its domain was retail marketing in the banking industry, and the meetings focused on new business opportunities for clients. Over a two-year period, the initial group of five to seven consultants attracted many others within the firm. Four years after the first meeting, the community had created a new line of marketing approaches for financial services companies. And it convened 200 people from the firm in New Orleans for its annual conference. The community acted like a petri dish for entrepreneurial insights that ultimately generated more clients, shaped the firm's strategy, and enhanced its reputation.

They solve problems quickly. Members of a community of practice know whom to ask for help with a problem. They also know how to ask questions so that peers can quickly comprehend and focus on the heart of the problem. At Buckman Labs, members of communities of practice from around the world routinely respond to practice-specific queries within 24 hours. In one case, an employee trying to help a pulp mill customer in the Pacific Northwest solve a dye-retention problem received several responses within a day from expert peers in Europe, South Africa, and Canada—and one response provided exactly the solution the customer needed.

They transfer best practices. A community of practice does much more than work on specific problems. It's also an ideal forum for sharing and spreading best practices across a company.

Consider how the former Chrysler made this work, beginning in the early 1990s when the company broke up its functional departments to organize around car platforms such as small cars and minivans. Chrysler's leaders feared they would lose functional expertise and the ability to keep up with leading-edge change. To address those concerns, senior managers and engineers formed communities of practice known as 'tech clubs,' which were composed of experts from different car platforms. The clubs helped the company successfully make the move to platforms, a change that cut R&D costs and car-development cycle times by more than half.

Today the tech clubs are an important part of the integration of DaimlerChrysler. The clubs meet regularly to discuss questions in 11 areas of product development, including body design, electronics, and vehicle development. They analyze variations in practice and set standards. Engineers who participate in the clubs are responsible for developing and maintaining an Engineering Book of Knowledge, a database that captures information on compliance standards, supplier specifications, and best practices.

They develop professional skills. Studies have shown that apprentices learn as much from journeymen and more advanced apprentices as they do from master craftsmen. It seems clear, then, that effective learning depends on the availability of peers and their willingness to act as mentors and coaches. That applies not only to the education of inexperienced workers but also to that of experts. The best neurosurgeons don't rely simply on their own brilliance; they read

(Continued)

peer-reviewed journals, attend conferences in which their colleagues discuss new research, and travel great distances to work alongside surgeons who are developing innovative techniques.

Some companies have found that communities of practice are particularly effective arenas for fostering professional development. At IBM, communities of practice hold their own conferences, both in person and online. Presentations, hallway conversations, dinners, and chat rooms are opportunities for members to exchange ideas, build skills, and develop networks.

They help companies recruit and retain talent. American Management Systems has found that communities of practice help the company win the war (or at least some of the battles) for talent. Thus a consultant who was planning to leave the company decided to stay after peers at a community forum found project opportunities for her that were tailor-made to her interests and expertise. Other valuable consultants—at least six, by one manager's count—stayed with the company after being invited to join a prestigious community of practice that would enable them to develop skills and find new clients.

different companies; for example, the CEOs who make up the Business Round-table meet regularly to discuss relationships between business and public policy, among other things. A community can be made up of tens or even hundreds of people, but typically it has a core of participants whose passion for the topic energizes the community and who provide intellectual and social leadership. Large communities are often subdivided by geographic region or by subject matter in order to encourage people to take part actively.

Communities of practice differ from other forms of organization in several ways. (For a summary of the differences, see the exhibit 'A Snapshot Comparison.') Consider, briefly, how communities differ from teams. Teams are created by managers to complete specific projects. Managers select team members on the basis of their ability to contribute to the team's goals, and the group disbands once the project has been finished. Communities of practice, on the other hand, are informal—they organize themselves, meaning they set their own agendas and establish their own leadership. And membership in a community of practice is self-selected. In other words, people in such communities tend to know when and if they should join. They know if they have something to give and whether they are likely to take something away. And members of an existing community, when they invite someone to join, also operate on a gut sense of the prospective member's appropriateness for the group.

To get a better sense of how communities of practice look in action, let's consider two examples.

At the Hill's Pet Nutrition facility in Richmond, Indiana, line technicians meet weekly to talk about recent successes and frustrations as well as challenges looming ahead. They formed the group several years ago after managers and technicians attended a retreat where they were introduced to the concept of communities of practice and learned how such groups could help the company develop and retain technical expertise. The group has a 'mayor' who's been chosen by his peers to keep things on track from week to week and see to it that

A Snapshot Comparison

Communities of practice, formal work groups, teams, and informal networks are useful in complementary ways. Below is a summary of their characteristics.

	What's the purpose?	Who belongs?	What holds it together?	How long does it last?
Community of practice	To develop members' capabilities; to build and exchange knowledge	Members who select themselves	Passion, commitment, and identification with the group's expertise	As long as there is interest in maintaining the group
Formal work group	To deliver a product of service	Everyone who reports to the group's manager	Job requirements and common goals	Until the next reorganization
Project team	To accomplish a specified task	Employees assigned by senior management	The project's milestones and goals	Until the project has been completed
Informal network	To collect and pass on business information	Friends and business acquaintances	Mutual needs	As long as people have a reason to connect

people with relevant expertise are present when needed. The plant grants people time to participate. Actual attendance fluctuates depending on the agenda.

At a recent gathering we observed, 12 technicians from the first and second shifts met around a large table in the glass-walled conference room overlooking the plant. Although it was mid-afternoon, they were soon joined by Roger, a technician from the third shift who would have to return seven hours later to begin his 'real' work. Roger made a special trip in on this occasion to help John hone his proposal to substitute pneumatic tubes for the balky conveyor belt that carried the pet food kibbles to the packaging bin; Roger's background in plumbing was thus particularly relevant.

Senior managers at the plant had not warmed to the pneumatic tube idea. They believed the conveyor system would work if people just operated it properly. They felt the new approach was unproven and, in any case, would be difficult to incorporate with the plant's current technology. Nevertheless, community members had encouraged John to continue pushing for change, and John had pressed on, buoyed by the knowledge that experts in his community of practice saw merit in his proposal.

Before the group members took up John's proposal, they followed their usual opening routine—going around the table and letting people vent about one thing or another, including the most recent Colts game. They also followed up on the previous week's discussion about rethinking how new technicians are certified. Then they turned to the proposal.

Vince began by reviewing management's concerns. John then explained that the latest revision of his proposal included evidence from colleagues in other plants that the technology was reliable and would be compatible with existing equipment. Roger was able to confirm the evidence based on his own experience and suggested that he go along the next time John presented his ideas to management.

The community support for John's work ultimately paid off. A year after the meeting, the company installed the new technology. The result? Significant reductions in downtime and wasted pet food related to packaging. In addition to benefiting the company in this way, the community provides important benefits for members: it gives them opportunities to solve nagging problems and hone their ability to run the plant effectively. Improvements in operations can lead to financial rewards in the form of bonuses that are tied to the plant's performance.

Our second example comes from Hewlett-Packard, where a community of practice consisting of product-delivery consultants from around North America holds monthly teleconferences. The community focuses on an HP software product called High Availability, which minimizes computer downtime for customers. The core group of consultants, who had been somewhat isolated, came together a few years ago with the help of facilitators from a knowledge management support team. The members discovered that they had many problems in common and that they could learn a great deal from one another. The community has succeeded in standardizing the software's sales and installation processes and establishing a consistent pricing scheme for HP salespeople.

Participation in the monthly calls is voluntary, but levels of attendance are steady. For one such call, the focus was meant to be on Maureen's experiences with a major customer for which she was installing the product. Before diving in, however, the consultants spent the first ten minutes chatting about the recent reorganization of their division—whether it was a good thing, what it meant for them, and so on.

Maureen had not spent a lot of time preparing a formal presentation; she knew that only by talking directly and openly could she spur the give-and-take that would make the call worthwhile for the group. As the call proceeded, community members interrupted her constantly with questions and examples from their own experiences—all of which helped Maureen understand how to work more effectively with her clients.

The conversation then turned to a persistent bug in the software. Rob, a member of the software division that developed the product, had been invited to take part in these calls to create a stronger connection between the product-delivery consultants and software developers. He'd already worked out a way to get rid of the bug, but he learned from the stories he heard in the teleconference how to make the fix even more effective. He told the group that he would follow up during next month's call.

The participants in these communities of practice were learning together by focusing on problems that were directly related to their work. In the short term, this made their work easier or more effective; in the long term, it helped build both their communities and their shared practices—thus developing capabilities critical to the continuing success of the organizations.

The strength of communities of practice is self-perpetuating. As they generate knowledge, they reinforce and renew themselves. That's why communities of practice give you not only the golden eggs but also the goose that lays them. The farmer killed the goose to get all the gold and ended up losing both; the challenge for organizations is to appreciate the goose and to understand how to keep it alive and productive.

A Paradox of Management

Although communities of practice are fundamentally informal and self-organizing, they benefit from cultivation. Like gardens, they respond to attention that respects their nature. You cannot tug on a cornstalk to make it grow faster or taller, and you should not yank a marigold out of the ground to see if it has roots. You can, however, till the soil, pull out weeds, add water during dry spells, and ensure that your plants have the proper nutrients. And while you may welcome the wildflowers that bloom without any cultivation, you may get even more satisfaction from those vegetables and flowers you started from seed.

The same is true for companies that grow communities of practice from seed. To get communities going—and to sustain them over time—managers should:

- identify potential communities of practice that will enhance the company's strategic capabilities;
- provide the infrastructure that will support such communities and enable them to apply their expertise effectively;
- use non-traditional methods to assess the value of the company's communities of practice.

Identifying Potential Communities

Communities of practice should not be created in a vacuum. In most cases, informal networks of people with the ability and the passion to further develop an organization's core competencies already exist. The task is to identify such groups and help them come together as communities of practice. At Shell, for example, a person who wants to develop a new community joins forces with a consultant and interviews prospective members. They look at challenges and problems that people across units and teams have in common and that would serve as bases for a community of practice. The interviews are not only a means of collecting information; they also generate enthusiasm for the embryonic community. After laying the groundwork, the coordinator calls the members of the community of practice together, and the group begins discussing plans for activities that will build individual and group capabilities and advance the company's strategic agenda.

A key task is defining a community's domain. If members do not feel personally connected to the group's area of expertise and interest once it has been defined, they will not fully commit themselves to the work of the community. The U.S. Veterans Administration found this to be true with a community it started in its claims-processing organization. The core group first defined its focus as 'technical capability,' an umbrella term covering employees' processing skills and the associated procedures and equipment. During the community's first year, the core group's participation was limited and progress was slow. The more active members decided they could move faster if they redefined the community's domain. They created subcommunities of first-line managers, customer service representatives, and training coordinators. As a result, the first-line managers are sharing tips about implementing a new team structure, the customer service reps are helping to set standards to reduce processing time, and the training coordinators are upgrading training modules across the organization.

Providing the Infrastructure

Communities of practice are vulnerable because they lack the legitimacy—and the budgets—of established departments. To reach their full potential, then, they need to be integrated into the business and supported in specific ways.

Senior executives must be prepared to invest time and money in helping such communities reach their full potential. That means intervening when communities run up against obstacles to their progress, such as IT systems that do not serve them, promotion systems that overlook community contributions, and reward structures that discourage collaboration. It also means linking communities to related initiatives such as a corporate university.

One way to strengthen communities of practice is to provide them with official sponsors and support teams. Such sponsors and teams do not design the communities or prescribe their activities or outcomes. Instead, they work with internal community leaders to provide resources and coordination.

Companies have done this using a range of approaches. Compare the cases of two organizations—American Management Systems (AMS) and the World

Bank—each of which has adopted the community of practice as the foundation of its knowledge management strategy. AMS takes an especially formal approach, while the World Bank combines formal and informal methods. A few years ago, AMS was going through an intense period of growth and globalization and, as a result, was losing its distinctive ability to leverage knowledge across the company. Then-chairman Charles Rossotti personally invited 'thought leaders,' who had been nominated by their business units, to spearhead the development of communities of practice in strategic areas. The company pays for two to three weeks of the leaders' time each year for these activities.

Community membership at AMS is a privilege. To join a community, a potential member must be recognized as an expert by his or her manager. Once on board, a participant has to complete one knowledge-development project per year—for instance, documenting a best practice—in order to remain in the community. Community members' participation is paid for by their business units, which fund their annual projects, cover their attendance at workshops, and send them to an annual conference that brings together all the company's communities of practice.

At the World Bank, president James Wolfensohn established the goal of making his organization the 'knowledge bank'—a global source for high-quality information on economic development—so that it could better fulfill its mission of eradicating poverty. Key people throughout the organization then took the initiative to start communities of practice. Membership is open, and members decide on the level of participation that suits their needs. Communities of practice receive funding for specific activities and manage their own budgets.

At both AMS and the World Bank, senior management boards sponsor communities. Support teams help with community development and coordinate annual community conferences, knowledge fairs, library services, and technical support. Both organizations also have started to fund positions for knowledge managers who assist community leaders. These facilitators coordinate the groups, organize events, respond to queries from members, and keep the communities current on information from external sources.

AMS is exploring ways of explicitly rewarding community members. It has a promotion system that formally acknowledges their work, and it grants non-financial rewards such as early access to innovative technology and special business cards that attest to the members' expertise. The World Bank also formally recognizes community participation through its personnel evaluation system, but to drive participation it relies primarily on the intrinsic benefits of community membership: the opportunities to solve problems, develop new ideas, and build relationships with peers who share a common passion.

At both AMS and the World Bank, communities of practice have brought together people and ideas, and they have spread knowledge throughout the companies' global operations. They have made demonstrable and significant contributions to the organizations' goals. These two cases show how different styles of formal commitment to communities of practice by senior managers can be very effective when aligned with the organization's culture.

Using Non-traditional Methods to Measure Value

Leaders intuitively recognize the benefit of developing people's capabilities. That said, most have difficulty understanding the value of communities. For one thing, the effects of community activities are often delayed. For another, results generally appear in the work of teams and business units, not in the communities themselves. And it's often hard to determine whether a great idea that surfaced during a community meeting would have bubbled up anyway in a different setting. Such complexity makes it very difficult for managers to assess the value of communities.

The best way for an executive to assess the value of a community of practice is by listening to members' stories, which can clarify the complex relationships among activities, knowledge, and performance. 'The idea we pursued at that meeting helped me persuade the customer to continue to buy our service.' 'Thanks to advice from the community, I got done in two days what normally takes me two weeks.' 'I took a risk because I was confident I had the backing of my community—and it paid off.'

The solution to the conundrum of valuing communities of practice is to gather anecdotal evidence systematically. You cannot just collect certain stories, perhaps the most compelling ones, because isolated events can be unrepresentative. A systematic effort captures the diversity and range of activities that communities are involved in.

At Shell, community coordinators often conduct interviews to collect these stories and then publish them in newsletters and reports. AMS organizes a yearly competition to identify the best stories. An analysis of a sample of stories revealed that the communities had saved the company $2 million to $5 million and increased revenue by more than $13 million in one year.

The New Frontier

Communities of practice are emerging in companies that thrive on knowledge. The first step for managers now is to understand what these communities are and how they work. The second step is to realize that they are the hidden fountainhead of knowledge development and therefore the key to the challenge of the knowledge economy. The third step is to appreciate the paradox that these informal structures require specific managerial efforts to develop them and to integrate them into the organization so that their full power can be leveraged.

Communities of practice are the new frontier. They may seem unfamiliar now, but in five to ten years they may be as common to discussions about organization as business units and teams are today—if managers learn how to make them a central part of their companies' success.

17 Knowing What We Know: Supporting Knowledge Creation and Sharing in Social Networks

Rob Cross, Andrew Parker, Laurence Prusak and Stephen
P. Borgatti

Crafting an Answer

'So the call came in late on Thursday afternoon and right away I wished I
hadn't answered the phone. We had received a last-second opportunity to bid
on a sizable piece of work that the Partner on the other end of the line really
wanted to pursue. I had no clue how to even begin looking for relevant
methodologies or case examples, so my first move was to tap into my
network to find some relevant info and leads to other people or databases.
And I relied pretty heavily on this group over the next couple of days. Seth
was great for pointing me to other people and relevant information, Paul
provided ideas on the technical content of the project while Jeff really helped
in showing me how to frame the client's issues in ways that we could sell. He
also helped navigate and get buy-in from the client given his knowledge of
their operations and politics...I mean the whole game is just being the
person that can get the client what they need with [the firm's] resources
behind you. This almost always seems to mean knowing who knows what
and figuring out a way to bring them to bear on your client's issue.'

—*Anonymous Interviewee*

The way in which this manager relied on his network to obtain information and
knowledge critical to the success of an important project is common and likely
resonates with your own experience. Usually when we think of where people
turn for information or knowledge we think of databases, the Web, intranets
and portals or other, more traditional, repositories such as file cabinets or policy

and procedure manuals. However, a significant component of a person's information environment consists of the relationships he or she can tap for various informational needs. For example, in summarizing a decade worth of studies, Tom Allen of Massachusetts Institute of Technology (MIT) found that engineers and scientists were roughly five times more likely to turn to a person for information than to an impersonal source such as a database or a file cabinet. In other settings, research has consistently shown that who you know has a significant impact on what you come to know, as relationships are critical for obtaining information, solving problems, and learning how to do your work.

Particularly in knowledge-intensive work, creating an informational environment that helps employees solve increasingly complex and often ambiguous problems holds significant performance implications. Frequently such efforts entail knowledge management initiatives focusing on the capture and sharing of codified knowledge and reusable work products. To be sure, these so-called knowledge bases hold pragmatic benefits. They bridge boundaries of time and space, allow for potential reuse of tools or work products employed successfully in other areas of an organization, and provide a means of reducing organizational 'forgetting' as a function of employee turnover. However, such initiatives often undervalue crucial knowledge held by employees and the web of relationships that help dynamically solve problems and create new knowledge.

As we move further into an economy where collaboration and innovation are increasingly central to organizational effectiveness, we must pay more attention to the sets of relationships that people rely on to accomplish their work. Certainly we can expect emerging collaborative technologies to facilitate virtual work and skill profiling systems to help with the location of relevant expertise. However, as was so poignantly demonstrated by reengineering, technology alone can only accomplish so much in the pursuit of business performance. Improving efficiency and effectiveness in knowledge-intensive work demands more than sophisticated technologies—it requires attending to the often idiosyncratic ways that people seek out knowledge, and learn from, and solve, problems with other people in organizations.

With this in mind, we initiated a research program to determine means of improving employees' ability to create and share knowledge in important social networks. In the first phase of our research, we assessed the characteristics of relationships that 40 managers relied on for learning and knowledge sharing in important projects. In the second phase, we systematically employed social network analysis to map these dimensions of relationships among strategically important networks of people in various organizations. Working with a consortium of Fortune 500 companies and government organizations, we developed empirical support for relational characteristics that facilitate knowledge creation and sharing in social networks as well as insight into social and technical interventions to facilitate knowledge flow in these networks.

Supporting Knowledge Creation and Sharing in Social Networks

In the first phase of our research we asked 40 managers to reflect on a recent project that was important to their careers and indicate where they obtained information critical to the project's success. As can be seen in Figure 17.1, these managers overwhelmingly indicated (and supported with vivid stories) that they received this information from other people far more frequently than impersonal sources such as their personal computer archives, the Internet or the organization's knowledge management database. And we found this in an organization that most industry analysts heralded as a knowledge management exemplar because of its investment in technology. This is not to say that the firm's leading edge technical platform and organizational practices for capturing, screening, and archiving knowledge were not helpful. Just to point out that 'impersonal' information sources were primarily leveraged only after the managers had been unsuccessful in obtaining relevant knowledge from colleagues (or when directed to a point in the database by a colleague).

We also asked the managers to identify the people most important to them in terms of information or knowledge acquired for that project, and had them carefully describe these relationships. Four features emerged that distinguished

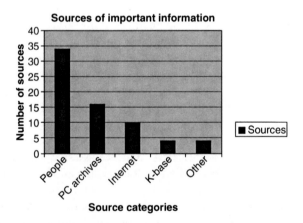

Fig. 17.1 *Where People Go for Information*
 [1] (Total sources exceed the number of interviews because several respondents indicated more than one critical source of information. In this case, prior material included computer or paper files or archives that the interviewees had used in prior projects.)

effective from ineffective relationships: (1) knowing what another person knows and thus when to turn to them; (2) being able to gain timely access to that person; (3) willingness of the person sought out to engage in problem solving rather than dump information; and (4) a degree of safety in the relationship that promoted learning and creativity. An in-depth review of these dimensions is beyond our scope here; however, a summary of these relational features and representative quotes can be found in Table 17.1.

Table 17.1 Relational Qualities that Promote Effective Knowledge Sharing

Relational Dimensions	Impact on Knowledge Seeking	Representative Quote
Knowledge	Knowing what someone else knows (even if we are initially inaccurate and calibrate over time) is a precursor to seeking a specific person out when we are faced with a problem or opportunity. For other people to be options we must have at least some perception of their expertise.	'At [Company X] we had access to background information and you know lots of case studies and approaches that were really well written up. I had no experience though of actually applying this approach on an engagement. So what was specifically useful to me was to talk with Terry who I knew had done several of these engagements. He helped me work some of the content in the database into a workable approach. I was lucky I knew him and could leverage some of his experience . . . '
Access	However, knowing what someone else knows is only useful if you can get access to their thinking in a sufficiently timely fashion. Access is heavily influenced by the closeness of one's relationship as well as physical proximity, organizational design, and collaborative technology.	'I have gotten less frustrated the more I have worked with him because I know how to get a hold of him. It took me a while to figure out that he was a phone guy and not an e-mail guy. And I have also learned how to ask him for help and what I can expect. It was important to learn what I could rely on him for and how to get his attention to make the relationship, which was initially frustrating, an important one for me . . . '

(Continued)

Table 17.1   (*Continued*)

Relational Dimensions	Impact on Knowledge Seeking	Representative Quote
Engagement	People who are helpful in learning interactions actively think with the seeker and engage in problem solving. Rather than dump information, these people first understand the problem *as experienced by the seeker* and then shape their knowledge to the problem at hand.	'Some people will give you their opinion without trying to either understand what your objectives are or understand where you are coming from or be very closed in their answer to you. [She] is the sort of person who first makes sure she understands what the issue is. I have been around people who give you a quick spiel because they think they are smart and that by throwing some framework or angle up they can quickly wow you and get out of the hard work of solving a problem. [She], for all her other responsibilities and stature within the firm, is not like that.'
Safety	Finally, those relationships that are safe are often most effective for learning purposes. Being able to admit a lack of knowledge or to diverge in a conversation often results in creativity and learning.	'[he] is always looking for the positive spin on something. I mean even if he thinks that is garbage and if he really thought that, he would make this known but in a positive way. So he might say 'Well I think we might be a little off track on that and here's why' and then say why and of course there is learning that comes from that.'

The managers we interviewed indicated that these four dimensions were key characteristics of relationships that were effective for acquiring information, solving problems or learning. In contrast, they also recounted numerous times when learning or knowledge sharing did not happen because of one of the above dimensions not existing in the relationship (e.g. someone knew what they needed to know, but did not make himself or herself accessible). Further, a separate quantitative study demonstrated that these dimensions consistently predict whom people seek out for informational purposes, even after controlling for such features as education or age similarity, physical proximity, time in organization, and formal hierarchical position. With the importance of these four relational characteristics established, the second step of our research was to use social network analysis to map information flow as well as these relational characteristics among strategically important groups to improve knowledge creation and sharing.

Social Network Analysis

Social network analysis (SNA) provides a rich and systematic means of assessing informal networks by mapping and analyzing relationships among people, teams, departments, or even entire organizations. Though managers are often adamant that they know their organization, studies are showing that they have different levels of accuracy in understanding the networks around them. By virtue of their position in the hierarchy, managers are frequently far removed from the day-to-day work interactions that generate an organization's informal structure, and so may have a very inaccurate understanding of the actual patterns of relationships. And the potential for inaccurate perceptions is only increased by our transition into a world of virtual work and telecommuting, where employees are engaged in work relationships increasingly invisible to superiors. Social network analysis can provide an X-ray of the way in which work is or is not occurring in these informal networks.

Mapping Information Flow among Executives

We conducted a social network analysis of executives in the exploration and production division of a large petroleum organization. This group was in the midst of implementing a distributed technology to help transfer knowledge across drilling initiatives and was also interested in assessing their ability as a group to create and share knowledge. As a result, we were asked to conduct a social network analysis of information flow among the top 20 executives within the Exploration and Production Division. As can be seen in Figure 17.2, this analysis revealed a striking contrast between the group's formal and informal structure.

Three important points quickly emerged for this group in relation to sharing information and effectively leveraging their collective expertise. First, the social network analysis identified mid-level managers who were critical in terms of

Rob Cross, Andrew Parker, Laurence Prusak, Stephen P. Borgatti

(A) **Formal organizational structure of exploration and production division**

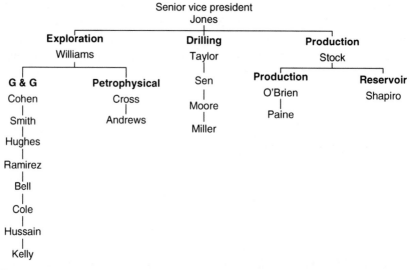

(B) **Informal organizational structure of exploration and production division**

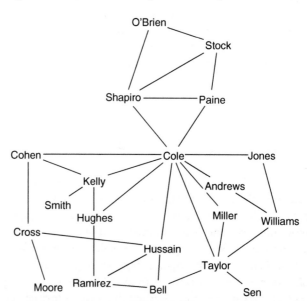

Fig. 17.2 *Formal versus Informal Structure in a Petroleum Organization* (Names have been disguised at the request of the company.)

276

information flow within the group. A particular surprise came from the very central role that Cole played in terms of both overall information flow within the group and being the only point of contact between members of the production division and the rest of the network. A facilitated session with this executive team revealed that over time Cole's reputation for expertise and responsiveness had resulted in his becoming a critical source for all sorts of information. Through no fault of his own, the number of informational requests he received and the number of projects he was involved in had grown excessive, which not only caused him stress but also frequently slowed the group as a whole, because Cole had become a bottleneck.

The social network analysis also revealed the extent to which the entire network was disproportionately reliant on Cole. If he were hired away, the efficiency of this group as a whole would be significantly impacted as people in the informal network reestablished important informational relationships. Of course, people would find ways to reconnect to obtain necessary information. However, the social network diagram made it very clear that if Cole left, the company would lose both his valuable knowledge, and the relationships he had established that in many ways were holding the network together. As a result, a central intervention that came from this analysis was to reallocate many of the informational requests coming to Cole to other members in the group. Simply categorizing various informational requests that Cole received and then allocating ownership of these informational or decision domains to other executives served to both unburden Cole and make the overall network more responsive and robust.

Just as important, the social network analysis helped to identify highly peripheral people who essentially represented untapped expertise and thus under-utilized resources for the group. In particular, it became apparent that many of the senior people had become too removed from the day-to-day operations of this group. For example, Figure 17.2 reveals that the most senior person (Jones) was one of the most peripheral in the informal network. This is a common finding. As people move higher within an organization, their work begins to entail more administrative tasks that makes them both less accessible and less knowledgeable about the day-to-day work of their subordinates. However, in this case our debrief session indicated that Jones had become too removed, and his lack of responsiveness frequently held the entire network back when important decisions needed to be made. In this case, the social network diagram helped to make what could have been a potentially difficult conversation with this executive non-confrontational, and resulted in more of his time being committed back to the group.

Finally, the social network analysis demonstrated the extent to which the production division (the subgroup on the top of the diagram) had become separated from the overall network. Several months before this analysis, these people had been physically moved to a different floor in the building. Upon reviewing the network diagram, many of the executives realized that this physical separation had resulted in loss of a lot of the serendipitous meetings that occurred when they were colocated. In this case, the executives decided that they needed to introduce more structured meetings to compensate for this recent loss of serendipitous communication (and they also adopted an instant messaging system to promote communication).

Beyond Information Flow

In addition to mapping information flow, we also use social network analysis to assess the relational characteristics of *knowledge, access, engagement,* and *safety* among a group. Sometimes, if we have only mapped an information network and find that certain people are not as connected as they should be, it is difficult to tell what to do. Simply proposing more or better communication is the oldest consulting recommendation in the book—and no one today really needs more meetings. By analyzing the dimensions of relationships that precede or lead to effective knowledge sharing, we can offer more precise ways to improve a network's ability to create and share knowledge. For example, if it is discovered that the *knowledge* network is sparse, it might make sense to consider a skill profiling system or new staffing practices—technical and social interventions designed to help a network know what it knows. In contrast, if the *access* network is sparse, then it might make sense to consider peer feedback or technical means of connecting distributed workers (e.g. video conferencing or instant messaging) to make sure that people within the network have access to each other in a timely fashion.

Throughout our research we have found organizations employing various practices to promote these relational dimensions in important networks. We have summarized some of these initiatives in Figure 17.3 on pp. 279–81, and now turn to specific case examples where we used social network analysis to assess these relational dimensions.

Knowledge Dimension: Do We Know What We Know?　　Other people can only be useful to us in solving problems if we have some awareness of their expertise. Even if we are wrong, our initial perception will determine whether and how we turn to them for information when faced with a new problem or opportunity. The managers we interviewed in the first phase of our research reported that people they turned to for information provided a critical extension to their own knowledge when the manager had at least a semi-accurate understanding of her or his contact's expertise. As a result, assessing this relational knowledge of 'who knows what' at a network level provides insight into the potential for members of a network to be able to tap others with relevant expertise when faced with a new problem or opportunity.

Knowledge Dimension: Do we know what we know?
- British Telecommunication's global effort to expand product lines and services was hampered because all of its six industry sectors were acting as silos. Employees in one industry sector were not aware of the knowledge and expertise of employees in the other sectors. To overcome this lack of awareness, they introduced virtual communities of practice that were connected through the Knowledge Interchange Network (KIN). This increased awareness of experts via the distributed technology and improved cross-sector collaboration.
- IBM Global Services, the management consulting division of IBM, has a strategic drive to ensure that the best expertise is brought to bear on client projects. To help employees better understand 'who knows what' in this complex and distributed workforce, they have adopted Tacit Systems EKG profiling system. This technology actively mines e-mail (that the employees permit the system to assess) and distributed databases to categorize kinds of knowledge that are being requested/shared and by whom. Though limited to electronic communications, the system is then able to generate and make available a profile of an employee's expertise that others in the organization can then seek out as necessary.
- Recently the World Bank made a strategic decision to reposition itself away from being a lending organization to being a provider of knowledge and services (a 'Knowledge Bank'). In order for its employees to meet the needs of its member organizations, it was necessary to increase awareness of the expertise throughout the organization. A critical step in this process has been to hold regular Knowledge Fairs, where people from each department and/or thematic group set up booths which inform others of their expertise. This helps to increase people's awareness of the experience of employees throughout the Bank.

Access Dimension: Can we access what we know in a sufficiently timely fashion?
- Alcoa, the world's leading producer of aluminum, wanted to improve access between its senior executives. When designing their new headquarters they focused on open offices, family-style kitchens in the center of each floor and plenty of open spaces. Previously, top executives would only interact with a couple of people in the elevator and those they had scheduled meetings with. Now, executives bump into each other more often and are more accessible for serendipitous conversations. This change in space has increased general accessibility as well narrowed the gap between top executives and employees.
- Shearman & Sterling, a top New York law firm, wanted to make its attorneys more accessible to each other in order to use the full expertise of staff on client cases. They implemented Same Time, an instant messaging system, throughout the organization. This quickly began to overcome barriers of physical distance that often precluded serendipitous interaction. It also allowed attorneys to send messages to each other while simultaneously being on conference calls with opposing counsel. The increased accessibility of their attorneys meant that the firm's human capital could be more effectively used.

(Continued)

(Continued)

- IBM Global Services has incorporated knowledge creation, sharing, and reuse measurements into performance metrics. Performance metrics and incentives, particularly at the executive rank, have driven collaborative behavior into the day-to-day work practices of executive networks. Further, knowledge sharing has been incorporated into personal business commitments, which are required for certification and effect promotion decisions. This encourages employees at all levels to be collaborative with and accessible to each other.

Engagement Dimension: Do we effectively engage with each other in problem solving?
- Deep sea oil drilling is a very expensive business, with lost production for a day costing up to $250,000. To minimize costs, British Petroleum has initiated a peer assist program that brings experts together to brainstorm with project teams. The peer assist program allows experts with relevant knowledge and experience to collaborate with and advise teams initiating a drilling project (or facing an important milestone). Peer assists facilitate active engagement in problem solving among the most current and relevant expertise that this organization has at a given point in time.
- An important issue for Skandia is improving the probability and frequency of innovation. Skandia has 'Future Centers' where employees can come together informally and discuss ideas about new products or ideas for the future of the organization. These brainstorming sessions can very often produce new ideas about products and directions for the organization.
- At Aventis, the pharmaceutical company formed with the merger of Rhone- Poulenc Rorer and Hoechst Marion Russel, they employ the GET program (Global Experience Transfer) to facilitate engagement between the marketing and research and development organizations. Selected employees from the R&D function and the Commercial Operations functions of specific therapeutic units are paired and go through a rotation program in each functional unit (with each employee alternating in the mentoring role). This process facilitates engagement in problem solving by developing a shared context between the functions and integrating social networks at a critical functional boundary.

Safety Dimension: How do we promote safety in relationships?
- Buckman Laboratories, a highly successful chemical company, aspires to support front-line workers with the knowledge they need to help the customer. At Buckman, they have introduced a code of ethics that explicitly states that every employee has the right to talk to any other employee. This has helped build an atmosphere of trust and decreased barriers between hierarchical levels in the organization.
- Russell Reynolds Associates, one of the world's premier executive search firms, believes a large part of its success is derived from the extent to which its recruiters and researchers share knowledge about candidates and openings. In an attempt to counter knowledge hoarding they have created a culture of openness, trust, and collaboration. In hiring, the company places a unique emphasis on demonstrated collaboration and trustworthiness. In orientation, all new hires engage in a 3–4 day New Associates Program that promotes cross-office collaboration. On an ongoing basis, weekly meetings within offices, monthly conference calls between

(Continued)

the different offices as well as face-to-face meetings of action committees all serve to promote an environment of trust.

- An important issue for Johnson and Johnson is increasing knowledge sharing throughout a highly decentralized organization that operates in over 50 countries. At Johnson and Johnson they have set up communities of practice around product areas. This has helped create a shared vocabulary around specific activities, a recognition of the knowledge of their peers, a higher degree of trust between employees and communal effort on projects rather than many individuals pulling in separate directions.

Fig. 17.3 *Initiatives Promoting Knowledge Sharing in Human Networks*

Supporting New Product Development

For example, we analyzed a network of immunologists in a Fortune 250 pharmaceutical company. By virtue of effectively integrating highly specialized knowledge in the drug development process, this group of people held the potential to provide strategic advantage to the organization. However, they also dealt with many impediments to effective collaboration, in that they were dispersed across five geographic sites and four hierarchical levels and attempting to integrate very different kinds of expertise. One telling view of this network emerged when we mapped the *knowledge* relation to get a better understanding of who understood and valued other people's expertise in this group.

What we found was that the *knowledge* network was very sparse compared with others that we had seen, indicating that an impediment to this group effectively creating and sharing knowledge was that they did not know what each other knew. Two characteristics of this group seemed to result in the sparse pattern. First, the group was physically dispersed, which precluded serendipitous inter-actions that help people learn colleagues' expertise and skills. Second, the group housed deep specialists who often struggled to find overlap with their colleagues. Stories emerging in interviews indicated that even when there were opportunities to incorporate each other's expertise, this was often not done, because one group of specialists did not know enough about what another group did to be able to 'see' a way to involve them in projects.

Conducting the social network analysis provided several intervention opportunities. A facilitated session with leaders allowed them to assess and discuss the relative isolation of the specialties, as well as more pointed concerns about certain members' expertise not being tapped while other members appeared to be bottlenecks in sharing information. As a result of the discussion around this social network, various changes were made to the group's operations. First, a variety of internal projects—ranging from process improvement to a project tracking database—were jointly staffed with people from various locations. This forced people to work together and so begin to develop an appreciation of each other's unique skills and knowledge. Second, several new communication forums were created—including weekly status calls, a short update e-mail done weekly, and a project tracking database that helped each person keep up to date on what other members of the group were doing. Finally, some simple changes in project management practices and restructuring of the project leaders' responsibilities helped people to connect around them.

Facilitating Merger Integration

In another scenario we assessed the top leadership network of a Fortune 250 organization (i.e. top 126 executives of this conglomerate). This was an organization that had grown by acquisition over the course of several years, with the strategic intent that acquired companies would combine their expertise in developing and taking to market new products and services. The chief executive office (CEO) of this organization had become acutely aware of the need to create a leadership network that knew enough of what others in the conglomerate knew to be able to combine the appropriate resources in response to new opportunities. As there was some evidence that this was not happening, he asked us to conduct a social network analysis of his top executives across these acquired organizations.

Mapping information flow among these executives showed that there was only limited collaborative activity in pockets of the organization and that in general this lack of collaboration was a product of people not knowing what other people knew. In fact, we found that the problem was so significant that a key executive would not only indicate that he or she did not know what a specific person in another division did, but also that the executive did not even know what that division did. Despite alignment of the organization's formal structure, this lack of collective awareness of 'who knows what' was having a significant impact on the organization's ability to execute strategically.

Two interventions were undertaken to begin helping to integrate this group. First, on a technical front, a customized technology was introduced for this group that combined a skill-profiling system with a new collaborative environment where executives posted project information. This system was quickly used, as the CEO pushed people into adopting it and also made it the primary forum by which these executives began to get information they needed to run their business. In addition, action learning sets were employed on internal projects. People from across these divisions were staffed together on small teams that each attacked a given project, but did so with reflective exercises, as the point of the initiative was both to solve problems for the company and to create connections across the executive team.

Creating Awareness of 'Who Knows What'   Overall, we are finding that it is important for organizations to pay attention to how strategic networks of employees develop an understanding of their collective knowledge. In more staid times, working relationships developed as a product of interaction over longer time periods. This is not so in today's business environment. Given the rapid turnover many companies experience today, it is important to find ways to help people become better connected so the organization can get the true benefit of their expertise more quickly. This is often a process that can be improved by focusing on the way that new people are brought into a group. Generally what most organizations do when hiring a new person is to hold orientation courses that teach the person about the computer system, benefits and, perhaps, some homilies about the culture and history of the company. It is rare to find practices that teach the group what the newcomers know. This is a critical shortcoming in increasingly project-based work, where people will be brought into the center of the network primarily as a result of what other people understand about their expertise and so how to tap them when new problems or opportunities arise.

However, knowingly or unknowingly, some organizations we worked with were employing different mechanisms that built this awareness of 'who knows what'. For example, on a technical front many organizations are implementing skill-profiling systems or corporate yellow pages. On an organizational front, organizations such as the World Bank have organized their employees into thematic groups that have Help Desks whom anyone connected with the organization can contact. The individuals staffing the Help Desks are able to route people to others within the thematic group who have expertise on a particular subject. Other companies and government organizations have regular Knowledge Fairs where teams, communities, or departments can set up a booth and distribute information about the expertise that they have. Although this has limited scope, it has proven effective in increasing awareness of the projects and knowledge activities taking place within the different departments and communities of the organization.

Access Dimension: Can We Access What We Know in A Sufficiently Timely Fashion?   Of course, knowing that someone else knows something of relevance does little good if we cannot gain access to their thinking in a timely fashion. Critical issues on which we may turn to others for help or advice often require turnaround within increasingly tight time frames. As with the *knowledge* dimension, we have found it helpful to map the *access* relation at a network level to understand who is able to reach whom in a sufficiently timely fashion.

....

Assessing Access in a Global Consulting Practice

We conducted a network analysis of the global consumer goods practice within a major consulting firm. One of the more telling networks in this analysis was the diagram reflecting who was sufficiently accessible to whom among this group of 46 people spread through Europe and the U.S. Despite the entire practice reporting to one overall partner and being subject to a common strategy, performance measurement and reward practices, we found significant clustering in the network when we assessed who was accessible to whom. The social network analysis of accessibility showed three tightly knit groups rather than one integrated network—two in North America and one in Europe—that were all highly centralized around different partners. In fact, only three employees served to bridge these fiefdoms, and these were not the people in charge of the group. Rather, they had been through rotating work assignments and so developed relations with many others in the network.

A first intervention for this organization was reconsidering staffing practices to help integrate people from the different locations on both client projects and internal initiatives. A key concern lay with developing relationships throughout the overall practice to improve knowledge sharing and the location of relevant expertise for both sales efforts and client engagements. Further, increasing overall connection within the network also reduced the extent to which the practice was exposed by the potential for any of these three central people leaving. In this and many other examples, we have consistently found that a network view makes it clear that, should certain central people in a network leave, they take more than just what they know—they also fundamentally affect the connectivity of the entire group.

The two groups in the U.S. represented another challenge for management. It turned out that the majority of people in these two groups not only had offices in the same building but also were interspersed along the same corridor. What we discovered in interviews was a political problem that had emerged and resulted in tensions between two subgroups. While management had suspected there were problems, the visual representation of the network diagram clearly showed the extent to which these issues were impeding the ability of the overall group to effectively leverage the expertise of its members. Various steps were taken to help resolve the problem including: executive coaching, revised performance management practices and an extensive off-site planning session, and organizational development (OD) interventions to help the group integrate.

Accessibility after a Transition to Teams

Reorganizations often shift the location and concurrently the accessibility of specific expertise. For example, we worked with one commercial lending organization in a transition from a functional to a team-based structure. To minimize inefficiencies resulting from cross-functional handoffs in the commercial lending process, the organization shifted to a team-based structure that co-located lenders, analysts, and servicers in industry teams. Before the transition, these groups had been housed together on different floors and so were able to tap into each other's functional knowledge with relative ease. With the redesign, it was far more difficult for inexperienced people to learn the basics of their function and also for experienced lenders and analysts to engage in collaborative problem-solving efforts on the more creative aspects of commercial lending (e.g. structuring a specific transaction).

Social network analysis showed that four months after the transition to teams, several key people had become significantly overburdened, as they were heavily sought out by both their past functional colleagues as well as their new team members. In particular, we found that the people who were reputed experts in their area were tapped for advice to such an extent that they were falling behind on their own work. While in the functional department these interactions were more controlled and observable, in the team-based environment it was difficult for management to see how instrumental these opinion leaders really were to the success of the whole system. In fact, from a cursory review of their individual performance metrics (e.g. loans serviced or loans booked) these people experienced a fairly significant decline in productivity. Further, the longer hours that these people were working, in tandem with declining individual performance metrics that influenced their bonus calculations, served to undermine their own morale. As a result of these findings, several steps were taken—such as new staffing practices, better orientation materials (to help bring new people up to speed more effectively) and a reallocation of tasks within teams.

Managing Accessibility Through the course of our research we have found that many organizations struggle with the notion of accessibility as people increasingly work from diverse locations. By and large, most solutions that companies considered were technical in nature and included such things as e-mail, asynchronous and synchronous collaborative environments, video conferencing, and instant messaging. However, we generally find that organizational design considerations and cultural norms are the more powerful indicators of who is accessible to whom.

Performance management systems promoting individualistic behaviors seem to be one of the primary drivers of sparse, disconnected networks. Further, though more of a trait of organizational culture, we often find that hierarchy has a marked impact on who is able to access whom. Again, this is a telling indicator for organizations trying to become more flexible and effective at information sharing. Some organizations have taken interesting steps to promote access across hierarchy such as making knowledge sharing a part of the mission or code of ethics. At Buckman Laboratories, all associates are empowered to speak with any associate at any level, and this is supported by a communication technology that gives each employee access to all other employees. Others are beginning to turn to creative uses of physical space to promote both intentional and serendipitous interactions among high-end knowledge workers. For example, Chrysler has gone full circle (from dispersion back to co-location) by recently bringing all the people involved in new car development into one building so that they can have face-to-face access to each other.

Engagement Dimension: How Do We Improve Engagement in Problem Solving? One of the most interesting findings from our interviews with the forty managers in the first phase of our research was the importance of the person sought out for information being willing to cognitively engage with the information seeker. People who were willing to engage in problem solving helped seekers to create knowledge with sufficient understanding and clarity as to be able to take action on it. And when we say engaging in problem solving, we do not mean a significant time investment on the part of the person sought out. Rather, we mean a simple two-step behavior whereby those contacted for information first ensured that they understood the other person's problem, and then actively shaped what they knew to the problem at hand. In short, these people taught rather than dumped information on the seeker—a behavior that, if developed among a network, can improve the effectiveness with which people learn from each other.

Integrating Specialized Expertise in Problem Solving

We conducted one network analysis of a specialist group supporting the internal knowledge management efforts of a global computer manufacturer. This group of 18 people was a virtual team that had been formed to combine expertise in both the technical and organizational/strategic aspects of knowledge management. While members of the group claimed to know and have access to each other's expertise, a quick review of the *engagement* network showed that in fact the group was having little success in integrating their expertise. Rather, what became apparent was a strong split in the network because of unique skill bases.

Despite people technically knowing at a high level what the skills and knowledge of people in the other discipline were, there were only two connections between the two groups on the *engagement* relation. This clustering was a significant concern, as it is in engagement in problem solving that true learning takes place and people effectively integrate specialized expertise in projects—rather than just doing what they know or have done before. Interviews revealed that each group's depth of specialization, and the fact that they were virtual and so had little slack, face-to-face, time to interact made it difficult for them to find common ground. Aside from the leader of the group, who had experience with both subgroups, there was little common language or occupational values that existed between the two subgroups.

Several organizational learning interventions have been undertaken in this group to help build engagement and trust. As always, a key component of these interventions has been the use of various network diagrams in facilitated sessions to help the group create common awareness and make sense of productive and unproductive dynamics. Further, a shift in performance measurement was made to encourage joint problem solving and de-emphasize individual project metrics. While in the midst of these initiatives, the group plans to periodically assess the *engagement* network and intervene as appropriate to improve their operations over time.

Supporting Engagement of Specialists in New Product Development

In another scenario, we conducted a network analysis of 78 members of a drug development community of practice. The community, which was geographically dispersed across eight sites in the U.S. and Europe, included people from the drug discovery stage all the way to clinical development. The analysis indicated that within this highly dispersed community there were many people who did not know each other. It also became apparent that, although the people within each functional unit engaged with each other on matters relevant to the community, there was little engagement between the functions. This was a critical problem for this group, given the need to combine unique expertise to effectively develop and market a specific drug.

Further, the network proved to be highly centralized around a few individuals. The six most central people resided in the main U.S. site. Although they had many connections to people within the site, they did not engage as often

Rob Cross, Andrew Parker, Laurence Prusak, Stephen P. Borgatti

with community members in the European locations. There were also several people who were totally disconnected from the group, which resulted in their skills and expertise being lost to the community. In this instance, a new collaborative technology was introduced that had both synchronous and asynchronous features. Secondly, different project management practices and a new role within the community were initiated to help bridge functional areas of expertise. Finally, the network diagrams were used to convince management to support staged face-to-face forums focusing on specific problems. These forums helped the different functional areas find common ground, while solving problems critical to the success of a project.

Engagement in Human Networks   Overall, as with the access dimension, we found that many of the things organizations were doing that had an impact on engagement were technical in nature and included synchronous technologies such as VP Buddy, Same Time, or white boarding applications that allow for dispersed engagement in a common problem. In many ways, instant messaging does seem to support the serendipitous kinds of interactions that are lost when employees are not co-located. However, there are limitations in the ability of these applications to richly convey knowledge across media that provide relatively few cues in comparison to face-to-face interactions. Videoconferencing for visual interaction between people in different locations does seem to help. This has been particularly important at British Petroleum, where experts have been able to assist technicians who are working on oil rigs thousands of miles away.

Is also unique in its recognition of the importance of engagement in problem solving early in projects where learning from others' experiences can have a disproportionate impact on the trajectory and success of a project. For example, BP has instituted a peer review process in its drilling initiatives as an effective way to tap into others' knowledge. Before engaging in any significant task, the individual or group invites peers to provide input. Because the focus is performance, those with the most relevant knowledge and recent experiences are tapped to participate. Through this peer review process not only is performance on the task at hand improved, but also people become much more aware of the unique skills and abilities of others. This creates a natural reason for meeting and developing the needed norms of reciprocity and trust that make engagement and sharing of expertise a natural process.

Safety Dimension: How Do We Promote Safety in Relationships?   Finally, the managers we interviewed in the first phase of our research indicated that safe relationships offered certain advantages in problem solving. First, they provided more learning, as people were not overly concerned about admitting a lack of knowledge or expertise. Asking someone for help often requires that the

288

seeker has some degree of trust in the person sought out for information. Such trust often shapes the extent to which people will be forthcoming about their lack of knowledge, as defensive behaviors can knowingly and unknowingly block learning in critical interactions. Secondly, several of the managers indicated that in more safe relationships they could be more creative. An important feature of these relationships was that they were more willing to take risks with their ideas and felt that this often resulted in more creative solutions.

Safety Promotes Learning in High-End Knowledge Work

Social network analysis provides us with a means of understanding the extent to which information and knowledge seeking is a safe behavior in important groups. For example, we assessed the safety network in the information resources group supporting a key research and development function of a Fortune 500 manufacturing organization. This group of 34 people was composed of two organizational units that had recently been merged under one leader. The *Safety* network represented an interesting point of intervention here because, unlike many networks we have seen, the *Knowledge, Access*, and *Engagement* networks were all very well connected, whereas the safety network was not.

Interestingly enough, the *safety* network split into two groups that reflected the two departments that had been merged several months before this analysis. This is a common finding in both restructuring and merger scenarios. We often have found that communication networks (i.e. network diagrams developed from asking people who they typically communicate with) form quickly in restructuring or merger scenarios. However, what simply assessing communication patterns obscures is the time and effort that must be put into developing trust among a group, if we truly want people to learn from each other. Safety is important and highly predictive of who is sought out when one engages in problem solving and so exposes a lack of knowledge or allows someone else to shape the course of a solution. Relationships that are safe, and therefore useful for deeper levels of knowledge sharing and true learning, take time to develop.

In this specific network analysis, there were two interesting points. First, two people who were low in the hierarchy had become important ambassadors between the groups. Several amusing anecdotes were discovered in our interviews, whereby people that were senior in this group often went to these more junior people when they needed information from a colleague in the other subgroup. A lighthearted but very effective intervention was created by using these anecdotes along with the network diagram in a facilitated session debriefing the overall group. Playfully illuminating the way in which members of each group had stereotyped the other, and the inefficiencies that this caused, resulted in a productive discussion of a potentially charged issue.

Second, there were different levels of safety between the two groups. In part this seemed to be a product of the physical environment, as the more tightly connected group had all worked in an open space environment that allowed frequent, face-to-face communication. We also found that leadership style differed in the two groups before the restructuring. In general, creating a greater degree of safety within networks of relationships is often a product of leadership style and organizational (or sometimes occupational) culture. The behaviors that leaders exhibit and those they reward shape the extent to which people will be forthcoming about their lack of knowledge on various topics. This varied widely by organization. In some, safety was never considered a concern, because it was an accepted norm to doggedly seek out the most relevant knowledge for the success of a given project. In others, safety was a critical concern, and employees were very cautious about exposing a lack of knowledge.

Just as important, our interviews indicated that relationships need time and some space (physical, cognitive, and social) to develop a sense of safety. Although communication technologies, such as e-mail, are helpful in maintaining relationships, when creating relationships we have found that it is important to increase the opportunity for face-to-face interactions between people. For example, though often chided, organizations that have instigated a program of brown bag lunches find that this process is effective for the development of safe relationships between people. One organization we worked with encouraged face-to-face contact by monthly meetings between different groups of researchers. These meetings consisted of a discussion session in the morning and a working session in the laboratory in the afternoon and allowed for a free flow of ideas within the context of a real working environment.

···

A Combined Network View and Organizational Learning

In addition to looking at each of the networks individually, it is also instructive to assess the dimensions cumulatively to get a better understanding of a network's underlying learning potential. In doing this, we can analyze networks where pairs of relationships exist (e.g. both *knowledge* and *access*) or networks where all of the relationships exist (e.g. *knowledge, access, engagement,* and *safety*). For example, we conducted a social network analysis of 38 employees constituting the telecommunications consulting practice of a Big Five accountancy. We first assessed the *knowledge* network to better understand who in this network of people indicated that they knew and valued other's expertise. Though relatively sparse, we found that the *knowledge* network showed a healthy, integrated pattern without distinct subgroups. However, the network diagram took on added life when we also considered the *access* network, where each person rated his or her colleagues on the extent to which they were accessible in a timeframe sufficient to help solve problems. Ultimately, both *knowledge* and *access* relations must be present for information sharing in a group to be effective. By combining the networks from these two questions, we had a view of the potential of a person to obtain information from others when faced with a new problem or opportunity.

Several things were interesting in this network. First, we noticed a fairly marked decline in the number of connections among the group in comparison to the *knowledge* network. While many central people remained central, several people higher in the hierarchy shifted out to the periphery of the network. As people move higher in an organization, their work begins to entail more administrative tasks, which makes them both less accessible and less knowledgeable about the day-to-day work of their subordinates. What network analysis affords in this picture is an opportunity to assess whether those in positions of formal authority are sufficiently central to the flow of knowledge, as well as to identify those people that truly are influential knowledge brokers in the group.

The third question asked of the 38 consultants was who in the group they could count on to actively engage in problem solving. When the *engage* network was added we were assessing a network where a line was drawn between two people only if all three dimensions of a relationship existed (knowing what the other knows, having access to their thinking and being willing to engage in problem solving). With the addition of the engagement network, we found a significant decrease in connections, which is not trivial in terms of the network's ability to solve problems. As outlined in the initial interviews, it is often those people who are willing to engage in problem solving who help both to create actionable knowledge (rather than information overload) and ensure that we are solving the right problem. The final question we asked of this consulting practice determined with whom each person felt safe discussing work-related issues. With the incorporation of the *safety* network there is very little change. This is because the *safety* network in this group was the densest of all the networks. Ultimately, this was a sound indicator of the culture of this group for knowledge creation, and is obviously not a place we would look to intervene. It is also important to note that based on our experiences, a dense safety network is not typical.

Rob Cross, Andrew Parker, Laurence Prusak, Stephen P. Borgatti

Interventions from a Combined Network View

Analyzing the combined network (i.e. *Knowledge* + *Access* + *Engagement* + *Safety*) provides a great deal of insight into who is critical as well as who is currently less utilized within a group in terms of knowledge creation and sharing. Understanding who is central to a group helps to indicate those people who might be either bottlenecks, or highly valued knowledge resources upon whom the group is reliant. Only interviews providing an in-depth understanding of a network can tell, but these people do pose interesting questions to management. Has the group become too reliant on these people—should they decide to leave? Are these people hoarding information and so have become bottlenecks in terms of the group's knowledge creation and sharing activities? In contrast, should these people be rewarded for the somewhat invisible role they play in supporting a group from a knowledge perspective?

If we discover that people are central in these networks for legitimate reasons, management has an opportunity to begin acknowledging the work that these people do for the group. In the words of one of the people central in the telecommunications practice, 'I spend about an hour and a half every day responding to calls and other informational requests . . . [and] . . . none of that time gets seen in my performance metrics.' Network analysis makes such interactions that are critical to a group visible, thus providing an opportunity for management to acknowledge these people and the critical role they play. For example, management might choose to better support knowledge creation and sharing by offering central people such things as:

- Monies for efforts that might stimulate knowledge flow in a group via face-to-face meetings, or to purchase technologies such as groupware.
- Cognitive and social space to allow room for both individual and collective creativity and bonding to occur.
- Executive focus such as rewarding or promoting network enabling people to both acknowledge their efforts and signal the importance of this kind of work to others within the organization.

In addition to central or core individuals, we also find it important to better understand why some people are peripheral in these networks. It might be that people in these positions do not know what we thought they knew when hired. In these cases they are peripheral for a legitimate reason and so reflect development or re-staffing opportunities. Alternatively, it might be that these people are peripheral because they are relatively new and the organization's assimilation processes do little to help them integrate into a network of colleagues. The important feature of this combined network view is that we can isolate why people are peripheral. Being peripheral because one is inaccessible is a different coaching process than if one is not considered safe.

292

Finally, on a more conceptual level, the combined network view offers unique purchase on the elusive concept of organizational learning. Some have claimed that an organization has learned when, through its processing of information, its range of potential behaviors has changed. Thus, if we are interested in promoting an organization's ability to react to new opportunities, we need to account for the ways in which people in networks become able to leverage each others' knowledge. Changes in the knowledge, access, engagement, and safety relationships underlying a network's future information processing behavior provide one means of both descriptive and prescriptive traction on organizational learning. Organizations have often been claimed to be path-dependent or constrained by what they know. Such notions as absorptive capacity, core rigidities, or architectural knowledge have been claimed to lead to this path dependence over time. While critically important, this work has often been done at a level of abstraction that makes interventions questionable. In contrast, the combined view of these networks provides some idea as to precisely whose knowledge is primarily responsible for what a group is likely to learn over time.

Conclusion

A critical resource embedded within organizations is the knowledge that workers bring to work on a day-to-day basis. However, aside from human resource policies targeted to the attraction, development, and retention of identified valuable workers, there has been little effort put into systematic ways of working with the knowledge that is embedded in social networks. Given the extent to which people rely on their own knowledge and the knowledge of their contacts to solve problems, this is a significant shortcoming. By introducing social network analysis to understand how a given network of people create and share knowledge, we are able to make these interactions visible and so actionable.

In applying these ideas in various organizations, we have found it particularly important to identify points of knowledge creation, and sharing within an organization, that hold strategic relevance. Typical domains yielding benefit include senior management networks, communities of practice, and collaborative initiatives such as new product development, R&D units, or joint ventures and alliances. It is particularly fruitful to map collaborative relationships that cross boundaries of some form. Such boundaries might be hierarchical, functional, geographical, or even organizational, as in joint venture or merger and acquisition scenarios. Understanding how knowledge flows (or more frequently does not flow) across these various boundaries within an organization

Rob Cross, Andrew Parker, Laurence Prusak, Stephen P. Borgatti

can yield critical insight into where management should target efforts to promote collaboration that has a strategic payoff for the organization.

....

Selected Bibliography

Much of the emphasis on organizational knowledge today (at least in terms of practice) is focused on efforts to capture, screen, store, and codify knowledge. To get a more popular view of what many organizations are doing under the rubric of knowledge management we suggest some of the following publications: T. Davenport and L. Prusak, *Working Knowledge* (Boston, MA: Harvard Business School Press, 1998); C. O'Dell & C. J. Grayson, *If Only We Knew What We Know* (New York, NY: Free Press, 1998); T. Stewart, *Intellectual Capital: The New Wealth of Organizations* (New York, NY: Doubleday, 1997); and R. Ruggles, 'The State of the Notion: Knowledge Management in Practice,' *California Management Review*, 1998, 40(3), 80–89.

Of course, our own perspective is that knowledge embedded in human networks is too often overlooked in these initiatives. Two streams of literature heavily influenced our thinking here. First is the rich ethnographic evidence accumulating within the situated learning and community of practice traditions. This work is making clear the large degree to which people learn how to do their work not from impersonal sources of information but through interactions with other people. Some important work in this tradition includes: J. S. Brown and P. Duguid, 'Organizational Learning and Communities-of-Practice: Toward a Unified View of Working, Learning and Innovation,' *Organization Science*, 1991, 2(1), 40–57; J. Brown and P. Duguid, *The Social Life of Information* (Cambridge, MA: Harvard Business School Press, 2000); J. Lave and E. Wenger, *Situated Learning: Legitimate Peripheral Participation* (Cambridge, UK: Cambridge University Press, 1991); J. Orr, *Talking About Machines* (Ithaca, NY: Cornell University Press, 1996); and E. Wenger, *Communities of Practice* (Oxford, UK: Oxford University Press, 1998).

The second stream of literature influential in our thinking came from the social network tradition, which has also shown, with very different methods, the extent to which information that affects what we do largely comes from other people. Some important works on how social networks influence information flow and diffusion in networks include: G. Simmel, *The Sociology of Georg Simmel* (New York, NY: Free Press, 1950); R. Burt, *Structural Holes* (Cambridge, MA: Harvard University Press, 1992); M. Granovetter, 'The Strength of Weak Ties,' *American Journal of Sociology*, 1973, 78, 1360–80; T. Allen, *Managing the Flow of Technology* (Cambridge, MA: MIT Press, 1984); P. Monge and N. Contractor, 'Emergence of Communication Networks,' forthcoming in F. Jablin and L. Putnam (eds), *Handbook of Organizational Communication*, 2nd edn. (Thousand Oaks, CA: Sage); and E. Rogers, *Diffusion of Innovations*, 4th edn. (New York, NY: Free Press, 1995).

294

VI FUTURE DIRECTIONS

Knowledge-Worker Productivity: The Biggest Challenge

Peter F. Drucker

The most important, and indeed the truly unique, contribution of management in the 20th century was the fifty-fold increase in the productivity of the *manual worker* in manufacturing. The most important contribution management needs to make in the 21st century is similarly to increase the productivity of *knowledge work* and *knowledge workers*. The most valuable assets of a 20th-century company were its *production equipment*. The most valuable asset of a 21st century institution (whether business or non-business) will be its *knowledge workers* and their *productivity*.

The Productivity of the Manual Worker

First, we must take a look at where we are. It was only a little over a hundred years ago that for the first time an educated person actually *looked* at manual work and manual workers and then began to study both. The Greek poet Hesiod (eighth century BC) and the Roman poet Virgil (700 years later) sang about the work of the farmer. Theirs are still among the finest poems in any language, but neither the work they sang about nor their farmers bear even the most remote resemblance to reality, nor were they meant to have any. Neither Hesiod nor Virgil ever held a sickle in their hands, ever herded sheep, or even looked at the people who did either. When Karl Marx, 1900 years after Virgil, came to write about manual work and manual workers, he too never looked at either, nor had he ever as much as touched a machine. The first man to do

both—that is, to work as a manual worker and then to study manual work—
was Frederick Winslow Taylor (1856–1915).

Throughout history there have been steady advances in what we today call
'productivity' (the term itself is barely fifty years old). They were the result of
new tools, new methods and new technologies; there were advances in what
the economist calls 'capital.' There were few advances throughout the ages in
what the economist calls 'labor'—that is, in the productivity of the worker. It
was axiomatic throughout history that workers could produce more only by
working harder or by working longer hours. The 19th-century economists
disagreed about most things as much as economists do today. However, they all
agreed—from David Ricardo through Karl Marx—that there are enormous
differences in *skill* between workers, but there are none in respect to productivity other than between hard workers and lazy ones, or between physically
strong workers and weak ones. Productivity did not exist. It still is an 'extraneous factor' and not part of the equation in most contemporary economic
theory (e.g. in Keynes, but also in that of the Austrian School).

In the decade after Taylor first looked at work and studied it, the productivity of the manual worker began its unprecedented rise. Since then, it has been
going up steadily at the rate of 3 percent per annum compound—which means
it has risen fifty-fold since Taylor. On this achievement rest *all* of the economic
and social gains of the 20th century. The productivity of the manual worker has
created what we now call 'developed' economies. Before Taylor, there was no
such thing—all economies were equally 'underdeveloped.' An underdeveloped
economy today—or even an 'emerging' one—is one that has not, or at least has
not yet, made the manual worker more productive.

The Principles of Manual-Work Productivity

Taylor's principles sound deceptively simple. The first step in making the
manual worker more productive is to look at the task and to analyze its
constituent motions. The next step is to record each motion, the physical effort
it takes, and the time it takes. Then motions that are not needed can be
eliminated; and whenever we have looked at manual work, we have found
that a great many of the traditionally most-hallowed procedures turn out to be
waste and do not add anything. Then, each of the motions that remains as
essential to obtaining the finished product is set up so as to be done the
simplest way, the easiest way, the way that puts the least physical and mental
strain on the operator, and the way that requires the least time. Next, these
motions are put together again into a 'job' that is in a logical sequence. Finally,

the tools needed to do the motions are redesigned. Whenever we have looked at any job—no matter for how many thousands of years it has been performed—we have found that the traditional tools are wrong for the task. This was the case, for instance, with the shovel used to carry sand in a foundry (the first task Taylor studied). It was the wrong shape, the wrong size, and had the wrong handle. We found this to be equally true of the surgeon's traditional tools. Taylor's principles sound obvious—effective methods always do. However, it took Taylor twenty years of experimentation to work them out.

Over these last hundred years, there have been countless further changes, revisions, and refinements. The name by which the methodology goes has also changed over the past century. Taylor himself first called his method 'Task Analysis' or 'Task Management.' Twenty years later it was re-christened 'Scientific Management.' Another twenty years later, after World War I, it came to be knows as 'Industrial Engineering' in the US and Japan, and as 'Rationalization' in Germany.

To proclaim that one's method 'rejects' Taylor or 'replaces' him is almost standard 'public relations.' For what made Taylor and his method so powerful has also made it unpopular. What Taylor *saw* when he actually looked at work violated everything poets and philosophers had said about work from Hesiod and Virgil to Karl Marx. They all celebrated 'skill.' Taylor showed that in manual work there is no such thing. There are only simple, repetitive motions. What makes them more productive is *knowledge*, that is, the way the simple, unskilled motions are put together, organized, and executed. In fact, Taylor was the first person to apply knowledge to work.[1]

This also earned Taylor the undying enmity of the labor unions of his time, all of which were craft unions and based on the *mystique* of craft skill and their monopoly on it. Moreover, Taylor advocated—and this is still anathema to a labor union—that workers be paid according to their productivity—that is, for their output, rather than for their input (e.g. for hours worked). However, Taylor's definition of work as a series of operations also largely explains his rejection by the people who themselves do not do any manual work: the descendants of the poets and philosophers of old, the Literati and Intellectuals. Taylor destroyed the romance of work. Instead of a 'noble skill,' it became a series of simple motions.

Nevertheless, every method during these past hundred years that has had the slightest success in raising the productivity of manual workers—and with it their real wages—has been based on Taylor's principles, no matter how loudly his antagonists proclaimed their differences with Taylor. This is true of 'work enlargement,' 'work enrichment,' and 'job rotation'—all of which use Taylor's methods to lessen the worker's fatigue and thereby increase the worker's productivity. It is also true of such extensions of Taylor's principles of task analysis and industrial engineering as Henry Ford's assembly line (developed after 1914, when Taylor himself was already sick, old, and retired). It is just as true of the Japanese 'Quality Circle,' 'Continuous Improvement' (*Kaizen*), and 'Just-In-Time Delivery.'

The best example, however, is W. Edward Deming's 'Total Quality Management.' What Deming did—and what makes Total Quality Management effective—is to analyze and organize the job exactly the way Taylor did. However, he also added Quality Control (around 1940) that was based on a statistical theory that was only developed ten years after Taylor's death. Finally, in the 1970s, Deming substituted closed-circuit television and computer simulation for Taylor's stopwatch and motion photos. Deming's Quality Control Analysts are the spitting image of Taylor's Efficiency Engineers and function the same way.

Whatever his limitations and shortcomings—and he had many—no other American, not even Henry Ford, has had anything like Taylor's impact. 'Scientific Management' (and its successor 'Industrial Engineering') is the one American philosophy that has swept the world—more so even than the Constitution and the Federalist Papers. In the past century, there has been only one worldwide philosophy that could compete with Taylor's: namely, Marxism. In the end, Taylor has triumphed over Marx.

During World War I, Scientific Management swept through the US together with Ford's Taylor-based assembly line. In the 1920s, Scientific Management swept through western Europe and began to be adopted in Japan.

During World War II, both the German achievement and the American achievement were squarely based on applying Taylor's principles to Training. The German General Staff, after having lost World War I, applied 'Rationalization' (i.e. Taylor's Scientific Management) to the job of the soldier and to military training. This enabled Hitler to create a superb fighting machine in the six short years between his coming to power in 1939. In the US, the same principles were applied to the training of an industrial workforce, first tentatively during World War I and then, with full power, during World War II. This enabled the Americans to outproduce the Germans, even though a larger proportion of the US than the German male population was in uniform and thus not in industrial production. Then, training-based Scientific Management gave the US civilian workforce more than twice—if not three times—the productivity of the workers in Hitler's Germany and in Hitler-dominated Europe. Scientific Management thus gave the US the capacity to outnumber both Germans and Japanese on the battlefield and yet still out-produce both by several orders of magnitude.

Since 1950, economic development outside the Western world has largely been based on copying what the US did in World War II, that is, on applying Scientific Management to making the manual worker more productive. All earlier economic development had been based on technological innovation—

first in France in the 18th century, then in Great Britain from 1760 until 1850, and finally in the new economic Great Powers, Germany and the US, in the second half of the 19th century. The non-Western countries that developed after World War II, beginning with Japan, eschewed technological innovation. Instead, they imported the training that the US had developed during World War II based on Taylor's principles and they used it to make highly productive, almost overnight, a still largely unskilled and pre-industrial workforce. (In Japan, for instance, almost two-thirds of the working population were still, in 1950, living on the land and unskilled in any work except cultivating rice). However, while highly productive, this new workforce was still—for a decade or more—paid pre-industrial wages so that these countries—first Japan, then Korea, then Taiwan and Singapore—could produce the same manufactured products as the developed countries, but at a fraction of their labor costs.

The Future of Manual-Worker Productivity

Taylor's approach was designed for manual work in *manufacturing*, and at first applied only to it. Nevertheless, even within these traditional limitations, Taylor's approach still has enormous scope. It is still going to be the organizing principle in countries in which manual work, and especially manual work in manufacturing, is the growth sector of the society and economy—that is, 'Third World' countries with very large and still growing numbers of young people with little education and little skill.

However, there is equal—or even greater—opportunity in the *developed* countries to organize non-manufacturing production (i.e. production work in services) on the production principles now being developed in manufacturing—and that means applying Industrial Engineering to the job and work of the individual service worker. There is equally a tremendous amount of knowledge work—including work requiring highly advanced and thoroughly theoretical knowledge—that includes *manual* operations. The productivity of these operations also requires Industrial Engineering.

Still, in developed countries, the central challenge is no longer to make manual work more productive—after all, we know how to do it. The central challenge will be to make knowledge workers more productive. Knowledge workers are rapidly becoming the largest single group in the workforce of every developed country. They may already compose two-fifths of the US workforce—and a still smaller but rapidly growing proportion of the workforce of all other developed countries. It is on their productivity, above all, that the future prosperity—and indeed the future survival—of the developed economies will increasingly depend.

What We Know About Knowledge-Worker Productivity

Work on the productivity of the knowledge worker has barely begun. In terms of actual work on knowledge-worker productivity, we will be in the year 2000, roughly where we were in the year 1900, in terms of the productivity of the manual worker. Nevertheless, we already know infinitely more about the productivity of the knowledge worker than we did then about that of the manual worker. We even know a good many of the answers. We also know the challenges to which we do not yet know the answers, and on which we need to go to work.

Six major factors determine knowledge-worker productivity.

1. Knowledge-worker productivity demands that we ask the question: *'What is the task?'*
2. It demands that we impose the responsibility for their productivity on the individual knowledge workers themselves. Knowledge Workers *have* to manage themselves. They have to have *autonomy.*
3. Continuing innovation has to be part of the work, the task, and the responsibility of knowledge workers.
4. Knowledge work requires continuous learning on the part of the knowledge worker, but equally continuous teaching on the part of the knowledge worker.
5. Productivity of the knowledge worker is not—at least not primarily—a matter of the *quantity* of output. *Quality* is at least as important.
6. Finally, knowledge-worker productivity requires that the knowledge worker is both seen and treated as an 'asset' rather than a 'cost.' It requires that knowledge workers *want* to work for the organization in preference to all other opportunities.

Each of these requirements (except perhaps the last one) is almost the exact opposite of what is needed to increase the productivity of the manual worker. In manual work, of course, quality also matters. However, lack of quality is a restraint. There has to be a certain minimum quality standard. The achievement of Total Quality Management—that is, of the application of 20th century Statistical Theory to manual work—is the ability to cut (though not entirely to eliminate) production that falls below this minimum standard.

In most knowledge work, quality is not a minimum and a restraint. Quality is the essence of the output. In judging the performance of a teacher, we do not ask how many students there can be in his or her class. We ask how many students learn anything—and that's a quality question. In appraising the performance of a medical laboratory, the question of how many tests it can run through its machines is quite secondary to the question of how many tests results are valid and reliable. This is true even for the work of the file clerk.

Productivity of knowledge work therefore has to aim first at obtaining quality—and not minimum quality but optimum if not maximum quality. Only then can one ask: 'What is the volume, the quantity of work?' This not only means that we approach the task of making more productive the knowledge worker from the quality of the work rather than the quantity, it also means that we will have to learn to define quality.

What Is the Task?

The crucial question in knowledge-worker productivity is: *What is the task?* It is also the one most at odds with manual-worker productivity. In manual work, the key question is always: *How should the work be done?* In manual work, the task is always given. None of the people who work on manual-worker productivity ever asked: 'What is the manual worker supposed to do?' Their only question was: 'How does the manual worker best do the job?' This was just as true of Frederick W. Taylor's Scientific Management as it was true of the people at Sears Roebuck or the Ford Motor Company who first designed the assembly line, and as it is true of W. Edward Deming's Total Quality Control.

Again, in knowledge work the key question is: What is the task? One reason for this is that knowledge work, unlike manual work, does not program the worker. The worker on the automobile assembly line who puts on a wheel is programed by the simultaneous arrival of the car's chassis on one line and the wheel on the other line. The farmer who plows a field in preparation for planting does not climb out of his tractor to take a telephone call, to attend a meeting, or to write a memo. *What* is to be done is always obvious in manual work.

However, in knowledge work the task does not program the worker. A major crisis in a hospital, such as when a patient suddenly goes into coma, does of course control the nurse's task and programs her; but otherwise, it is largely the nurse's decision whether to spend time at the patient bed or whether to spend time filling out papers. Engineers are constantly being pulled off their task by having to write a report or rewrite it, by being asked to attend a meeting, and so on. The job of the salesperson in the department store is to serve the customer and to provide the merchandise the customer is interested in or should become interested in. Instead, the salesperson spends an enormous amount of time on paperwork, on checking whether merchandise is in stock, on checking when and how it can be delivered, and so on—all things that take salespeople away from the customer and do not add anything to their productivity in doing what salespeople are being paid for, which is to sell and to satisfy the customer.

The first requirement in tackling knowledge work is to find out what the task is so as to make it possible to concentrate knowledge workers on the task and to eliminate everything else—at least as far as it can possibly be eliminated. This requires that the knowledge workers themselves define what the task is or should be—and only the knowledge workers themselves can do that. Work on knowledge-worker productivity therefore begins with asking the knowledge workers themselves: *What is your task? What should it be? What should you be expected to contribute?* and *What hampers you in doing your task and should be eliminated?*

Knowledge workers themselves almost always have thought through these questions and can answer them. Still, it then usually takes time and hard work to restructure their jobs so that they can actually make the contribution they are already being paid for. However, asking the questions and taking action on the answers usually doubles or triples knowledge-worker productivity, and quite fast.

Nurses in a major hospital were asked these questions. They were sharply divided as to what their task was, with one group saying 'patient care' and another saying 'satisfying the physicians.' However, they were in complete agreement on the things that made them unproductive. They called them 'chores'—paperwork, arranging flowers, answering the phone calls of patients' relatives, answering the patients' bells, and so on. All—or nearly all—of these could be turned over to a non-nurse floor clerk, paid a fraction of a nurse's pay. The productivity of the nurses on the floor immediately more than doubled, as measured by the time nurses spent at the patients' beds. Patient satisfaction more than doubled and turnover of nurses (which had been catastrophically high) almost disappeared—all within four months.

Once the task has been defined, the next requirements can be tackled, and they will be tackled by the knowledge workers themselves. These requirements are:

- Knowledge workers' *responsibility* for their own contribution. It is the knowledge worker's decision what he or she should be held accountable for in terms of quality and quantity with respect to time and with respect to cost. Knowledge workers have to have autonomy and that entails responsibility.
- Continuous innovation *has to be built into the knowledge worker's job.*
- *Continuous learning* and *continuous teaching* have to be built into the job.

One central requirement of knowledge-worker productivity remains. We have to answer the question: What is quality? In some knowledge work—and especially in some work requiring a high degree of knowledge—we already measure quality. Surgeons, for example, are routinely measured, especially by their colleagues, by their success rates in difficult and dangerous procedures (e.g. by the survival rates of their open-heart surgical patients or the full recovery rates of their orthopedic-surgery patients). By and large, we mainly have judgments rather than measures regarding the quality of a great deal of knowledge work. The main trouble is, however, not the difficulty of measuring quality. It is the difficulty—and more particularly the sharp disagreements—in defining what the task is and what it should be.

The best example of this is the American school system. As every one knows, public schools in the American inner city have become disaster areas. Next to them—in the same location and serving the same kind of children—are private (mostly Christian) schools in which the kids behave well and learn well. There is endless speculation to explain these enormous quality differences. A major reason is surely that the two kinds of school define their tasks differently. The typical public school defines its task as 'helping the underprivileged,' while the typical private school (and especially the Parochial Schools of the Catholic Church) define their task as 'enabling those who want to learn, to learn.' One therefore is governed by its scholastic failures, the other one by its scholastic successes.

Similarly, the research departments at two major pharmaceutical companies have totally different results because they define their tasks differently. One sees its task as not having failures, that is, in working steadily on fairly minor but predictable improvements in existing products and for established markets. The other one defines its task as producing 'breakthroughs' and therefore courts risks. Both are considered fairly successful—by themselves, by their own top managements, and by outside analysts. Yet each operates quite differently, and quite differently defines its own productivity and that of its research scientists.

To define quality in knowledge work and to convert the definition into knowledge-worker productivity is thus to a large extent a matter of defining the task. It requires the difficult, risk-taking, and always controversial definition as to what 'results' are for a given enterprise and a given activity. We therefore actually *know* how to do it. Nevertheless, the question is a completely new one for most organizations and also for most knowledge workers. To answer, it *requires* controversy, *requires* dissent.

The Knowledge Worker as Capital Asset

In no other area is the difference greater between manual-worker productivity and knowledge-worker productivity than in their respective *economics*. Economic theory and most business practice sees manual workers as a *cost*. To be productive, knowledge workers must be considered a *capital asset*. Costs need to be controlled and reduced. Assets need to be made to grow.

To be sure, in managing manual workers we learned fairly early that high turnover (i.e. losing workers) is very costly. The Ford Motor Company, as is well known, increased the pay of skilled workers from eighty cents a day to $5.00 a day on January 1, 1914. It did so because its turnover had been so excessive as to make its labor costs prohibitively high; it had to hire 60,000 people a year to keep 10,000. Even so, everybody (including Henry Ford himself, who had at first been bitterly opposed to this increase) was convinced that the higher wages would greatly reduce the company's profits. Instead, in the very first year, profits almost doubled. Paid $5.00 a day, practically no workers left—in fact, the Ford Motor Company soon had a waiting list.

However, short of the costs of turnover, rehiring, retraining, and so on, the manual worker is still being seen as a cost. This is true even in Japan, despite the emphasis on lifetime employment and on building a 'loyal,' permanent work-force. The management of people at work, based on millennia of work being almost totally manual work, still assumes that with few exceptions (e.g. highly skilled people) one manual worker is like any other manual worker.

This is definitely not true for knowledge work. Employees who do manual work do not own the means of production. They may, and often do, have a lot of valuable experience, but that experience is valuable only at the place where they work. It is not portable. Knowledge workers, however, *own* the means of production. That knowledge between their ears is a totally portable and enormous capital asset. Because knowledge workers own their means of production, they are mobile. It may not be true for most of them that the organization needs them more than they need the organization. For most of them it is a symbiotic relationship in which they need each other in equal measure. It is not true, as it was for the manual worker in modern industry, that they need the job much more than the job needs them.

Management's job is to preserve the assets of the institution in its care. What does this mean when the knowledge of the individual knowledge worker becomes an asset—and, in more and more cases, the *main* asset—of an institution? What does this mean for personnel policy? What is needed to attract and to hold the highest producing knowledge workers? What is needed to increase their productivity and to convert their increased productivity into performance capacity for the organization?

The Technologists

A very large number of knowledge workers do both knowledge work *and* manual work. I call them 'technologists.' This group includes people who apply knowledge of the highest order.

Surgeons preparing for an operation to correct a brain aneurysm before it produces a lethal brain hemorrhage, spend hours in diagnosis *before* they cut— and that requires specialized knowledge of the highest order. Again, during the surgery, an unexpected complication may occur which calls for theoretical knowledge and judgment, both of the very highest order. However, the surgery itself is manual work—and manual work consisting of repetitive, manual operations in which the emphasis is on speed, accuracy, and uniformity. These operations are studied, organized, learned, and practiced exactly like any manual work—that is, by the same methods Taylor first developed for factory work.

The technologist group also contains large numbers of people in whose work knowledge is relatively subordinate—though it is always crucial. The file clerk's job—and that of the clerk's computer-operator successor—requires a knowledge of the alphabet that no experience can teach. This knowledge is a small part of an otherwise manual task, but it is its foundation and is absolutely crucial.

Technologists may be the single biggest group of knowledge workers. They may also be the fastest-growing group. They include the great majority of health-care workers: lab-technicians; rehabilitation technicians; technicians in imaging such as X-ray, ultrasound, magnetic resonance imaging; and so on. They include dentists and all dental-support people. They include automobile mechanics and all kinds of repair and installation people. In fact, the technologist may be the true successor to the 19th- and 20th-century skilled workers.

Technologists are also the one group in which developed countries can have a true and long-lasting competitive advantage. When it comes to truly high knowledge, no country can any longer have much of a lead the way 19th-century Germany had through its University. Among theoretical physicists, mathematicians, economic theorists, and the like, there is no 'nationality.' Any country can, at fairly low cost, train a substantial number of high-knowledge people. India, for instance, despite her poverty, has been training fairly large numbers of first-rate physicians and first-rate computer programers. Similarly, there is no 'nationality' in respect to the productivity of manual labor. Training based on Scientific Management has made all countries capable of attaining— overnight—the manual-worker productivity of the most advanced country, industry, or company. Only by educating technologists can the developed countries still have a meaningful and lasting competitive edge.

The US is so far the only country that has developed this advantage through its unique nationwide systems of community colleges. The community college was actually *designed* (beginning in the 1920s) to educate technologists who have *both* the needed theoretical knowledge *and* the manual skill. On this, I am convinced, rests both the still huge productivity advantage of the American economy and the (so far unique) American ability to create, almost overnight, new and different industries.

Peter F. Drucker

Currently, nothing quite like the American Community College exists in any other nation. The famous Japanese school system produces people who are either prepared only for manual work or prepared only for knowledge work. Not until the year 2003 is the first Japanese institution devoted to train technologists supposed to get started. The even more famous German apprenticeship system (started in the 1830s) was one of the main factors in Germany's becoming the world's leading manufacturer. However, it focused—and still focuses—primarily on manual skills and slights theoretical knowledge. It is thus in danger of becoming rapidly obsolete.

Other developed countries should be expected to catch up with the US fairly fast. 'Emerging' or 'Third World' countries are, however, likely to be decades behind—in part because educating technologists is expensive, in part because in these countries people of knowledge still look down with disdain, if not with contempt, on working with one's hands. 'That's what we have servants for' is still their prevailing attitude. However, in developed countries—and again foremost in the US—more and more manual workers are going to be technologists. To increase knowledge-worker productivity, increasing the productivity of technologists deserves to be given high priority.

The job was actually done more than seventy years ago by the American Telephone Company (AT&T) for its technologists, the people who install, maintain, and replace telephones. By the early 1920s, the technologists working outside the telephone office and at the customer's location had become a major cost center—and at the same time a major cause of customer unhappiness and dissatisfaction. It took about five years or so (from 1920 until 1925) for AT&T—which had by that time acquired a near monopoly on providing telephone service in the US and in parts of Canada—to realize that the task was not installing, maintaining, repairing, and replacing telephones and telephone connections. *The task was to create a satisfied customer.* Once they realized this, it became fairly easy to organize the job. It meant, first, that the technicians themselves had to define what 'satisfaction' meant. The results were standards that established that every order for a new telephone or an additional telephone connection would have to be satisfied within forty-eight hours, and that every request for repair would have to be satisfied the same day if made before noon, or by noon the following day. Then it became clear that the individual service people—in those days all men, of course—would have to be active participants in such decisions as whether to have one person installing and replacing telephones and another one maintaining and repairing them or whether the same people had to be able to do all jobs (which in the end turned out to be the right answer). Then these people had to be taught a very substantial amount of theoretical knowledge—and in those days few of them had more than six years of schooling. They had to understand how a telephone works. They had to understand how a switchboard works. They had to understand how the telephone system works. These people were not qualified engineers nor skilled craftsmen, but they had to know enough electronics to diagnose unexpected problems and be able to cope with them. Then they were trained in the repetitive manual operation or in the 'one right way' (i.e. through the methods of Scientific Management) and *they* made the decisions (e.g. where and how to connect the individual telephone to the system and what particular kind of telephone and service would be the most suitable for a given home or a given office). They had to become salesmen in addition to being servicemen.

Finally, the telephone company faced the problem how to define *quality*. The technologist had to work by himself. He could not be supervised. He, therefore, had to define quality, and he had to deliver it. It took another several years before that was answered. At first the telephone company thought that this meant a sample check, which had supervisors go out and look at a sample (maybe every 20th or 30th job done by an individual service person) and check it for quality. This very soon turned out to be the wrong way of doing the job, annoying servicemen and customers alike. Then the telephone company defined quality as 'no complaints'—and they soon found out that only extremely unhappy customers complained. It then had to redefine quality as 'positive customer satisfaction.' In the end, this then meant that the serviceman himself controlled quality (e.g. by calling up a week or ten days after he had done a job and asking the customer whether the work was satisfactory and whether there was anything more the technician could possibly do to give the customer the best possible and most satisfactory service).

I have intentionally gone into considerable detail in describing this early example because it exemplifies the three elements for making the worker who is both a knowledge worker and a manual worker both effective and productive.

- First, there is the answer to the question 'What is the task?'—the key question in making every knowledge worker more productive. As the example of the Bell System shows, this is not an obvious answer. As the Bell System people learned, the only people who knew the answer to this were the technologists themselves. In fact, until they asked the technologists, they floundered. However, as soon as the technologists were asked, the answer came back loud and clear: 'a satisfied customer.'
- Then, the technologists had to take full responsibility for giving customer satisfaction, that is, for delivering quality. This showed what *formal knowledge* the technologist needed. Only then could the *manual* part of the job be organized for manual-worker productivity.
- Above all, this example shows that technologists have to be treated as *knowledge workers*. No matter how important the manual part of their

work—and it may take as much time as it did in the case of the AT&T installers—the focus has to be on making the technologist knowledgeable, responsible, and productive as a knowledge worker.

Knowledge Work as a System

Productivity of the knowledge worker will almost always require that the *work itself* be restructured and be made part of a *system*. One example is servicing expensive equipment, such as huge and expensive earth-moving machines. Traditionally, this had been seen as distinct and separate from the job of making and selling the machines. However, when the US Caterpillar Company, the world's largest producer of such equipment, asked 'What are we getting paid for?' the answer was 'We are not getting paid for machinery. We are getting paid for what the machinery does at the customer's place of business. That means keeping the equipment running, since even one hour during which the equipment is out of operation may cost the customer far more than the equipment itself.' In other words, the answer to 'What is our business?' was 'Service.' This then led to a total restructuring of operations all the way back to the factory in order that the customer could be guaranteed continuing operations and immediate repairs or replacements. The service representative, usually a technologist, has become the true 'decision maker.'

As another example, a group of about 25 orthopedic surgeons in a midwestern US city have organized themselves as a 'system' to: produce the highest quality work; make optimal use of the limited and expensive resources of operating and recovery rooms; make optimal use of the supporting knowledge people such as anesthesiologists or surgical nurses; build continuous learning and continuous innovation into the work of the entire group and of every member thereof; and, finally, minimize costs. Each of the surgeons retains full control of his or her practice. He or she is fully responsible for obtaining and treating the individual patient. Traditionally, surgeons schedule surgeries early in the morning. Hence, operating and recovery rooms are standing empty most of the time. The group now schedules the use of operating and recovery rooms for the entire group so that this scarce and extremely expensive resource is utilized ten hours a day. The group, as a group, decides on the standardization of tools and equipment so as to obtain the highest quality at the lowest cost. Finally, the group has also built quality control into its system. Every three months three surgeons are designated to scrutinize every operation done by each of the members—the diagnosis, the surgery, the after-treatment. They then sit down with the individual surgeons and discuss their performance. They suggest where there is need for improvement and they also may recommend that a certain surgeon be asked to leave the group when his or her work is not satisfactory. Each year, the quality standards that these supervising committees apply are discussed with the whole group and are raised, often substantially. As a result, this group now does almost four times as much work as it did before. It has cut the costs by 50, half of it by cutting back on the waste of operating and recovery rooms and half by standardizing tools and equipment. In such measurable areas as success rates in knee or shoulder replacements and in recovery after sports injuries, it has greatly improved its results.

What to do about knowledge-worker productivity is thus largely known. So is *how* to do it.

How to Begin?

Making knowledge workers more productive requires changes in basic attitude, whereas making the manual worker more productive only required telling the worker how to do the job. Furthermore, making knowledge workers more productive requires changes in attitude not only on the part of the individual knowledge worker, but on the part of the whole organization. It therefore has to be 'piloted,' as any major change should be. The first step is to find an area in the organization where there is a group of knowledge workers who are receptive. (The orthopedic surgeons, for instance, first had their new ideas tried out by four physicians who had long argued for radical changes.) The next step is to work consistently, patiently, and for a considerable length of time with this small group. The first attempts, even if greeted with great enthusiasm, will almost certainly run into all kinds of unexpected problems. It is only after the productivity of this small group of knowledge workers has been substantially increased that the new ways of doing the work can be extended to a larger area, if not to the entire organization. At this point, the main problems will be known, such as where resistance can be expected (e.g. from middle management) or what changes in task, organization, measurements, or attitudes are needed for full effectiveness. To bypass the pilot stage—and there is always pressure to do so—only means that the mistakes become public while the successes stay hidden. It only means discrediting the entire enterprise. If properly piloted, a great deal can be done to improve knowledge-worker productivity.

Knowledge-worker productivity is the biggest of the 21st-century management challenges. In the developed countries, it is their first *survival requirement*. In no other way can the developed countries hope to maintain themselves, let alone maintain their leadership and their standards of living. In the 20th century, this leadership very largely depended on making the manual worker more productive. Any country, any industry, any business can do that today using the methods that the developed countries have worked out and put into practice in the 120 years since Frederick Winslow Taylor first looked at manual work. Anybody today, any place, can apply those policies to training, the organization of work, and the productivity of workers—even if they are barely literate, if not illiterate, and totally unskilled.

Above all, the supply of young people available for manual work will be rapidly shrinking in the developed countries—in the West and in Japan very fast, in the US somewhat more slowly—whereas the supply of such people will still grow fast in the emerging and developing countries for at least another thirty or forty years. The only possible advantage developed countries can hope to have is in the supply of people prepared, educated, and trained for knowledge work. There, for another fifty years, the developed countries can expect to have substantial advantages, both in quality and in quantity. Whether this advantage will translate into performance depends on the ability of the developed countries—and of every industry in it, of every company in it, of every institution in it—to raise the productivity of the knowledge worker and to raise it as fast as the developed countries have raised the productivity of the manual worker in the last hundred years.

The countries and the industries that have emerged as the leaders in the last hundred years in the world are the countries and the industries that have led in raising the productivity of the manual worker—the US first, Japan, and Germany second. Fifty years from now, if not much sooner, leadership in the world economy will have moved to the countries and to the industries that have most systematically and most successfully raised knowledge-worker productivity.

The Governance of the Corporation

What does the emergence of the knowledge worker and of knowledge-worker productivity mean for the *governance of the corporation*? What does it mean for the future and structure of the economic system?

In the last 10 or 15 years, pension funds and other institutional investors became the main share owners of the equity capital of publicly owned companies in all developed countries. In the US, this has triggered a furious debate on the governance of corporations. With the emergence of pension funds and mutual funds as the owners of publicly owned companies, power has shifted to these new owners. Similar shifts in both the definition of the purpose of economic organizations (such as the business corporation) and their govern-ance can be expected to occur in all developed countries.

Within a fairly short period, we will face the problem of the governance of corporations again. We will have to redefine the purpose of the employing organization and of its management as both satisfying the legal owners (such as shareholders) and satisfying the owners of the human capital that gives the organization its wealth-producing power—that is, satisfying the know-ledge workers. Increasingly, the ability of organizations—and not only of businesses—to survive will come to depend on their 'comparative advantage' in making the knowledge worker more productive. The ability to attract and hold the best of the knowledge workers is the first and most fundamental precondition.

However, can this be *measured* or is it purely an 'intangible'? This will surely be a central problem for management, for investors, and for capital markets. What does 'capitalism' mean when knowledge governs rather than money? And what do 'free markets' mean when knowledge workers—and no one else can 'own' knowledge—are the true assets? Knowledge workers can neither be bought nor be sold. They do not come with a merger or an acquisition. In fact, although they are the greatest 'value' they have no 'market value'—that means, of course, that they are not an 'asset' in any sense of the term.

These questions go far beyond the scope of this article. However, it is certain that the emergence as *key questions* of the knowledge worker and of the knowledge-worker's productivity will, within a few decades, bring about fun-damental changes in the very structure and nature of the economic system.

....

Note

1. For work in the oldest knowledge profession—that is, in Medicine—Taylor's close contemporary William Osler (1849–1919) did what Taylor did and at the same time in his 1892 book *The Principles and Practice of Medicine* (arguably the best textbook since Euclid's *Geometry* in the third century BC). Osler's work has rightly been called the application of Scientific Management to Medical Diagnosis. Like Taylor, Osler preached that there is no 'skill', there is only *method*.

19 Just-in-Time Delivery Comes to Knowledge Management

....

Thomas H. Davenport and John Glaser

Dr. Bob Goldszer is the associate chief medical officer and head of the Special Services Department at Brigham and Women's in Boston, one of the nation's leading hospitals. A professor at the Harvard Medical School, Goldszer has both an MD and an MBA. He's a high-end knowledge worker at the top of the medical profession.

Yet Dr. Goldszer has a big problem—one common to all physicians. There is so much knowledge available about his work that he cannot possibly absorb it all. He needs to know something about almost 10,000 different diseases and syndromes, 3,000 medications, 1,100 laboratory tests, and many of the 400,000 articles added each year to the biomedical literature. Even if he were to consult only those articles written by his colleagues at Partners HealthCare (the Boston-based umbrella organization that includes Brigham and Women's, Massachusetts General, and several other hospitals and physicians' groups), he would need to choose among 202 on hypertension, 139 on asthma, and 313 on diabetes. As a primary care physician, he must know something like a million facts, and those facts are constantly changing. Clearly, it is difficult for Goldszer to stay on top of even a fraction of all the new knowledge being generated in his field and still do his job.

This is not a trivial problem. It is, quite literally, a matter of life and death. Over the past decade, researchers have done a series of studies on medical errors. The results are sobering. The Institute of Medicine's 1999 report *To Err Is Human* suggests that more than a million injuries and as many as 98,000 deaths each year are attributable to medical errors. Partners' own research in 1995 suggested that more than 5 percent of patients had adverse reactions to drugs while under medical care; 43 percent of those inpatient reactions were serious, life threatening, or fatal. Of the reactions that were preventable, more than half were caused by inappropriate drug prescriptions. About a third of the marginally abnormal pap smears and mammograms received no documented follow-up. A study of the six most common laboratory tests ordered by physicians in Brigham and Women's surgical intensive care unit found that almost half of the tests ordered were clinically unnecessary. Another study at the Brigham found that more than half of the prescriptions for a particular heart medicine were inappropriate.

Some of these mistakes result from carelessness, but far more of them, we believe, occur because the clinicians must track such massive amounts of complex information. The problem of staying on top of all the knowledge available in a given profession is not restricted to medicine, of course. Knowledge workers in many other fields have problems similar to Dr. Goldszer's, though generally theirs are less life threatening. No matter what the industry, knowledge workers often cannot keep up with the knowledge being generated. And although failure to keep up with current information may not result in deaths, it can lead to less successful projects and products, wasted resources, and broken businesses.

Knowledge management, which was all the rage in the mid- to late-1990s, is still a good idea, but it needs a new approach. In the early years of knowledge management, companies established employee networks and communities of practice, built knowledge repositories, and tried to encourage information sharing. Knowledge workers were expected to participate in these activities in addition to doing their regular jobs. That meant staying a little later each night to share what they'd learned in the course of doing their jobs and coming in a little earlier each morning to learn from others. As a result, the programs, many of which continue today, have been only marginally successful. Even the successful ones require motivational schemes and some arm-twisting from senior executives.

But there is a better approach to information sharing and retrieval. The key to success, we have found, is to bake specialized knowledge into the jobs of highly skilled workers—to make the knowledge so readily accessible that it cannot be avoided. This is the main approach Partners HealthCare has taken to address Dr. Goldszer's problem. Partners has made his job easier by helping him avoid mistakes, learn from other employees' experiences, and access important information when he needs to make decisions. While there are several ways to bake knowledge into knowledge work, the most promising approach is to embed it into the technology that knowledge workers use to do their jobs. That approach ensures that knowledge management is no longer a separate activity requiring additional time and motivation.

We believe that this method could revolutionize knowledge management in the same way that just-in-time systems revolutionized inventory management—and by following much the same philosophy. In this article, we shall discuss how just-in-time knowledge has been embedded into Dr. Goldszer's work and other physicians' work at a few Partners hospitals. We shall also consider the circumstances that make it possible—or impossible—to bake knowledge into the work processes of other high-end professionals.

Partners' Ambitious Project

Embedding knowledge into everyday work processes is time-consuming and expensive. It is not an undertaking that anyone in his right mind would tackle without a very good reason. A decade ago, Partners had that reason. Researchers at the Harvard School of Public Health and Harvard Medical School found that there were surprisingly high numbers of medical errors and adverse drug reactions at Partners hospitals. That these institutions could be unconsciously acting in direct opposition to their healing mission was deeply troubling.

Under the direction of H. Richard Nesson, CEO of Brigham and Women's at the time, Partners undertook an ambitious and risky project to link massive amounts of constantly updated clinical knowledge to the IT systems that supported doctors' work processes. The project was ambitious because it had the potential to substantially improve the quality of physicians' decision making—and hence improve the quality of patient care. But it was also risky because knowledge-based systems had a very spotty record of success in their first incarnation two decades ago and because Partners did not really know if it would be able to codify the millions of facts and data points that doctors use to make complex decisions about treatment.

So the project was defined relatively narrowly at first. Partners professionals targeted an essential work process—physician order entry—and a problem that was well documented—errors in drug prescriptions and lab-test ordering. Drug interactions are relatively straightforward and easy to program; this fact, too, improved the project's chances for success.

The decision to focus on the order-entry system was important because the system is central to physicians delivering good medical care. When doctors order tests, medications, or other forms of treatment, they are translating their judgments into actions. This is the moment when outside knowledge is most valuable. Without the system, doctors would have no easy way to access others' knowledge in real time. Automated order entry addresses this need in several ways. It increases efficiency and safeguards against errors due to poorly written orders. Even more important, it allows physicians easy access to massive amounts of up-to-date medical knowledge while they go about their daily work. Indeed, the order-entry system forces physicians to engage with queries or recommendations (although, as we shall see, they can always override the system's recommendations).

Order entry is a key work process in this system, but it is not the only one. Partners' approach is built on a set of integrated information systems—including on-line referral and medical-records systems—that physicians can use to manage patient care. These all draw from a single database of clinical information and use a common logic engine that runs physicians' orders through a series of checks and decision rules.

Here is how it works. Let us say Dr. Goldszer has a patient, Mrs. Johnson, and she has a serious infection. He decides to treat the infection with ampicillin. As he logs on to the computer to order the drug, the system automatically checks her medical records for allergic reactions to any medications. She has never taken that particular medication, but she once had an allergic reaction to penicillin, a drug chemically similar to ampicillin. The computer brings that reaction to Goldszer's attention and asks if he wants to continue with the order. He asks the system what the allergic reaction was. It could have been something relatively minor, like a rash, or major, like going into shock. Mrs. Johnson's reaction was a rash; Goldszer decides to override the computer's recommendation and prescribe the original medication, judging that the positive benefit from the prescription outweighs the negative effects of a relatively minor and treatable rash. The system lets him do that, but it requires him to give a reason for overriding its recommendation.

The fact that the order-entry system is linked not just with the clinical database but also with the patient's records increases its usefulness by an order of magnitude. The system may inform Goldszer that a drug being prescribed is not economical or effective, but it can also tell him that the patient is taking another drug that interacts badly with the new medication or one that might exacerbate a condition other than the one being treated. When it comes to ordering tests for a patient, the system may note that a particular test is generally not useful in addressing the symptoms identified or that it has been performed on the patient enough times that a retest would not be useful.

That is a relatively simple explanation of what the integrated system does, but, in fact, the logic engine and the knowledge base can serve as very sophisticated screens for the physician's decisions. For instance, imagine that a patient with a history of sleep apnea is prescribed a narcotic to mitigate pain after surgery. Narcotics can cause people with sleep apnea to go into respiratory arrest, but, as long as the history of sleep apnea is noted in the patient's medical records, the system will alert the physician to that potential problem. It also takes into account the patient's age, likely metabolism, probability of renal failure, maximum allowable life-time amounts of a chemotherapy agent, and hundreds of other factors.

The logic engine and knowledge base at Partners are used more during order entry than at any other time. But they are used increasingly during normal review of patient medical records as well. For example, the system alerts the physician, as he or she reviews Mrs. Smith's record, to follow up on her marginally abnormal mammogram or to recheck her cholesterol levels. In addition, it may remind a physician that a particular patient should receive a call or schedule a follow-up appointment.

There are, of course, times when a physician is not treating a patient directly yet still needs to know that something has happened. For these times, Partners developed an event-detection system that alerts a physician when a hospitalized patient's monitored health indicators depart significantly from what is expected. The physician is notified through a pager and can then visit the patient directly or call in a new treatment. Minor variations are routed to the nurses' station, and the nurse can decide whether to call in the physician.

The power of knowledge-based order-entry, referral, computerized medical-record, and event-detection systems is that they operate in real time. Knowledge is brought to bear immediately without the physician having to seek it out. In some situations, physicians can consult with other experts in real time, via teleconferencing and other technologies. Such practices are still in their early stages, but they show great promise. For example, if a patient on Nantucket island experiences what his doctor suspects is a stroke, he needs to be diagnosed and treated within an hour or his chances for full recovery drop precipitously. By the time he is flown to Cape Cod Hospital, it might be too late. If a specialist in Boston, or for that matter in Tel Aviv, can interview the patient over a videoconference screen, observe how he speaks and moves, and review scan results, the likelihood of effective treatment will go way up.

Partners has also assembled many other knowledge resources that are not accessible in real time but are valuable nonetheless. These sources are more extensive than what is in the clinical-information database. However, they are like traditional knowledge-management systems in that users need to seek them out. The organization's on-line sources (collectively called *The Handbook*) include on-line journals and databases, care protocols or guidelines for particular diseases, interpretive digests prepared by Partners physicians, formularies of approved drugs and details on their use, and even on-line textbooks. All of these resources are accessible through an integrated intranet portal. It is an unusually good set of resources, but they are not different in kind from those that practitioners at other hospitals can consult. *The Handbook* is accessed, across all Partners institutions, about 3,000 times a day. Contrast this with the 13,000 orders submitted a day at Brigham and Women's alone; even though it is invisible to the clinicians, the information embedded in the order entry system is used far more intensively than *The Handbook* is.

While Partners' embedded-knowledge program has been under development for more than a decade, it is still not complete. The on-line order-entry system and related knowledge are only accessible within the organization's two flagship hospitals, Mass General and Brigham and Women's. Medical knowledge has not yet been codified for all the diseases that Partners physicians treat. But the approach is clearly beneficial. A controlled study of the system's impact on medication errors found that serious errors were reduced by 55 percent. When Partners experts established that a new drug was particularly beneficial for heart problems, orders for that drug increased from 12 percent to 81 percent. When the system began recommending that a cancer drug be given fewer times per day, the percentage of orders entered for the lower frequency changed from 6 percent to 75 percent. When the system began to remind physicians that patients requiring bed rest also needed the blood thinner heparin, the frequency of prescriptions for that drug increased from 34 percent to 54 percent.

These improvements not only save lives, they also save money. For starters, the system now recommends cheaper as well as more effective drugs. Even more important, it helps prevent longer hospital stays and repeat tests that result from adverse drug events (ADE). That can save a facility large sums of money, since a 700-bed hospital will normally incur about $1 million per year in preventable ADE costs. Order entry with embedded knowledge is still rare enough that US insurers have not yet seen their costs go down, nor have national malpractice figures changed. However, Partners, which insures itself for malpractice, has some early data suggesting that malpractice reserves can be smaller because of fewer drug-related claims.

Keys to Success

Developing a system like Partners' is not easy—from either a technical or a managerial standpoint. Few off-the-shelf software packages used for knowledge-intensive business processes allow individuals and organizations to embed their own knowledge into systems. Partners had to develop most of its systems from scratch, creating a complex information and technology infrastructure that pulled together the knowledge base and logic modules with an integrated patient-record system, a clinical-decision support system, an event-management system, an intranet portal, and several other system capabilities. Other hospitals have some or all of these capabilities, but Partners' real-time knowledge approaches are undoubtedly at the cutting edge.

The technical under-pinnings of an embedded-knowledge system are key, but just as important are the non-technical, managerial aspects required to keep the system running smoothly. Several of these aspects—each of which would be relevant to any organization seeking to bake knowledge into its work—are described below.

Support from the Best and Brightest

Building a system like Partners' is a challenging IT project, to be sure. But then comes an even harder task: convincing knowledge workers, no matter what environment or field they are in, to support the system and the new way of working. The growing concern over medical errors provided that motivation at Partners; absent a similar sense of pressing need, it probably would not have gotten off the ground.

An Expert and Up-to-Date Knowledge Base

If Partners' clinical database included idiosyncratic, untested, or obsolete knowledge, it would put patients—and Partners itself—at high risk. Thus, only clinicians at the top of their game can create and maintain the knowledge repository. Partners has addressed this issue by forming several committees, and empowering existing ones, to identify, refine, and update the knowledge used in each domain. For instance, the medication recommendations in the system come from drug therapy committees. Teams of specialists design care protocols for particular diseases. And radiology utilization committees have developed logic to guide radiology test ordering. Participation in these groups is viewed as a prestigious activity, so busy physicians are willing to devote extra time to codifying the knowledge within their fields.

Prioritized Processes and Knowledge Domains

Since these initiatives are difficult and expensive, they should only be undertaken for truly critical knowledge work processes. At Partners, it was relatively easy to identify which medical care processes were the most crucial, but important decisions still needed to be made about which disease domains and medical subprocesses to address—for example, ordering medications versus referring a patient to a specialist—and in what order. Fields with many disease variations and multiple treatment protocols, such as oncology, are more difficult to include in the knowledge systems. In general, it's preferable to develop systems in fields with low levels of ambiguity, a well-established external knowledge base, and a relatively low number of possible choices facing the decision makers.

Final Decisions by the Experts

With high-end knowledge workers like physicians, it would be a mistake to remove them from the decision-making process; they might end up resenting or rejecting the system if it challenged their role—and with good reason. Because over-reliance on computerized knowledge can easily lead to mistakes, Partners' system presents physicians with recommendations, not commands. The hope is that the physicians will combine their own knowledge with the system's. Out of the 13,000 orders entered on an average day by physicians at Brigham and Women's, 386 are changed as a result of a computer suggestion. When medication allergies or conflict warnings are generated, a third to a half of the orders are canceled. The hospital's event-detection system generates more than 3,000 alerts per year; as a result of these alerts, treatments are changed 72 percent of the time—a sign that the hybrid human-computer knowledge system at Partners is working as it should.

A Culture of Measurement

In order to justify the time and money spent on an embedded knowledge system, and to assess how well it is working, an organization needs to have a measurement-oriented culture. Partners has always had a strong measurement culture because it is an academic medical center and because most of its senior clinicians are also researchers. Its knowledge management approach has only furthered the emphasis on measurement. The tracking mechanisms within the order-entry system can detect whether the physicians use the knowledge and change their treatment decisions, which is the only way to know that the system is working. The measures are used as justifications and progress reporting tools for efforts to reengineer and continuously improve care processes.

The Right Information and IT People

Whenever knowledge technologies are applied to business problems, it is tempting to attribute any success to the technology. But in the case of Partners' system, and in many others we have seen, success is based mostly on the people behind the technology. An IT organization that knows the business and can work closely with key executives and knowledge-rich professionals is important. A 'back room' IT group could never successfully build a system of this type. Also important is a staff that is skilled in information management. In health care, this discipline is called medical informatics, and Partners has recruited leaders in this field. It has several medical informatics departments, including Clinical and Quality Analysis, Medical Imaging, Telemedicine, and Clinical Information Systems R&D. The leaders of each of these departments are doctors, but they also have advanced degrees in fields such as computer science, statistics, and medical informatics.

In general, it is easier to embed knowledge into the work of less-skilled workers; the higher you go, the harder it gets. But organizations are gradually learning how to make the concept work at all levels. Customer service representatives without a great deal of technical skill now have highly scripted jobs. Many highly skilled reps at high-tech firms like Hewlett-Packard, Dell, and Xerox work with computer systems that rapidly supply knowledge to help them resolve customers' problems. Mid-level knowledge workers—programers, engineers, designers—depend increasingly on knowledge repositories built into the technology they use to do their jobs. GM's Vehicle Engineering Centers, for example, program information about the desirable dimensions of new vehicles and the parameters of existing components into the company's computer-aided design systems so that car and truck designers cannot help but employ the knowledge.

Baking knowledge into the work processes of high-end professionals like physicians is relatively new. Such professionals are different from other knowledge workers: They are generally paid more and receive more intensive training; they make decisions based largely on intuition and years of experience; they have historically enjoyed high levels of autonomy; they are sufficiently powerful that the organizations they work for are reluctant to tinker with their work processes; and, perhaps most important, they do most of their work away from a computer screen. All those factors make it harder to embed knowledge into their work processes. But the Partners example illustrates that it is indeed possible to inject knowledge directly and effectively into the work these professionals do, dramatically improving their performance. And for people like Dr. Goldszer and his patients, such improvements can make all the difference.

Seeing Knowledge Plain: How to Make Knowledge Visible

Leigh Weiss and Laurence Prusak

Several years ago, one of the authors was asked to help a large agricultural collective get over some difficulties they were having in formulating a strategy for the organization. When meeting with and interviewing the individual executives, everyone seemed to agree on what the environment looked like, what were realistic goals, who the major competitors were, and so on. Yet the organization was having a very difficult time formulating the proposed strategy. We had an intuition that the executives did not mean at all the same things when they spoke of competitors, threats, opportunities, and other factors that would affect strategy. The words were often the same or very similar but the meanings and usage were different due to the very diverse backgrounds and experiences of the members of the executive team, which included farmers, MBAs, and marketers.

We suggested that the group try to illustrate, or make visible, their proposed strategy and its component pieces. This idea was initially met with very quizzical looks. But when they tried to actually draw on a poster what they were talking about, the results confirmed our hunch. People were using words quite differently as exemplified by how we were drawing them. For example, the group tried to express the three main competitors in their size-ratio to the organization. Everyone had said how 'powerful' or 'important' they were. Yet when they tried to express this in a drawing, significant differences were revealed as to the relative size of these other firms. Before long it was clear that there was very little consensus or agreement as to the relative size and importance of the competitors. These differences only emerged by literally drawing the competitive landscape on a chart. The words were significantly misleading until they were represented visually.

As this story demonstrates, there is an increasing realization that visualization can be an extremely potent tool and method for working with knowledge.[1] 'Making knowledge visible,' of course, is somewhat of a contradiction as knowledge is by its very nature invisible. Short of very complex neurological machinery, it cannot be seen, touched, or measured. However, knowledge can be, and often is, visualized.

Examples of visualized knowledge abound—explanatory diagrams, maps, taxonomies, and social network analyses. These all fall into the larger category of cognitive artifacts—tools, either mental or actual things, that aid human cognition and understanding. One's sense of direction is such a tool, as well as knowing how to read a map and of course the map itself.[2] A map, for example, is a visual representation of a landscape that allows people to navigate based on a particular intended use. It is representative because 'the map is not the territory.' So maps for hikers have elevation contours while maps for motorists show roads, intersections and important landmarks. This is somewhat analogous to the ways that verbal and written stories make ideas and concepts come to life because they put them in the context of a narrative that makes them much more useful.

A PowerPoint presentation with graphs, charts, and text arranged graphically visualizes knowledge and can provide a more complete picture than knowledge that is disembodied, abstracted, and eviscerated, as often happens when it is simply presented in lists or other context-less forms. In fact, the very widespread success of PowerPoint is illustrative of just how great an appetite there is for more visual displays of knowledge and information. However, PowerPoint is quite often used merely to present words, usually in truncated phrases, and diagrams and charts can often be reductive or merely fatuous. PowerPoint has not done much more than point out the need for better approaches to knowledge visualization.[3]

A good proportion of the research to date in this area has focused on how individual knowledge is or could be visualized.[4] While this is a fascinating and important subject, it is not the emphasis of this chapter. We are concerned here with how organizational knowledge can be made visible. What has served up to now, more or less, for visualizing organizational knowledge is the traditional organization chart, process maps, Gantt charts, and all the various forms thrown off by PowerPoint and its imitators. While there have been a few exceptions, overall their effectiveness as cognitive artifacts is questionable.

Precursors to Knowledge Visualization

What we are discussing here has a long lineage, like most seemingly innovative business ideas. For example, semiology, the science of signs, was developed in the 19th century by the philosophers Saussere and Peirce, and was based on earlier thinking going back as far as Plato. Almost all psychological theorists have shown an interest in how individual knowledge is symbolized and represented within the mind. In more modern times, cognitive science is strongly focused on this area, and of course researchers in artificial intelligence and information science have also been doing much work in this arena. Knowledge visualization is also strongly rooted in the literature of information- and knowledge-based products, for example by Edward Tufte and Richard Saul Wurman.[5]

There is also a tradition of sorts, going back several decades, that has attempted to analyze and offer tools for creating visible organizational knowledge. For example, causal mapping was first discussed in the 1970s[6] and one can argue that the popularization of system theory by Peter Senge in *The Fifth Discipline*[7] was a significant step along this road. Decision trees and all of their near and far relations also began to gain currency, at least in the Academy in the 1970s,[8] heavily influenced by computer models of individual cognition. One can also argue that scenarios are an offshoot of this stream of work.

There were several significant branches of attempts at schematic knowledge visualization that came out of the artificial intelligence and expert system movement. Case-based reasoning, requirements engineering and knowledge engineering, and modeling are the better known of these attempts.

However, neither any of these, nor the many other lesser known variants on this theme, have ever seriously caught on with management as true knowledge tools. For one thing they were often described and presented in jargon that was nearly impenetrable—Senge being a notable exception. More importantly, they were either too reductionist—often trying to reduce a rich or complex situation to one or two company rules, propositions, or statements that could be visualized or modeled—or they were too inclusive, using very wide, encompassing words so as to include an entire system.

Social network analysis is perhaps one exception—an example of a knowledge visualization tool that has been used, albeit to a limited extent, by management. Social network analysis involves the mapping and measuring of normally invisible relationships between people. Network maps are visual representations of people's friendships, social capital and communication patterns, and include meaningful information like social distance, which could refer to frequency of contact or emotional closeness. Social network analysis emerged out of sociology and an effort to understand the informal structures that are important in people's lives. Thus, for example, a company might have a formal organizational chart showing who reports to whom, but a social network analysis shows the informal relationships among people and how work actually gets done—an organizational X-ray. Social network analysis can be applied at the level of individuals, departments or groups, organizations, or entire industries or markets.

Social network analyses can be powerful ways of visually communicating collaboration or information flows in companies. Imagine a drawing where each person in a division is represented by a dot or node. When two people share information or knowledge, a line is drawn between those two nodes. Now imagine that the diagram has a primary cluster of many nodes with links between them closely clustered together, a second cluster of many nodes with links between them but only one node linking the two clusters. That one node is the lynchpin between the two groups. If that person were removed, the two groups would be isolated, and important information might not flow between them. When this type of picture is shown to the head of a department, he or she can visually identify the places where coordination might need to be improved and take appropriate action.[9]

Just imagine if you tried to write down in a traditional way how a network was configured: John knows Jane but talks mostly to Jim who works closely with Jill ad infinitum. Clearly a diagram would be an essential navigation tool for doing this.

Why the Current Interest?

There are at least three main factors creating a need for people to find ways of making sense of their world and their work through knowledge visualization. First, technological advances in the past century have created enormous numbers of various signals. This change has resulted in all of us receiving a high volume of data, information, and static noise that is difficult to prioritize and understand. Second, global economic changes, such as the increased mobility of capital, a more liberal approach to regulation, and the globalization of markets, are creating a business environment that has become significantly more confusing (risks due to knowing less than competitors about certain opportunities, or simply knowing less than can be known), complex (risks due to interdependent variables whose relationships are difficult to understand), and uncertain (risks due to unknown events that nobody can anticipate).[10] Third, virtual and distributed work, and its resulting distributed cognition, has made it increasingly difficult for people to make sense of their own work environments such as knowing who knows what within an organization and where knowledge can be found.[11] These and other changes make it increasingly difficult for people to make sense of the world around them and necessitate new ways to create understanding.

Take, for example, the research and discovery process in pharmaceutical companies. Over the past decade, the number of inputs to discovery has escalated as have the number of sources that contribute information and knowledge. Formerly, a pharmaceutical company might rely on its own internal research and inputs from a small number of other institutions. The proliferation of small biotechnology companies is one example of how the sources of innovation have increased. Today, almost all pharmaceutical companies have formed alliances and collaborations with industry partners and academic institutions to develop new products, acquire platform technologies, and access new markets. Simply keeping track of the collaborations, much less the content that flows across the relationships, is a monumental task.

What Can Be Done about Knowledge Visualization?

When we talk about knowledge 'visualization,' we mean showing or displaying knowledge in ways that will help people better navigate a knowledge environment and act on it. It is a technique that makes it easier to better understand shared experience and expertise and take action based on that understanding. Visualizing knowledge is especially important in a world where it is increasingly difficult to recognize patterns because knowledge is more and more complex and interrelated. Making knowledge visible has several distinct advantages. These include:

- Creating a rich picture of what is known so that knowledge connections are visible and comprehensible
- Better communicating complex relationships
- Showing time, space, and activities in a multi-dimensional setting
- Showing multiple levels of relationships and causation
- Stimulating new knowledge—the act of making knowledge visible creates new knowledge, so it is not just the output but the process that is valuable
- Exposing what is not known
- Displaying patterns that were previously unknown
- Creating common symbols to foster group coherence

For managers, making knowledge visible has advantages that enable them and their employees to do their jobs more effectively. For example, making knowledge visible can improve knowledge worker productivity by reducing the transaction costs associated with finding, understanding, assimilating, and applying knowledge. A research report by analysts at IDC estimated that an organization employing 1,000 knowledge workers might easily incur a cost of more than $6 million per year in lost productivity as employees fail to find existing knowledge they need, waste time searching for nonexistent knowledge, and recreate knowledge that is available but could not be located.[12] One can imagine the impact on an organization with 100,000 or more employees.

Additionally, making knowledge visible helps cut through the thickets of information overload. A recent article in the *Wall Street Journal* described visualization software that helps managers cut through this clutter.[13] Infinity Pharmaceuticals is using visualization software to analyze the properties of millions of chemical compounds in search of the tiny percentage that have the potential to be developed into drugs. And the UK mobile telephone retailer Carphone Warehouse Group PLC, one of Europe's largest mobile phone retailers, uses visualization to reduce customer acquisition costs because they are able to more efficiently direct resources to the most effective sales channels. There is even an evolving subindustry of advisory companies aiming to help organizations visualize and thus make sense of their knowledge and information to produce actionable results, including redesigning business processes, enhancing product or service delivery, and identifying organizational and human resource needs.

Since many people are primarily visual learners, visuals present knowledge in a way that can often be more easily absorbed. One need only look at the increasing number of books being published that show complex and interrelated knowledge in a visual format. Some examples include *Understanding Healthcare* by Richard Saul Wurman, a visual guidebook to personal health and *You Are Here: Personal Geographies and Other Maps of the Imagination*, by Katharine Harmon, a wide-ranging collection of personal maps about everything from a dog's perspective on an ideal country estate to a trip down the road to success.[14]

Knowledge visualization can be a useful approach for helping customers or clients find what they are looking for. For instance, Thinkmap is an innovative company addressing this challenge using proprietary software to help knowledge workers make sense of the vast experience and expertise in an organization. Their approach employs a kinetic, graphic interface that enables users to see connections between content (e.g. documents) and additional information about the content itself. One of the benefits of their approach is that it enables knowledge workers to make better decisions.

Thinkmap helped Sony Music Entertainment develop an approach enabling creative professionals to easily find appropriate songs and create sound tracks from among the company's large, diverse catalog of musical recordings. Thinkmap worked with Sony to develop a site that allows customers to select songs from Sony's library of over 200,000 songs using a visual, intuitive web-based navigation tool. Customers can search songs based on artist name, song title, date published, and subject matter. They are then presented with a list of appropriate songs, alongside a graphical, kinetic display of related topics, built with Thinkmap's proprietary software. The result is that users see information on songs and artists and the connections between them. In all of these examples, the enriched context makes it easier for one to make sense of the vast content available to them and increases the likelihood that they will make meaningful, appropriate applications of it.

Visualizing knowledge can also help employees find knowledge they need within the organization. A number of years ago one of the authors was involved in a research program focusing on information ecologies.[15] One of the participants was a woman who worked in the large IT center of a major financial services/credit card company. She was particularly interested in how fragmented the knowledge and information inherent in the firm's IT units was. In particular, she found the lack of locational understanding frustrating. 'No one really knew where all the firm's data-centers were, and what was worse, no one knew what was in them,' she stated.

Prodded by some of the research groups' activities, she set out to map where all the data centers were and what was in them. This activity took over six months for her to do (it was in addition to her regular work) and involved much negotiating, bargaining, pleading, and promising. Eventually she got the information, she needed and managed to get 200 copies of a world map produced that rather elegantly displayed the world of the company's data centers.

She sent them out to all her far-flung correspondents and expected that would be the end of her activities. She was amazed by the flood of responses requesting the map and eventually had to print thousands of copies. She even received an extremely rare thank you note from the CEO, stating that he found the map quite useful. No one had ever thought before to do such a thing, and she actually got a promotion and began to work on other such projects within the company.

However, the sad reality is that most organizations provide information and knowledge to employees and clients or customers, in a context-free, stand-alone way. Often, this form of documentation does not have sufficient context to enable employees to make connections between other related materials. Consequently, they often fail to identify other material that might be useful, or make the material itself more meaningful.

One example of a company trying to do things differently is Motorola. Motorola has a history of innovation and a rich archive of documents. Their Archive Team has developed a context-rich intranet site, Motorola History Online, that helps employees access these materials, making it easier to do their jobs by more easily identifying and applying lessons learned in already codified knowledge.[16] The site is highly visual and provides a variety of ways to learn—interactive timeline, spider map, interactive educational animations, and plain text. The contextual interface ensures that employees searching for a specific document will find related materials. For example, an employee might be looking for a specific image for a sales presentation or may want a document describing how Motorola first entered the semiconductor market. The search results will take the employee to these images and documents and also show them related material in the form of a spider map that uses kinetic, connected words and phrases to illustrate visually the links between Motorola's themes, people, and products. In addition, the timeline helps employees see the evolution of Motorola's products. This approach of visualizing content in context reduces the chances that an employee will miss important content or will misinterpret the content because the context is missing. Motorola employees find their visual, context-rich intranet extremely helpful. Seeing the knowledge in context makes it easier for employees to understand and appropriately apply knowledge.

Another example of an effective approach to visualizing knowledge was work done by one of the authors in a development project to help the South American Andean nations better understand their knowledge assets in the context of emerging economic clusters. There were several standardized and established ways to accomplish this, mostly involving listing and classifying things such as 'technical information sources,' which is the way this work is often done. Such reports often have very low impact for those who most need them because the information is presented in such static, reductive, achrono-logical ways. We decided not to follow this road and tried to present the material in ways that expressed the development of the knowledge *over time*, and how all the major actors and components and institutional factors inter-acted together to bring the cluster together. This literally could only be done by doing some form of event mapping. This was the only way we could develop the rich interactive picture we wanted so that others could use it when we and the principles were not there to explain it and provide context.

The use of this map was successful with the South American client, CAF (Corporación Andina de Fomento), and especially with actual participants whose work was being 'visualized,' so to speak. They quickly recognized how the visualization was analogous to the stories they had been telling us about the growth of the cluster. In one or two maps we had at the least captured some of the dynamism, interactivity, and interplays that exist in any complex activity.

Characteristics of Knowledge Visualization Tools

Tools to visualize knowledge have become increasingly sophisticated. They usefully illustrate knowledge contexts and contrasts. Contexts show relationships such as how a set of introductory training materials for employees is related to a larger body of materials on similar and different subjects. *Contrasts*, a subset of *context*, shows differences between two pieces of information such as the fact that Joe is taller than Jill.

Four properties are especially worth noting for their impact—dynamic/ kinetic displays, graphic representation, chronological meaning, and meaning of colors, shapes and lines. The Sony Music Entertainment example earlier provides a useful example of *dynamic* and *kinetic* properties. As creative professionals used the Sony approach and input words they wanted to find in songs, the display changed automatically. Based on the choices a user made about topics of interest and relevant songs, a picture would emerge of one or several options that might fit the users needs. This example also shows the value of *graphical* properties of visually represented knowledge.

The Motorola Online History example discussed earlier illustrates how visualizations can add value by displaying information *chronologically*, in this case a timeline of the major milestones in the company's history. This way, a Motorola employee can either search the representation by date, to find out what was happening in the company at that time, or search by topic and find out when an important event occurred. Finally, visualizations can help people navigate by embedding *colors, shapes and lines* with meaning. In the social network example discussed earlier, the lines represented connections between people where information was flowing between them.

Conclusion

When the great physicist Richard Feynman was still in his mid-twenties, he wrote several papers on quantum mechanics that expressed many of his ideas in 'odd little diagrams' rather than in linear words or equations. Although they were initially met with skepticism by the prestigious *Physics Review*, 'it turned out that the method they reflected proved to be not only correct and useful but revolutionary. ... In the *Physics Review* his diagrams were now ubiquitous. They were as famous as diagrams get.'[17] His 'odd little diagrams' were visualizations that helped readers make sense of the extremely complex ideas he was describing.

The social science of semiology, and even just some ordinary reflection, tells us that all physical artifacts send messages and can be seen as types of signs. Architects have known this forever, and have designed buildings that convey meaning as well as serve a function. Modern rhetoricians and even some management theorists have shown us that verbal artifacts such as stories and narratives are also cognitive artifacts in that they too convey a type of meaning that allows one to know where one is—socially, psychologically, and politically.[18]

It is perhaps worth ending on the point that while computing power and technological advances have enabled many of the more sophisticated ways of visualizing knowledge, computers cannot visualize knowledge on their own. All of the examples described in this chapter required considerable human agency and experience to determine what type of visualization would be useful and how it would best deliver value to the people who used it.

✎ Knowledge visualization has been missing from the repertoire of knowledge management thinking, and has important implications for managers. The field of knowledge management emerged, in part, in response to the realization that the main source of an organization's competitive advantage is the proprietary knowledge it possesses (e.g. tacit and explicit knowledge of processes and routines, competitors, products, customers, research, etc.), and that embedding, retaining and transferring that knowledge among employees is critical to exploiting the value of that very knowledge. Making knowledge visible makes it easier for employees to locate and use. It reduces the transaction costs associated with finding knowledge in an organization and even facilitates effective knowledge markets—the creation and exchange of knowledge based on market principles where 'sellers' or authors receive a fair return for the time and effort they put into sharing knowledge and 'buyers' or knowledge seekers have appropriate incentives to search for what is known.[19]

We would argue that knowledge visualization is a real and important future direction for companies looking to derive greater value from their information and knowledge assets. Knowledge developments, roles, relationships, dynamics, embodiments, and conceptualizations can all be represented in visual form often far more effectively than in words or lists. Just as the great anthropologist Clifford Geertz called for the development of 'thick descriptions' to describe other cultures, we are also advocating these 'rich pictures' in helping individuals understand the often foreign terrain of the very organizations in which they work.[20]

Notes and References

1. This subject is even gaining attention in the press, as demonstrated by the article 'Get the Picture,' in the *Wall Street Journal* on January 12, 2004.
2. See Hutchens. 'Cognition in the Wild.' MIT Press for a sophisticated discussion.
3. See Edward Tufte's critical analysis of PowerPoint in 'The Cognitive Style of Power Point' (2003).

4. A very popular example of the representation of individual knowledge are Tony Buzan's many books.
5. See the popular views of information design by E. Tufte (all published by Graphics Press): *The Visual Display of Quantitative Information* (2001), *Visual and Statistical Thinking: Displays of Evidence for Decision-Making* (1997), and *Envisioning Information* (1990). Wurman's thinking can be found in *Information Anxiety* Volumes 1 and 2 published by Pearson Education.
6. See *Visible Thinking* by J. Bryson, F. Ackermann, C. Eden and C. Finn (2004), John Wiley & Sons, Ltd (NY) for a current perspective on this subject.
7. Senge, P. (1994). *The Fifth Discipline.* Currency.
8. A good survey is the 1990 book *Influence Diagrams, Belief Nets and Decision Analysis,* edited by R. Oliver and J. Smith. Wiley (NY).
9. Rob Cross discusses the value of social networks and the ways in which they usefully represent knowledge in his recent book with Andrew Parker, *The Hidden Power of Social Networks: Understanding How Work Really Gets Done in Organizations.*
10. Bryan, Lowell (2002). 'Just-in-Time Strategy for a Turbulent World'. *McKinsey Quarterly,* pp. 17–27.
11. Hinds, Pamela J. and Sara Kiesler (eds) (2002). *Distributed Work.* MIT Press.
12. S. Feldman and C. Sherman, 'Industry Developments and Models: The High Cost of Not Finding Information,' IDC report, April 2003.
13. J. Borzo, 'Get the Picture,' *Wall Street Journal,* January 12, 2004, (Section R4, Technology Special Report).
14. Wurman, R. S. (2004). *Understanding Healthcare.* Quad Graphics (USA). And Harmon, K. *You Are Here: Personal Geographies and Other Maps of the Imagination* (2003). Princeton Architectural Press (NJ).
15. See Davenport, T. and Prusak, L. (1997). *Information Ecology.* Oxford University Press (New York).
16. The intranet was collaboration between Motorola and Thinkmap using Thinkmap's proprietary technology. Motorola created the content and specified the relationships. Thinkmap developed the interface to visually expose the content and context globally across the company.
17. L. Mlodinow (2003). *Some Time with Feynman.* Penguin Books (London).
18. A recent example is Brown, Denning, Groh and Prusak (2004). *Storytelling in Organizations.* Jossey-Bass.
19. See L. Bryan, 'Making a Market for Knowledge,' *The McKinsey Quarterly* (2004) and T. Davenport and L. Prusak (2000) *Working Knowledge,* Harvard Business School Press (Boston, MA) for a detailed description of knowledge markets.
20. See especially chapter 1 of Clifford Geertz's 1973 book, *The Interpretation of Cultures,* published by Basic Books (New York).

21 Do You Know Who Your Experts Are?

Michael Idinopulos and Lee Kempler

Expertise can be surprisingly difficult to find, even in institutions that have spent millions to attract and retain world-class experts. Take the experience of one manager at a biotechnology company.

Early in the project, it needed someone with deep technical knowledge of a particular protein. We spent weeks looking for an expert—calling HR, asking around the office, scanning personnel records. Finally, we concluded the expert didn't exist. Three days later, I'm in an elevator complaining about this to a colleague, when the woman next to me turns and says, 'I wrote my doctoral thesis on that protein. What do you need to know?'

Such inefficiency and reliance on chance would normally be unthinkable for corporate resources. Project managers don't find cash lying around in elevators. Store managers don't idly speculate on the whereabouts of their inventory. IT managers don't spend weeks rummaging through offices for spare computer terminals. Companies, after all, follow well-established processes to connect valuable resources (cash, inventory, equipment) with the people who need them.

The same cannot always be said of expertise. In some instances a formal process has not been necessary. For companies with small, simple organizational structures, informal social networks have been reasonably effective at putting experts in touch with those who are in need of their services. 'Around here, people know one another' is a common refrain. 'If I need help, I know whom to call.'

But the days of knowing whom to call may be over. Mergers, growth, globalization, and employee turnover have diminished the ability of informal social networks to ferret out experts. As a result, many companies are no longer willing to let serendipity dictate how their experts interact. A growing number of companies, including BP and IBM—afraid that their productivity may fall, their time to market be slow, or their competitive position erode—have adopted more systematic approaches to both finding and leveraging expertise.

Unfortunately, there has never been a good way to get the job done. Until recently, companies had two primary ways of capturing their expertise: document repositories and expertise databases. Neither can help seekers of expertise very much. Written documents reflect only a fraction of what an expert knows, while expertise databases suffer from inadequate classification schemes and tend to be out-of-date almost from the moment of inception. (One large high-tech company spent tens of millions of dollars developing a state-of-the-art expertise portal, which it rarely uses and even more rarely updates.)

A new approach, however, can change all this. The typical company already tracks information about the experience of its employees—what projects they are working on, what papers they have written, what they studied in school. It can therefore use search technologies to mine this information and find expertise in a way that it simply cannot do using document repositories or static directories. And depending on the state of a company's data systems, the solution can be surprisingly affordable and easy to implement.

Context Is King

Expertise is difficult to find largely because it can be difficult to pin down. Suppose a colleague asked you to describe your expertise. How would you respond? If the question came from a stranger in a distant corner of your company, you might give a general answer such as 'market research' or 'clinical-trial design.' But if the question came from the next desk, you would probably be more specific, giving your area of specialization within market research or mentioning the clinical trials you managed. To a colleague in another country you might give a geographic answer, while you would tell a local about your product expertise. And so it goes.

That is because the answer to 'What expertise do you have?' depends on who is asking and why. The question, by itself, is too abstract to invite a meaningful reply. People looking for expertise are doing so within the context of specific problems. Cash, inventory, and equipment are always the same, but expertise is defined by its context. That makes it an unusually difficult asset to identify.

Moreover, in most cases, finding an expert is less about identifying the world's leading authority on a recognized topic and more about reaching the person who happens to fit the demands of a particular situation, as our biotech case shows. Sometimes, the expertise wanted can be very narrow—the call might be for someone who has launched a product in a particular geography or worked for a potential customer. This type of expertise can be the most valuable of all. But it is often the most elusive because those who have it might not think of themselves as experts.

The problem of context befuddles most of the expertise directories that are in use today. Such directories contain short, context-free summaries of a person's areas of expertise. These summaries have their benefits—especially in small companies that have relatively few experts, so informal social networks can complement the directories. But the abstracts generally are not up to the challenge of identifying the large amount of highly specialized expertise that is available in large companies with tens of thousands of employees.

So companies must characterize expertise in ways that are sensitive to different contexts. How can these companies do so?

Actions Speak Louder Than Words

What matters in seeking expertise is not what people say they have done but what their achievements say about them. Consider a related challenge: hiring. Here too a company, constrained by certain organizational needs, is operating within a particular context. Companies generally evaluate candidates first by looking at what they have done, screening resumés with an eye to the specific needs of the job. Those who pass the first screening advance to more subjective types of evaluations, such as interviews and reference checks, which give the company a more complete understanding of whether and how a candidate's experience satisfies the contextual requirements.

All other things (basic qualifications, salary requirements, fit with the company's culture) being equal, the person with experience relevant to the specific context of the job is more likely to get hired. A packaged-goods company about to introduce a salty snack to a new market might see two candidates with general product-management experience, but the one who had just successfully launched a potato chip in that same region would attract the real interest.

Internal expertise searches can work in much the same way. Seekers of expertise want to know what qualifies a person for internal 'hire' to an expert 'position,' so they examine a candidate's track record: background, work experience, and references. Armed with this information, expertise searches tend to be highly effective. In an external search, descriptions on resumés are subject to interpretation and spin by the candidates, but descriptions in internal databases can usually be assessed with considerable precision. Companies have a set of norms—shared meanings, processes, and roles—that allow considerably more, and more reliable, information to be extracted from a given data point. On a resumé, for instance, the statement 'led a project team' raises questions: how big a project, for how long, with what success? But a comparable description in a company record will be imbued with a higher level of contextual knowledge, since the details and outcomes of the project, and even the role played by its team leader, are better understood.

Although this type of information seldom appears in expertise directories, it can often be found distributed across a company in various databases, such as those used in human resources, accounting, and patent registration. But trawling through that information can be time-consuming and haphazard; it involves getting access to these different databases, triangulating among them, and using a number of processes (intranet searches, phone calls to peers) to search for the right person, who even then may not be found.

Today's search engines, by contrast, can retrieve and rank thousands, indeed millions, of records in seconds. Everything that makes up the collective experience of the company and its employees can be found almost instantly. Rather than settle for the simplifications required to force-fit expertise into a static directory, companies will have a greatly enhanced expertise locator tool—something like Google.

Google for Experts

A small but growing industry is trying to improve the whole process of locating expertise by devising enterprise-software-based solutions, many of which combine new search technologies, profiling capabilities, and unique user interfaces. Several products use natural-language parsing technologies, for example, to distill an individual's areas of activity and interest by automatically combing through e-mails, instant messages, and other types of self-refreshing content.

In many respects, such products represent a real advance over the usual expertise location methods, including static expertise directories. Especially in industries where expertise needs are deep and narrow (software development, for instance), the products can extract helpful descriptions of what people have worked on without exposing personal or classified information. Some products also codify frequently asked questions (FAQs) and can thus greatly reduce the time experts spend answering them.

But as with most vendor-driven enterprise solutions, companies need to invest time and effort in understanding exactly what they want the technology to do before they decide which, if any, vendor solution suits them. Some companies abandon their discussions with vendors after realizing the privacy implications of mining their employees' private correspondence. Others have been disappointed to find that the software returned a high number of false positives. Depending on a company's particular expertise needs, professional vocabularies, and methods of communication, vendor technologies just might not deliver the right information in the right ways.

Companies should start by understanding their specific needs. Successful companies have found that the best way to do so is to bring together a cross-functional team from IT, knowledge management, and line functions to ask three fundamental questions: (1) What specific expertise-related needs do employees have? (2) What information will enable them to meet these needs? (3) How will that information be delivered to them? Only when the questions are answered can companies implement an effective expertise search system, with or without a third-party solution.

Format Follows Function

Mapping out specific business processes and knowledge needs is the first step. Whose productivity is suffering from limited access to expertise? In which situations is expertise needed? People looking for expertise may share certain characteristics: seniority, function, geographic location, or specific activity (for instance, responding to a service issue, starting a new project, or preparing for a stage-gate review). And the reasons for wanting experts—to provide quantitative data, to share high-level insights, to join a team, to attend a client meeting—also tend to be limited.

This analysis typically teaches companies which groups have their own definition of what they mean by 'expert' and what sort of experience qualifies a person to be one. A pharmaceutical company, for example, might learn that project leaders have trouble finding relevant technical knowledge during early-stage research design. Enabling them to search quickly and easily for experts by looking at the education, research experience, white-paper authorship, and patent filings of the company's employees could significantly reduce the difficulty. A consumer products company wanting geography-specific expertise might look no further than where its employees were educated or had previously worked.

From the Source

Companies have a great deal of information about their people stored in HR, accounting, knowledge-management, intellectual-property, and even recruiting systems. Most is captured for other purposes, but it can be precisely what expertise seekers need. Before companies invest in new software or ask their employees to fill out lots of new forms, they should see what they already have in their systems.

They may be disappointed. Most databases have been designed for a limited purpose—storing documents, tracking time, reimbursing expenses—and have little or no extraneous information. But companies shouldn't necessarily be discouraged by these gaps in individual databases. By integrating them, companies can offset gaps in one with data from others.

If an employee of that packaged-goods company needed help launching a salty snack in Ohio, for example, he or she might search a traditional expertise directory and find several people with general product-launch experience. But if the employee could triangulate among the company's various databases, they would quickly reveal one particular person's geographic familiarity with Ohio (college in Dayton) and product experience with salty snacks (a previous internship at Frito-Lay). Thus rather than finding several general experts, the employee would uncover a single person uniquely qualified to help with the product launch (exhibit).

Where gaps are a problem, companies can improve the quality of their databases by selectively introducing mechanisms to capture more information about what their workers are doing. Unlike traditional expertise surveys, which collect data outside normal business processes, databases of experience can be upgraded within the flow of existing work. An updated project description can, for instance, be a required part of the documentation for stage-gate reviews. A summary of a conference presentation might be required for travel reimbursement.

The more an expertise locator system can use existing data and existing processes for data collection, the greater the likelihood of success. Using existing data lets the system deliver value from the day of rollout. And because the information, as part of the everyday flow of work, is constantly updated, the system is not in danger of growing stale—a problem with expertise directories that can be 'refreshed' only with new rounds of surveys.

Build and Buy

The final question is what technology should be used for the search. Many IT departments approach this choice as a question of 'build versus buy.' The optimal answer is likely to involve a bit of both. From an IT standpoint, an expertise locator has three distinct pieces: a user interface, a search engine, and database integration facilities.[1] Most companies will want to take different approaches to each of these three components.

Generally, companies will want a custom-designed user interface. Depending on the specific expertise they require, their users might need to manipulate results in very different ways. In a large high-tech company with data from many sources, for instance, tech-savvy users might want to 'slice and dice' results using a number of filtering and sorting criteria. In a global corporation, geography and even time-zone information might play a prominent role in the display and manipulation capabilities of the system. So even if the work of developing it is outsourced to a contractor, companies should think twice about relying on vendor templates to display their search results.

The search engine itself is another matter: with the availability of off-the-shelf products from Google, Verity, and the like, companies have little need to develop their own. Many have already licensed these products for other purposes (document databases, for instance) and can use them for expertise locators. Depending on the exact needs of the company, customization could be minor (a few days to tweak priority weightings) or more significant (weeks of customization by a seasoned developer to optimize the engine for searches of a number of databases). Alternatively, companies could negotiate with vendors to buy just the search component of a larger solution optimized for expertise searches.

Database integration is likely to be the most labor-intensive aspect of implementation. Some companies have already created enterprise data warehouses to track all their data in a single, easily accessible repository. For those companies, implementation should be relatively straightforward—a three- to four-month effort. For other companies, migrating enterprise-wide data to an integrated, centralized data warehouse might demand extensive resources. (A company of 10,000 employees could expect to spend up to $500,000 on servers and data-migration software.) Setup is likely to take three months for a team of four to six full-time employees. The act of migrating information and tagging it with the Extensible Markup Language (XML) can take at least three months more for each database migrated.[2]

Whether a company decides to invest this much time and money will depend on how well it understands its expertise problem and on the nature of the opportunity to be had from the solution. A pharmaceutical company whose blockbuster drug launches were constantly plagued by delays partly attributable to the challenge of finding expertise would probably view millions of dollars in potential new revenue as sufficient justification.

Expertise should be identified through experience, its frequent companion. While many point out that the two should not be confused, there is nonetheless a strong correlation between them. By letting the employees' experience speak for itself, companies can quickly find experts when and where they are needed.

....

Notes

1. Companies that must capture new content need a fourth component, which allows experts to create new descriptions of their expertise.
2. The ability to find experts is just one benefit of data warehousing, which is used mainly to facilitate enterprise-wide reporting, analysis, and decision making.

22 Using Supplier Networks to Learn Faster

Jeffrey H. Dyer and Nile W. Hatch

Last year, Toyota Motor Corp. posted profits that exceeded the *combined* earnings of its three largest competitors. In today's world of hypercompetition, how did Toyota accomplish this? In searching for the answer, many business gurus and researchers have overlooked—or have not fully understood—the importance of knowledge-sharing networks. Certainly, knowledge management has become a hot topic. But how exactly do firms learn, and why do some companies learn faster than others? Furthermore, does learning go beyond the boundaries of the organization?

Many companies keep their suppliers and partners at arm's length, zealously guarding their internal knowledge. In sharp contrast, Toyota embraces its suppliers and encourages knowledge sharing with them by establishing networks that facilitate the exchange of information. By doing so, Toyota has helped those companies retool and fine-tune their operations, and the results have been stunning: 14 percent higher output per worker, 25 percent lower inventories and 50 percent fewer defects compared with their operations that supply Toyota's rivals. Such improvements have provided Toyota with a significant competitive advantage, enabling the company to charge substantial price premiums for the enhanced quality of its products. As Koichiro Noguchi, a Toyota director and former purchasing head, puts it, 'Our suppliers are critical to our success. We must help them to be the best.'

Toyota is not alone. More and more, companies are recognizing the competitive advantage that springs from the manner in which they work with their partners. Even powerful Microsoft Corp. has to rely on companies around the world to localize and translate its products in markets as diverse as those of China, Chile and the Czech Republic. Ultimately Microsoft's speed to market and even the quality of its offerings in those countries depend directly on how well it works and shares knowledge with those firms. For computer-systems company Dell Inc., suppliers are the very lifeblood of its business, and effective knowledge sharing with those partners is crucial for the company's success (see 'Knowledge Sharing at Dell,' p. 59). Other firms like Boeing, Harley-Davidson and Xilinx, a semiconductor manufacturer headquartered in San Jose, California, have also realized the importance of knowledge sharing with partners, and they are looking at strengthening those processes. As Xilinx vice president Evert Wolsheimer states, 'I think our partnership relationships will evolve in a similar direction over time to look like what Toyota has done.'

Learning at Toyota

So what exactly has Toyota done? To answer this, we performed an in-depth study of Toyota and its suppliers and found that the company has developed an infrastructure and a variety of *inter*organizational processes that facilitate the transfer of both explicit and tacit knowledge within its supplier network. (See 'Two Types of Knowledge,' p. 60.) The effort, headed by the company's purchasing division and its operations management consulting division (OMCD), consists of three key processes: supplier associations, consulting groups and learning teams. (See 'How Toyota Facilitates Network Learning,' p. 61)

Supplier Associations

In 1989, Toyota started an association for its U.S. suppliers. Named the Bluegrass Automotive Manufacturers Association (BAMA), the group was modeled after Toyota's supplier association in Japan (called *kyohokai*). The initial objective was to provide a regular forum for Toyota to share information with and elicit feedback from suppliers. Membership was voluntary, but word gradually spread about the value of joining the association. By 2000, BAMA had grown to 97 suppliers from an original membership of just 13. According to Toyota's Chris Nielsen, general manager for purchasing planning, 'We really didn't know if this would work in the U.S. ... Before BAMA, it was not very natural for supplier executives to talk and share information. ... Over the years, that has changed as suppliers have built relationships at senior levels.'

Details of the *kyohokai* reveal the various mechanisms through which knowledge is shared. The supplier association holds both general-assembly meetings

Knowledge Sharing at Dell

Knowledge sharing with partners is the foundation of Dell Inc.'s efforts toward 'virtual integration.' According to CEO Michael Dell, ' "Virtual integration" means you basically stitch together a business with partners that are treated as if they're inside the company.'[1] To achieve that, Dell has implemented a variety of measures.

First, Dell has taken minority equity stakes in a few key vendors. Second, it encourages its top suppliers to locate their resources inside or near Dell's design centers and factories. Third, it has implemented a certification program that is unique among major PC manufacturers. According to Scott Perry, senior director of global sales at Maxtor Corp., a manufacturer of computer hard drives, 'Dell's certification process teaches our engineers the language, processes and metrics used by Dell. In short, it teaches them how to think like Dell. This is critical because Dell wants our engineers to monitor processes both in our factories and at Dell factories using the tools, processes and metrics preferred by Dell.' Fourth, Dell engineers routinely visit supplier plants to monitor performance, share process knowledge for improving quality and yields, and encourage the better vendors to share their know-how with others. Fifth, Dell has worked on its own internal operations to facilitate greater and faster knowledge transfer. For example, the company returns defective parts much more quickly than its competitors do, providing suppliers with valuable data earlier on. 'Returned parts on Dell's products usually reach us in 30 days versus 90 days for competitors,' says Maxtor's Perry. 'As a result, we can work together to fix problems quickly, which keeps warranty costs low.' Sixth, suppliers' engineers visit Dell plants to help both Dell and the suppliers improve product quality and process capabilities. These engineers conduct failure analyses at Dell's factories, after which they transfer the resulting knowledge to their own facilities for corrective and preventive actions. Seventh, Dell coordinates its knowledge-sharing activities by meeting weekly with key suppliers and by holding quarterly business reviews with their top executives. Lastly, Dell is one of the first PC makers to establish a Web portal for supplier collaboration, providing vendor partners with access to Dell systems and key information regarding product design and engineering, cost management and quality. This system is part of a greater effort to share important information with suppliers, including detailed data regarding product demand, backlogs, pipelines and inventories.

The importance of such knowledge-sharing practices at Dell should not be underestimated. 'Our business model is based on direct relationships, not only with our customers but also [with] our partners,' notes Dell President and COO Kevin B. Rollins. 'Close supplier relationships influence everything from planning and forecasting to improved quality, pricing, inventory management, production and fulfillment. We're constantly looking for ways to integrate our suppliers and partners more closely into our business through substituting information for inventory and cost.'

[1] J. Magretta, 'The Power of Virtual Integration: An Interview With Dell Computer's Michael Dell,' Harvard Business Review 76 (March–April 1998): 72–84.

(bimonthly) and topic committee meetings (monthly or bimonthly). The former enable high-level sharing of explicit knowledge regarding production plans, policies, market trends and so on within the supply network. The latter allow more frequent interactions on four specific subject areas—cost, quality, safety and social activities—which are generally of benefit to all members of the network. The quality committee, for example, picks a theme for the year, such as 'eliminating supplier design defects,' and meets bimonthly to share knowledge with regard to that particular topic. The quality committee also sponsors various activities, including basic quality training for more than 100 engineers each year, tours of 'best practice' plants both inside and outside the automotive industry, and an annual conference on quality management that highlights in-depth supplier cases of quality improvement selected by a panel. Such efforts, in conjunction with those of the other committees, not only provide a forum for sharing valuable knowledge, they also help develop relationships among the participating suppliers.

Consulting/Problem-Solving Groups

As early as the mid-1960s, Toyota began to provide expert consultants to assist its suppliers in Japan. To that end, the company established the OMCD for acquiring, storing and diffusing valuable production knowledge residing within the Toyota Group. The OMCD consists of six highly experienced senior executives (each of them has responsibility for two Toyota plants and approximately 10 suppliers) along with about 50 consultants. About 15 to 20 of those consultants are permanent members of the OMCD, while the rest are fast-track younger individuals who deepen their knowledge of the Toyota Production System (TPS) by spending a three- to five-year rotation at the OMCD. Toyota sends these in-house experts to suppliers, sometimes for months at a time, to help those companies solve problems in implementing the TPS. Interestingly, Toyota does not charge for its consultants' time, instead making the OMCD a resource available to all members of the Toyota Group. Our survey of 38 of Toyota's largest first-tier suppliers in Japan revealed that, on average, they received 4.2 visits per year, each lasting 3.1 days.

In 1992, Toyota established the U.S. version of the OMCD. Originally called the Toyota Supplier Support Center (now TSSC Inc.), the group has since grown to more than 20 consultants and is headed by general manager Hajime Ohba, who is a former OMCD consultant. Like the OMCD, the TSSC requires that participating suppliers share their project results with others. This policy allows Toyota to showcase 'best practice' suppliers that have successfully implemented various elements of the TPS, and it encourages the suppliers to open their operations to one another. This is critical because the ability to see a working template dramatically increases the chances that suppliers can successfully replicate that knowledge within their own plants. Companies can, however, designate certain areas of their plants—where Toyota hasn't provided any assistance—as off-limits to visitors in order to protect their proprietary knowledge.

To date, transfers of TPS know-how have been difficult and time-consuming. Although the goal is to achieve success in six months, no project in the United States has been completed in less than eight months and most consume at least a year and a half. 'It takes a very long time and tremendous commitment to implement the Toyota Production System,' says Ohba. 'In many cases it takes a total cultural and organizational change. Many U.S. firms have management systems that contradict where you need to go.' Consider Summit Polymers Inc., a manufacturer of plastic interior parts, based in Kalamazoo, Michigan, which was one of the first U.S. suppliers to use the TSSC. According to Tom Luyster, who was vice president of planning at the time, 'The TSSC sent approximately two to four consultants to our plant *every day* for a period of three to four months as we attempted to implement TPS concepts in a new plant.' And after that initial phase, Toyota continued to provide ongoing support to Summit Polymers for more than five years.

But the results have been impressive. On average, the TSSC has assisted suppliers in increasing productivity (in output per worker) by 123 percent and reducing inventory by 74 percent. These improvements clearly demonstrate that, although the TSSC's knowledge-transfer processes require considerable effort, they can dramatically improve supplier performance.

Take, for example, Continental Metal Specialty (CMS), a supplier of metal stampings, such as body brackets. The consulting process began with Toyota sending people to teach the TPS to CMS personnel, after which the two companies jointly examined CMS's production process to identify each step, flagging those that were value-added versus those that were not. Out of 30 steps, four were designated as value-added: blanking, forming, welding and painting. Toyota and CMS then reconfigured the production system to eliminate as many of the non-value-added steps as possible. One important change brought welding into the plant and placed it next to the forming process, thereby eliminating 12 non-value-added steps. Over time, CMS has eliminated a total of 19 non-value-added steps, reducing set-up times from two hours to 12 minutes. In addition, inventories on most parts have been reduced to almost one-tenth of previous levels. Then CMS chairman George Hommel described the benefits: 'We wouldn't be where we are now if we hadn't worked with Toyota. I'd say that 75 percent to 80 percent of all that we've learned from customers has come from Toyota.'

It should be noted that Toyota does not ask for immediate price decreases or a portion of the savings from the improvements. Suppliers keep all of the initial benefits, in contrast with the General Motors Corp. (GM) typical practice of asking for a price decrease after offering assistance at a supplier's plant. As one supplier executive declared, 'We don't want to have a GM team poking around our plant. They will just find the "low-hanging fruit"—the stuff that's relatively easy to see and fix. ... We'd prefer to find it ourselves and keep all of the

Jeffrey H. Dyer and Nile W. Hatch

Two Types of Knowledge

Most scholars divide knowledge into two types: *explicit* and *tacit*.[1] The former can be codified easily and transmitted without loss of integrity once the rules required for deciphering it are known. Examples include facts, axiomatic propositions and symbols that provide information on the size and growth of a market, production schedules and so on. In contrast, tacit knowledge is 'sticky,' complex and difficult to codify,[2] and it often involves experiential learning. One example is the know-how required to transform a manufacturing plant from mass production to flexible operation. Because tacit knowledge is complex and difficult to imitate, it is most likely to generate competitive advantages that are sustainable. In fact, in *The Knowledge Creating Company*, researchers Ikujiro Nonaka and Hiroyuki Takeuchi make the case that the really powerful type of knowledge is tacit because it is the primary source of innovative new products and creative ways of doing business.[3]

[1] B. Kogut and U. Zander, 'Knowledge of the Firm, Combinative Capabilities, and the Replication of Technology,' Organization Science 3, no. 3 (1992): 383–97; R. Grant, 'Prospering in Dynamically-Competitive Environments: Organizational Capability as Knowledge Integration,' Organization Science 7, no. 4 (1996): 375–87; and G. Ryle, 'The Concept of Mind' (Chicago: University of Chicago Press, 1984): 29–34.
[2] R. Nelson and S. Winter, 'An Evolutionary Theory of Economic Change' (Cambridge: Belknap Press, 1982); B. Kogut and U. Zander, 'Knowledge of the Firm' (1992); and G. Szulanski, 'Exploring Internal Stickiness: Impediments to the Transfer of Best Practice Within the Firm,' Strategic Management Journal 17 (1996): 27–43.
[3] I. Nonaka and H. Takeuchi, 'The Knowledge Creating Company' (New York: Oxford University Press, 1995).

---

savings.' Of course, Toyota does eventually capture some of the savings through its annual price reviews with suppliers, but the company is careful to keep activities that *create* value completely separate from those that *appropriate* value. For example, Toyota has typically used a 'target-pricing' system by which the company lets suppliers know the prices it thinks are fair for certain parts for the duration of a contract.[1] This motivates suppliers to cut costs continually to reap higher profits on those parts.

Voluntary Learning Teams

In 1977, the OMCD organized more than 50 of its key suppliers in Japan into voluntary study groups (called *jishukenkyu-kai*, or *jishuken*) to work together on productivity and quality improvements. With the help of an OMCD consultant, the teams determined a theme and spent three months addressing the problems of each of its members' plants. *Jishuken* are an advanced knowledge-sharing mechanism through which members learn as a group, exploring new ideas and applications of TPS. The team then transfers any valuable lessons to Toyota and throughout the supplier network.

In 1994, Toyota replicated the *jishuken* concept in the United States by establishing three plant development activity (PDA) core groups among 40

346

suppliers. As with the supplier association, membership was voluntary. For the first year, the theme was quality improvement because, as Toyota's Chris Nielsen noted, 'everyone agrees that they can improve quality.' Each PDA member was asked to select a demonstration line within a plant as a place to experiment with implementing certain concepts.

Our interviews with U.S. plant managers revealed the value of the PDA projects. According to one manager, 'When you bring a whole new set of eyes into your plant, you learn a lot. ... We've made quite a few improvements. In fact, after the [PDA] group visits to our plant, we made more than 70 changes to the manufacturing cell.'

A key reason that PDA transfers of tacit knowledge have been particularly effective is that they involve learning that is context-specific. The plant manager from Kojima Press Industry Co. Ltd., a supplier of body parts, describes an example: 'Last year we reduced our paint costs by 30 percent. This was possible due to a suggestion to lower the pressure on the paint sprayer and adjust the spray trajectory, thereby wasting less paint.'

The Evolution of a Knowledge-Sharing Network

The successful structures and collaborative relationships of the three knowledge-sharing processes—the supplier association, consulting groups and learning teams—did not appear by happenstance. Rather, Toyota established these institutions in the same order in both the United States and Japan. The intent was first to create weak, non-threatening ties that could later be transformed into strong, trusting relationships. As each structure evolved and the relationships matured, the processes became a vehicle for a shared identity among Toyota suppliers. As one supplier executive put it, 'We're a member of the *Toyota Group*. That means we are willing to do what we can to help other group members.'

In the initiation phase of Toyota's U.S. network (roughly from 1989 to 1992), the network structure was a collection of dyadic ties with Toyota as a hub that heavily subsidized activities. (See 'Evolution of Toyota Network,' p. 62.) Toyota's help came in two forms: financial (for instance, funds for planning and organizing meetings) and valuable knowledge. It was important for Toyota to subsidize network knowledge-sharing activities early on to motivate members to participate. The supplier association was the vehicle through which links to suppliers were established and explicit knowledge was transferred. In that early stage, the connections between suppliers were weak, and there were numerous holes because most suppliers did not have direct ties to each other. Companies

Jeffrey H. Dyer and Nile W. Hatch

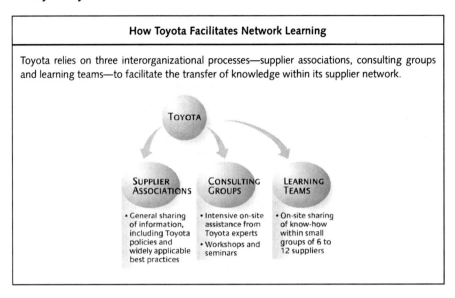

How Toyota Facilitates Network Learning

Toyota relies on three interorganizational processes—supplier associations, consulting groups and learning teams—to facilitate the transfer of knowledge within its supplier network.

were motivated to participate in the supplier association primarily to demonstrate their commitment to Toyota with the hope that they would then be rewarded with additional future business. At this point, the network was just beginning to develop an identity, and suppliers did not yet perceive a strong sense of shared purpose with other members.

Next, Toyota gradually increased the strength of its bilateral relationships with suppliers by sending consultants to transfer valuable knowledge at minimal cost. Consequently, suppliers increasingly participated in the network not only to demonstrate their commitment to Toyota but also to learn from the company. Although the supplier association facilitated the exchange of information that was primarily *explicit*, the personal visits of consultants were effective in transferring *tacit* knowledge of greater value. And the consultants created an atmosphere of reciprocity: Suppliers began to feel indebted to Toyota for sharing knowledge that significantly improved their operations.

In the final phase, the PDA learning teams developed and strengthened multilateral ties between suppliers and facilitated the sharing of tacit knowledge among them. Today, suppliers have two primary motivations for participating. First, they now appreciate how important it is, as a Toyota supplier, to keep up to pace. They are aware that the profit-creating potential of past productivity enhancements declines steadily, and they know they are in a learning race with rival suppliers because business from Toyota is allocated based on relative performance improvements. This creates strong incentives for suppliers to learn and improve as quickly as possible. Second, suppliers now strongly identify with the network and feel obligated to reciprocate in the

---

Evolution of Toyota Network

In the early stages of a knowledge-sharing network, Toyota establishes bilateral relationships with suppliers (left). At this point, the supplier network resembles a hub (Toyota) with many spokes. Later, the suppliers begin to form ties with each other in nested subnetworks (right). These multilateral relationships greatly facilitate the flow of knowledge so that members are able to learn much faster than rival, non-participating suppliers.

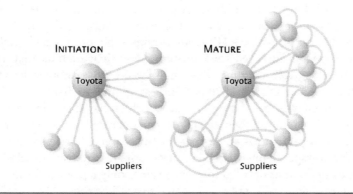

---

information exchange so they begin to share knowledge more freely with other members. This strengthens multilateral ties among suppliers and creates sub-networks for knowledge sharing within the larger system. In this mature stage, multiple pathways exist for transferring both explicit and tacit knowledge, and the amount of tacit knowledge being transferred is substantial (whereas in the initiation phase it was almost non-existent).

The Competitive Advantages

For manufacturing in the United States, Toyota now buys more than 70 percent of its parts from U.S. companies. Consequently, the company is increasingly using the same suppliers as its U.S. competitors, which raises an interesting question: How can Toyota achieve a competitive advantage through these vendors? Traditional economic theory suggests that the only possible way is by extracting lower unit prices based on greater relative bargaining power.[2] In the United States though, Toyota has lower unit volumes than its U.S. competitors, placing the company at a disadvantage. But Toyota has been able to overcome that handicap and has instead achieved competitive advantages with its U.S. suppliers by providing them with knowledge and technology to improve their productivity for just their operations that are dedicated to Toyota.

The results of our survey of those vendors help illuminate the reasons for Toyota's success.

Compared with the Big Three (GM, Ford and Daimler-Chrysler), Toyota has engaged in significantly more knowledge-sharing activities with its U.S. suppliers. Toyota sent personnel to visit the suppliers' plants to exchange technical information an average of 13 days each year versus six for the Big Three. As one plant manager noted, 'We have received a great deal of knowledge from Toyota. ... We have learned about in-sequence shipping, *kanban* [a system for reducing inventory], one-piece production and standardized work. We have even learned some of Toyota's HR-related training philosophy and methods.' The plant managers surveyed were unanimous in their opinion that Toyota provided more valuable assistance than their largest U.S. customer despite the fact that they sold an average of 50 percent less volume to Toyota.

The greater knowledge sharing has had a substantial effect. From 1990 to 1996, the suppliers reduced their defects (in parts per million) by an average of 84 percent for Toyota versus 46 percent for their largest Big Three customer. Similarly, the average supplier slashed its inventories (as a percent of sales) by 35 percent in its operations devoted to Toyota versus only 6 percent for its largest Big Three customer. And suppliers increased their labor productivity (sales per direct employee) by 36 percent for Toyota versus just 1 percent for their largest Big Three customer. Furthermore, by 1996 the suppliers had achieved 10 percent higher output per worker, 25 percent lower inventories and 50 percent fewer defects in their manufacturing cells for Toyota, as compared with what had been achieved for their largest U.S. customer. These results are all the more amazing given that the suppliers were manufacturing a similar component for a U.S. customer *within the same plant!*

Sustaining the Advantages

If suppliers have achieved such significant improvements by sharing knowledge with Toyota, why then don't they utilize that know-how for their other customers? In fact, one-third of the U.S. suppliers in our study reported that they *did* transfer the knowledge acquired from Toyota to manufacturing cells devoted to their largest U.S. customer. But the remaining two-thirds did not. Many plant managers reported that even when they wanted to transfer knowledge to other manufacturing cells in the same plant, they often couldn't because of two types of barriers: network constraints and internal process rigidities.

Network Constraints

In some instances, plant managers reported being unable to transfer knowledge because of a particular customer's policies or other constraints. For example, one supplier was required by its Big Three customer to use large containers, approximately 4 feet by 6 feet and weighing 200 to 300 pounds when filled. By comparison, Toyota had the supplier use smaller containers, about 2 feet by 3 feet and weighing 40 pounds when filled. This had a number of important ramifications. The manufacturing process using large containers required more floor space, and the supplier needed to purchase forklifts and hire forklift operators to move the containers. Not only were the large containers unwieldy, they were also tougher to keep clean, which affected product quality. Furthermore, the large containers made it more difficult to label and sort products into a particular sequence for production at the assembler's facility. But the large containers fit well into the Big Three assembler's system (which also used forklifts and a lot of floor space), so the customer would not allow a change to a smaller size. Thus, the supplier was unable to replicate the processes that it was using for Toyota.

Internal Process Rigidities

Suppliers were much less likely to transfer knowledge from Toyota to one of the Big Three when the manufacturing cells for that customer had a high level of automation or a large capital investment in heavy equipment. Such internal process rigidities—large machines bolted or cemented in place, trenches in the floor, utilities hardwired to equipment and so on—increased the costs of transferring knowledge. As one plant manager reported, 'When you invest in automation, you do everything you can to run that job for as long as you can. When you have to change a highly automated process, you have a devil of a time. It just never works.' Internal process rigidities help explain why suppliers had relatively low rates of productivity improvement for their U.S. customers. Plant managers could not make the changes they wanted, or they were forced to wait until the customer terminated a vehicle model before they could implement a new process. Thus, at the very least, internal process rigidities created a significant time lag. In contrast, Toyota's production network has been designed as a dynamic system with flexibility built directly into the manufacturing processes. Most machines, for example, are on rollers so they can be moved easily to new locations.

Other factors can also impede the transfer of knowledge to production cells dedicated to Toyota's rivals. A number of plant managers refrained from even requesting a major change from a U.S. customer because they perceived the approval process to be time consuming and difficult. Furthermore, significant changes to a manufacturing cell often require considerable down time, which a customer might be unwilling to endure. Or the customer might refuse to accept the possibility that the new processes might initially have bugs. According to the president of one supplier, 'Sometimes it's just not worth the risk to try something new if the customer isn't supportive and involved. If you cause a recall, or even if they think you caused a recall, it could put you out of business. And if you shut down their plant, they charge you $30,000 a minute.'

In summary, taking know-how learned from one customer and applying it to another can be extremely difficult, mainly because knowledge is so context-dependent. But the ability to transfer and adapt knowledge can, in and of itself, be a competitive advantage. As Michio Tanaka, the general manager in purchasing at Toyota, asserts, 'The ideas behind the [TPS] have basically diffused and are understood by our competitors, but the know-how regarding how to implement it in specific factories and contexts has not. Toyota Group companies are better at implementing the ongoing... activities associated with the [TPS]. ... I think we are better at learning.'

The Bottom Line

The trickle-down benefits of knowledge sharing can be substantial. By transferring its know-how to suppliers, Toyota has helped those firms greatly improve their performance, and this in turn has generated tremendous competitive advantages for Toyota. Consider the significant price premiums that Toyota vehicles enjoy (relative to U.S. cars in the same class): an average of 9.7 percent for new cars and 17.6 percent for used ones.[3] Higher quality is a major reason why Toyota vehicles can command such prices. The J. D. Power and Associates Initial Quality studies have found that between 1990 and 2000 Toyota cars had roughly 40 percent fewer problems (per 100 vehicles) than did autos from the Big Three.[4] The total cost of the knowledge-sharing activities that have contributed to the enhanced quality of Toyota vehicles was between $50 million and $100 million for the United States and Japan. That amount might seem considerable, but it was relatively small for a $100 billion company like Toyota, and it was certainly a wise investment that has more than paid for itself in increased profits for the Japanese automaker.

The experience of Toyota strongly suggests that competitive advantages can be created and sustained through superior knowledge-sharing processes within a network of suppliers. We believe those principles have broader applicability, for example, in other types of alliance networks, including those with partners in joint ventures. In fact, establishing effective interorganizational knowledge-sharing processes with suppliers and partners can be crucial for any company trying to stay ahead of its competitors. As one senior Toyota executive observes, 'We are not so concerned that our knowledge will spill over to competitors. Some of it will. But by the time it does, we will be somewhere else. We are a moving target.'

Indeed, Toyota's dynamic learning capability, enabled through a network of knowledge sharing, might turn out to be the company's one truly sustainable competitive advantage.

....

References

1. L. Chappel, 'Toyota: Slash—But We'll Help,' *Automotive News* 77 (Sept. 16, 2002): 4.
2. M. Porter, 'Competitive Strategy' (New York: Free Press, 1980).
3. J. H. Dyer and N. Hatch, 'Network-Specific Capabilities, Network Barriers to Knowledge Transfers, and Competitive Advantage' (paper presented at the Strategic Management Society Conference, Orlando, Florida, Nov. 7–10, 1998).
4. J. H. Dyer, 'Collaborative Advantage' (New York: Oxford University Press, 2000).

Index

absorptive capacity, and strategic
    alliances 132
Accenture:
  and approach to knowledge
    management 26
  and knowledge storage and
    organization 24
accessibility, and social network
    analysis 273–4, 279–80, 283–4
  global consulting practice 284–5
  impact of reorganization 285
  managing accessibility 285–6
advanced knowledge 38–9
Alcoa 279
Allen, Tom 271
Amazon.com 206
ambidextrous organizations 216
America Online 206
American Management Systems, and
    communities of practice 262,
    266–8
Amoco 186
Andersen Consulting 232
Andrews, Frank 98
Apple, and knowledge exploitation 42
Argyris, C. 146
Aristotle 1
Arrow, Kenneth 2
AT&T 16
  and technologist productivity 308–9
availability heuristic 108
Aventis 280
awareness, and strategic alliances 130–31

Banc One (Bank One), and replication of
    best practice 196–97
Bay of Pigs 104
Bay State Shippers, and industry
    positioning 46–7

best practice 175
  and communities of practice 261
  and identifying 175–8
  and replication/sharing of 202–3
    adaptation 201
    Chevron 184–7, 191
    copy in detail 199–201
    copying the template 195–98
    difficulties with 192–5, 200,
     216
    Ford Motor Co. 215, 219
    IBM 220, 221
    Intel 199–203, 219
    Nucor Corporation 232
    Partners HealthCare System
     Inc. 220–21
    Rank Xerox 199, 201
    referring to original template 201–2
    Starbucks 197
    suitability for copying 198
    Toyota supplier networks 344–5
    use active template 198–9
    Xerox 178–80
  see also performance variability
Bethlehem Steel Corporation, and fair
    process 253–6
biotechnology industry, and collaborative
    ventures 44
Bluegrass Automotive Manufacturers
    Association 342
Boeing 342
Bohmer, Richard 66
Booz-Allen and Hamilton 24
Boyle, Dennis 112
brainstorming 108–10
  and Skandia 280
British Petroleum 3, 186
  and best practice 221
  and oral debriefings 145

Index

Index

Index

Index

Index

Index

Lightning Source UK Ltd.
Milton Keynes UK
UKOW040227300113

205571UK00001B/26/P